PIONEER PUBLIC SERVICE

CANADIAN GOVERNMENT SERIES

R. MacG. Dawson, *Editor*

1. DEMOCRATIC GOVERNMENT AND POLITICS
    By J. A. Corry

2. THE GOVERNMENT OF CANADA
    By R. MacGregor Dawson

3. CONSTITUTIONAL AMENDMENT IN CANADA
    By Paul Gérin-Lajoie

4. THE CANADIAN HOUSE OF COMMONS: REPRESENTATION
    By Norman Ward

5. THE GOVERNMENT OF PRINCE EDWARD ISLAND
    By Frank MacKinnon

6. CANADIAN MUNICIPAL GOVERNMENT
    By Kenneth Grant Crawford

7. PIONEER PUBLIC SERVICE: AN ADMINISTRATIVE HISTORY OF THE UNITED CANADAS, 1841–1867
    By J. E. Hodgetts

PIONEER PUBLIC SERVICE

AN ADMINISTRATIVE HISTORY OF
THE UNITED CANADAS, 1841-1867

BY

J. E. HODGETTS

*Associate Professor of Political Science
Queen's University*

TORONTO
UNIVERSITY OF TORONTO PRESS
1955

Copyright ©, Canada, 1956
University of Toronto Press
Reprinted 2015
London: Geoffrey Cumberlege
Oxford University Press
ISBN 978-1-4875-9167-0 (paper)

FOREWORD

This book is a new venture in the study of Canadian politics. Some years ago Professor Leonard White published *The Federalists*, a book which traced the early development of ideas about public administration in the young American republic: it is no accident that Professor Hodgetts, who studied under Professor White, should now perform the same service for the study of politics and administration in Canada. The pupil has proved himself worthy of his master and has turned in an equally brilliant performance. The administrative approach which has been used, moreover, not only produces a large volume of new material but examines some old material in a somewhat different light, and the result is a most welcome addition to our knowledge of Canadian government and its antecedents. If anyone has been inclined to question the development of public administration as a study in its own right, research projects such as this should place the matter beyond dispute. Conceivably either history or politics might have taken on this task, but they did not; it remained for the specialist in the field to perceive the neglect and to fill the gap.

Few students, one suspects, appreciate how great has been the influence of the permanent officials in the years before Confederation, nor do they have an adequate comprehension of the degree to which administrative decisions of those days, both by Ministers and officials, determined many of the present practices. An astonishingly large number of the problems, moreover, will be found to have remained substantially the same for the past hundred years. The scheme of departmental organization, the delegation of authority and the allotment of responsibility, the application of financial controls, the intricate give and take between the political non-technical Minister and the technically trained specialist—these in some aspect or another have been the constant concern of the administrator: a different time, a different place, has simply shifted the emphasis a little one way or the other.

"These adminstrative pioneers deserve better of us than oblivion," writes Professor Hodgetts, and he himself has taken the surest means to see that their careers are recorded and that they receive their just credit or blame for the work they performed. Canadian political and economic history has acquired depth and colour in the process.

R. MacGregor Dawson

PREFACE

THREE OBJECTIVES underlie this study. It is intended, first, to provide a description of the evolution and structure of the administrative machine which, with few fundamental changes, still serves the Canadian nation. When the new Dominion of Canada came into being on July 1, 1867, it inherited from the United Provinces of Upper and Lower Canada their system of government departments together with a body of experienced civil servants. These departments and officials had been located in Ottawa since November 1865 and, naturally, the new federation, seeking a smooth transition from the smaller to the larger union, took over the already well-established system. The Maritime Provinces for several years after Confederation had virtually no representation in the bureaucracy at headquarters. Consequently, they could claim only a minor influence in shaping the structure and operations of the new federal civil service. This situation, it has been felt, justifies the limitation of the present study to the administrative history of the United Canadas during the formative years 1841 to 1867.

A by-product, so to speak, of this first objective has been the attempt to acknowledge and appraise the hitherto unsung contributions of the public servant to the welfare of a pioneer community. Historians and sculptors have rescued most of our leading political figures from oblivion, but a mantle of silence has enveloped the personalities and labours of our early public servants. The anonymity of the stage hands behind the scenes should not be permitted to conceal their usefulness to the players who have for so long postured in front of the backdrops. Unfortunately, the record of their labours lies concealed in forbidding departmental reports and in the bulky proceedings of official investigating bodies. These dry, factual records, however, yield many reminders that serving the government in these early days could often be an exciting and rewarding task, attractive to courageous, inventive, and self-sacrificing men. For men such as these, the restless progressive nation to the south perpetually stood as a challenge to the unclaimed wilderness of the two Canadas. When, in the course of official duty, they traversed our vast hinterland and caught a glimpse of its natural potential, such officials became convinced exponents of early Canadian nationalism. Their genuine enthusiasm was ultimately transferred to those political leaders who began to envisage a broader union from sea to sea.

A second objective of this study is to disclose the presence in the pioneer public service of certain basic administrative issues which today still rise to perplex both the student and practitioner of public administration. The public service today, it is true, is larger and more complex than our pre-Confederation civil service. Perhaps this is a good reason for turning back to the smaller, less intricate structure in order to observe the same administrative problems without the confusion and distraction produced by bigness. However, in order to use the administrative history of our early civil service as a means of throwing light on contemporary administrative issues, a special procedure has been followed. An examination of the administrative mechanism is not particularly rewarding unless the policies which that mechanism is designed to implement are also described. And these policies, in turn, are understandable only in terms of the broader social, political, and economic environment to which they are a response. Consequently, each of the later chapters in this study dealing with specific departments approaches their administrative history by means of this threefold line of analysis. First, the features of the environment which have a bearing on policy are described; second, the policy decisions in response to these environmental problems are assessed; finally, the efficiency of the administrative machine is examined in relation to the policies it was supposed to implement. This procedure, admittedly, forces the administrative historian to aspire to the higher artistry of the social historian. While disclaiming such lofty pretensions, this study at least attempts to take into account those environmental factors which have helped to shape the structure and have given impetus to the administrative machine. Administrators do not work in a social vacuum and they cannot rise higher than their source of power, the community itself.

Finally, this study, it is hoped, will reveal a neglected aspect of the winning of responsible government in Canada. The formal victory of this constitutional principle was dramatically high-lighted in 1849 with the mob pelting Lord Elgin in the streets of Montreal. It is a major thesis of this study that the recognition of this principle on the political level did not, in fact, coincide with its practical implementation at the administrative level. In administrative terms, responsible government was won only when the provincial authorities obtained full control over their public services. In certain services, such as the

Customs, Post Office, Ordnance lands and canals, Indian Affairs and Militia, the transfer was only made during the period 1849 to 1862. Moreover, in the most vital area of government, control of the purse, the legislature had by no means obtained the power to make responsible government a working reality. Legislative control of the executive's expenditures on the public service was barely established by the time of Confederation. The earlier chapters in this study, particularly the chapter entitled "Tightening the Purse Strings," are concerned in part with elaborating this neglected aspect of Canadian history.

It is a pleasure to record the many obligations which I have incurred, both to institutions and individuals, during the writing and production of this book. The Nuffield Foundation's award of a travelling fellowship gave the original impetus to the study and various grants from the Arts Research Committee of Queen's University kept the project from flagging along the way. Publication was made possible by the generous financial support provided by the Social Science Research Council and the University of Toronto Press. I wish to extend both my thanks and apologies to my friends who have generously shared their knowledge and patiently endured my enthusiasms. In particular, I am indebted to the judicious counsel of my chief, J. A. Corry, and the helpful suggestions of my colleague, John Meisel. Dr. R. MacG. Dawson's careful editing and perceptive comments have saved me from numerous intellectual blunders. I have relied constantly on my wife's discriminate taste in literary matters and on her powers of endurance in maintaining the domestic peace. I should also like to thank Mrs. Murie Meisel for designing and drafting the charts and Miss M. Jean Houston for an editing of the manuscript on behalf of the Press which extended far beyond the call of professional duty. The customary absolution for all those named and for those whose ideas have been incorporated unacknowledged into the text is hereby granted; the author's personal liability is fully admitted. Finally, this book is affectionately dedicated to my mother and father whose personal sacrifices and steady support throughout the years epitomize the loyalty of all parents to the cause of education.

CONTENTS

	FOREWORD	v
	PREFACE	vii
I	The Canadas: Perspectives	3
II	Lord Durham Proposes	12
III	Lord Sydenham Disposes	24
IV	The Bureaucracy from Within	35
V	The Bureaucracy from Without	55
VI	The Top Command	73
VII	Tightening the Purse Strings	96
VIII	The Crown Lands Department: "A Fair Subject of Discussion"	118
IX	Nature Provides, Man Divides	128
X	Administering the Natural Resources: Three Problems	156
XI	Public Works: Department of Transport and Housekeeper Extraordinary	176
XII	A "One Man Power" versus the Engineers' Empire	189
XIII	Indian Affairs: The White Man's Albatross	205
XIV	Agriculture: Departmental Potting-Shed	226
XV	Immigrants or Itinerants	240
XVI	Pioneer Public Service: Retrospect	269

APPENDIX *following* 280

Chronological Perspective of Public Departments 1841–1867

Departmental Organization in 1867: Department of Finance, Department of Crown Lands, Department of Public Works, Department of Agriculture

INDEX 285

PIONEER PUBLIC SERVICE

CHAPTER I

THE CANADAS: PERSPECTIVES

"The *Tour of Europe* has become stale. Every flower by the way has been picked up, smelt, and flung aside. The *Tour of the West* would be found a thousand times more interesting, instructive and beneficial." Thus, in 1822, did Robert Gourlay permit his enthusiasm for the North American colonies to outrun his animosity toward the rulers of Upper Canada who had unjustly confined him for several months to a bleak prison.[1] Anyone who had the temerity in the 1830's to undertake the Grand Tour proposed by Gourlay would probably have been satisfied that the grandeurs of nature lived up to all advance notices. Even the well-travelled Lord Sydenham found Niagara Falls "the most magnificent sight on earth."[2] But certainly man and all his works must have appeared extremely insignificant when set against the overpowering majesty of Nature.

Visitors from the Old Country touring the provinces of Upper and Lower Canada at the time of their union in 1841 (after paying tribute to Nature's wonders) would have been first impressed by the difficulties attending their journeys "up-country."[3] Having endured for three or four weeks the discomforts of ocean travel by sail, they must have found the process of tacking upriver to drop anchor at Quebec or Montreal almost interminable. Undoubtedly, they would have been properly impressed with the magnificent locations of Quebec and Montreal, finding in each of these centres of the colonial world active populations of about 35,000. But this first glimpse of concentrated population, as the tourists would soon discover, was misleading. In fact, the crude early census would have shown that the combined population of the two colonies was not much over one and a half million. With our own hindsight of an additional hundred

---

[1]Robert Gourlay, *A Statistical Account of Upper Canada* (3 vols., London, 1822), vol. I, p. iii. For his treatment at the hands of the Canadian government see W. Stewart Wallace, *The Family Compact*, vol. xxiv in the "Chronicles of Canada" series, ed. by George M. Wrong and H. H. Langton (Toronto, 1915), pp. 27 f.
[2]G. Poulett Scrope, *Memoirs of the Life of the Right Honourable Charles Lord Sydenham, G.C.B.* (London, 1843), p. 192.
[3]The best descriptions of local travelling and social conditions have been assembled by Edwin C. Guillet, *Early Life in Upper Canada* (Toronto, 1933).

years we are in a position to realize that today the population of either of the two big metropolitan centres of Toronto and Montreal surpasses by many thousands the total population of the United Canadas in 1841.[4]

It is likely that our tourists would soon have been diverted from vital statistics in facing the physical hardships of travelling inland from Montreal. Ahead of them, as far as Prescott, lay many miles of dangerous rapids, crude roads, narrow trails which had to be covered by a variety of conveyances: sooty, uncomfortable steamboats, bateaux, stage coach, wagon, and horseback. While an alternative route was available via the Ottawa River and thence down the Rideau military canals to Kingston, it was even more arduous than the more direct route. At Prescott the traveller could obtain surprisingly luxurious steamboat accommodation on such vessels as the *Great Britain* which plied Lake Ontario as far as Toronto, Hamilton, and Niagara ports. Shortly, fleets of steam-driven mail packets were to be competing for passengers and mails, on a route that extended from the western end of Lake Ontario to Prescott. Even the Grand Trunk Railway which went through to Toronto in 1856 failed to match the cleaner, more splendid facilities provided by the lake steamers, although the railway reduced travel time from Montreal to Toronto from three or four days to fourteen hours. Every town had its harbour or anchorage: the lakeshore and even the rivers flowing into the lake were alive with vessels of all descriptions carrying on an active local trade.

Travel by road was accompanied by the greatest inconveniences and delay. Sydenham's famous non-stop stage-coach run in 1840 from Toronto to Montreal in under thirty-six hours remained an unbroken record. Regular stage-coach service for the mails was inaugurated in the early forties but the roads were best travelled in winter, were almost impassable in spring, and at other seasons constantly threatened the imminent disintegration of the vehicles and left the passengers bruised and exhausted. Even where gravelled or primitive "macadamized" roads were laid out, there was seldom enough traffic to smooth down the surface and establish a solid road bed. Because travel by water was so popular, the roadside facilities were notoriously poor.[5] Our imaginary tourists most probably would have added

[4]As a later chapter will show, the early census figures are not particularly reliable but they provide a crude over-all view of the colony and are conveniently assembled in volume IV of *Censuses of Canada, 1665 to 1871* (Ottawa, 1876). The census of Upper Canada, 1840, lists a population of 432,159; for Lower Canada, 1844, a population of 697,084.

[5]Gourlay, *Statistical Account of Upper Canada*, vol. I, p. 250.

their complaints to those of their predecessors against the crude inns and the cruder "Yankee" manners of the innkeepers.

Pushing on beyond Toronto and Hamilton into the western peninsula, the visitors would begin to notice that settlements were becoming smaller and separated often by large tracts of tangled forest, threaded by little better than ancient Indian trails. If they travelled north a few miles they would become conscious of the fact that the wilderness hovered on the back porch of all those active little communities they had observed scattered along the lake front. The situation was similar in the Lower Province where tiny villages were strung out like coloured beads on the silver thread of the St. Lawrence or clustered in the Eastern Townships.

Despite the narrowness of the settled fringe, the observer would have been impressed with the vigorous economic activities everywhere in evidence.[6] Connecting the fringe with the hinterland were many rivers and small lakes which provided a natural route for timber to reach the settlements and often produced the motive power for operating the hundreds of saw mills in each province. Roughly 8,000 men were engaged in this staple industry contributing both to local needs and to the vital export of lumber in all forms that annually moved across the seas from Quebec, happily protected by Imperial preference tariffs.[7] At the time of Union, the Gore and Home Districts feeding into Hamilton and Toronto were at the centre of the lumbering activities in the Upper Province. A decade later the Ottawa region had become the major area of supply, the cut from the rest of the province being reduced in comparison to a trickle. In the Lower Province, the industry was more widely scattered, but with some concentration in the counties on the south side of the river opposite Quebec. In a few years, as in the Upper Province, the source of supply was to shift to the north in the St. Maurice and Saguenay areas.

[6]However, had our tourist possessed both hindsight and foresight, he would have observed that this particular economy—based on staple products—was subject to extreme boom-and-depression conditions. Had he been present in the spring of 1838, for example, he would have experienced the apathy and defeat noted by prominent settlers; again, with the modification in Imperial tariff policies in 1842 and, more especially, in 1846, he would have witnessed a serious depression. See D. G. Creighton, *Dominion of the North: A History of Canada* (Boston, 1944), chap. v.

[7]Early trade returns of the province can be little better than rough estimates, although the tariff wall required fairly accurate accounts of the value of goods imported. For the extensive list of lumber products shipped out (but to which no value has been assigned) see "Schedule of Imports and Exports 1841, 1842," in *Journals*, Legislative Assembly, Canada, 1843, Appendix S.S.

Important as was the lumbering industry to the colonial economy, the foundation of settlement everywhere was agriculture, probably between seventy to eighty thousand farmers being employed in each province.[8] Many of these, of course, carried on timber-cutting operations in the winter to supplement their cash crops of wheat, oats, barley, potatoes, and the like. Estimates of the acreage under cultivation showed nearly two million acres in Upper Canada and over two and one-half million acres in Lower Canada under the plough.[9]

As with the lumber industry, rivers provided both transportation and power for processing the grain crops. Grist mills were even more numerous than saw mills and more widely scattered throughout the farm lands in both colonies. The British preferential trade policy accounted in great measure for the activity in processing grain, for producers in the United States shipped their grain to Canada for milling and then exported to the British market, enjoying the benefits of the preference extended to colonial flour.[10] The adoption of free trade in 1846 was a serious blow to this enterprise and when an economic depression struck in the late forties the names of many Canadian entrepreneurs were appended to the Annexationist Manifesto of 1849.[11]

Apart from the two basic colonial enterprises, agriculture and lumbering, there were many small-scale domestic industries that had grown up mainly to supply local needs. The pot and pearl asheries, useful in the production of soap and glass, were actually productive enough to feature as important export industries.[12] Presumably the well-known thirst of the inhabitants—especially in Upper Canada—accounted for the impressive development of domestic breweries and distilleries.[13] There was also a large household manufacture of cloth, linen, flannel, and woollens in both the Canadas; wool carding and

[8]These figures are rough calculations based on census figures for 1851, the first occasions that the occupational breakdown was attempted.

[9]*Censuses of Canada, 1665 to 1871*, vol. IV, Upper Canada Census, 1841, Table II, p. 131; Lower Canada Census, 1844, Table VII, p. 154.

[10]See A. R. M. Lower, *Colony to Nation* (Toronto, 1946), chapter XXI; also G. N. Tucker, *The Canadian Commercial Revolution, 1845–1851* (New Haven, 1936), chap. v. Over 300,000 barrels of flour were shipped out of Quebec and Montreal in 1841; see "Schedule of Imports and Exports 1841, 1842."

[11]See Tucker, *The Canadian Commercial Revolution*, chap. IX.

[12]Exports of pot ashes from Quebec and Montreal in 1841 amounted to 14,066 barrels, pearl ashes to 7,287 barrels.

[13]The 1842 Census for Upper Canada (Table XI), p. 140, lists 96 breweries and 147 distilleries. The import lists display thirteen different types of wine arriving in the colony in substantial quantities.

fulling mills, local tanneries and foundries were liberally scattered throughout both colonies.[14]

Congregated in the larger cities and towns there were perhaps six to seven thousand merchants engaged in the export of staples and the forwarding trade. Testifying to the higher standard of living enjoyed by this class and by the professional class of about the same size, the census listed about twenty thousand domestic servants for both colonies.[15]

From the economic point of view then, our early visitors would have confronted a population whose solid core was made up of agriculturists, spread out along the great water route to the interior and rapidly thinning out as the "back townships" were reached. At this period nearly all the farms would have been heavily wooded and consequently the two staple crops—wheat and timber—could be harvested in a complementary fashion. Such industries as existed were small, often household concerns and linked either with the processing of the two staples or designed to meet the colonists' everyday demands for such items as tools, nails, leather, and cloth. Since the export trade and forwarding services were all-important in the economic life of the colony, a substantial group of merchants had congregated, notably at Quebec, Montreal, Kingston, Toronto, and Hamilton. There were few businessmen with sufficient capital to embark on large-scale projects; even the government had to use its fullest powers of persuasion to bring the capital resources of the Imperial authorities to its aid. Fifteen years later with the railway building boom in the air and visions of great colonization projects colouring the thinking of Imperial authorities, capital was more easily attracted into the United Provinces.

[14] The figures are as follows:

	Wool carding	Fulling	Tanneries	Foundries
Census, U.C., 1842	186	144	261	22
Census, L.C., 1844	169	153	335	69

It may be surmised that the affluent colonists did not ordinarily patronize local textile products for we are told that, as a mark of their patriotism in 1837, they vied with one another in the conspicuous wearing of clothing made from domestic cloth. See Alfred D. Decelles, *The "Patriotes" of '37*, vol. xxv in the "Chronicles of Canada" series (Toronto, 1916), pp. 62 f.

[15] These estimates are based on the census figures of 1844, Table VI (Lower Canada), p. 153, and of 1851, Table VI (Upper Canada), p. 193, Table VII (Lower Canada), p. 217. Contemporary letters suggest that the chief topic of female conversation, after the inadequacies of local transportation had been fully canvassed, was the problem of securing, training, and retaining adequate domestic help. See, for example, *A Gentlewoman in Upper Canada: The Journals of Anne Langton*, ed. by H. H. Langton (Toronto, 1950), *passim*.

From a broader point of view, the observer in the 1840's confronted a population in which young people were numerically much more significant than they are today, over half the population in both colonies being under the age of sixteen.[16] In the Lower Province practically all the inhabitants were born in Canada, while in Upper Canada about half the settlers had been born in the British Isles or the United States.[17] This contrast was important for it revealed not only the newness and mobility of the people in the Upper Province but also the tendency for the rising tide of immigrants to bypass the Lower Province. Proudly attached to the soil, the church, and their cultural heritage, the French-speaking Canadians watched the population of the energetic, restless sister province gradually pull ahead, thereby disturbing the precarious balance of political power.[18] The religious homogeneity of the population in Lower Canada provided a solid conservative counterweight to the advancing numbers in Upper Canada. In the latter province, religious factions were numerous and no one predominated.[19] They also tended to become identified with political movements[20] thereby intruding extra emotional notes into a public opinion that was already sufficiently divided by other factors.

The increasing agitation of public opinion in the colonies and the ultimate precipitating causes of the open rebellion in 1837 have been well and amply described in most Canadian histories. In the Lower Province the battle line was drawn on the civil list question and the demand for an elective second chamber. The demands of the "Patriotes" became increasingly exorbitant with each refusal of co-

[16]Today, even with the "baby boom," the number of young persons under sixteen is less than 30 per cent of the population.

[17]The population figures reduced to rough percentages reveal the following situation:

	Born in province	British Isles	U.S.
Census, U.C., 1842	52%	40%	6.8%
Census, L.C., 1844	87%	9%	1.7%

[18]Once again the census figures reveal the shift in the population balance:

	Population of U.C.	Population of L.C.
Census U.C., 1842, L.C., 1844	487,053	697,084
Census, 1851	952,004	890,261
Census, 1861	1,396,091	1,111,566

[19]A rough outline of the relative strength of the major denominations is as follows:

	Catholic	Church of England	Methodist	Presbyterian
Census, L.C., 1844	82%	6%	—	—
Census, U.C., 1842	13%	22%	17%	20%

[20]See Lower, *Colony to Nation*, pp. 164 f.

operation from the executive. In the case of the civil list the executive wished to protect its independence by assuring a fixed annual sum to cover the salaries of political, administrative, and judicial officers. The Assembly, dominated by the exigent Papineau, insisted on asserting a control over the executive which the Mother of Parliaments itself did not at that time possess, namely, the power to vote all costs of government on an annual basis. The immovable executive confronted the irresistible force of the legislature; refused its "supplies" by the Assembly, the executive government was deprived of the way and the will to provide good administration. Factiousness hitherto confined to loud words and noisy votes was transformed in the fall of 1837 into a brief but serious show of force.

In the Upper Province the agitation which eventually produced a parallel rebellion centred on a curious mingling of political, religious, and economic complaints. In the Act of 1791 Pitt had foisted an appointive Legislative Council on the colonies, hoping thereby to provide the form by which a local aristocracy might be developed to offset the creeping disease of republicanism. This appointive Council was criticized as much by Upper Canadian as by Lower Canadian reformers. In addition, however, a slavish adherence to British forms had induced Pitt to provide the Upper Province with all the trappings of an Established Church, endowing the "protestant clergy" with one-seventh of the surveyed lands. The clergy reserves and the establishment of the Church of England were a source of real discontent amongst the many powerful competing religious groups. The census indicated that the privileged church could claim less than one-fifth of the population. The reserves were also an obvious source of economic discontent for they were an inseparable part of the most complicated problem facing colonial administrators—the equitable disposal of the public lands. From the manner of their laying out, the reserves resulted in the interposing of large tracts of wild, uncultivated land between the cleared and settled tracts. It was common testimony, from Gourlay's controversial questionnaire in 1818 to the later committees investigating the "wild lands" in the 1850's, that the reserves by scattering settlements had rendered uneconomical the building of roads and schools.[21] Similarly, the reserves were the centre of political discord. The ruling clique in Upper Canada, led by John Beverley Robinson and John Strachan, were nearly all members of the Established Church. The Reform party drew much of its strength from

[21]See Wallace, *The Family Compact*, p. 30.

the Methodists who undoubtedly felt most discriminated against in receiving no share of the reserves and who were often stigmatized as disloyal because of their connections in the United States. When Sir John Colborne, the Lieutenant-Governor, by his last official act, endowed forty-four rectories in Upper Canada this proved to be one of the most important grievances which drove the extreme wing of the Reformers, under Mackenzie and Rolph, to rebel.

Sailing boldly into the tense atmosphere of the post-rebellion period came Lord Durham, vested with extraordinary powers as commander-in-chief and high commissioner "for the adjustment of certain important questions depending in . . . the Provinces of Lower and Upper Canada." Between June and the end of October 1838, Durham and his staff busily collected the raw material for his famous report which was presented to the British House of Commons in February 1839. The administrative implications of the report are examined in the following chapter and we need recall here only its three major features. First, it proposed a legislative union of the two Canadas. Second, it presumed the long-run assimilation of the French-speaking population and the consequent disappearance of the problems arising from "the two races warring within the bosom of a single state." Third, it maintained that local self-government could be made compatible with colonial dependency if a clear-cut division of functions was made, leaving one area entirely within the autonomous control of local authorities. On the third proposition Durham proved an accurate prophet. His second assumption was incorrect, although the division between the races has since been bridged in less drastic ways than through assimilation. His first proposal, that of legislative union, proved unworkable. By the 1860's the legislative union had become politically bankrupt and was bailed out only by the achievement of a broader federal union in which each unit was permitted to retain its local powers and privileges.[22]

Charles Poulett Thomson (or Lord Sydenham as he was soon to become) arrived in Canada in mid-October 1839, after having been well briefed by his predecessor. A man endowed with the same self-confidence and energy as Lord Durham, Sydenham possessed a subtler political touch which was immediately called into play as he sought to bring the two provinces into a union which neither was keen to

[22]Thus in 1867 Canada employed the same principle of functional division that Durham had proposed in 1839 when trying to combine Imperial control with local self-government in the colony.

effect. Taking advantage of the suspension of the normal governmental processes in Lower Canada, he had the special Legislative Council of fourteen, chosen by himself, approve of the Union. A rapid barnstorming tour of the Upper Province accompanied by an active lobby of the Assembly then in session resulted in a similar agreement from that section. The Imperial Parliament, with certain amendments and deletions, approved his Act of Union in July 1840 and on the first anniversary of the Queen's marriage, February 1841, the Union was proclaimed in force. In April elections for the new legislature were held throughout both sections. On June 14, 1841, the first legislature of the United Canadas met in Kingston with Lord Sydenham frankly superintending operations in order to get the Union well launched.

The political and legislative achievements of Sydenham have been as carefully considered by the historians as those of his predecessor. But probably his outstanding permanent achievement was in laying the foundations of the administrative services of the provinces. Lord Durham diagnosed the administrative weaknesses of the provinces and conceived the grand design for reform but, as is suggested in chapter III, Lord Sydenham must receive full credit for his ingenious implimentation of those parts of the plan which had administrative implications.

CHAPTER II

LORD DURHAM PROPOSES

LORD DURHAM'S REPORT on the affairs of the British North American colonies was a scathing indictment of the civil services of the two Canadas before Union. "No country in the world," he wrote indignantly, "ever demanded from a paternal government, or patriotic representatives, more unceasing and vigorous reforms, both of its laws and its administrative system. . . . From the highest to the lowest offices of the executive government no important department is so organized as to act vigorously and completely throughout the Province and every duty which a government owes to its subjects is imperfectly discharged."[1] Poulett Thomson confirmed Durham's views when he despairingly wrote home to his brother in March 1840 saying of Lower Canada: "The hand of the Government is utterly unknown and unfelt at present out of Montreal and Quebec."[2] And yet, less than eighteen months later, Lord Sydenham was writing with unrestrained optimism to the Colonial Secretary, Lord John Russell:

The task . . . which I undertook two years ago is entirely completed, and I have the satisfaction of feeling assured that the great objects of my

[1]*Lord Durham's Report on the Affairs of British North America*, ed. by Sir C. P. Lucas (3 vols., Oxford, 1912), vol. II, p. 98 (all citations from the report are from the Lucas edition). Some Canadian historians agree with Beverley Robinson, a severe contemporary critic of Lord Durham's report, that Durham's portrayal of the state of the administrative services in Upper Canada was too gloomy. During the course of a short visit Durham could have gained only an impressionistic view of these services, but even so, his description does not appear to have been too inaccurate in the larger outlines. Ten, even twenty years later, as subsequent chapters on the individual departments will attempt to show, the public service was still trying to shake itself clear from its unfortunate administrative legacies. Durham tended to oversimplify when he attributed administrative deficiencies to the personal failings of the ruling clique. As will appear there were many institutional reasons for other deficiencies which persisted long after responsible government had been won.

An indispensable supplement to Durham's report is the series of surveys of Upper Canadian departments made by a royal commission in 1839–40 to which reference will subsequently be made. Most of the members of this large investigating body were themselves directly concerned in administering the affairs of the province. And yet, even with their understandable bias in favour of the status quo, the commissioners and those appearing before them were surprisingly frank in substantiating in detail some of Lord Durham's hasty generalizations.

[2]See G. Poulett Scrope, *Memoir of the Life of the Right Honourable Charles Lord Sydenham*, (London, 1843), p. 176.

mission are answered. The Union of the two Canadas is fully perfected. . . . Effective departments for every branch of the public service in this province have been constituted, and the future harmonious working of the constitution is, I have every reason to believe, secured.[3]

This glowing self-congratulatory letter surely could have been written only in that excess of physical well-being which we are told attended the cessation of one of Sydenham's periodic attacks of gout. Certainly the course of true administrative reform, following Sydenham's death in 1841, did not run smooth. Nevertheless, Sydenham, working within the framework of Durham's report, must receive full credit for setting up the modern departmental system of public administration. He must have built wisely and well, for a quarter century later at Confederation the departmental structure remained virtually the same as that which he had first proposed in 1840.

The significance and value of Sydenham's contribution can best be appreciated by following Lord Durham through his critical exploration of the decrepit administrative services prior to the Union. According to the dictum of Adam Smith, defence, preservation of public order, and the provision of a few major public works were the activities to which any government ought to confine its attention. The administrative apparatus required to provide these three services in the colonies was, so far as Lord Durham could judge, in a very sorry state. The protective services were under the jurisdiction of the Lieutenant-Governor of each province, such officials having been chosen in the past for their military experience. An uneasy supervision of the British Army Commissariat was divided between the Lieutenant-Governors and the War Office in London. The local militia was under the Adjutant General's office. In Lower Canada, according to Durham, the militia was so disorganized that it could not be used even for local police duties.[4] The situation could have been little better in Upper Canada because commissions in the militia had become notorious political plums much sought after by the type of person who would never be suspected of carrying a marshal's baton in his knapsack.

The administration of justice, a second central responsibility of the state, was chaotic and unregulated.[5] A Solicitor General, located in Montreal, tried unsuccessfully to control the sheriffs in each judicial district as well as the justices of the peace. The latter served at the

[3]Sydenham to Russell, July 21, 1841; quoted in O. A. Kinchen, *Lord Russell's Canadian Policy* (Lubbock, Texas, 1945), p. 164.
[4]Durham's *Report*, vol. II, p. 133.
[5]*Ibid.*, pp. 116 f.

parish level as a substitute for non-existent local governments in Lower Canada. In Upper Canada there was more adequate provision for courts, but sheriffs and clerks of Crown pleas operated in splendid isolation. Since these officers of the judicial branch were eligible, at the time, to hold a seat in the legislature, the dispensation of justice was attended by unsavoury political favouritism that did not lend prestige to the system.

Disorganized and inefficient as were the administration of protective services and justice, Durham found even worse conditions in the management of other state functions. Provision of public works, Adam Smith's third major category of state activity, was of profound importance to the colonists. Canals, roads, bridges, county court houses and post offices, harbours, timber booms and slides, lighthouses and navigational aids were matters on which great elections turned and objects of daily speculation amongst isolated and dependent colonists. The brave figure of the sturdy self-reliant pioneer has perhaps been overdone. Even the bravest and most self-reliant were prepared to fight tooth and claw for a government-built bridge or road that might save them days or weeks of unpleasant travel by awkward water routes;[6] or for a port or postal station that would mean all the difference between lonely isolation and some regular contact with friends and relatives outside the country. Just as the income tax, rent controls, and social services loom large to us today, so for the pioneer community a projected road, a canal lock, or a postal connection became a matter for constant agitation. In perspective we see these matters not as they would be for us today, insignificant and petty, but rather as issues of vital concern. The government had a slender purse to meet the insatiable demands of the colonists. Competition was so keen that legislators were under the constant pressure of interested parties.

Normally such pressure would have been exerted upon local authorities rather than upon the provincial government. But since competent local authorities at that time were lacking, "the great business of the assemblies" as Durham revealed "is literally parish business"—much of it concerned with local bridges and roads. Profligacy was encouraged by the use of that free-for-all system still peculiar to the United States whereby any private member of the legislature had the right to introduce his own measure calling for the expenditure of public funds. "When they [the members of the Legisla-

---

[6]See, for example, *A Gentlewoman in Upper Canada: The Journals of Anne Langton*, ed. by H. H. Langton (Toronto, 1950), pp. 183 f.

ture] came to their own affairs, and, above all, to the money matters," Sydenham wrote in amazement to his brother, "there was a scene of confusion and riot of which no one in England can have any idea. Every man proposes a vote for his own job; and bills are introduced without notice, and carried through all their stages in a quarter of an hour!"[7] The lack of executive control over the raising of funds for public works was accompanied by a decentralized system of superintending the expenditure of the money so voted. *Ad hoc* commissioners were appointed by the legislature to take charge of each separate work. Lord Durham found one astonishing case in Nova Scotia where £10,000 having been voted for local improvements, 830 commissioners were appointed to superintend the expenditure of the fund. Since each commissioner received five shillings per day and 2½ per cent commission, little remained after these "expenses of management" had been covered.[8] Canal builders, like William Hamilton Merritt, had complained to Durham about the lack of capital for undertaking badly needed public works, but, as Sydenham quickly realized, no help could be expected from the Imperial authorities until a more efficient system of management had been introduced. As will be seen, Sydenham thought his new Board of Works was one of his greatest contributions to the future welfare of the colonists.

Durham's criticism of colonial public administration reached its climax when he considered the arrangements for managing public lands.[9] Executive and legislative councillors competed with one another in the speculative purchase of lands, large sections of which had been granted to United Empire Loyalists. The Attorney General in Upper Canada set an example for the rest of the colony by inventing the most ingenious ways of evading the regulations which were designed to prevent single individuals from monopolizing large tracts of land. The common man often despaired of obtaining clear title to his land. "The necessity of employing and paying agents acquainted with the labyrinths of the Crown Lands and Surveyor General's departments," according to Durham, forced many militia men to sell out their military land grants at great personal loss. Then when title was granted, faulty surveys performed by dishonest or incompetent surveyors could lead to years of heart-breaking litigation over disputed boundaries. In Lower Canada settlers had to be patient, for a land

[7]Scrope, *Memoir of Lord Sydenham*, p. 172.
[8]Durham's *Report*, vol. II, p. 93.
[9]*Ibid.*, pp. 203 f. Durham reserved a section of the *Report* for his examination of the "Disposal of Public Lands." See also special report in Lucas, vol. III, **Appendixes**, Appendix B.

patent might take from six weeks to eight years to pass through the labyrinth.

The Crown Lands Department, which at Union was required to administer this tragic mess, fumbled about for years searching to overcome its unfortunate heritage. Its task was rendered more difficult by the astonishing assortment of odd-job agencies which finally took refuge under its hospitable roof. The history of its misadventures will be taken up in a later chapter.

Another major concern of the Durham mission was the state of the emigration service. With the zealous but not altogether balanced Gibbon Wakefield on his staff it was inevitable that Durham's report should have much to say on the subject of colonization.[10] The last part of the report contains harrowing tales of the arrival in Canada of diseased and destitute immigrants for whom the government was prepared to assume very little responsibility. Conjoined with these tales of horror Durham ironically included a statement from the British authorities in which the policy of voluntary emigration was complacently approved. When Sydenham became Governor, he supported Durham in expressing his indignation of a policy that simply dumped paupers "under the Rock" at Quebec leaving them to shift for themselves. As a member of the middle class, he could not resist a further gibe, commenting in satirical vein that there were now so many inexperienced *émigrés* idling about looking for positions that it reminded him of home and the endless search for jobs for "second sons."[11] The justice of this *laissez-faire* immigration policy had been slightly tempered with mercy (or at least medical aid) by the establishment in 1834 of a quarantine station on Grosse Isle. But it was not until the black year of 1847, as will be noted later, that the colony obtained the right to regulate its own immigration service.

One would not have expected much in the way of state-directed education at a time when England still left this subject to voluntary (mainly religious) associations. Charles Buller, who investigated the educational system of Lower Canada on behalf of Lord Durham, discovered that half the money appropriated in the form of grants to local educational institutions had been squandered on unrelated local works.[12] The system of appointing local commissioners, generally politicians, to administer these grants was obviously unsatisfactory. In Upper Canada a series of grants both in land and in money had also failed to produce any remarkable development in educational

[10]*Ibid.*, vol. II, pp. 242 f.
[11]Scrope, *Memoir of Lord Sydenham*, pp. 210–11.
[12]Durham's *Report*, vol. II, p. 95.

facilities. Buller's report, which was accepted by Durham, served as a basis for a revitalized educational system in both sections of the United Provinces after 1844. By 1855 the editor of the *Massachusetts Teacher* was able to inform his readers, after touring Upper Canada, that "a system of education in some respects more complete and more imposing than that of Prussia [then regarded as a pioneer in state-controlled education] has sprung up on our own borders."[13] Dr. Ryerson was largely responsible for this advance in Upper Canada, and the tactics he employed to implement his strong opinions make the reference to Prussia rather appropriate.[14]

All public services depend upon the provision of adequate funds. Consequently, the efficient administration of a country's revenue collecting services would appear to be essential for the development of a successful administrative machine. Unfortunately, since these agencies had to be dispersed in the Canadas the revenue-collecting services tended to be isolated and vulnerable to patronage hunters and to peculation. Lord Durham apparently did not pay much attention to these agencies, but contemporary reports clearly reveal that an unfortunate situation had grown up.[15]

The revenues from the sale of Crown lands were supposed to support a great variety of public services. But in practice their value remained potential, because sales were limited by the slow settlement of the country, and such revenue as was obtained was quickly swallowed in the exorbitant costs of management. Apart from the Crown lands, then, the chief sources of current revenues were the Post Office, the Customs, and the Inland Revenue Offices.[16]

While it may seem odd to include the Post Office in this category,

---

[13] Quoted in J. G. Hodgins "Historical Sketch of Education in Upper and Lower Canada," in H. Y. Hind *et al*, *Eighty Years' Progress of British North America* (Toronto, 1863), p. 374.

[14] Since much has already been written on the subject of education, this aspect of colonial administration has not been pursued. See, for example, J. G. Hodgins, *Documentary History of Education in Upper Canada* (28 vols., Toronto, 1894–1910), and C. B. Sissons, *Egerton Ryerson: His Life and Letters* (2 vols., Toronto, 1937–47). For a thorough examination of earlier developments which qualifies the traditional view of Ryerson as educational innovator, see George W. Spragge, "Elementary Education in Upper Canada, 1820–1840." *Ontario History*, vol. XLIII (1951), pp. 107–22.

[15] An especially valuable study of the difficulties in the early customs service is in "Report of the Select Committee on Customs Collections of Upper Canada," *Journals*, Legislative Assembly, Canada, 1841, Appendix V.V.

[16] Territorial revenues for the year 1842 amounted to £51,775 from which costs of management equal to £27,202 had to be deducted. Revenues in 1842 from the Post Office came to about £56,392 less £43,978 for management.

Customs (net) £265,386
Inland revenue (net) £ 31,925

actually at this time England listed the Post Office amongst her tax-collecting agencies.[17] And in the British North American colonies there was even more reason to think of the Post Office as a taxing instrument. Its charges were so high and its services so inadequate that most colonists must surely have regarded it primarily as a tax-gathering rather than a servicing agency.[18] This attitude was fortified by the practice of sending back all "profits" on the postal service to the British Treasury rather than using them to improve or expand services in the colony. Nor were this Department's relations with the colonists enhanced by having its affairs under the control of an Imperial officer, the Deputy Postmaster, Thomas Stayner. This official made all appointments and approved all mail contracts and applications for new post offices. Next to the Governor himself he was the highest paid colonial official and also one of the most heartily detested. The colonial legislature was thinking particularly of Stayner when one of its committees reported in 1838 that

> there is a growing impatience and unwillingness on the part of the Colonists . . . to have the measures of Government, whether connected with their general system of government, legislation or patronage, controlled by persons who are utter strangers to them, not responsible in any way to themselves or the British Parliament, and who perhaps, being advanced to their office from length of service, or other like cause, are not regarded as competent (perhaps unjustly) to manage and direct measures which they (the Colonists) deem of vital importance.[19]

Lord Durham clearly believed that the effort to assert an absentee control even over trivial local matters was a major source of unrest in the colony as well as an important cause of administrative delay and inefficiency.

The Customs Service was responsible for collecting duties imposed on imports under both Imperial and colonial legislation. Theoretically this service was also run from a Whitehall office but in practice control was exercised effectively only over the older branch of the service—that is, the customs officials, particularly those at Quebec and Montreal, who collected duties based on Imperial legislation. Under the terms of the Canada Trade Act, 1822, the Upper Province was given one-

---

[17]During the 1840's, for example, the "Board of Taxes and Stamps" was listed as one of the main revenue departments. See Great Britain, *Parliamentary Papers*, 1843 session, vol. XXX, no. 551.

[18]See William Smith, *The History of the Post Office in British North America, 1639–1870* (Cambridge, 1920), chaps. XII and XIII.

[19]Quoted by Durham in his *Report*, vol. II, p. 106.

fifth of the collections made at the ports of Lower Canada. This proportion was increased to over one-third by 1836. Meanwhile, in the 1830's the provincial legislature imposed duties on imports into Upper Canada from the United States. The staff of these inland customs ports were under the general supervision of a provincial official, the Inspector General. Reliable investigators[20] claimed that Upper Canada collected only one-half the revenue which the current duties on American goods ought to have produced. There was widespread sympathy for the smuggler, the value of goods smuggled into the province being estimated as much greater than the value of the goods upon which duty of any sort was paid. Isolated local collectors, under only nominal supervision, were left to their own discretion in applying the high, unpopular duties on such articles as books, tea, and tobacco. The collector quickly learned that the lot of the "revenuer," unless he wished to co-operate, was not an 'appy one!

The Excise—or Inland Revenue—Service was much less important as a revenue producer, but it appeared to be run on the same slipshod lines under the Inspector General. While it appears that some licences were indeed issued by the Courts of General Quarter Sessions, for some reason the provincial Inspector General's Office was required to license such miscellaneous items of local concern as public houses, billiard tables, "hawkers, pedlars and petty chapmen." The cost of administration was, for that reason, grotesquely out of line with the revenues produced.

While this detailed picture of the administrative services could give Lord Durham little pleasure, he was even more concerned by the situation existing at the top of the provincial civil service. A sound axiom for good administration is that there must be unified responsible direction at the top. Lord Durham found neither unity nor responsibility.[21] Instead he found a hostile legislature which insisted on overstepping what Durham called "the proper limits of Parliamentary interference" in order to show the executive that it was quite independent.

[20]See "Report on State and Management of Customs in Canada," *Journals*, Legislative Assembly, Canada, 1843, Appendix B.B. Referring to the 30 per cent duty on books, Malcolm Cameron, the investigator, noted that theology and law books bore the brunt of the duty. In the first instance, presumably, the claims of conscience necessitated a declaration of the goods; in the case of the lawyers "because they can make more in the time out of the people, than by evading the revenue law." Cameron was not the first colonial businessman to cast aspersions on the legal fraternity. See the remarks of W. H. Merritt cited below in chap. IV.

[21]Durham's *Report*, vol. II, p. 81.

Having no influence in the choice of any public functionary, no power to procure the removal of such as were obnoxious to it merely on political grounds, and seeing almost every office of the Colony filled by persons in whom it had no confidence, it entered on that vicious course of assailing its prominent opponents individually and disqualifying them for the public service by making them the subjects of inquiries and consequent impeachments . . . and when nothing else could attain its end . . . it had recourse to that *ultima ratio* of representative power . . . a general refusal of supplies.

Thus did Durham summarize a situation which verged on a state of guerrilla warfare. The temptation to intrude on the executive's administrative responsibilities proved too great to resist, and it early developed in the legislature the feeling that the public service was its special target.[22]

But even without the disruptive pressures of the legislature on the administrative branch, unity of command would not have prevailed. Lord Durham discovered that both the Governors and Lieutenant-Governors in the colonies were, as he neatly put it, only "slightly responsible." The closest parallel to their constitutional position would have been that of a state governor or the so-called "weak governor" in the states of the American union before the reforms of the 1920's strengthened his hands. Administrative power did not come to a focus in the Governor for he could be (and was) short-circuited by certain officials who were technically his subordinates. This situation was most marked in the Post Office and in the Imperial portion of the Customs Branch where departmental officials took their orders from and carried on their correspondence with the parent departments in Whitehall.[23] Lord Durham, as has already been noted, considered absentee direction to be at the root of much of the administrative weakness he had uncovered.

[22]As the patronage was gradually transferred from the hands of Imperial officials to the Canadian executive in the years after 1840, the legislature fought even harder to assert its control over the civil service. While it had to concede the right of individual appointment to the Canadian ministry, the legislature was able by statute to curb the executive's discretion. In this respect it asserted itself more successfully than did the Imperial Parliament, for in Great Britain the executive managed, throughout the reform period 1850–70, to retain complete command of the civil service. To this day, no general British Civil Service Act has been passed comparable to the Canadian Civil Service Act first passed in 1857.

[23]The Commission, dated July 17, 1827, appointing Peter Robinson Commissioner of Crown Lands in the Province of Upper Canada, provides a good illustration of the divided allegiance of an official in the colony. After a long recital of his duties, he is directed in the execution of the said office "to obey all such orders and directions as you may from time to time receive from the Commissioners of the Treasury, or of one of His Majesty's Principal Secretaries of State, or from the Governor, or Officer administering the Government for the time being."

But a more disturbing factor was the ambiguous relation of the Governor to his Executive Council. Ostensibly, the Council existed to advise the Governor on all matters which were referred to it.[24] In some matters, the Governor, operating under his instructions, was compelled to consult his Council; in other cases, he used his own discretion in deciding to request or accept the Council's advice. According to Durham's findings, the Council, usurping the prerogatives of the Governor, effectively dispensed patronage, made land grants, handled appeals, pardons, and reprieves, and directed the issuance of proclamations which authorized the establishment of inland customs ports, markets, judicial circuits, and polling booths. If, in the exercise of these powers, public indignation was aroused, the members of Council could shift responsibility to the Governor. His short tenure and lack of knowledge of local politics, coupled with his theoretically complete responsibility, made him a convenient scapegoat.[25] Vociferous attacks on the administration brought on the recall of the Governor, while the Council continued undisturbed in office. Since all Councillors, from 1820 on, had been required to take an oath of secrecy, the public could never determine who was, in reality, responsible for the advice upon which presumably the Governor had acted. Indeed, even the members of Council could not be sure which of them had the ear of the Governor. This position of partial responsibility remained embarrassing for the Governor so long as he was viewed as the formal head of state in the colony. Lord Sydenham, for example, who automatically assumed this role, found his incomplete powers particularly galling. But this was a problem which, after all, would disappear once the local executive became responsible for policy.

It was precisely because Lord Durham counted on this constitutional change that he attached so much importance to the creation of a proper departmental system, with responsible ministerial heads capable of advising the Governor on local problems.[26] Durham went to the root of the matter and suggested the remedy.

The mere ordinary administration [he wrote] would require the superintendence of persons competent to advise the Governor, on their own responsibility, as to the measures which should be adopted, and the additional labours which fall on the heads of such departments in other countries, in devising improvements of the system and the laws relating

[24]For a brief description of the early duties of the Executive Council, see *Preliminary Inventory, Record Group 1, Executive Council, Canada, 1764–1867* (Public Archives of Canada, Manuscript Division, 1953), pp. 5–7.
[25]Durham's *Report*, vol. II, pp. 75 f.
[26]Durham's *Report*, vol. II, pp. 108–9.

to each, would certainly afford additional occupation. . . . Yet, of no one of these departments is there any responsible head, by whose advice the Governors may safely be guided. There are some subordinate and very capable officers in each department, from whom he is, in fact, compelled to get information from time to time. But there is no one to whom he, or the public, can look for the correct management and sound decision on the policy of each of these important departments.

As Durham concluded, "it is really difficult to conceive how a desirable responsibility could be attained except by altering the working of the cumbrous machine, and placing the business of the various departments of Government in the hands of competent public officers."

The Executive Council of Lord Durham's time, then, differed in at least three fundamental respects from our modern cabinet. First, the Council did not contain individual ministers, each one having responsibility for the administration of a particular department of state. This change, as will be noted, was Sydenham's contribution to the evolution of cabinet government. Second, the Council was not responsible to the legislature, but was viewed strictly as the Governor's council to use or abuse as he pleased. Lord Elgin was to acknowledge formally in 1849 the primary allegiance of the Council to the representatives of the colonists gathered in parliament. Finally, the Council did not operate as a unified team either in tendering advice to the Governor or in confronting the legislature. The growth of a collegial spirit depended upon the Governor's willingness to treat his cabinet as a team frankly and openly, without resorting to secret manipulation and private deals with individual members of the Council. It also depended upon the maturing of true parties out of jealous factions so that party loyalty could reinforce the formal ties of cabinet solidarity. It is impossible to say exactly when these two conditions were finally fulfilled but it is clear that throughout the whole period before Confederation the growth of team spirit within the cabinet suffered many set-backs. As will appear later, the position of the Prime Minister in this period lacked the magnetic force which it acquired after Confederation. Furthermore, it will also be shown that the organization of the cabinet for handling business tended to discourage joint decisions.

In summary, Lord Durham had discovered in the colony a most disheartening scene of administrative incompetence. The administrative agencies set up to provide public works, to manage natural resources, emigration, and education, and to collect various taxes revealed many shortcomings. But the debility of these services was really the fault of feeble, unco-ordinated or non-existent administrative leadership. At the top of the hierarchy Durham could discover no real heads of departments who were capable of assuming both individually and collectively full responsibility for administrative services. A Governor owing responsibility to the Colonial Secretary; an atomized Executive Council tendering discordant secret advice to the Governor who need pay no attention if he so desired; a Legislature swinging rudderless in the full tide of its own passions, tied to the unstable mooring of the colonial electorate; uncivil and unfruitful squabbles between Governors and Assemblies, resulting often in hopeless deadlock; and, finally, a group of poorly informed Whitehall departments, with snail-like pace passing references on colonial matters back and forth, issuing detailed instructions, sometimes over the head of the Governor, to officials of their own choice who were responsible for administering local services: obviously vigorous administration could not be expected while these conditions prevailed.[27]

A single reform or a lone reformer could not reduce this chaos to order. But the attack begun in 1839 by the Colonial Secretary Lord John Russell and the new Governor Lord Sydenham prepared the civil service of the colony for assuming the full weight of responsible government when that constitutional change was formally acknowledged at the political level by Lord Elgin in 1849.

[27]Sir James Stephen at the Colonial Office expressed great irritation at receiving criticism from the colonies for delays and confused orders when, in his experience, the fault rested with such departments as the Treasury and the Board of Trade jealously trying to safeguard their own jurisdiction and patronage preserves. For illuminating evidence on this point see Paul Knaplund, *James Stephen and the Colonial System, 1813–1847* (Madison, 1953), chap. III, especially at pp. 41 f.

CHAPTER III

LORD SYDENHAM DISPOSES

IN HIS EFFORTS to do full justice to the memory of Lord Durham, Charles Buller wrote that Sydenham had reaped what Durham had sown. Lord Durham, he contended, "saw the defects, and devised the remedies; others have stepped in to appropriate the honour of the execution."[1] No one could refuse to acknowledge the justice of Buller's claim on Durham's behalf. But it is important to realize that the colonists themselves were not idly standing by while Durham diagnosed their political and administrative ills. On May 9, 1839 (nearly six months before Sydenham landed at Quebec) the legislature of Upper Canada sent a joint address to the Lieutenant-Governor, Sir George Arthur, asking that he appoint a royal commission to inquire into the state of the public departments. Arthur had in fact precipitated this request on the part of the legislature by himself undertaking a reorganization of the office of the Provincial and Civil Secretary (an office which was really his staff agency on civil matters in the colony).[2] The Lieutenant-Governor, therefore, gladly acceded to the request by appointing the Commission on October 21, 1839. It was a very large body, made up almost entirely of men in public office. It proceeded on a business-like basis, allocating to one or other of eight subcommittees the responsibility for investigating one specific branch of administration. Two committees reported on the administration of justice, others dealt with the Executive Council, Receiver General, Inspector General, Indian Department, Education, and the Adjutant General's Office.[3] Arthur was not destined to receive the reports of his Commission, but Sydenham (though he apparently never acknowledged the Commission's work) certainly must have relied on the

[1]Durham's *Report* (Lucas ed.), vol. III, *Appendixes*, "Part III, Sketch of Lord Durham's Mission to Canada in 1838" (by Charles Buller), p. 374.

[2]*The Arthur Papers*, ed. by Charles R. Sanderson (3 parts, Toronto, 1949), part III, pp. 100 f, 115.

[3]"Report of the Royal Commission Set Up to Investigate Business, Conduct and Organization of Various Public Departments of Upper Canada," *Journals*, Legislative Assembly, Upper Canada, 1839–40, vol. II. An interesting modern parallel to their procedure was that of the Hoover Commission on the Organization of the Executive Government in the United States. While the Upper Canadian Commission failed to obtain an integrated report comparable to the Hoover Report, the special studies give us the best available picture of the state of the public services prior to the Union.

analysis of administrative weaknesses provided in these special studies. They filled in many details which Durham in his hasty survey of Upper Canada had overlooked.

Lord Sydenham was well equipped to undertake the incredibly difficult task of bringing about the union of the two Canadas and reorganizing the administrative departments of government.[4] As a young man he entered the family business, and travelled widely on the continent, developing that debonair self-confidence which is often associated with men of a slight physical frame. He needed all of it when he arrived in Canada. He also acquired, on his business travels, the observant eye, the mastery of detailed facts, the tact, and the sound business sense which are the necessary virtues of the first class administrator. He had been associated with Huskisson in the task of consolidating the British customs service, and in the late 1820's he was a member of the famous Parnell committee on the improvement of public accounts. His friendship with the economist Bowring and such stalwart reformers as Joseph Hume and Jeremy Bentham provided additional evidence of his interests and abilities. All of these were brought into play when he embarked on his great campaign to make some of Lord Durham's report a working reality.

Any measure which Sydenham had to propose was, of course, subject to the overriding jurisdiction of the Colonial Office. It is important to observe, therefore, what views Lord John Russell, then Colonial Secretary, entertained with respect to implementing Lord Durham's report. Russell has been blamed for his short-sighted attitude toward the report's major recommendation.[5] He was not prepared to accept the principle of a colonial executive responsible on strictly local matters to a colonial assembly. Nor could he accept Durham's view that the dilemma of combining local responsible government with over-all Imperial control could be solved by carving out two separate spheres of action and responsibility. Although increasingly difficult to maintain with each new concession to colonial pressure, his view was that cabinet responsibility in the colony was incompatible with the retention of a colonial governor responsible to the Imperial government.

[4]Short sketches of the career and character of Sydenham are to be found in his brother's *Memoir* (London, 1843), part I and pp. 295 f.; in Adam Shortt, *Lord Sydenham*, "Makers of Canada" series, vol. XXV, ed. by D. C. Scott, Pelham Edgar, and W. D. LeSueur (Toronto, 1908); and in J. C. Dent, *The Last Forty Years: Canada since the Union of 1841* (2 vols., Toronto, 1881), vol. I, pp. 37 f.

[5]See, for example, Rosa W. Langstone, *Responsible Government in Canada* (Toronto, 1931), pp. 105 f., and the introduction by Sir C. P. Lucas to Durham's *Report*, vol. I, pp. 142 f.

In one important respect, however, Russell's cautious approach was justified. Unless there was a complete reorganization of the departmental structure, any grant of responsible government would be dangerous. It would be dangerous because, as Durham himself had so clearly revealed in his report, as long as there was no executive leadership and guidance, flaccid, dishonest, ineffective government would prevail throughout the colony. The Colonial Secretary apparently realized the need for a top-level reorganization as a preliminary to the adoption of any further steps in the direction of responsible government. In an important despatch addressed to Sydenham on July 23, 1840, Russell outlined what he called his three "rules of administration."[6] These are worth developing, for Sydenham's reforms followed them very closely. "It may be understood as a cardinal maxim," he wrote, "in constitutions where the Executive has the character of a Monarchy, and the Legislature in one of its branches has derived from the choice of the people, that the Executive should be charged with the administration of the Public Revenue and that the Representative Assembly should check and control abuse, profusion, or misapplication." If the Assembly was to be deprived of the power to handle the expenditure of public funds, Russell admitted that a second and compensating principle must be recognized: "Every Office should be so constituted that all proceedings carried on in it should be a matter of daily record, and where no superior measure of state intervenes, such proceedings should, when requested, be laid before the Assembly." Clearly, if control of executive expenditures was to be effective, the legislature needed to be fully informed.

Had Russell intended to sponsor the complete cabinet system his despatch at this point would have set forth additional principles governing the relation of the executive to the legislature. However, the despatch says nothing further on this issue and, indeed, Russell had, in a previous despatch of October 14, 1839, already stated that it was not the policy of the Imperial government to appoint all members of the Executive Council from the majority group in the Assembly.[7] Furthermore, while he was prepared to let the Assembly exercise "a due control over the officers appointed, or kept in office by the Governor, and over the distribution and expenditure of public funds," he was not willing to give the executive the same status as the ministers in England because the Governor of the colony must still

---

[6]Public Archives of Canada, R.G. 7, G. 1, vol. 48, pp. 274–7. These rules are also conveniently cited in part by O. A. Kinchen, *Lord Russell's Canadian Policy* (Lubbock, Texas, 1945), Appendix 9.

[7]Russell to Thomson, Oct. 14, 1839, cited in Kinchen, Appendix 7.

take his orders from the Imperial government rather than his colonial advisers.

The third rule of administration propounded in Russell's despatch was designed to guide Sydenham's reorganization of the departments. He directed that the functions of the departmental heads should be clearly explained to them and that all were to be directly responsible to the Governor for the conduct of public business. Recognizing the importance of unity of command, Russell wanted to provide each department with a responsible ministerial head. Unlike modern cabinet ministers, however, the departmental heads were to be responsible primarily to the Governor rather than to the legislature.

Lord John Russell's conception of colonial government as expressed in these three rules of administration harmonized with Sydenham's own view of his role in Canada which has been aptly described as that of combined Governor, Prime Minister, and party manager.[8] It required energetic action in all three capacities to implement Russell's rules of administration, but Sydenham with justifiable pride was able to report substantial progress in a despatch which he sent to the Colonial Office shortly before his death. Explaining his efforts to apply Russell's first two principles he wrote:

I have appointed to the Executive Council none but the principal officers of the Government, who are responsible both to the Governor, and the public for their acts. . . . For the satisfactory conduct of public affairs, it has appeared to me absolutely necessary, that on the one hand, the Governor should be able to rely upon the zeal and attention of the Heads of Departments not merely to act under his immediate directions upon every minute point, but also to feel themselves really responsible for their conduct of their different offices—and on the other hand, their being members of one or other House of Parliament, the public would possess a wholesome control over their acts, and the security would be obtained for the general administration of affairs being in accordance with the wishes of the legislature.[9]

Sydenham also attached much importance to the requirement that the executive initiate all money matters. He was able to write this principle into section 57 of the Act of Union, stating at the time that without this section "I would not give a farthing for my bill."[10]

[8]J. L. Morison, *British Supremacy and Canadian Self Government, 1839–1854* (Glasgow, 1918), pp. 88 f. "I actually breathe, eat, drink and sleep nothing but government and politics," Sydenham reported after one hectic session of parliamentary management. Sydenham was convinced that only a skilled parliamentary tactician could survive successfully as Governor of the province.
[9]Public Archives of Canada, R.G. 7, G. 12, vol. 57, pp. 289–94.
[10]Quoted in Scrope, *Memoirs of Lord Sydenham*, p. 172.

These decisions conformed with Russell's directives, for the members of the Executive Council, despite Sydenham's offhand reference to their acting in accordance with the wishes of the legislature, were really responsible to him. The council was literally *his* council "for the governor to consult," as he frankly admitted, "but no more."[11] The conception of joint cabinet responsibility was also incompatible with Sydenham's view of his councillors. It consorted better with his capacity as canny party manager to be free to consult his councillors separately and often secretly. Nevertheless, Sydenham's reforms did establish unity of command within each department and then brought the reins of control into his own hands. Sydenham's handling of the first two rules of administration was, of necessity, equivocal. The colonists expected responsible government; the Colonial Office instructed him to withhold it. Steering between these two opposite demands, Sydenham placated the colonists by his tact and brilliant manœuvring but in the process he conceded enough either by promise or implication to compel his successors Bagot and Metcalfe to take further steps along the road to fully responsible government.[12]

Sydenham's major contribution, then, was made as an administrative reformer, rather than as a constitutional innovator. Detailed administrative reform, however, depended upon the accumulation of much technical information concerning the internal structure and operations of each department. Lord Durham's *Report* and the accompanying special studies on land management, immigration, education, and municipal government were especially helpful in reconstructing the administrative services in Lower Canada. In the Upper Province, as has been noted, a royal commission on the public departments produced detailed studies of the various agencies which added much to Sydenham's knowledge. And in July 1840 Russell instructed the Governor to appoint a commission to investigate the Post Office—an administrative agency which had escaped both Lord Durham and the Royal Commission, but which had been the subject of an exhaustive inquiry in 1835.[13] In the following year a select committee was also appointed to investigate intensively the Customs Ser-

[11]*Ibid.*, p. 143.
[12]Bagot moved more or less willingly in the direction of responsible government; Metcalfe, arguing that Sydenham had betrayed the Imperial cause, fought a grim rearguard action against the advocates of responsible government.
[13]The inquiry resulted in the comprehensive and valuable "Report of the Commissioners Appointed to Enquire into the Affairs of the Post Office in British North America," *Journals*, Legislative Assembly, Canada (henceforth *J.L.A.C.*), 1846, Appendix F. See also William Smith, *The History of the Post Office in British North America* (Cambridge, 1920), pp. 233 f.

vice in Upper Canada.[14] Apparently Sydenham felt that he was much better briefed on the situation in Upper Canada than in Lower Canada. Echoing Lord Durham, he wrote to his brother: "Not a man [in Lower Canada] cares for a single practical measure. . . . There is positively no machinery of government. Every thing is to be done by the governor and his secretary."[15]

Despite his enormous energy, Sydenham was not able to prepare remedies for all the administrative ills which these investigators had diagnosed. The commission on the Post Office, for example, did not report until Sir Charles Bagot, his successor, had been appointed.[16] Even so Sydenham boldly took up the cudgels against the Deputy Postmaster General, that most independent Imperial administrator, forcing him to bow to his superior authority. Indeed, he carried his battle for concentrating power in the Governor's hands right back to headquarters where, over the head of Freeling, the Secretary of the Post Office, he forced a reduction in colonial postal rates.[17] Reform of the Customs Service, which one might have assumed from his earlier work with Huskisson would have been a logical objective, had to await the attentions of his successors. The same was true of the Indian Department. Despite these important omissions, Sydenham's reorganization of the other departments created, in fact, the necessary underpinning for the cabinet system that he himself was unable and probably unwilling to introduce. This achievement was all the more remarkable when it is realized that he had little more than a year in which to build.

What precisely were the measures he took? Reporting to the Colonial Office in July 1841, Sydenham described them in detail.[18] Working from the departments which had existed separately before the Union, he rearranged their functions in order to provide a more coherent and efficient system. Starting with the office that was most closely affiliated with the Governor, the so-called Civil Secretary's

[14]"Report of Select Committee on Customs Collections of Upper Canada," *J.L.A.C.*, 1841, Appendix V.V.
[15]Scrope, *Memoir of Lord Sydenham*, p. 175.
[16]The report was dated December 31, 1841, but was at first regarded as confidential—hence its later appearance in the *Journals* for 1846.
[17]See Smith, *History of the Post Office*, p. 233. For detailed evidence of Sydenham's struggle with Stayner see "Return re Correspondence between Home and Provincial Government re Post Office Department etc. . . . ," *J.L.A.C.*, 1844-5, Appendix I.
[18]Public Archives of Canada, Sydenham to Russell, no. 92, July 18, 1841, R.G. 7, G. 12, vol. 57, pp. 239-94. I am indebted to Professor Paul Knaplund for copies of Colonial Office papers (Public Record Office, C.O. 323/57) containing James Stephen's interesting reactions to Sydenham's prodigious legislative programme.

Office, Sydenham sought to reduce its duties. Both he and Durham had commented on the fact that nearly all colonial business was handled by or routed through the Civil Secretary. This concentration of power in the hands of the Civil Secretary was objectionable for, as Sydenham wrote to Russell in July 1841:

> It is evident that that officer who is and always must be the confidential Servant of the Governor and whose tenure of office should therefore terminate with the Governor's, can never on his first arrival, and scarcely indeed at any time, profess that intimate local knowledge which is necessary to carry on a correspondence . . . [relating to] the whole internal arrangements of the Province.[19]

Sydenham, therefore, planned to restrict the Civil Secretary to "the conduct of the correspondence with the Secretary of State and the Lieutenant-Governors, the British Minister at Washington, and all Foreign authorities or individuals as well as such general questions as pertain to both Provinces."

The former duties of the Civil Secretary relating to purely local matters Sydenham now proposed to place in a newly created Provincial Secretary's Office headed by "two gentlemen resident in the Province and the terms of whose offices will not end with the Governor, but be on the same footing as any other office in the Province."[20] Organized in a fashion reminiscent of the British Home Secretary's Department prior to the 1780's, this Office had an Eastern and Western division.[21] This was a regrettable acknowledgement from the administrative point of view of the truth of Lord Durham's famous statement, "I found two nations warring in the bosom of a single state." This dualistic note is struck again and again, in many of the administrative agencies which were designed to execute programmes for the United Provinces. Sydenham attached to the Eastern division of the Provincial Secretary's Office a new agency, the Registrar's Office. He viewed this agency as one of his key innovations for he was trying to abolish feudal tenures in Lower Canada and substitute a more convenient form of tenure which required a business-like system of registering property transactions.

As will appear later Sydenham's efforts to re-route government business through the Provincial Secretary's Office were not immediately successful. The Colonial Office and several of his successors

---

[19]Public Archives of Canada, R.G. 7, G. 12, vol. 58, p. 118.

[20]*Ibid.* Sydenham was following, in part, the rearrangement in the office made by Lieutenant-Governor Sir George Arthur in 1839.

[21]See Sir Frank Newsam, *The Home Office* (London, 1954), chap. II. The original division of the Secretary of State's Office into a Northern and a Southern Department was, says Newsam, "primarily religious and political."

in Canada did not agree with his view that the Civil Secretary was primarily a private secretary to the Governor. They envisaged him essentially as the permanent head of the colonial civil service. And indeed throughout the greater part of this period the Civil Secretary retained a variety of responsibilities such as supervisor of the Montreal police and superintendent of Indian affairs.

The Executive Council had degenerated, according to Sydenham, to a mere committee for passing on claims for land grants and for the intermittent audit of public accounts. Both of these tasks were transferred, land matters moving to the Commissioner of Crown Lands and auditing to the Inspector General. However, in practice the Executive Council was unable to escape from either the detailed consideration of land patents or the careful scrutiny of revenues and expenditures. For that reason Sydenham created the new position of President of Committees of Council, designed to supervise the handling of this type of work.[22]

Another new administrative adjunct was Sydenham's Board of Works. Successful negotiation of an Imperial loan of one and one half million pounds to be used for public works had been the succulent bait with which Sydenham had tempted Upper Canada into the Union. On the other hand, Sydenham had to guarantee to the Imperial authorities that the money would be better spent than had been the case in the past. In June 1839 a Board of Works had been set up in Lower Canada, and in August 1841 the Board's jurisdiction was extended to the United Provinces "conferring," as Sydenham reported to Russell, "the most extensive powers upon that department, and thus enabling us to proceed safely and securely in whatever may be undertaken on the public account or with public aid."[23] Sydenham's prophecy, as the subsequent administrative history of this agency makes abundantly clear, was not very accurate. However, the creation of one central authority in the place of the dozens of separate agencies was a distinct improvement.

The management of the public lands had been in the hands of a Commissioner of Crown Lands appointed for each province and Sydenham now tried to concentrate all land management operations in his new Crown Lands Department which he expected to work in

[22]For a more extended description of this position see below, chap. VI. Today, the cabinet, mainly through Treasury Board, has found a way of checking the tiresome flood of petty financial detail that would otherwise waste its valuable time. The early struggle to make the cabinet a more efficient committee of management will also be examined in chap. VI.

[23]Public Archives of Canada, Sydenham to Russell, Toronto, Sept. 16, 1840, R.G. 7, G. 12, vol. 57, pp. 35–44.

close conjunction with the long-established Surveyor General's Department. He could not have envisaged the amazing accretion of odd jobs which over the next twenty years made of the Crown Lands Department the largest and most amazingly polyglot administrative agency in the province.

Sydenham's account of his rearrangement of the financial agencies of the province is rather vague. He appears, however, to have had the British Treasury as his model in trying to strengthen the Inspector General's Department. That Department had traditionally been responsible "for the sufficiency of the authority and the correctness of the calculations, etc." of all departmental expenditures, the Executive Council merely deciding "upon questionable items" and confirming or overruling "the allowance or disallowance of the Inspector General."[24] In short, not only was a pre-audit or "comptrol" function expected of the Inspector General but also a post-audit of expenditure. Sydenham apparently wished to add to these responsibilities the duties of a department of finance. This was, in fact, the arrangement then prevailing in the British Treasury. For many years, in both countries, auditing remained a subordinate branch of the financial department. Writing of the qualities which he required in his Inspector General, Sydenham claimed that he must be not only "acquainted with accounts and competent to superintend the routine business of his Office, but also capable of proposing the financial arrangements from time to time necessary and of explaining and indicating these arrangements in the House of Assembly." Apparently Sydenham envisaged a man who could combine the practical accounting abilities of an Auditor General with the financial skill of a Minister of Finance.

With a reorganized Inspector General's Department to look after expenditures Sydenham coupled a Receiver General's Office to look after revenues. However, the practice of paying the cost of managing various departments out of gross revenues often left the Receiver General with nothing to receive. This was a practice that persisted with remarkable tenacity for a number of years in both England and Canada, and one that Sydenham, pursuing a common prejudice of businessmen in colonial public life, himself encouraged. Reform of the postal and customs services, the other two agencies connected with administering the finances of the province, was never properly undertaken during Sydenham's régime.

[24]See "Report on the Public Departments," *Journals*, Legislative Assembly, Upper Canada, 1839–40, "Third Report of General Board on Inspector General's Office," pp. 32 f, and "Fifth Report on Executive Council Office," pp. 13–14.

Creation of a system of local government was, in Sydenham's mind, very closely associated with his other administrative reforms. Taking to heart Lord Durham's criticism that the business of the legislature was mainly parish business, the Governor believed that the only cure was to create vigorous local governments. He greatly feared that his efforts to assert the Executive's power over money bills would be wasted if there were no local governments to handle minor public works financed by local rates. If the attention of the Executive was to be diverted from the broader tasks of administering the affairs of the United Provinces by the need to introduce and defend a host of local money measures, Sydenham felt there would be no improvement. Moreover, he realized how important it was to devolve authority to local governments in a frontier community with inadequate means of communication. Writing to Russell in September 1840 to record his disappointment at the Imperial government's refusal to adopt his local government bill, he said:

. . . whilst the Government is thus brought directly in contact with the people it has neither any officer in its own confidence, in the different parts of these extended provinces, from whom it can seek information, nor is there any recognized body, enjoying the public confidence, with whom it can communicate, either to determine what are the real wants and wishes of the locality, or through whom it may afford explanation.[25]

This serious gap between the senior government and the colonists was only partially filled by the introduction of Sydenham's District Councils. Nevertheless, many of the administrative problems which it will later be shown confronted large departments like Public Works and Crown Lands could be traced to the colonists' desire to establish direct contact with the senior government in lieu of any effective local government. The expensive and administratively cumbersome system of local agencies was the central government's response to this pressure.

In assessing the contributions of Lord Sydenham to the creation of the public service of the new Province of Canada it is necessary to recall Charles Buller's statement that Sydenham reaped the harvest after others prepared the soil and planted the seed. Even before Lord Durham planted the seeds of reform, critical colonists had been loosening the soil. In the 1830's the Post Office had been up for legislative scrutiny and the Committee on Grievances had not missed the opportunity in 1835 to complain of the failings of the government services.

[25]Public Archives of Canada, Sydenham to Russell, Aug. 4, 1841, R.G. 7, G. 12, vol. 57, pp. 301–3.

Reformers in Upper Canada had seized the opportunity afforded by Lieutenant-Governor Arthur's reform of his own Civil Secretary's office to request a full-scale investigation of the public departments. Durham's *Report* put the finishing touches to these earlier inquiries, especially documenting the sad state of affairs in Lower Canada and presenting what in effect became the long-term programme of action. However, having admitted that much preliminary work had been done by the time Sydenham arrived on the scene, it is still true that Sydenham knew how to go about the difficult task of making the programme an administrative reality. Restricted by Lord John Russell's colonial policy, Sydenham none the less built a substantial foundation for the modern civil service.

The key to his administrative reorganization was to be found in the assertion of the principle of unity of command. In so far as the colonial situation permitted, Sydenham succeeded in his object of converting the "slightly responsible" Governor into the real executive of the province. Except for the suzerainship of the Imperial authorities, Sydenham's relations with his departmental heads approximated those which the President of the United States now entertains with his cabinet. As strong governor, Sydenham was more than a Prime Minister, more than captain of a team of colleagues. Like the President of the United States he alone was responsible for policy and over-all administration; but unlike the President his primary responsibility was not to the electorate but to the Imperial government.

The principle of unified command and co-ordination was carried down from the Governor to the head of each department. Sydenham, following Durham's advice, created a separate political head for each major department. This measure necessitated a reshuffling of duties amongst existing departments and the creation of several new agencies. This process of administrative "rationalization" was responsible for reforms in the Executive Council, Civil and Provincial Secretary's Offices, and the Offices of the Inspector General and Receiver General. At the same time new departments like Crown Lands and the Board of Works were created. Sydenham's insistence upon the adoption of the British practice of having all money bills introduced by members of the executive further tightened the reins of control held at the top. Since each departmental head was made individually responsible to the Governor rather than jointly responsible to the popular assembly, Sydenham's plan obviously fell far short of the modern cabinet system. This achievement awaited a change in the attitude of the Imperial government as well as a Governor more sympathetic to the objectives outlined in Lord Durham's *Report*.

CHAPTER IV

THE BUREAUCRACY FROM WITHIN

THE DEPARTMENTAL FRAMEWORK which Lord Sydenham bequeathed to the province in 1841 remained almost intact throughout the whole period of Union. As new duties were undertaken, new branches were appended to the existing departments. The agencies hitherto under Imperial control, such as the Post Office, parts of the Customs Service, the Emigration Office, Indian Office, and Adjutant General's Office, when transferred to the local authorities became either full-fledged departments or were incorporated as branches of older agencies. Only one significant addition to the departmental structure, apart from these agencies, was required before Confederation; this was the creation of an embryonic Department of Agriculture.

Later chapters will be devoted to detailed studies of some of the more important agencies in the departmental constellation; it may be useful at this point, however, to review the general outlines of the administrative structure and examine some of the working conditions obtaining within the bureaucracy. The chart in the Appendix, "Chronological Perspective of Government Departments," depicts the departmental structure of 1841 for which Sydenham was responsible. The merging of departments and the addition of new branches can be followed through to Confederation; while the agencies listed on the right give an indication of what happened to the departmental structure when the new Dominion was created.

The following table shows the departments grouped into five categories based on the similarity of function: "Administrative"; "Financial"; "Defence"; "Education and Welfare"; "Natural Resources and Development." The relative size of each unit at selected dates is evidenced by the figures of the number of staff employed.

Within the first category headed "Administrative" is a group of four departments whose tasks related mainly to the servicing or co-ordinating of the work of other departments. Generally speaking, the fortunes of the first of these agencies, the office of the Governor's Secretary, followed the rise and decline of the personal powers of the Governor. In the early 1840's, the Secretary was the nerve centre of the entire colonial civil service. By 1850, reflecting the chief executive's loss of power, the Secretary's responsibilities gradually declined, until at Confederation they consisted of handling the

TABLE
Pre-Confederation Departments: Staff in 1842, 1852, 1867*

Department	1842 HQ.	1842 Field	1852 HQ.	1852 Field	1867 HQ.	1867 Field
I. Administrative Departments—Total	31	—	33	—	63	—
1. Governor's Secretary's Office	7	—	5	—	10	—
2. Executive Council Office	6	—	8	—	11	—
3. Provincial Secretary's Office	15	—	15	—	17	—
3a. Provincial Registrar's Office (Prov. Sec. *ex officio*)	3	—	5	—	16	—
4. Crown Law Office	—	—	—	—	9	—
II. Revenue & Finance Departments Total	23	101	57	281	98	844
5. Receiver General's Office	3	—	8	—	12	—
6. Inspector General's Office (Dept. of Finance)	7	—	10	—	16	35
6a. Customs Branch	—	75	6	200	18	472
6b. Inland Revenue Branch	—	23	—	34	—	105
6c. Audit Branch	—	—	—	—	11	—
7. Post Office†	13	3	33	47	41	232
III. Internal Order & Defence—Total	9	—	8	—	32	62
8. Adjutant General's Dept. (Dept. of Militia)	9	—	8	—	32	62
IV. Education & Welfare—Total	9	59	20	113	38	688
9. Indian Department‡	3	28	3	20	8	69
10. Emigration Office‡	3	—	4	7	5	34
11. Education Office ||	3	24	13	37	25	42
12. Public Institutions¶	—	7	—	49	—	543
V. Natural Resources & Development—Total	23	182	58	310	123	712
13. Board of Works (Dept. of Public Works)**	4	92	9	200	18	551
14. Crown Lands Department	6	45	33	110	61	152
14a. Surveyor General	10	45				
14b. Geological Survey	3	—	3	—	18	—
15. Agriculture and Statistics (including Census)	—	—	13	—	26	9
Total	95	342	176	704	354	2306
		437		880		2660

*The large judicial establishment and the employees of the legislative branch have been excluded from this list of "civil servants."

†These figures exclude the postmasters. In 1842 there were over 450 post offices staffed by local postmasters paid by fees; in 1852 there were over 600 and in 1867 over 2,300 post offices.

‡The Indian Department became a branch of Crown Lands in 1860 and the Emigration Office was absorbed by Agriculture and Statistics. The staff have been separated to make comparisons possible over the three selected years.

\|\|In 1842 assistant superintendents of education for Upper and Lower Canada were appointed; there was one clerk in the Upper Canada Office. The masters of grammar schools in Upper Canada (by 4 & 5 Vic., c. 19) were nominated by the Boards of Trustees but the Governor affirmed their appointments and their salaries came out of the public purse. The figures for the field staff in 1852 and 1867 include as well the salaried inspectors and the staff of the normal schools in Lower Canada. No figures for the normal and model School in Upper Canada could be located.

¶There was no department by this title but the figures for 1842 and 1852 record the staff of the provincial Penitentiary; in 1867 they also include provincial asylums, other prisons, district jails, and the Marine and Emigrant Hospital. This explains the great increase in staff under the 1867 column.

**Figures for all three years include staff of Trinity Boards at Quebec and Montreal, although in earlier years these were independent of the Department of Public Works. The field staff of 200 in 1852 is an approximate figure.

SOURCES: detailed, accurate figures for 1867 may be found in the "Blue Book" published as a supplement to the Annual Report of the Minister of Agriculture and Statistics in Province of Canada, *Sessional Papers*, no. 42, 1867–8. Earlier figures of headquarters' staff are to be found in the similar compilation made out in quadruplicate for the Colonial Office. A complete file of these dating back to Union is available in the Public Archives of Canada. Other returns against which these figures have been checked are found in the *Journals*, Legislative Assembly, Canada, 1841, Appendix J.J.; 1843, Appendixes P and A.A.; 1852–3, Appendix F.F.F.F.; 1856, Appendix 60; *Sessional Papers*, Canada, 1864, no. 58.

correspondence with the departments in Whitehall and with other agents of the British government abroad—such as the Ambassador at Washington.[1]

The Executive Council Office registered all decisions or applications of the other departments where the approval of His Excellency in Council was required. Orders in Council resulting from Council consideration of these matters were transcribed by the Office for the information of the departments. In a minor way, as will be shown, the Office, under the President of the Committees of Council, was performing some of the duties of a modern cabinet secretariat.

The Office of the Provincial Secretary, the third agency in the "Administrative" category, inherited many of the duties shed by the Governor's Secretary. When Sydenham first created the office in 1841 its duties were comparable to those exercised today by the Department of Municipal Affairs—attending to such matters as the appointment of municipal councillors whenever the local electorate had failed to elect them, finding securities for county registrars, dispatching Commissions of the Peace, and superintending the financial returns from District Councils (the local government units designed by Sydenham). In addition, the office became an agency for recording and registering the transactions of other governmental officials. Legal appointments and the many applicants for government positions were cleared through it. Various institutions such as the prisons and asylums reported through the office, as did the Education Department. Through his control of the Great Seal and Privy Seal, the Provincial Secretary ratified all important appointments and commissions. Questions raised in the House requiring parliamentary returns were channelled through the Office and all applications for payment of money required a warrant signed by the Provincial Secretary before payment could be made.

The Crown Law Department was not properly organized until 1855, until that time consisting merely of the Attorneys General and Solicitors General of both sections of the province. These law officers were required to give opinions on points of law, to draft proclamations, deeds, and other legal documents, and to examine bills prepared for the legislature. Theoretically, the Solicitors General were

[1]For a description of the duties of this office see the indispensable historical account prepared for Council by Thomas D'Arcy McGee, "Report on the Origin and Organization of the Public Departments," Public Archives of Canada, M. 837, 1863. This report is a loose folio of sixty or seventy pages, revealing several different penmen at work. However, McGee requested the report and sponsored it in cabinet. The brief descriptions of the other departments appearing in the rest of this section have largely been taken from McGee's "Report."

supposed to conduct the "non-political" legal work of the government such as preparing and conducting cases in the courts. In practice, they seem to have shared with the Attorneys-General "referential work" which involved rulings on points of law submitted by the other departments.

The offices of the Governor's Secretary, Provincial Secretary, Executive Council, and Crown Law Department have all been classified here as "administrative" because they were not really operating departments but concerned rather with facilitating the work of other agencies: they recorded, registered, and transmitted the multitude of official papers which passed in a relentless, deliberate flow from one agency of government to another. Throughout the whole period, as the table indicates, their combined staffs, all of which were employed at headquarters, remained very small and relatively static. Nevertheless, they were essential parts of the mechanism of "top command" and as such they will be reconsidered at greater length in chapter vi.

The second functional group, "Financial," in the table, includes the three departments concerned with government revenues and expenditures. The Post Office and the Customs Branch within the Inspector General's Office were the tax-gathering agencies. When the provincial authorities took command of the Post Office in 1851, an immediate expansion of facilities took place—a fairly strong indication that the servicing rather than the taxing functions of the Post Office were now to be stressed. A money order branch was added in 1855; the following year railway mail carriage and sorting along with fortnightly ocean mail service were introduced; the parcel post came in 1859. In the ten years after 1852 postal revenues trebled and, as the table reveals, there was a corresponding increase in staff.

The other revenue-collecting agency, the Customs Branch, remained until 1849 under the rather ambiguous system of dual control described in chapter ii: Imperial duties levied in Canada under British legislation were collected at the ports of Quebec and Montreal by a staff under the general direction of the Commissioner of Customs in England, and Imperial authorities audited the books; at the same time a purely "domestic" section of the Customs Service had grown up in connection with the trade between the province and the United States, and a growing list of inland customs "ports," forming a wholly Canadian Customs, came under the supervision of the Inspector General. When Imperial control was withdrawn after 1849 the whole service was placed under the Inspector General (in 1859 renamed the Minister of Finance).

At Confederation, in addition to over eighty customs ports there were 54 revenue districts for the collection of excise taxes and 18 offices to receive the tolls on shipping. One of the most important duties of the Inspector General's Department was to assemble annually for Parliament uniform trade and navigation statistics. Between 1840 and 1867 the Customs Branch expanded enormously; during the Sydenham régime, for example, there were only 44 customs officers; twenty years later there were nearly five hundred.

The three agencies chiefly concerned with regulating the financial affairs of the province were the offices of the Receiver General, Inspector General, and Auditor.[2] Like the departments listed in the first category as "administrative," the Receiver General, Inspector General, and Auditor were all in charge of offices of record and account, their relations being largely with the inner circle of officialdom itself or with a few financiers and bankers at home and abroad. The combined staffs of the three offices never numbered more than forty, despite the circumlocutory technique then in vogue for checking the inflow and outgo of public money.

The only agency in the third category, "defence," was the Adjutant General's Department which in 1861 became the Department of Militia. Unless a state of emergency or war was declared the Department remained almost moribund. As long as Imperial control of the militia prevailed the Governor as Commander-in-Chief was given the discretion to create new military districts, prepare muster rolls, and have the officers of militia report directly to him. In 1861, however, a Canadian Minister of Militia was appointed and all officers were placed under his authority.

The fourth category, "Education and welfare," would in any country today be one of the largest and still-growing classifications, and even during this early period it comprised several of the most important administrative agencies in the province: the Indian Department, the Emigration Office,[3] the Education Offices for Canada East and West, and various penal, reform, and charitable institutions (generally grouped together as "Provincial Institutions"). The Immigration Office and the Indian Department were two of the last Imperial agencies to be transferred to the province. Formally, neither these two agencies nor the educational authorities enjoyed the status of autonomus

[2]Since fiscal control is of critical importance to the public service, the whole of chap. VII below has been devoted to that topic. It will be convenient, therefore, to postpone until that point the analysis of the functions of these three agencies.

[3]The obvious Imperial origins of this Office are to be detected in the name "Emigration" Office; from the Canadian viewpoint it ought to have been Immigration Office (a title which has been preferred in this study).

departments. In practice, however, each agency, whether under Imperial or Canadian control, tended to operate quite independently.

The superintendents of the Education Offices for Canada East and Canada West, both working on shoe-string budgets, owed a formal allegiance to the Provincial Secretary. They corresponded with the schools at all levels in the educational hierarchy, distributed the governmental grants, assembled statistics, and poured forth an astonishing stream of textbooks and informative pamphlets.[4] The normal and model schools were also administered by the superintendents. In Lower Canada, the relations between the Department and individual schools were more direct because there were not, as in the upper part of the province, well-organized municipal authorities to administer the educational grants.[5]

Immigration affairs were supervised by a Chief Agent at Quebec who reported directly to the Governor or his Secretary. The Imperial phase of administration was formally closed in 1853 when the newly created Bureau of Agriculture took charge of immigration agencies located at Quebec, Montreal, Ottawa, Kingston, Toronto, and Hamilton.[6] The administrative problems connected with immigration interlocked with those arising from colonization and land settlement policies and are of sufficient importance to warrant a later chapter in this study.[7]

The Indian Department also started as an Imperial agency, remaining for most of the period under the superintendence of the Governor's Secretary. In 1860, after protracted negotiations, Indian affairs were thrust into the hands of reluctant Canadian authorities to be placed in a special branch of the Crown Lands Department. Historically, the chief duty of the Indian Department had been to disburse the annual "presents" to the Indians. During the period of Union the Department, pledged to the principle of "civilizing" its wards, continued an earlier policy of segregating the Indians on reserves and

[4] A brief glimpse of the activities of these two officials is to be obtained from "First Report of the Select Committee re State of the Public Income and Expenditure of the Province," *Journals*, Legislative Assembly, Canada, (*J.L.A.C.*), 1850, Appendix B.B.; see evidence of Ryerson and Meilleur. The fruits of Ryerson's labours have been preserved in J. G. Hodgins, *Documentary History of Education in Upper Canada* (28 vols., Toronto, 1894–1910).

[5] J. B. Meilleur, Superintendent of Education for Lower Canada, argued that this was one important reason why his administrative costs were higher than Ryerson's. See his evidence before the Select Committee on Public Income and Expenditure, *J.L.A.C.*, 1850.

[6] However, the Chief Emigration Agent at Quebec appears to have retained his autonomy until the Minister of Agriculture and Statistics took a firm grip on the affairs of the Department in 1862.

[7] See below, chap. xv.

provided each "Indian Superintendency" with its complement of missionaries, teachers, agents, and the like. Through various treaty arrangements, each tribe had funds or assets which had to be administered for them by the Department. This agency was an excellent example of what today would be called a "clientele" department— that is, an administrative agency which had the responsibility of serving all the needs of one particular section of the public. How this programme was implemented and the difficulties attending the clientele organization are matters for extended comment in another chapter.[8]

The most important pre-Confederation departments were located in the fifth category, "Natural Resources and Development." The Departments of Public Works and Crown Lands were the giant planets of the early public service, each drawing numerous administrative satellites within its orbit of power. Attached to the Department of Public Works, for example, were the Trinity Houses of Quebec and Montreal which managed the navigational aids on the St. Lawrence and the Gulf. Shortly before Confederation, a Board of Railway Examiners was also attached to the Department, its responsibilities being confined to checking financial probity of various railway companies.[9] The direct concern of the Department of Public Works was with the canals, locks, harbours, slides, and booms scattered along the internal waterways of the province. Its most troublesome responsibility was as a housing agency for all government departments. The chief administrative problems of the Department arose from its two most important features: first, by far the largest portion of the provincial budget was spent by it; second, its staff consisted primarily of technicians, such as engineers, architects, and draughtsmen.[10]

While the Department of Public Works was the great spendthrift, Crown Lands was expected to be the great revenue producer, acting in its capacity as government real estate agent. But administering and disposing of the public lands was only one side of this complex department's activities. In addition to the various land branches, there were branches to administer surveys, woods and forests, fisheries, mines, the Indians, colonization roads, and, more on the fringe of its responsibilities, the Geological Survey. The administrative problems of the Crown Lands Department, as will appear in later chapters, were attributable to the semi-autonomous nature of its constituent

[8]See below, chap. XIII.
[9]By 1867, however, the Board of Railway Examiners was attached to the Department of Finance rather than to Public Works.
[10]The implications of these features, together with a more extended commentary on the activities of this Department, are presented in chaps. XI–XII.

branches, the tremendous geographic range of its responsibilities, and the infinite opportunities for "spoils."[11]

The only significant addition to the original departmental roster established by Sydenham was the Department of Agriculture and Statistics. From its first appearance in 1853 until Confederation, it tended to become a repository for odd jobs that apparently could not be fitted into other departments. Maintaining a paternal though casual eye on a host of voluntary agricultural societies, the Department also assumed responsibility for collecting statistics (including the Census returns), registration of patents, and immigration affairs, and for a short period had a formal concern for the colonization roads programme. This Department was potentially one of the most valuable but unfortunately one of the weakest departments in the whole pre-Confederation administrative system.[12]

A bureaucracy consists of more than the departmental structure outlined above. Something must now be added about bureaucrats and their working conditions. The detailed statistics of staff in the table reveal that we are dealing with a small group which, during this entire period, never exceeded 2,700 employees. There was great variety, nevertheless, in the tasks performed, especially in the so-called "outside service," that portion of the staff employed in other than headquarters' offices (the so-called "indoors service"). In the outside service such varied occupations were available as lighthouse keeper, customs collector, steamboat inspector, canal superintendent, mail sorter, fisheries overseer, agent for land sales or colonization roads, Indian or immigration agent, and so forth. Many casual or seasonal labourers paid on an hourly, daily, or monthly basis—generally a rough and obstreperous crew—were employed by the Departments of Public Works and Crown Lands. Headquarters employed a more standardized array of clerks, copyists, bookkeepers, accountants, draftsmen, and a few engineers.

Recruitment of staff, with the exceptions of a few professional groups noted below, also followed the haphazard, politically influenced methods which were common in other jurisdictions. In 1857, however, a Civil Service Act formally approved the creation of a Civil Service Examining Board whose task it was "to examine all who may present themselves in accordance with regulations of the Board."[13] This

[11]See below, chaps. VIII–X.
[12]See below, chap. XIV.
[13]20 Vic., c. 24 (June 10, 1857). The Board consisted of all permanent heads of the departments plus the Commissioner of Customs, the Auditor, and the Deputy Provincial Registrar. It was directed to meet once a month.

measure was inspired by a wave of reform in England which had resulted in the creation in 1855 of a Civil Service Commission. Despite this step forward both the British Commission and its Canadian counterpart apparently suffered from the same weaknesses: neither had been granted powers to compel departments to submit candidates for examination, and the tests, being elementary and set up on a non-competitive basis, were scarcely capable of discriminating between good and bad candidates.[14]

In his special report to Council in 1863 Thomas D'Arcy McGee (then President of Council) made a strong indictment of the Act.

The system of examination [he wrote] has no doubt sometimes prevented grossly incompetent persons from being imposed on the service—but on the other hand the provision of the Act has tended to raise a presumption in the minds of those examined that they have some claim or right to public appointments, which others, however well known their qualifications, have not. . . . Another inconvenience of the same description is found in this, that the Act in reality authorizes no appointment of higher grade than a fourth class clerkship or at all events, no salary of a higher amount for those admitted under it, than $500. per annum. In making some of the most important civil appointments during the last five years, the Act was consequently set aside, by its very authors, as inconvenient and impracticable. The examination required by the Act has also been frequently evaded by the appointment as "Extra Clerks" of applicants for public employment. By the present law, no Extra Clerk is supposed to remain in office for a longer period than one month, unless by order in council; if he so remains the order in council is presumed—a species of prescription is established, and the "extra clerk" may be promoted in three months to a position and salary, to which the duly examined and appointed candidate cannot attain for two or four years.[15]

Summing up, on the basis of five years' experience with the Act, McGee concluded:

As a matter of fact, our system of examination has not, hitherto, proved either a passport or a hindrance to admission to the public service. There have been examined since 1857, 668 applicants; of these 516 were certified, and 152 rejected; of the certified we can identify as appointed at the seat of government something less than 10 percent. There were also, it may be remarked, 81 notices of intention received which were never acted on by the parties—making over thirty-three percent of the whole, who either declined the examination, or were rejected . . . What seems conclusive against that act, is the absolute right and title to position given to mere

[14]By 1870, the British administrative reformers succeeded in pressing home the principle of open competition and made the commission a truly effective instrument. But in Canada the system remained almost unchanged and relatively ineffective until after 1908.

[15]McGee's "Report," final section on Civil Service Act.

seniority; the absurdity of expecting the best men who may apply to enter the service at the foot of the ladder, the open evasions of the law, rendered sometimes unavoidable by its too stringent conditions; the discouragement of special capacities; and the general derangement and disorganization which must follow in time, from a system regulated by seniority alone.

In the interest of both the country and the civil service McGee asked that the Act be repealed. A bill introduced for this purpose failed to receive approval,[16] so that both the Act and the situation provoked by it were inherited by the post-Confederation civil service.

Apart from this formal and clearly unsatisfactory provision governing the recruitment of staff for regular clerical positions there were scattered evidences of a concern for the development of professional standards in other branches of the service. It should be remembered that in the 1840's few, if any, professions had been established in the colony—or, for that matter, in the mother country. The period after 1840 witnessed a remarkable growth in professional associations in Britain.[17] Each association sought to determine the qualifications for entry into the profession, administer its own entrance examinations, and regulate the group with its own code of professional behaviour.

In Canada a similar movement seems to have affected the lawyers and doctors, for repeated efforts were made around 1850 to organize under government auspices a bar association for Lower Canada and medical associations in both parts of the United Provinces.[18] More important from the civil service's point of view was the development of professional qualifications for the land surveyors. Indeed, the first rigorous entrance requirements for the civil service were set up in conjunction with the recruitment of land surveyors. It is interesting to observe that the department in England which pioneered the examination system was the Customs and Excise Service. This difference in emphasis probably suggests the relative importance of the two types of service to the two countries. Britain required capable and honest officials to handle one of the major sources of governmental revenue, whereas Canada's need for settlement was reflected in the early insistence on an efficient surveyor's branch. Moreover, in both

[16]See *J.L.A.C.*, 1861, pp. 36, 345; 1863 (Feb. Session), pp. 140, 280. Apparently the measure, introduced by McGee, received third reading in the Assembly but was not proceeded with.

[17]For an excellent survey of the growth of "professionalism" see A. M. Carr-Saunders and P. A. Wilson, *The Professions* (Oxford, 1933).

[18]For evidences of this interest see *General Index to Journals, Legislative Assembly of Canada 1841-1851*, under "Bar of Lower Canada" and "Medical Profession." See also *The Canadian Journal*, vol. I, 1852-3 (Council of the Canadian Institute, Toronto, 1853), pp. 1-6.

cases the specific qualities required for the position could be clearly stated and could be ascertained by examinations.

Whatever the explanation, in 1849 a provincial statute provided for a Board of Examiners consisting of the Commissioner of Crown Lands and six others appointed by the Governor.[19] Candidates had to be at least twenty years of age and were to provide evidence of having taken courses in geometry, trigonometry, mensuration, map drawing and plotting, and astronomy. A three-year apprenticeship was necessary, followed by a public examination held by the Board to test the candidate "with respect to his ability, and the sufficiency of his instruments"; certificates of character and sobriety were also required. In the years that followed, various amending acts were passed each of which contributed to the evolution of a real engineering profession. In 1857, for example, the apprenticeship period was reduced to one year, and a two-year university course leading to a degree in civil engineering, natural philosophy, or geology was introduced. The final stage was reached in 1860 when the Association of Provincial Land Surveyors and the Institute of Civil Engineers and Architects were incorporated.[20] The chief feature of these associations was that they were now self-governing, the state having withdrawn from the examining board. In the 1840's and 1850's, however, the government was probably the most important employer of men possessing such technical abilities; it was necessary, therefore, for it to assume the initiative in helping the profession establish itself.

In quite a different sphere, although just as important for the Canadian economy as were the surveyors and engineers, we find another instance of the effort to establish rigorous entrance requirements. Government regulation of the timber trade required the presence of a special official located at Quebec and known as the Supervisor of Cullers. The cullers employed under the Supervisor were responsible for measuring and grading various types of timber as it lay floating in rafts moored in the inlets around Quebec. In the case of the cullers, however, the trade itself first took an interest in determining what qualifications were necessary to make good cullers. According to early legislation dating back before the Union, the Supervisor could hire only those cullers who had shown to a Board of Examiners their "skill, experience, age, character, and knowledge of this [the Timber] Act

[19]12 Vic., c. 35 (1849). Amending statutes were 14 & 15 Vic., c. 4 (1851), providing for two Boards of Examiners; 18 Vic., c. 83 (1855), and 20 Vic., c. 37 (1857), making alterations in examinations and apprenticeship requirements.
[20]23 Vic., c. 139 (1860).

and factually acquainted with the department or departments of culling and measuring for which [they apply] to be licensed."[21] Prior to 1842 the government did not have any part in these arrangements: the Mayor of Quebec and the Board of Trade appointed both the Supervisor of Cullers and the Board of Examiners. In 1843 a statute empowered the Governor to appoint the Supervisor, and this official, acting with the Quebec Board of Trade, chose the Examiners.[22] The Supervisor, together with a small office staff, appears to have been treated as part of the public service, whereas the sixty or seventy approved cullers were definitely not civil servants. As late as 1865 a select committee was forced to report that, despite these careful arrangements for building up a selected corps of officials, the majority of them were "only third-class men."[23]

Given the feeble examinations and the rather undeveloped state of the professions throughout this period, it is not surprising to find politicians clinging to the traditional methods of personal appointment. At the lower level patronage appointments seldom give pleasure to the minister involved. Most good departmental heads would have agreed with the Honourable P. M. Vankoughnet when he said in 1860: "The distribution of patronage was never a pleasing task to the Government. There were so many applications for vacant offices that the death of an officer, whose office would have to be filled up, was as much a cause of sorrow to the Government as to the relatives of the deceased."[24] But in filling the key permanent posts, ministers would equally have agreed with D'Arcy McGee's previously quoted view that being tied to an inflexible and poor examination system would constitute an "inconvenience which must be felt by every administration."

Vankoughnet's comment suggests another aspect of the patronage system which is seldom recognized. A close inspection of the lists of public employees reveals that wholesale house-cleaning, as was practiced in the United States at this time, was not popular in Canada. If vacancies occurred in due course, patronage appointments would be made; but there are no instances of mass discharges and mass replenishment. Governments always found reason for expanding the service and thereby creating new patronage resources, but there were

[21]8 Vic., c. 49 (1845).
[22]7 Vic., c. 25 (1843).
[23]See "Report of the Select Committee in Relation to the Supervisor of Cullers' Office," *J.L.A.C.*, 1865 (1st session), Appendix 4.
[24]Reported in *Thompson's Mirror of Parliament, 1860*, speech on April 23, 1860.

limits to this form of favouritism as well. Imperial authorities (probably impressed by their own experience) were persistently suspicious of the colonists' abilities to resist the temptations of patronage which were so great in such departments as the Customs and Post Office. And the expansion of these services shortly after Imperial shackles were cast off, in 1849 and 1851 respectively, suggests that those suspicions were not unfounded and reveals that the temptation to expand these services unnecessarily was too great to resist.[25] Since the patronage aspect of recruitment is one of the few features of the early civil service that has received attention elsewhere, the discussion of this problem can be cut off at this point.

Presuming that a candidate, by hook or by crook or even by examination, gained an entrance to the pre-Confederation civil service, what sort of conditions did he find? Had he been one of the two or three hundred officials employed at headquarters he could count on a scenic boat trip either up or down the St. Lawrence every four years, as the seat of government after 1849 was rotated between Toronto and Quebec.[26] Apart from the personal inconvenience of these removals, the civil servant often had to work in uncomfortable offices with poor light, heat, and ventilation. The necessity of maintaining duplicate establishments in two capitals resulted in the rental of old buildings quite unsuitable for government offices, since, as the Department of Public Works insisted, they constituted magnificent fire traps. Even in Toronto where the renovated Parliament Buildings provided better accommodation for the various departments, disastrous fires periodically demolished valuable records.[27]

The Victorian schoolmaster must have had some hand in the preparation of office regulations, although discipline was easier to invoke on paper than in practice. Office hours usually ran from 9 to 4, clerical workers at first insisting on extra pay for overtime.[28] That seasoned colonial administrator, Sir Charles Metcalfe, put an end to overtime pay in 1843 and at the same time required attendance books to be kept to record entrances and exits. Two years later Metcalfe had to

[25]The expansion in these services must also, in part, be attributed to the anxiety of provincial authorities to expand facilities (as in the Post Office) which had been financially starved under Imperial control.

[26]This feature of life in the pre-Confederation civil service is sufficiently novel to warrant special consideration in the next chapter.

[27]For an interesting brief account of the vicissitudes of these buildings see Frank Yeigh, *Ontario's Parliament Buildings* (Toronto, 1893).

[28]See Public Archives of Canada, State Book B, May 26, 1843, p. 478, for list of regulations.

request that these regulations be called to the attention of the clerks.[29] In 1852 a minute of Council sought to standardize hours of work, during the winter months from 9.30 to 3 and during the summer from 9 to 4 without intermission.[30] The detailed regulations for Crown Lands officials suggest a much more rigorous regimen.[31] In addition to the general rule about working "without intermission" (which raises an interesting speculation about eating habits of civil servants), the clerks in the Crown Lands Department were forbidden to communicate verbally or in writing with any outsider unless they first obtained approval of their superior officers. Newspapers were to be kept safely isolated in the waiting room. Conversation with fellow employees was taboo except on business matters. Chief clerks were instructed to tutor juniors and brief them on these regulations. In 1862 supplementary regulations appeared.[32] Smoking in the building was now forbidden, whether on moral grounds or as a safety precaution is not clear. Clerks who visited around or were absent without leave from their desks for more than one hour were to be reported for breach of discipline. Perhaps the most significant regulation was that which read: "All Departmental letters and telegraphic despatches must be signed by the Commissioner or Assistant Commissioner." Since such communications flowed through the Department at the rate of about 10,000 per year, one can appreciate how this rule would create an awkward administrative bottleneck. And yet, as will be seen, the Department needed much more than this type of regulation to hold it together at the top. Even finicky regulations which attempted to place the department's relations with the public on a highly formalized footing were absolutely essential.[33]

Attendance regulations could not have been very carefully supervised. Sir John A. Macdonald, for example, in his capacity as Minister of Militia was forced in July 1862 to call to the attention of Council

[29]*Ibid.*, State Book D, June 2, 1845, p. 364.

[30]This regulation also had to be repeated; see State Book O, Feb. 3, 1855, p. 603. These regulations are the reverse of modern arrangements which normally require longer hours in winter than in summer. The inadequacy of artificial lighting must have necessitated the earlier winter closing hour.

[31]For these regulations see "Return re Crown Lands Department," *J.L.A.C.*, 1847, Appendix XX, item no. 4, "Rules and Regulations to be observed in the Crown Land Department."

[32]See "Annual Report of Commissioner of Crown Lands for the year 1862," *Sessional Papers*, Canada, 1863, no. 5.

[33]A later chapter will indicate how the offices tended to be overrun by land speculators who boldly walked off with departmental records or received inside information from a crony on the staff.

the case of three officials in that department: one, with forty years' service, suffered from epilepsy and had not been to work since November 1859; a second after working for three years had lost his eyesight about the same time; a third was of advanced age and delicate health, making attendance at his desk impossible.[34] In 1863, the Auditor reported that the Deputy Inspector General was still on the payroll although he had not been to work for the last eight years.[35] (This does not say much for the position which today is regarded as perhaps the most important permanent office in the civil service.) This laxity might be one way of compensating for the lack of a pension plan, but it certainly did not help the cause of departmental discipline and efficiency.

The payment of civil servants apparently followed no set principle. Rather rudimentary classifications existed for clerical, postal, and customs employees, but the civil service did not succumb to the grim logic of the classification analyst until the end of World War I. Meanwhile, the Civil Service Act of 1857 made some effort to establish coherence by setting out in attached schedules the salary scales which were to prevail in the various departments. But in 1862, Galt, who was then Minister of Finance, thought it necessary to appoint a special committee to consider and report on "the salaries to be paid to employees and their classification, especially with a view to equalizing the salaries in the Departments having due regard to the responsibility and labour falling upon each."[36] The committee, consisting of expert civil servants, made several reports, none of which seems to have been published. Before the Government could act in this matter, however, it was put out of office.

Civil servants themselves seemed to share with their modern counterparts the view that salaries should be adjusted to the cost of living. A woeful petition presented in 1857 by employees of the Legislative Assembly pointed out how inadequate were their fixed salaries when confronted with what they alleged was a 100 per cent increase in the cost of necessities. The government had responded to a similar plea in 1854 by recommending increases in salaries amounting in the case of lower paid clerks to as much as 25 per cent.[37]

An interesting sidelight is thrown on the attitude towards official salaries by the proceedings of a legislative committee of 1850,

[34]State Book X, July 24, 1862, p. 405.
[35]State Book Y, Aug. 6, 1863, p. 659.
[36]See Galt's memorandum to Council in State Book X, Jan. 27, 1862, p. 23.
[37]See *J.L.A.C.*, 1857, pp. 306, 567.

summoned for the purpose of considering economies in the civil service.[38] Agreeing to a proposal to reduce ministerial salaries by £200 to "meet public expectation," Francis Hincks nevertheless argued that it was not "wise policy to reduce salaries below what talent would command in other avocations, on the ground that public men should be actuated by patriotic motives, and that they are repaid by the honour which their offices confer." We may suppose that Hincks would have vehemently contested Jeremy Bentham's plan of putting public offices up to Dutch auction—the lowest bidder presumably having the highest motives and thereby qualifying for the post. The committee was inclined to agree that high salaries coupled with newly won responsible government would not, as some critics suggested, attract needy politicians to office for the emoluments and patronage involved. A majority agreed that salaries had to be high enough to make a public career available to any poor but capable citizen.

Actually the salaries paid in the civil service appear, by colonial standards, to have been quite attractive. Heads of departments at Confederation were paid $5,000; deputy heads generally received about $3,500; subordinate senior officials received between $1,400 and $2,400; clerks were hired at $500 and, moving by seniority, could expect at the end of fourteen years to be earning about $1,500. It is difficult to find the figures for making direct comparisons with salary scales in private employment. Nevertheless, in a country where cash incomes were often supplemented or even entirely supplanted by income in kind, civil service salaries were clearly quite inviting. The indirect evidence appears in the mail of every politician, for it was filled with requests for civil service appointments often suggesting as well a salary to which they felt their "services" had entitled them. There was never any danger that the demand for jobs would ever be exceeded by the supply. Compared with the teaching profession, one of the few salaried groups in the community, civil servants did very well indeed. At Confederation the average salary for a teacher was about $430; the highest salary paid in 1861, for example, was $1,300. So the clerical workers could expect ultimately to do better than any teacher. Salaries of professors at the University of Toronto ranged in the 1850's between $1,000 and $3,500. The earnings of a permanent head of a department, then, would have compared very favourably with the academicians' salaries.

Agitation for a pension plan for the Canadian civil service coincided

[38]See "Report of Select Committee on Public Income and Expenditure," *J.L.A.C.*, 1850.

with a major reform in the superannuation arrangements for British civil servants in 1859. Indeed, the Honourable Sidney Smith presented a resolution to the Assembly in 1859 which contained the details of a contributory pension fund modelled on the first superannuation scheme created for the British Civil Service in 1834. The plan got as far as third reading in the Assembly but seems to have been withdrawn by Vankoughnet in the Legislative Council in 1860. Nothing further was done about pensions until after Confederation when a rather similar plan was approved in 1870.[39]

An official's progress in the pre-Confederation civil service remorselessly followed the seniority principle. Seniority, as opposed to the merit principle, is a great pacifier because it works automatically. As one British administrator put it, "seniority is a matter of fact, while merit is a matter of opinion." The best men, of course, are not brought to the top or do not reach it soon enough if the seniority plan is followed. When coupled with secure tenure, seniority produces a contented although seldom brilliant public service. This weakness was recognized as early as 1843 by a royal commissioner who was investigating the Customs Service, and twenty years later D'Arcy McGee had occasion to complain in bitter terms of its evil effects:

> ... of the two hundred officers and clerks permanently employed at the seat of government and of the much larger number employed in the external civil service, the specialité of every man depending for its reward upon the sole test of seniority, the public service must be deprived in many instances, year after year, of the best services of some of the best men. On the other hand, it is apparent that the elevation of an officer, by seniority alone, from a position for which he has shown special aptitude and to which he has grown familiar, to another, a new and untried position, must lead to confusion and disorganization.[40]

At another point, he added, "a sterile seniority, standing alone, seems to be rather a ground for removal, than for invariable advancement."

---

[39]For the record of legislative failure to implement the pension project see *J.L.A.C.*, 1859, pp. 282, 349, 399, 485, 550, and 1860, pp. 290, 316, 320–1. The debate in the Legislative Council is reported in *Mirror of Parliament*, May 4, 1860. Vankoughnet claimed that the bill was not really a pension measure but a scheme to force civil servants to tax themselves for posterity. Even this defence failed, however, and Vankoughnet dropped the bill.

The new Dominion approved the first pension scheme in 1870, 32 & 33 Vic., c. 4. It is interesting to note that in England in 1859 a non-contributory pension scheme replaced the contributory one that had been provided since 1834. Experience suggests that the contributory scheme which the Canadians were trying to introduce at this same date was a wiser arrangement.

[40]See McGee's "Report," final section.

It is easier, however, to criticize seniority than to find a satisfactory substitute for it. Up to Confederation and, one can add, well beyond, seniority governed most promotions from the bottom to the top of the departments. There were exceptions in the case of positions requiring technical skill—positions in the Surveyor's Branch, for example, or the engineer, assistant engineer, and architect in the Public Works Department, or book-keepers in the financial departments. But the permanent heads of departments usually rose through the ranks; at Confederation, of nine deputy heads, at least six had come up by promotion. William Henry Lee, clerk of the Executive Council, was dean of the permanent civil servants, for he had entered as an extra clerk in 1821, thirty years later became permanent head, and by Confederation was still going strong with forty-three years' service behind him. Three others had more than twenty years of service. This longevity was not confined to the top ranking public officials but was found all the way down the hierarchy.

Promotion in the outside service tended to be restricted by the small size of the local establishments and the limited opportunities for transfer. There were far too many local pressures to be placated to make possible the transfer of "outsiders" into such positions as that of Postmaster or Customs Collector. The "locality rule" which is today a standard part of the civil service legislation in both Dominion and provincial jurisdictions had its counterpart in the informal convention of pre-Confederation days that jobs went to home-town boys.

Perhaps the emphasis on seniority partially contributed to the respect for paper work and complicated procedures in the various government departments. Long association with a given way of handling business must have developed in elderly clerks a strong defensive mechanism against any changes. On the ground that departments must be made accountable, bulky records were not only built up in the department concerned but frequently duplicated in several other "control" agencies as well. The book-keeping system was so cumbersome that departmental accounts were always in arrears, as the new Auditor quickly discovered after he was appointed in 1855.

Another factor contributing to the heavy paper work of government departments was the existence of a large force of agents in the field. These agents were required to make numerous financial returns, reports on transactions, and references for decisions back to headquarters. Most clerical workers at the seat of government spent their time assembling, tabulating, and analysing these figures or occupied themselves in the routine task of copying out in fair hand the letters submitted by the agents. Many years were to pass before the typewriter and the telephone could disturb this routine.

The public became conscious of the world of red tape inside the civil service whenever it had business with a department. The most notorious department and the one which probably had the closest connection with the colonial settlers was the Department of Crown Lands. Hamilton Merritt in 1850 presented to a parliamentary committee an analysis of the work-methods in that Department.[41] Taking the case of a militia man desiring to get his claim to land honoured, he found that eighteen different entries had to be made to convert the claim into land scrip, and that in order to obtain land with the scrip another sixteen entries were required. The processing of the claim involved the following departments or their agents: Department of the Adjutant General, the Lands Branch of the Crown Lands Department, the Executive Council Office, the Surveyor's Branch of the Crown Lands Department, the local land agent, the Provincial Secretary's Office, the Governor General, and the Provincial Registrar's Office. Sometimes applicants waited several years for claims to thread their way through the maze so diligently contrived by the bureaucrat.

In summary, the profile of the civil service which emerges out of the pre-Confederation period reveals a small working force totalling about 2,700, two-thirds of this staff being employed in scattered outposts throughout the provinces. Appointment was generally based on patronage considerations, although by 1857 lip-service was being paid to the principle of simple pass examinations, and in certain professions a movement to improve standards was having its influence on the quality of engineers, surveyors, and other technicians hired by the government. While patronage governed entrance to the service, there was no indication of wholesale house-cleanings with each change of government. In any event, governments in the last part of the period tended to rise and fall too rapidly to make practicable such changing of the guard inside the civil service as occurred in the United States. Promotions were determined almost entirely on the seniority principle and such primitive plans for classification and pay as existed also revealed the importance of this principle. A pension plan had been bruited but had fallen before the onslaught of the Upper House. Salary scales compared well with those (such as for

[41]See his evidence and detailed memoranda presented to Select Committee on Public Income and Expenditure, *J.L.A.C.*, 1850.

teachers) prevailing outside the service, and there was always a waiting list of hungry place-hunters in every Member's file. Working conditions within the civil service were not ideal and efforts were made to impose a rather gloomy Victorian discipline on the clerks. The short working day of clerical workers was taken up with making tedious entries in a vast number of clumsy ledgers, copying out letters, or passing bulky files busily to and fro between various departments. Without shorthand, typewriters or telephone, the written word became a living presence to which civil servants daily made their obeisance. The means became a much venerated end.

CHAPTER V

THE BUREAUCRACY FROM WITHOUT

THE PRE-CONFEDERATION CIVIL SERVICE was marked by the cleft which separated the French-speaking and English-speaking members of the Canadian community. The Union of 1841 was, as Sir Richard Cartwright commented, a "mariage de convenance," one political consequence of which was the dual premiership, almost a revival of "the old Roman custom of selecting two Consuls, each representing one of the great parties in the state."[1] Majority opinion would, no doubt, have supported Attorney General Baldwin when he remarked before a legislative committee in 1850 "Canada is not, and for a period much longer . . . cannot be in a situation in which an Administration can be advantageously formed, wholly irrespective of what may be called the separate confidence of each section of the Province. . . ."[2] In the United States, John C. Calhoun had arrived at a similar interpretation of the mechanism necessary to preserve the political equilibrium on the slavery issue in his doctrine of the "concurrent majority."

Until Confederation, then, hyphenated ministries were the inevitable response to the forces of dualism. But the response was not restricted to the political forms or the party leadership. Equally important was the way in which dualism was reflected in the administrative branch. Some of the departments were split right down the middle, starting at the top with the political head and going down to the subdivisions of the various branches. There were many complaints, even from lawyers, that four seats in the cabinet for the Law Department was a trifle unfair.[3] And yet, since the party leaders generally took the portfolio of Attorney General and since the system demanded two leaders, then two Attorneys General were necessary. Furthermore, with the amount of political work vested in the Attorneys, their legal duties had to be delegated to a Solicitor General. And once again, two Solicitors were required, one for each section and both with seats in the cabinet. The Provincial Secretary's Office was, for a short time

[1]See Sir Richard Cartwright, *Reminiscences* (Toronto, 1912), p. 5.
[2]"First Report of the Select Committee re State of the Public Income and Expenditure of the Province," *Journals*, Legislative Assembly, Canada, (J.L.A.C.), 1850, Appendix B.B., Q. 105, evidence of Attorney General Baldwin.
[3]*Ibid.*, evidence of J. H. Cameron, one-time Solicitor General, and of Attorney General Draper.

after the Union, also directed by a Provincial Secretary for Canada East and one for Canada West. The Department of Public Works was headed by two political officials, a Commissioner and an Assistant Commissioner, the offices being carefully rotated and exchanged amongst representatives of the two groups. After 1851 the Assistant Commissioner became in fact a permanent official without a seat in the legislature; but not until 1859 did this change receive formal statutory acknowledgement.

The imprint of dualism, however, carried well below the top level. The Provincial Secretary's Department, for example, had two complete establishments, one for Canada East and one for Canada West. This division was a pure reflection of dualism, for the two branches did not operate separately in their respective portions of the province; they were *both* located at the seat of government. The same was true of the Surveyor's Branch in the Crown Lands Department: it was divided into two sections, corresponding to the old provinces of Upper and Lower Canada, but both sections were located in the one building. The Crown Lands Department, in fact, presented ample evidence that the Union of 1841 from the administrative point of view was only skin deep. All the branches which it inherited at Union continued to operate as if the provinces were still separate. Land sales, clergy reserves, and land claims as well as surveys were run by separate establishments for Canada East and Canada West. But, curiously, once again no attempt was made to divide them geographically. It was perhaps a reflection of increasing maturity and a more conciliatory attitude that when new branches such as Woods and Forests and Fisheries were added in 1854 and 1857 they were set up and even described as "Canadian" branches. That is, there was only one head for each branch, and where the branch was further subdivided into the old "Canada East–Canada West" pattern, the heads of these subdivisions reported to that single branch head. This may seem like an extremely small concession to the claims of proper co-ordination but in fact it was at that time a rousing administrative victory over the forces of dualism.

There was often great rivalry between the administrative units representing the separate sections of Canada. Sometimes it was far from healthy, erupting into bitter invective which revealed the deep-seated animosities dividing the two communities. William Spragge, head of the surveys in Upper Canada, did not hesitate, for example, to criticize the excessive cost of administering the land sales branch headed by his opposite number in Canada East.⁴ The Education Office also witnessed displays of this critical rivalry. Egerton Ryerson, the vigorous, opinionated head of the Upper Canada Education Office, seldom missed the opportunity of drawing comparisons between his work and that of his counterpart, Dr. Meilleur, in Lower Canada.⁵ Nor was the tension significantly eased when administrators in Lower Canada offered, as an excuse for higher costs, larger staffs, and poorer results, the fact that in Canada East there was no efficient junior level of government, the local authorities, to share the burden. Critics in Upper Canada, of course, treated this lack of local authorities as additional evidence of the backwardness of the French Canadians.

The deep misunderstandings between the two groups were aggravated by the normal competition between administrators for personnel, new offices, supplies, and ample appropriations. A standard complaint of the French group, which has a familiar ring today, was that the English-speaking race monopolized the bulk of the positions in the civil service and, in particular, that they tended to gravitate to all the key managerial posts.⁶ A list of 450 headquarters' staff in 1863 contained only 161 (about 35 per cent) who were French and these were obviously employed on less important tasks, for they received less than 20 per cent of the total payroll.⁷ The English-speaking community might raise the political battle-cry, "rep by pop," but the French-speaking community were entitled to answer, "you already have far more than your share of the civil service offices." The basic animosity as well as the superficial aggravations are brought out in the following extract from a letter written to the Commissioner of Public Works by an engineer on the staff:

I suppose you [the chief Commissioner] are aware that the "natives" below Quebec supposed that you were going down for no other purpose than to build them wharves in every parish for their pilot boats—and are therefore much dissatisfied with your visit. Cauchon has done me the honor to abuse me repeatedly in his paper in the good company of your name. I con-

⁴See his evidence before the Select Committee on the Present System of Management of the Public Lands, "Report," *J.L.A.C.*, 1854–5, Appendix M.M.
⁵For example, see the exchange between these two officials before the Select Committee on Public Income and Expenditure, *J.L.A.C.*, 1850.
⁶See *Mirror of Parliament*, 1860, also the list contained in *Elgin-Grey Papers, 1846–52*, ed. by Sir Arthur Doughty (4 vols., Ottawa, 1937), vol. I, pp. 387–90. This list showed, as Elgin sardonically observed (p. 382) that "in this French ridden colony about one-tenth of the sum paid in salaries goes to Frenchmen!"
⁷See *Sessional Papers*, Canada, 1864, no. 58, "Return to an Address . . . for Certain Statements Relative to Employees in the Public Departments."

gratulate myself with the reflection that no white men read his paper and that very few of his own color can read anything. . . . I shall finish myself with the French by my report on their wants—but I will also have the satisfaction of finishing the impudent scheming of these priest-ridden drones who can raise $6,000 to $8,000 for a Church—but nothing for a wharf, a steamer, or a road.[8]

If these remarks typified the general attitude of Upper Canadians, one must assume that ten years of legislative union had done little to close the breach between the two races which Durham noted when he remarked that representatives of the two groups would not even serve on juries together. The task of harnessing such ill-matched and often antagonistic teams together did not make the minister's task of co-ordination—difficult under any circumstances—any easier. Indeed, the evidence suggests that the solution which was almost immediately adopted was precisely the one which has been employed when necessary in the contemporary Canadian civil service: a single agency was created in the name of unity and then separate branches were allowed to go their own way in handling the problems peculiar to each group. That some departments also created two-headed ministries and that a dual premiership was acknowledged simply contributed to the divisive influences within the Service. There are a few evidences of administrators attempting to give a broader "nationalistic" emphasis to policy but on the whole they tended to share the jealousies and narrow-minded animosities of their political chiefs.

Perhaps the most remarkable testimony to the strength of the forces of dualism, however, and certainly the most notorious example of the compromise typically required by these forces was to be found in the system of perambulating capitals.[9] Scarcely had the public departments been housed in Kingston, after the Union, when the Governor General, Lord Metcalfe, issued marching orders. Perhaps, like Dickens (who said of Kingston, "one half of it appears to be burnt down, and the other half not built up"), Metcalfe believed that Kingston could never provide adequate facilities for the capital of the United Provinces. In any event, in March 1844 Montreal became the new seat of government. While this move undoubtedly brought the public services closer to the business community of the province, accom-

[8]Public Archives of Canada, Merritt Papers, vol. 6, T. C. Keefer to Merritt, Dec. 20, 1849(?).

[9]I am indebted to the publishers of the *Queen's Quarterly* for permission to reprint the following material which appeared substantially as in the text in the autumn issue, vol. LIX (1952), at pp. 316–22, "Our Early Peripatetic Government."

modation was still far from luxurious. The Department of Public Works, whose unhappy lot it was to handle the housing problems of the government, reported that public duties had to be "carried on in inconvenient tenements, separated from each other and held at high rents from private individuals."[10] Before Public Works could solve this housing shortage, the disastrous riot and fire of April 1849 induced the government to abandon Montreal. In October, with Lord Elgin's consent, the cabinet, unable to agree upon a permanent seat of government, approved the Assembly's curious decision to rotate the capital every four years between Toronto and Quebec.[11]

This decision was probably beneficial from the political point of view, but it produced many problems for the civil service and those members of the public having business with it. Sir Richard Cartwright in his *Reminiscences* testified to the beneficial results of the "perambulating system," explaining that it "had undoubtedly the effect of making not only the public men but all men of large affairs in either province very much better acquainted with the state of things and the temper of the people in Quebec and Ontario, respectively, than they ever were before or since." For the Ontario members, Sir Richard contended, "it was a sort of revelation to be dropped and kept for several months at a time in a city which was almost a bit of Old France. . . ." Unfortunately, he felt, when the Quebec members came to Toronto "they complained . . . not without reason, that they were ignored and treated with but scant courtesy . . . and in fact were looked down upon as members of an inferior race . . . as a rule they returned home with a very strong determination not to give up any privileges they possessed."[12]

These regular migrations of headquarters' divisions must have occasioned the public much delay and confusion in the handling of questions, returns, instructions, and finances. The disadvantages to the public service of this quadrennial interruption were probably even more serious than the delays and inconveniences forced upon the public. In the first place, accommodation for the various departments, as well as for the legislature, had to be found and kept available in two cities. Some permanent government buildings were erected or purchased in each centre, extra accommodation being provided by makeshift rental arrangements. At Toronto, especially after renovation

[10]The annual reports of the Commissioner of Public Works carry many interesting details concerning the housing problems of the government. See especially J.L.A.C., 1848, Appendix N.
[11]See *Elgin-Grey Papers*, vol. I, pp. 362–3.
[12]Cartwright, *Reminiscences*, pp. 6 f.

of the Parliament Buildings in 1855, a fairly concentrated grouping of government departments became possible. But at Quebec accommodation was less satisfactory, involving the leasing of two hotels and several private houses.[13] The inconvenience of these quarters for transacting business was a matter of much complaint, and on February 1, 1854, the forebodings of the Department of Public Works were confirmed when a fire destroyed the recently enlarged Parliament Buildings at Quebec. Indeed, in both Toronto and Quebec disastrous fires were of such frequent occurrence (the Parliament Buildings in Toronto were also partially destroyed by fire in 1862) that one might be inclined to suspect deliberate incendiarism on the part of irate citizens. One explanation is that often government buildings which were lying unused were requisitioned for quartering military personnel. There was always a high correlation between tenancy by the military and the sudden outbreak of fires.

Possibly the most stubborn administrative problem confronting colonial civil servants was that of controlling the activities of the various branches within the separate departments. The frequent migration of the seat of government prevented a sensible consolidation of various branches in a few central buildings, and administrators found themselves especially handicapped in their efforts to co-ordinate the business of government. This problem was accentuated by more than the assortment and scattered nature of the accommodation in each city. Control over the regional outposts of such departments as Public Works or Crown Lands was often drastically affected by the sudden change of headquarters. For example, so long as the Public Works Department remained at Toronto, fairly direct supervision of the public works in Canada West was possible. When the Department moved to Quebec, however, an expensive regional office had to be maintained at Toronto.

Perhaps the most interesting problem connected with the removal of the seat of government was the task of transferring from one end of the St. Lawrence system to the other three or four hundred civil servants with all their retinue and furniture, the records and furnishings of about a dozen departments, and a portion at least of the parliamentary library.[14] Our Public Archives have, unfortunately,

[13]See "Annual Report of Commissioner of Public Works," *J.L.A.C.*, 1852, Appendix Q; *ibid.*, 1854–5, Appendix O.
[14]Public Archives of Canada, State Book U, May 26, 1859, p. 60. The report of the Assistant Commissioner of Public Works to Council in 1855 indicates the careful preparations required for each move. See State Book P, July 31, 1855, p. 371.

large gaps in their collections of departmental records which mutely testify to the hazards attending this great expedition.[15]

The technical arrangements attending this migration of officials were left to the Commissioner of Public Works. At the outset, the Department of Works was instructed to contract with some private agency to transfer both the personal effects of each civil servant and the furnishings and records of each public department. This cabinet decision must have caused more than a mild flutter of disapproval in the households of the bureaucrats, for the original plan was soon altered so that each family could make its own arrangements. The "Passage Ticket" issued to each head of the household, it is interesting to note, provided for so many cabin passengers, so many children, and so many *servants*! Obviously, our colonial civil servants could lay claim to a scale of living comparable to their colleagues in Victorian England.

With two months' salary advanced to him, each civil servant was able to meet the costs of removing his personal effects. But his packing apparently had to be done by his wife—or servants, of course—since he himself received explicit instructions to appear daily at his office and assist with the packing or storing of the government's property. Anyone interested in acquiring a rug—somewhat worn, but cheap—could do so by waiting for the great sale of such articles which occurred on the occasion of the removal of the seat of government. New furnishings would, of course, be acquired in the new location and besides it was scarcely worthwhile transferring worn-out furnishings a distance of five hundred miles. Timing of the removal was also important. A general exodus was impossible. Consequently an order of departure was drawn up. In 1855, for example, the financial departments moved first, then Public Works, Crown Lands, the Adjutant General, and the Department of Agriculture. The Post Office and the Provincial Secretary's Office brought up the rear. In 1859 the movement was even more protracted, departments leaving in slow procession between June 10 and November 1.[16]

The cost of these periodic transfers was substantial. In 1855, for

[15]State Book Q, 1856, July 14, p. 415. The records of the cabinet for July 14, 1856, reveal that Hon. L. T. Drummond must have had a large part of his personal law library damaged during the course of its shipment by water from Quebec to Toronto as a then part of the library of the Crown Law Department. Unfortunately, it had been insured against total loss only and since it had been damaged rather than destroyed Drummond had to fall back on the cabinet for reimbursement.
[16]State Book P, 1855 Sept. 11, p. 463.

example, over £70,000 was spent on moving personnel and chattels from Quebec to Toronto and in preparing the buildings in Toronto.[17] The relative importance of this sum in the budget of the province may be appreciated by noting that it nearly equalled the revenue obtained from the tolls on the Welland Canal for that year.

One might have expected the Public Works Department to have registered a special vote of thanks to Queen Victoria when, in 1857, Her Majesty chose Ottawa as the permanent seat of government. There may have been some civil servants who, at the thought of being transferred to Ottawa, would have fervently seconded the legislator who exclaimed, "I tell you candidly gentlemen you might as well send the Seat of Government to Labrador." But on the whole most departments must have welcomed the change—not so much for the reason given by one newspaper in the United States that "the invaders would inevitably be lost in the woods trying to find it," but because it promised to end their nomadic existence.[18]

As will appear later, however, the Public Works Department had no reason to thank the Queen for her decision.[19] In 1859 contracts were let and construction of three main government buildings was commenced on Parliament Hill. The contractors, unfortunately, had such an exalted notion of what the dignity of the state required and were so badly supervised that they prematurely exhausted the first and subsequent appropriations. In the long-drawn-out controversy that followed, the public buildings remained at a standstill and public servants patiently waited in Quebec for a call that seemed increasingly unlikely to come. Finally, with an acrimonious arbitration still in full swing, the departmental buildings were completed and in January 1865 civil servants were notified to make preparations to move for what they fondly hoped would be the last time. By mid-November of that year the government had opened for business at the new stand and the perambulating public service finally reached a fixed abode. At least this was one problem created by the forces of dualism with which the post-Confederation civil service did not have to contend.

While dualism was undoubtedly the major environmental influence in the shaping of the early civil service, there were several other subordinate conditioning factors worthy of comment. One of these was

---

[17]See State Book Q, 1856, Feb. 18, p. 153; also "Seat of Government Removals," *J.L.A.C.*, 1859, Appendix 2, where a detailed tabulation of the costs of "removals" between 1849 and 1858 presents an over-all total of £140,613.

[18]Both comments quoted in L. Brault, *Ottawa Old and New* (Ottawa, 1946), at p. 147 and p. 153.

[19]See below, chap. XII.

the instability of governments. Ministers rose and fell with a celerity matched only by cabinets in modern France. For example, the political heads of the two largest departments, Public Works and Crown Lands, were each changed seventeen times in a period of twenty-six years. The effects of such rapid turnover are not difficult to imagine. Few political heads were in office long enough to obtain a comprehensive grasp of the business of their departments—particularly the larger and more complex departments. This meant that even a strong-minded minister with sound ideas for improving the administration or even the policy of his department was seldom able to carry through his reforms. Or, if he was successful in instituting the reforms, he never remained in power long enough to see that they became firmly rooted.

This weakness at the centre meant that the role of the permanent official was enhanced. The minister's subordinates were free to make what they could out of their jobs: they could rest easy on their oars, quietly bobbing up and down in a bureaucratic back-wash, or they could pull themselves into position of power and influence which even the strongest political heads would not dare to assail. Certain permanent officials—notably in the sprawling departments of Crown Lands and Public Works—adopted towards their political superiors an attitude of independence, even indifference, that would never be found today. Later chapters will give special attention to this matter.

Another conditioning factor was the small size of the public service in pre-Confederation times and the important influence of individual personalities. Even in the larger federal civil service of today the personal factor is of vital significance in determining relationships both within departments and between departments. The telephone call and the chat in the Chateau's cafeteria (or, at higher levels, in the Rideau Club) perpetuate the informal and highly personalized relationships which characterized the public service when it was much smaller. The outsider can study the statutes, orders, regulations, and organization charts which formally outline the duties and structures of governmental agencies; but for a realistic picture of the administrative machine in operation he must also have access to the "gossip" that flows within the hierarchy and some information about the informal structure of authority that stems from personal relations. It is not easy for the observer to uncover these domestic but nevertheless important administrative details and his difficulty grows greater as he tries to move backwards in history: not only are the scraps of gossip more inaccessible but the importance of the personal factor in an even smaller bureaucracy is greatly enhanced.

Given the importance of personalities in the small civil service, it is interesting to speculate upon the qualities and attitudes of the men drawn from those professions which tended to provide the political heads of government departments. The legal profession supplied the bulk of the recruits, journalism and business coming in a poor second and third.

It is easy to understand why the lawyer predominated in our political system. The nature of his work and the fact that he often had a partner enabled him to divide his time more easily between his professional career and politics. Moreover, the political process, particularly where it has to work within a divided community, requires leaders who are prepared to compromise, men who will not defend a principle to the death, and men who (as J. C. Dent remarked of R. B. Sullivan) have "enlightened views but no convictions." The lawyer's discipline prepared him to accept a dual premiership or a two-headed department or a perambulating capital as a cheap price to be paid for holding the Great Compromise (the legislative Union of 1841) together. Probably, this explains why lawyers tended to make good party men. The mills of justice grind slowly and the lawyer having regulated his mental gait to correspond was especially well adjusted to the demands of pre-Confederation politics. It was no place for the man in a hurry, the man with ideals impatient for fulfilment. Moreover, the lawyer was not only mentally adapted to the life of politics which he found in the Canadian cabinet, he also entertained what other groups felt was a conceited view of his natural right to monopolize public office. We find Attorney General Baldwin confidently informing a parliamentary committee in 1850 that the leading men in the community were bound to be lawyers and it was natural, therefore, for the head of the government to choose the post (i.e. Attorney General) which kept him in touch with the Profession. Baldwin added condescendingly that it was not essential for the Attorney General to be the Prime Minister.[20]

There was an additional reason why lawyers tended to dominate. Cabinet portfolios were seldom assigned on the strength of a particular individual's special abilities. The exigencies of cabinet making, if Sir Francis Hincks's description of the process in his *Reminiscences* is accurate, placed the candidate's personal capacity as an administrator at the bottom of the list of essential requirements. Is he a friend? Can he be trusted? What are his personal claims on the government?

[20]Evidence before Select Committee on Public Income and Expenditure, *J.L.A.C.*, 1850, Q. 105.

And, most important, can he carry a bloc of parliamentary supporters with him, to help bolster the cabinet? These were the important questions. If he knew anything about public finance, public works, or crown lands, as well as meeting the other more important tests, the cabinet was just lucky![21] Lawyers seemed somehow to be in a better position to cultivate these personal contacts which enabled them to pass the important tests and occasionally they also qualified as good administrators. Sir John A. Macdonald, for example, needs no eulogies as an adroit politician, but opinions concerning his administrative abilities are divided. Sir Richard Cartwright, not altogether an unbiased witness but an extremely penetrating observer, considered that Sir John neglected his departmental duties in favour of his true love—political manipulation.[22] Other commentators considered that he was a clear-headed administrator as well as an unexcelled politician.

The journalist also did rather well in politics. William Lyon Mackenzie, Joseph Cauchon, George Brown, and D'Arcy McGee were all journalists who became political luminaries. But they all possessed one common characteristic which tended to reduce their chances of political longevity. It was said of Joseph Cauchon, for example, that his newspaper made him notorious and thus brought him political success, but journalism had its weaknesses so far as political advancement was concerned or so far as the moulding of a real statesman was concerned. Newspapers were platforms from which the owner-editors addressed each other and their critics, often with bitter invective and always in extravagant terms.[23] The emphatic language required to capture readers and draw attention to one's ideas might prove a source of embarrassment in the journalist's subsequent political career. Mackenzie's experience illustrated this point; Cauchon was only temporarily successful as a politician and was finally neutralized by being sent as Governor to the North West Territories;

[21]See the *Globe*, Tuesday, Nov. 4, 1851, for a violent but illuminating comment on the abilities of new ministers to undertake the administrative duties attached to specific departments. Included in *Elgin-Grey Papers*, vol. III, pp. 941 f.

[22]Cartwright, *Reminiscences*, pp. 46–8.

[23]See W. Notman and F. Taylor, *Portraits of British Americans* (2 vols., Montreal, 1865), vol. I, p. 406: "The observation not infrequently made, that 'The Journal' made Mr. Cauchon is, we think, deficient in accuracy. . . . Indeed newspaper journalism has its serious drawbacks as well as its manifest advantages for those who aspire to political influence. . . . Certainly the school of newspaper journalism is not the best school for the education of statesmen; for it appears to be a condition of success that an American or Canadian newspaper should not only express sentiments and influence the aims of a party, which is fair and right enough, but that it should be required to do so in an unhealthy way. . . . They too often write as if society had lost its civilization. . . . "

McGee was assassinated; and although George Brown long assumed the role of "tribune of the people" he enjoyed but a brief career as a pro consul. What was said of George Brown might well have been said of other journalists who turned to politics: "He was so thoroughly convinced that he was always on the right side, that he never appears to have been able to enter into the convictions, equally strong and sincere, which moved others to oppose him. Hence much of the caustic writing in which he indulged as a journalist, and the denunciatory vein which runs through most of his utterances. . . ."[24] A successful politician cannot be a scolding "schoolmarm"; the people soon tire and turn back to a Macdonald and slip him on with a sigh of relief as they would an old shoe or a beloved hat. Nevertheless, because the journalist tended to pursue his schemes more passionately than the lawyer and because he was trained to simplify complex issues for the average citizen, he frequently proved himself a good administrative head. In a recent life of D'Arcy McGee, Josephine Phelan has contrasted McGee's enthusiasms with the cautious art of passive government practised with such rare intuition by Sir John A. Macdonald:

No contrast could be more striking that Macdonald's passivity and D'Arcy McGee's mulitple activities. Macdonald ignored the specific duties of the Attorney General's Department of which he was the formal head. But McGee, as Minister of Agriculture, although admittedly he knew next to nothing about the subject, explored the functions of his department in every detail. Fortunately his Deputy Minister, Dr. J. C. Taché proved a congenial co-worker, sharing many of McGee's interests and ideas. Together they reorganized the department and planned many improvements in its sub-departments which included statistics and immigration.[25]

McGee's interest in administrative reorganization was not restricted to his own Department, for in 1863 he presented to Council that valuable report on the history, current organization, and duties of the whole civil service from which extensive quotations have been borrowed throughout this study.

Joseph Cauchon had an unfortunate faculty for stirring up political enemies, but he was, nevertheless, one of the ablest administrators of his time. The annual report of the Crown Lands Department for the year 1856 must be regarded as a basic document in early Canadian

[24]W. J. Rattray, *The Scot in British North America* (4 vols., Toronto, 1880), vol. II, p. 576.

[25]Josephine Phelan, *The Ardent Exile: The Life and Times of Thomas D'Arcy McGee* (Toronto, Macmillan, 1951), p. 267.

public administration and serves as a strong testimonial to his logical, incisive analytical powers as Commissioner of Crown Lands.[26] Like most other political heads of the day he did not remain in office long enough to see his proposed reforms completely accepted, but his successors long had cause to thank him for his tremendously comprehensive survey of the complex operations of the Crown Lands Department. A few years later Cauchon's keen administrative insight also made its mark on the pages of the annual report of the Department of Public Works over which he presided for a time.[27] W. L. Mackenzie never had a chance to test his powers as an administrator, but in his declining years as a reinstated exile, he showed his true worth as a leading member of the public accounts committee. In no small measure he inspired that movement of reform in the 1850's which established the foundations of our modern system of financial accountability.[28]

The third group from which cabinets drew their members was the business community. If the journalist's political life tended to be relatively unsuccessful because of convictions too strongly expressed in earlier days, the businessman suffered even more for his dogmatism and self-righteousness. Unlike the journalist the businessman was not embarrassed by his dogmas but clung to them with such tenacity that he was distrusted, even ridiculed, by the lawyers who always outnumbered him in the cabinet. The businessman was always convinced that the problems facing Canada could be easily solved by the application of a few standard policies, like poultices applied to a sore. The subtleties and subterfuges of the legal brotherhood who largely dominated the political scene were beyond his comprehension. He did not understand that in Canadian politics the shortest distance between two points is not a straight line. Dual premiers and double-barrelled ministries seemed sheer extravagances. Moreover, the businessman could not join in the lawyer's mutual adulation society: he believed, in fact, that one of the causes of high taxation, insolvency, and lax administration was the presence of lawyers in high places. Merritt, one of the leading representatives of the businessman in politics, confided his prejudices to his diary on Saturday, March 11, 1848.[29] He

[26]See "Annual Report of the Commissioner of Crown Lands for the Year 1856," *J.L.A.C.*, 1857, Appendix 25.
[27]See "Annual Report of the Commissioner of Public Works for the Year 1861," *Sessional Papers, Canada*, 1862, no. 3.
[28]See below, chap. VII.
[29]Merritt Papers, Note Books.

had been kicking his heels in Montreal awaiting announcement of the formation of a new ministry so that the legislature could assemble. The announcement was finally made in the *Pilot* newspaper. Merritt listed the officers, their portfolios, and their occupations. He toted up the columns. Result: a ministry of twelve, seven from Lower Canada, five from Upper Canada. His gloomy conclusion:

I very much fear the Cabinet selected will not adopt the measures the country requires. [He has already neatly written in his diary what measures he knows are required.] Besides 7 lawyers neither [*sic*] of whom profess to understand anything about the finances of the country we have 4 gentlemen from Montreal . . . leaving Malcolm Cameron to represent the business of Upper Canada or say United Canada.

If those departments were filled by individuals selected from or by the people would the above choice [have] been made? One of the evils of the present system appears to be that in the composition of the Government some half a dozen Individuals select the men—fitness for the situation is not looked for, it is the hope of strengthening a party—I have from the first session had my misgivings as to the proper working of the system.

In a letter written to Baldwin at about the same time Merritt claimed that "the true cause in my judgement [for the mounting costs of government] consists in the want of financial Talent or information in those who have the direction of this branch of the public service—Pride, prejudice and ignorance seems to have combined to shut our eyes and close our senses against those measures which have been so successful in the state of New York."

When Merritt was persuaded to enter the cabinet he accompanied his acceptance of appointment with a long memorandum on the measures which he considered ought to be pressed. In a few weeks of hard work he had investigated all the departments and rearranged the public accounts in the same neat columns in which he customarily set down his own personal expenditures and banking transactions. It was really the same thing on a larger scale as far as he was concerned.[30] He insisted on a formal inquiry into his proposed reforms and at the hearings the country was treated to the unusual spectacle of the President of the Council (Merritt) being rudely disowned by every one of his colleagues. Mr. Merritt in their eyes was asking too many questions and discovering too many strange answers. As Fennings Taylor aptly put it in his biographical note on Merritt:

[30]In the same note book in which he entered his own detailed personal expenditures, Merritt had tabulated in similar form the expenditures of the province, with brief comments concerning various economies.

The restraints of office were . . . in the last degree irksome to him. He had accustomed himself to speak when he liked, to say what he thought, and to do as he pleased; and the obligation, therefore, of speaking by the card and in accordance with the decisions of Council, must have been as new to his experience as it was foreign to his taste. . . . Those who most admired him doubted whether he would find his colleagues in the government an applauding auditory, or the Executive Council a congenial place for airing successfully some of his peculiar crochets on government, currency and finance; crochets by which he had, as we think, impaired the influence of his grander and more statesmanlike views. . . . The truth seems to have been that [he] was neither a party man nor a politician. . . . His popularity sprang from his independence, his purity of character, and from the practical nature of his aims.[31]

Certain other members of the business community such as John Young, Isaac Buchanan, Robert Christie also tended to share Merritt's predicament. They were extremely able—obvious choices for such "working" departments as Crown Lands or Public Works and financial departments such as Receiver General or Inspector General. And yet, they lacked flexibility and possessed no intuitive feelings for the requirements of the political process directed by the cabinet. As a result their talents as administrators and financiers were never fully employed: they were too insensitive to the political forces which could sustain a cabinet in uneasy power. Even Francis Hincks, who is an exceptional case of the businessman turned successful politician, was not a good team player—he just happened to possess a financial acumen that made him for a time indispensable. Metcalfe's official biographer described Hincks as a man having "a tongue that cut like a sword, and no discretion to keep it in order."[32]

W. J. Rattray's summary of the life of Isaac Buchanan, another leading businessman, may stand as a sort of valedictory for the whole business community of pre-Confederation times:

From early life up to this moment, he has been a busy man, endowed with singular power of character and indomitable perseverance. It will be a matter of surprise . . . to find that so little advantage has been taken of his rare business and administrative abilities. That he would have been no mere figurehead in a working department of government is clear from the record of his whole life. Perhaps the strong will which chafes at routine,

[31]Notman and Taylor, *Portraits of British Americans*, vol. II, pp. 285–96, "William Hamilton Merritt."
[32]See J. W. Kaye, *The Life and Correspondence of Charles, Lord Metcalfe* (2 vols., London, 1854), vol. II, p. 489.

the love of carrying out cherished convictions or subjects of public importance, and a certain want of pliability in his moral texture, had something to do with this apparent neglect.[33]

These somewhat extended comments on three occupational groups were initiated, it will be recalled, because it was earlier argued that personal factors inevitably played an important part in the operations of our tiny pre-Confederation civil service. If the foregoing observations, which are offered as tentative hypotheses at this stage, are reasonably valid, they suggest that, in addition to the problems and enmities raised by dualism, the Canadian civil service also confronted an interplay of conflicting personalities and interests amongst its high command which made co-operation and over-all control very difficult to obtain. Cabinet solidarity was an illusive ideal so long as strong party loyalties remained undeveloped and so long as these personal incompatibilities prevailed.

A final factor which influenced the pre-Confederation public service was the widely held view that government services ought to be self-sustaining. In part this notion derived from the long-standing practice of meeting the costs of the administration of justice by charging fees, fines, and court "costs." Wherever a government agency was performing a task which had semi-judicial qualities, it was commonly assumed that those who derived the benefits should bear the costs. For example, the Fisheries Branch of the Crown Lands Department was at first financed entirely by the licence fees and fines it collected. Even when these resources were proven quite inadequate, the Department had difficulty in convincing the legislature that funds be appropriated out of the public treasury for regulating the use of and protecting this essential natural resource.[34]

The business community favoured the self-sustaining service because it felt that it was unfair to burden the general tax-paying public with the cost of services which were directed to special groups. For this reason, almost until Confederation, many services were maintained by contributions from the interests concerned. The Culler's Office, which supervised the grading of timber, was supported by direct levies made upon the timber dealers; the Emigration Office met most of its costs by charging an immigrant head tax; the River Police at Quebec were paid out of tonnage dues and the Marine Hospital

---

[33]Rattray, *The Scot in British North America*, vol. II, pp. 542–3.

[34]For a list of these "self-sustaining" enterprises, see the report of the Auditor prepared for Council, appearing in State Book T, 1858, Sept. 18, pp. 164–5.

was maintained from similar funds; the steamboat inspectors and railway inspectors were financed by those who had to submit to their scrutiny.

The "self-sustaining service" ideal found further support in the businessman's belief that any department which was in a position to receive a revenue from its services ought to make both ends meet. This belief found full expression in relation to the Public Works Department. It was hopefully maintained that the public works would all liquidate the debts created by their erection. Merritt even expected that the revenues from the Welland Canal would soon pay not only the costs of the Public Works Department but also *all* costs of government. His dream of a tax-free community was never fulfilled. Other departments, such as Crown Lands, the Post Office, and the Indian Office, which derived substantial revenues from their operations were also expected at least to meet all costs, if not to show a "surplus." Indeed, the revenues from the sale of Crown lands were milked for a variety of public functions having little or no relation to the major responsibilities of the Department.

There were two basic weaknesses in the "self-sustaining service" conception. First, it assumed that an ideal which was appropriate for private business was equally appropriate for public business. It implied that government services should be maintained only if they could pay their operating costs. On this assumption, if a customs house collected only a few dollars but spent many more on keeping up a large establishment, that service ought to be discontinued.[35] But the argument is based on the objectives of private administration which must ever weigh the profit motive in the balance. If it can be established that a service is essential, then so far as public administration is concerned it must be service at any cost. Failure to appreciate the significance of this difference in objectives accounted for the early conception of the "self-sustaining service." Current criticisms of the bureaucracy often display the same confusion.

The "self-sustaining service" doctrine also tended to overlook the indirect benefits which the whole public might derive from a service presumably directed to one sector of the community. It was this sort of thinking that gave rise to the belief that some services ought to be paid for by a direct levy on the group concerned. In fact,

[35]Opinions differed, for example, as to whether the officials at various ports of entry ought to be paid in accordance with the class of position or in accordance with the amount of business done by the port. For many years, the second alternative was chosen and ports were graded to correspond with their annual "take."

however, services such as steamboat inspection, timber culling, immigration promotion, or the maintenance of a marine hospital were all indirectly benefiting the Canadian public and could, therefore, become legitimate charges on public funds.

But an even more important weakness of the "self-sustaining service" ideal was that it seriously hampered the development of adequate parliamentary control over the administrative branch. The businessman might think it better to keep costs of administration out of the budget by permitting departments to pay their own expenses out of current revenues.[36] But this did not give Parliament any opportunity to discover what the costs really were; the legislature had to content itself with net receipts. If a large part of the public revenue was left in the hands of separate administrative agencies, how could the legislature assume full responsibility for controlling the public purse? Even at Confederation the logic of this position had not penetrated to all parts of the civil service and some revenue-raising departments were still paying their costs of management returning only their net proceeds to the Receiver General.

[36]Merritt, for example, strongly opposed any suggestion to make revenue-receiving departments, like Crown Lands, pay in their gross revenues to the treasury; he preferred to have these revenues applied against the service. See his evidence and memoranda submitted to the Select Committee on Public Income and Expenditure, *J.L.A.C.*, 1850.

CHAPTER VI

THE TOP COMMAND

THE VITAL CENTRE of the Canadian public service to-day is the cabinet. Here important policies are co-ordinated, departmental disputes arbitrated, financial requirements sifted and approved, and a comprehensive vigilance exercised over the whole sprawling bureaucracy. In performing these tasks the cabinet operates as if it were a single entity because of the joint responsibility which all its members assume towards the legislature and towards each other. The top command is also unified by the prestige and influence of the Prime Minister.

As supreme co-ordinator of the public service the cabinet receives assistance from several sources. A small staff drawn from the Privy Council Office has, since the Second World War, provided the cabinet with a secretariat. Almost since Confederation the multifarious measures involving public expenditures have been sifted for the cabinet by Treasury Board, a subcommittee of cabinet headed by the Minister of Finance and provided with a capable staff. In conjunction with the Civil Service Commission, this Board has also assumed the burden of personnel management for most of the service. The day-to-day outflow of funds from the Treasury is watched by a large staff under the Comptroller General—a high official within the Department of Finance. Finally, within each department the political head has for a long time now enjoyed the benefits of a permanent deputy who provides continuity and a more direct supervision of staff than the minister himself would be capable of providing.[1]

The structure of command in the pre-Confederation civil service was much less unified and coherent. Because this was a period marked by significant transformations in constitutional status, the relations between the various controlling authorities were transient and ill-defined. In the first decade after the Union of 1841 the Governor and his Secretary were still capable of exerting a strong co-ordinating influence over the local administration. But as their personal prerogatives waned, various "domestic" instruments began to share the

[1]For recent analysis of civil service controls see Taylor Cole, *The Canadian Bureaucracy* (Durham, N.C., 1949), chap. III.

functions of over-all control. At Confederation the Executive Council had clearly taken over all the reins of authority, but its grip was that of an inexperienced driver, uncertain of the strength of his own hands, unsure of the holding power of the traces, a little uneasy about his ill-matched team, and all too aware of the untried equipage which he was attempting to drive.

The Governor and His Secretary

Lord Sydenham's major concern, as was previously emphasized, was to achieve unified command at the top of the public service. The next three Governors were keen to preserve and improve upon the system which was designed by Sydenham to make them administrators-in-chief. The régime of Lord Metcalfe—a meticulous, conscientious administrator—possibly marks the high point of this effort to make the Governor the directing head of the public service. After his time, and particularly with the coming of responsible government under Lord Elgin, the directing and co-ordinating powers of the Governor and his Secretary were rapidly transferred to other agencies.

In the first eight years of the Union, however, the position of the Governor in administrative matters, like that of the President of the United States, depended very much on the personal inclinations and abilities of the incumbent. By diplomacy and party management Sydenham got legislative approval for his policies. His view of the ideal relationship between Governor and Council was expressed in a despatch to Lord John Russell in 1840: "They [the Executive Council] are a body upon whom the Governor must be able to call at any or at all times for advice—with whom he can consult upon the measures to be submitted to the Legislature, and in whom he may find *instruments*, within its walls, to introduce such amendments in the Laws as *he* may think necessary, or to defend *his acts* and *his policy*."[2] Seven years later, the Colonial Secretary, Lord Grey, was still able to approve Sydenham's view of the proper functions of the Council.[3]

Nevertheless, the insistent demands of the colonists for "responsible government" gradually wrought a significant change in the Governor's conception of his position and duties. Bagot, Lord Sydenham's successor, hesitated to press his formal powers as chief executive, although

---

[2]Quoted with apparent approval by Lord Grey in a despatch to Lt.-Gov. Sir John Harvey, March 21, 1847. See *Elgin-Grey Papers, 1846–52*, ed. by Sir Arthur Doughty (4 vols., Ottawa, 1937), vol IV, p. 1360, italics added.
[3]*Ibid.*, p. 1361.

his winning personality gained the necessary co-operation from the French-Canadian leaders.[4] Metcalfe, an administrator seasoned in India, took a more high-handed, direct-action approach, typified by his handling of the local patronage problem.[5] But Lord Elgin's experience in the office quickly led him to a more subtle conception of the Governor's directing role—a conception, as he himself admitted, that would be most difficult to sustain in practice. In a long letter to Lord Grey in July 1847, Elgin thus stated his convictions:

It is very satisfactory to me to find that you respond so cordially to the view which I have propounded in reference to the position and duties of the Governor of this Colony. I feel very strongly that they are substantially just, and that a Governor General by acting upon them with tact and firmness may hope to established [sic] a moral influence in the Province which will go far to compensate for the loss of power consequent on the surrender of patronage to an Executive responsible to the local Parliament. Until, however, the functions of his office under our amended colonial constitution are more clearly defined—until that middle term which shall reconcile the faithful discharge of his responsibility to the Imperial Government and the Province with the maintenance of the quasi monarchial relation in which he now stands towards the community over which he presides, be discovered and agreed upon—he must be content to tread along a path which is somewhat narrow and slippery, and to find that incessant watchfulness and some dexterity are requisite to prevent him from falling, on the one side, into the néant of mock-sovereignty, or on the other, into the dirt and confusion of local factions.[6]

In short, Lord Elgin had come very close to accepting that view of the personal prerogative of the representative of the Crown which Walter Bagehot was to describe twenty years later: "... the sovereign has, under a constitutional monarchy such as ours, three rights— the right to be consulted, the right to encourage, the right to warn. And a King of great sense and sagacity would want no others."[7]

At first glance, the official records of the Executive Council reveal scarcely a trace of this important transformation of the role of the

[4]G. P. de T. Glazebrook, *Sir Charles Bagot in Canada* (London, 1929), pp. 45 f.
[5]J. C. Dent, *The Last Forty Years: Canada since the Union of 1841* (2 vols., Toronto, 1881), vol. I, pp. 320 f., has a full account of Metcalfe's refusal to accept the popular ministry's advice on appointments. A sympathetic view of Metcalfe's action is to be found in J. W. Kaye, *The Life and Correspondence of Charles, Lord Metcalfe* (2 vols., London, 1854), vol. II, pp. 499 f.
[6]*Elgin-Grey Papers*, vol. I, p. 58.
[7]W. Bagehot, *The English Constitution* (Worlds Classics ed., London, 1933), p. 67.

Governor.[8] The formal procedure used in Sydenham's time differs in no important way from that used in 1867. In 1841 as at the end of the period, a distinction was made between a meeting of the Council and a meeting of the Executive Committee of the Council. In the first instance, the Governor always presided and reports approved by him were issued as Orders in Council. In the case of the meetings of the so-called Committee of the Executive Council, the Governor was not present and decisions taken were treated as "Reports" which then had to be referred to formal Council meeting for the Governor's signature. The two bodies consisted of exactly the same members with the Governor added as chairman at formal Council meetings.

Behind this unchanging formal façade, however, one can discern, even in the minutes of the Council, evidences of the great political transformation which was consummated in Lord Elgin's régime. There is a marked contrast, for example, between Metcalfe's handling of the Council in 1844 and Elgin's treatment of Council in 1848 and 1849. The records show that Metcalfe himself brought forward his own proposals for the consideration of the Council.[9] Furthermore, he carefully initialed his approval to practically every report presented to him by the Committee of the Executive Council. Metcalfe's successor, Lord Cathcart, was a temporary appointment who appears to have initiated few if any proposals of his own and in registering his approval of reports sent up from the Committee of Council did so with one signature which covered all reports.[10] The official minutes show increasing evidences of cabinet initiative. In 1847, for example, individual heads of departments began to submit their own reports for His Excellency's consideration and approval,[11] sometimes actually in the form of draft Orders in Council which required only the signature of the Governor to make them effective.[12]

The changing responsibilities of the Governor are also illustrated by the attitude of rigorous neutrality which Lord Elgin proposed to adopt toward the matter of disbursing local patronage. The Colonial Secretary, Lord Grey, considered that the formal confirmation of all important colonial officials—legal and administrative—ought to be continued by the traditional method of issuing warrants under the Sign Manual and having the Secretary of State in London counter-

[8]The impression presented in the text is derived from sampling the proceedings of Council as reported in the State Books held in the Public Archives of Canada.
[9]See, for example, State Book C, 1844.
[10]See State Book D, 1845.
[11]See State Book G, 1847.
[12]See State Book H, 1848.

sign them.[13] He criticized Elgin's practice of making the formal appointment himself without this final confirmation by the home government. Elgin's reply indicated his sure sense of the tense atmosphere in colonial politics.

I am disposed to believe [he argued] that the less you meddle in Canadian appointments even by the issue of Royal warrants the better. . . . You cannot effectually control them. By seeming to endeavour to do so you enable on the one hand designing colonial administrations to make you share the odium of obnoxious nominations, while on the other you rouse that jealousy of imperial interference which has heretofore produced such mischievous effects in Canada. I would allow the responsibility of appointing to office to rest upon the Provincial Ministry and to weigh upon them as heavily as possible. An intelligent Governor and a watchful opposition will generally succeed in preventing abuses from growing too rank.[14]

The Colonial Secretary was convinced by Elgin's reasoning and in February 1848 wrote to say that he would follow his advice.[15] Thus another milestone in the long journey toward colonial autonomy was passed. With the exception of such few remaining Imperial services as the Post Office, parts of the Customs Service, Indian Affairs, Immigration, and Militia, all administrative positions were thereafter filled without the formal sanction of the home government or the direct intervention of the Governor.

One of the best indications of the waning executive authority of the Governor during this decade 1840–50 is to be found in the arrangements made for the Governor's personal aides. Sydenham's plan had been to restrict the duties of the Civil Secretary, shifting his administrative responsibilites to two Provincial Secretaries, one for the Eastern and one for the Western division. He had also insisted that the Civil Secretary "being the Confidential Servant of the Governor must change with him." Subsequent correspondence between the Colonial Secretary and the Governors who succeeded Sydenham reveals that the matter of the Civil Secretary was not immediately settled by these arrangements. The Colonial Office apparently considered that the position of the Civil Secretary was almost as important as that of the Governor to the preservation of the Imperial

---

[13]*Elgin-Grey Papers*, vol. I, pp. 38–9. Grey's position was much more flexible than that expressed in *Regulations Relative to Appointments to Public Offices in the Colonies*, dated Oct. 15, 1843 (Public Archives Pamphlet, no. 1502). All important public positions in the colony were to be filled provisionally by the Governor, subject to formal approval of His Majesty. The regulations loftily suggest that in the larger, more populous colonies local talent will be kept in mind.

[14]*Elgin-Grey Papers*, vol. I, pp. 119–20.

[15]*Ibid.*, vol. I, p. 121.

connection against the colonial politicians' demand for responsible government. For example, in 1842 Lord Stanley, the Colonial Secretary, explained to Bagot, the new Governor, why he thought the Civil Secretary ought to be a permanent office: "The Civil Secretary in Canada, as you are now well aware, is practically the Chief officer of the Executive Government next after the Governor, and is exactly what the Government or Public Secretary is in all three Eastern Colonies."[16] Reversing Sydenham's plan of a temporary appointee, Stanley "advised the Queen to make the Civil Secretary in Canada dependent for his continuance in office on the pleasure of the Queen, and not a mere attaché to the Governor."

Bagot was quite prepared to endorse this view, as his prescription for a "Heaven-born Secretary" reveals: "He should be ready, very laborious, very phlegmatic—very courteous—thoroughly master of all forms and technicalities and terms of office correspondence—and without any latent design of being Vice-Roi over me. He should speak French tout bien que mal, and have the patience of Job. Now, how am I to find such a Phoenix?—and how am I to get on an inch on an hour without one?"[17]

Stanley was able to find in Rawson W. Rawson, a young permanent civil servant who had been employed by Gladstone, a man who seemed to possess all these qualities, but as Sydenham had foreseen the presence of such a powerful "alien" official remained a thorn in the flesh of those who advocated responsible government.[18] Ostensibly their criticism was directed against the high salary of the Secretary. But their real complaint was registered in an Address to the Queen which was moved by the Assembly in 1843. The address called for the abolition of the office and the transfer of the duties to the Provincial Secretary "responsible to your Majesty's faithful Commons, as a member of Your Majesty's Executive Council in this province and in that quality a responsible advisor to His Excellency . . . the Governor General."[19]

Lord Metcalfe attempted to assuage the colonists' suspicions by dropping the title "Chief Secretary" which successive civil secretaries had borne. He contended that this title "was merely nominal, no duties

[16]Stanley to Bagot, Private, July 11, 1842, Public Archives of Canada, R.G. 7, G. 1, vol. 102, pp. 138–9.
[17]Bagot to Stanley, May 28, 1842, Public Archives of Canada, Bagot Papers, vol. IV, Jan.–July, 1842, pp. 226–9.
[18]Stanley to Bagot, June 18, 1842, *ibid.*, vol. IX, pp. 96–102.
[19]Quoted in E. Thompson, *The Life of Charles, Lord Metcalfe* (London, 1937), pp. 372–3.

of superiority over the other Provincial Secretaries being assigned to his office; but it was a subject of jealousy and offence in the Colony ... and quite unnecessary...."[20] This gesture apparently did not have the desired effect, for Lord Cathcart, Metcalfe's successor, was compelled to advise the Colonial Office in 1846 that "the office of Civil Secretary has always been looked upon with much jealousy by those who style themselves advocates for Responsible Government." With great anxiety he noted that the current attempt to remove the office from the Civil List revealed the "ultimate intention that the whole correspondence with the Government at home should pass through the Department of the Provincial Secretary, leaving the Governor without any discretion as respects this responsible branch of his office, and entirely in the hands of his Executive Council."[21] Cathcart was obviously exaggerating, but his prediction did finally become a reality in this century: the Canadian executive now deals directly with its British counterpart without the mediation of the Governor General.

During Lord Elgin's term the tenure and status of the Civil Secretary reverted once more to Sydenham's conceptions of the office. In Jamaica, Elgin had become accustomed to a private secretary who was expected to leave when the Governor left. Consequently, even though the notion of a fixed tenure had developed in the Canadas, he replaced the former Civil Secretary with his own appointee, apparently with the approval of many in the colony. In June 1847 the government was successful in rejecting the hardy perennial motion for the abolition of the Civil Secretary's position, and from that time on no other serious effort was made to deprive the Governor of his Secretary.[22] Moreover, since the Secretary's direct administrative responsibilities were gradually transferred to provincial authorities, the original cause for colonial jealousy was removed.[23]

During the same years, the minutes of Council record that thenceforth departments having accounts to render for expenditures on "contingencies" would no longer direct them to the Civil Secretary but rather to the Clerk of the Executive Council.[24] It was not until

---

[20]Metcalfe to Stanley, no. 20, Jan. 20, 1844, Public Archives of Canada, R.G. 7, G. 12, vol. 64, pp. 150–1.
[21]Cathcart to Grey, Aug. 28, 1846, *ibid.*, vol. 65, p. 84.
[22]*Elgin-Grey Papers*, vol. I, p. 51.
[23]The direct administrative responsibilities are described in the excellent introductory essay appended to *Preliminary Inventory, Record Group 4 & 5, Civil and Provincial Secretaries' Offices, Canada East and Canada West* (Public Archives of Canada, Manuscript Division, 1953), pp. 5–8.
[24]See State Book G, Sept. 1, 1847, p. 347.

1860, however, that the Imperial authorities succeeded in passing over full responsibility for the Indians to a provincial ministry, thereby relieving the Civil Secretary of his last direct administrative duty, that of acting as the Governor's deputy in administering Indian Affairs.[25] By Confederation he had become in fact, as in name, the Governor General's personal secretary, his administrative and co-ordinating power having disappeared completely.

The Executive Council

These transformations which gradually weakened the executive powers of the Governor and his personal aides confronted colonial officials with the task of strengthening and expanding their own machinery for overhead direction and control. The agency which came to occupy the central position in this development was the Executive Council. At the time Lord Durham made his report, three functions were performed by the Council.[26] Its main task was to advise the Governor on all matters which were referred to it. Secondly, it exercised judicial functions as a court of clemency in criminal cases, a function undertaken today by the Minister of Justice. Thirdly, the Council acquired a number of administrative functions, operating usually as a referee in matters of dispute. The major portion of its administrative business related to the disposal of the public lands. In the 1830's an average of 1,500 petitions and applications respecting lands grants came before the Council each year. Only about 300 items classified as "state business" were dealt with by the Council during the same period. Another major managerial responsibility of Council was the audit and review of public accounts—a task which was never taken seriously.

After the Union of the two Canadas in 1841, the Executive Council had to function in a new and, for a time, uncertain constitutional environment. In the first place, the Act of Union provided that all financial measures were to be initiated by the executive.[27] This provision implied a central scrutiny of departmental budgets which the Council, for many years, was not properly equipped to undertake.

---

[25]See "Annual Report of Commissioner of Crown Lands for the Year 1862," *Sessional Papers*, Canada, 1863, no. 5, Appendix 44 on the Indian Department. The transfer was achieved by 23 Vic., c. 151 (1860).

[26]See above, chap. II. See also a fuller account in Report of Committee on Executive Council in "Report on the Public Departments," *Journals*, Legislative Assembly, Upper Canada, 1839-40, Appendix, vol. II.

[27]*Imperial Statutes*, 3 & 4 Vic., c. 35, s. 57 (1841). The Act was proclaimed in force on February 10, 1841.

Second, the evolution of responsible government also necessitated a drastic reorientation of the traditional functions of the Council. From the shadowy (and often irresponsible) adviser to the Governor, the Council had to become the active, responsible, policy-forming agency for the colony. Colonial politicians soon realized the significance of this constitutional change. It was one thing to be in a position to offer secret advice to a Governor who alone could be held accountable for the decisions based upon such advice; it was quite another matter to be thrust into the harsh glare of a partisan colonial legislative inquisition and forced publicly to assume responsibility for the formal acts of a Governor who now made perfectly clear his passive role as an instrument of the Council.

Even in the early stages of the evolution of responsible government Lord Sydenham was struck by the reluctance of the Council publicly to seize the initiative. In 1840, he remarked that "the most serious defect in the Government, is the utter absence of power in the Executive, and its total want of energy to attempt to occupy the attention of the country upon real improvemens, or to lead the Legislature in the preparation and adoption of measures for the benefit of the Colony."[28] Sydenham's criticism was probably accurate, but he ought not to have been surprised to find colonial statesmen reluctant to assume a positive and directing role when the traditional policy of the home government had been to smother the growth of such independent attitudes. Indeed, Sydenham's own actions as a partisan leader of the government suggest that he would have been the first to resent a strong manifestation of that spirit of initiative which he claimed was lacking. Certainly by 1843 we find Lord Metcalfe complaining to Stanley at the Colonial Office that the local cabinet was becoming too obstreperous. "The Council," he wrote, "are now spoken of by themselves and others generally as 'the Ministers', 'the Government' and so forth. They regard themselves as a responsible Ministry. . . ."[29]

Metcalfe's observation suggests that colonial statesmen quickly adapted themselves to the new constitutional environment and showed that they were more than willing to take over the co-ordinating and directing powers of the Governor. Indeed, perhaps the convention of joint responsibility within the cabinet took firm root in this early effort to counteract the personal powers of the Governor. Both Syden-

[28]Quoted by Grey in his despatch to Sir John Harvey, March 31, 1847, *Elgin-Grey Papers*, vol. IV, p. 1360.
[29]Quoted by Thompson, *The Life of Charles, Lord Metcalfe*, pp. 372–3.

ham and Metcalfe learned that the strength of their personal prerogatives depended on a policy of divide (the Council) and rule. By closing ranks and presenting a united front the cabinet was in a better position to master the Governor—as Metcalfe obviously realized.

The process of closing ranks and developing a united front not only strengthened the Executive Council against the Governor, it also gave it the power to direct the legislative branch. Lord Elgin saw that the grant of responsible government would educate colonial statesmen so that they would be capable of taking over the leadership hitherto provided by the Governor and the mother country. At the same time he could see that the concession of responsible government exposed the colony "to those demoralizing influences which are apt to prevail extensively under Party Government, in communities where such distinctions [i.e., party distinctions] exist, not so much for the assertion of great principles, or the defence of important interest, as for the advantage of persons seeking employment in the public service."[30] This risk, however, had to be taken if the colony was ever to grow into a mature political community.

The limited evidence of contemporary observers clearly indicates that in the formative years the cabinet spent long hours grappling with the problems of legislative strategy and with ways and means of maintaining its command over a somewhat turbulent legislature. By 1850, indeed, W. H. Merritt could raise the now familiar outcry against cabinet dictation; the executive, he contended, through its ability to introduce all financial legislation could dragoon the backbenchers into supporting any money measure.[31] On the other hand, it was not an easy task to maintain cabinet solidarity at a period when party lines were extremely fluid—as the record of changing administrations proved. Much of the cabinet's time was taken up— if we can rely on Merritt's observations—with planning the detailed strategy for holding on to its tenuous legislative support. The following exasperated notation appears in Merritt's diary on March 24, 1849: "We meet every morning in Council at 9 to 10 o'clock, discuss each subject brought before the House, and determine on advocating or opposing it [presumably the cabinet then had little control over the agenda of the legislature]—this is left to the two Attorney Generals [sic] for Upper and Lower Canada and detains the other members

[30]Elgin to Grey, Sept. 25, 1847, *Elgin-Grey Papers*, vol. IV, p. 1378.
[31]See his remarks before Select Committee re State of the Public Income and Expenditure of the Province, *Journals*, Legislative Assembly, Canada (*J.L.A.C.*), 1850, Appendix B.B.

of the Cabinet, as listeners—adjourn at 2 and meet again in the Legislative Assembly at 3 o'clock—thus loosing [sic] the greater part of the day—continue to 11-12 or 1 o'clock."[32] Merritt's reference to the dominant position of the Law Officers in these special planning sessions of the cabinet largely explains why the Prime Ministers usually occupied the position of Attorney General for Upper and Lower Canada.

Indeed, it is clear that the Law Officers of the Crown provided much of the central co-ordination which was expected of the cabinet as a body. Not only were they responsible for directing political strategy in Parliament but also their legal abilities induced the other departments to appeal to them for rulings—not always on points of law—which in turn came to be treated as rulings of the whole cabinet. D'Arcy McGee's informative report on the state of the public departments in 1863 reveals that during the preceding ten years departmental references to the Attorneys had increased tremendously.[33] The Eastern Branch of the Attorney General's Office, for example, handled 157 cases in 1851 whereas in 1862 there were 1,176 references. McGee considered that this was a most unwarranted trend. It arose, he contended, "not so much from necessity as from some confusion of ideas on the subject of departmental responsibility." Explaining his opposition to the increased "referential" work of the Attorneys, McGee reported:

That either of the chief law officers may happen to be Premier—and therefore to be consulted on grounds of public policy—cannot of itself relieve the head of any department from his own proper official responsibility. It is neither desirable for the sake of the departments, nor for the political head of the government, if he should happen to be also an Attorney General, that the former should shelter themselves under the written opinions of the latter in cases falling properly within their own jurisdiction.

It is not altogether clear from McGee's report whether this system of referring matters for decision to the Crown Law Officers came about merely because the opinion of a legal authority was required or because the legal authority usually also happened to be the political head of the cabinet. Perhaps the two tendencies developed hand in hand: the Premier came to be recognized as the head of a united team and consequently one whose opinions on all major issues it was expedient for departmental heads to obtain; the Attorney

[32]Public Archives of Canada, Merritt Papers, Note Books.
[33]"Report on the Origin and Organization of the Public Departments," Public Archives of Canada, M. 837, 1863, section on the Executive Council.

General, as the highest legal adviser of the government, came to be consulted and his written decisions regarded as binding on his colleagues because it was an easy way for departmental heads to shift responsibility to another's shoulders. What more natural, then, that the two positions of informal political head and formal legal adviser should merge, with the acknowledged Premiers accepting the portfolios of Attorney General for Canada East and Canada West?

Apart from its work as a joint board for political strategy and a central clearing house for legal decisions involving the work of various departments, the cabinet also had to replace the Governor as the centre for formulating policy and supervising or co-ordinating the financial affairs of the province. The scattered complaints recorded against the cabinet's performance of these two important duties reveal that even at Confederation the executive had not managed to develop altogether satisfactory methods of handling the nation's business through collective consideration.

After a brief unsatisfactory experience with the working methods of Council, Merritt openly criticized the system before a legislative committee in 1850:

> Here we combine the duties of separate Departments with the Executive Council, in whom the power is vested, and on whom the responsibility rests. . . . Here, each separate measure comes up [in the Council] in its turn, day by day, and is acted upon without the possibility of any other member than the one bringing it forward, understanding the subject; it is then filed away, and forms part of the general transactions of the Government.[34]

Since Merritt's cabinet colleagues had not really given their full confidence to him, it is possible that his criticism of procedure was exaggerated. Nevertheless, the minutes of Council testify to the general accuracy of Merritt's conclusions. They record several attempts to improve the methods of bringing business before cabinet and of providing all the information necessary for reaching decisions. One may surmise that as the powers of the Governor waned there was a tendency for each department to take an independent line in policy formation—often consulting the cabinet after the event. Moreover, the presence in most departments of well-entrenched permanent officials further encouraged this autonomous spirit. Orders in Council,

---

[34]Merritt's evidence before the Select Committee on the Public Income and Expenditure, *J.L.A.C.*, 1850. One hundred years later it is interesting to read the same strictures applied to the British cabinet by one with long experience in its operations. See L. S. Amery, *Thoughts on the Constitution* (London, 1947), pp. 86–7.

for example, were drafted by the heads of separate departments for "His Excellency's consideration and approval." These orders often had to be blindly approved by Council because supporting petitions, reports, and memoranda were not provided at all by the department concerned, or reached the Council unauthenticated by any department. An extract from the minutes of Council dated April 8, 1858, suggests the nature of the general problem confronting the cabinet:

> The Committee [of Council] beg to observe that the letter of the Assistant Commissioner [of Public Works] contains matter of very great importance in reference to the Tug Service which should have been in the possession of the Council while the contract was under discussion. Two [sic] much stress cannot be laid upon the strict adherence to the regulations made by the Council that all documents, papers and information bearing upon subjects brought before the government for executive action should accompany the Report from the Department forwarding the same.[35]

The repetition of these cabinet admonitions to the separate departmental heads indicates that the sense of departmental autonomy tended to override the demand for collective consideration of departmental policies. For example, in an entry dated October 30, 1862, the Council records in its minutes a recommendation that all reports and petitions be presented uniformly to Council under a minister's signature, or if the particular Minister is unable to act, that one of his cabinet colleagues authenticate the documents.[36] A year later, in February 1863, Thomas D'Arcy McGee returned to the attack, submitting for the approval of Council an elaborate scheme designed to improve the business methods of cabinet.[37] McGee proposed that all departmental reports and memoranda in which the expenditure of public money was recommended should state explicitly the statute, order, or other authority (if any) under which the report or recommendation was submitted and the fund to which it was proposed such payment would be charged. Recommendations to Council were to carry the signature of the Minister of the proper department or one authorized to act for him. No Order in Council was to be approved unless the working papers associated with it had been lodged with the Clerk of the Council one day in advance. If an emergency required suspension of this rule, a note to that effect was to be recorded in the minutes.

[35]State Book S, April 1858, p. 485.
[36]State Book Y, Oct. 30, 1862, p. 6.
[37]*Ibid.*, Feb. 9, 1863. The same date appears at the end of McGee's "Report," which obviously provided a basis for this recommendation for improving arrangements in Council.

We may suppose that McGee's plan, though formally endorsed by the departmental heads as a group, was not consistently applied by the departmental heads acting in their individual capacities. A month later, in April 1863, the minutes of Council record once again the hostility of the departmental heads towards any efforts to standardize business procedures. On April 7, Council recommended that where an Order in Council was required by statute and had to be published, all information relating to the order was to be passed over to the Crown Law Department which was to prepare the first draft. At the next meeting of Council, this recommendation was rescinded with the instruction that all preliminary drafting of orders be left with the separate departments.[38]

One of the interesting differences between British and Canadian legislative practices has been the tendency for Canadian statutes to confer discretionary powers on the "Governor General in Council" (i.e., the cabinet) rather than, as in England, to confer such powers on individual ministers. It is difficult to discover an historical explanation of this difference. The record of the early Canadian cabinet suggests that it failed to secure satisfactory collective consideration of policy matters or administrative issues upon which the statutes called for joint decision. Thus, while in principle the Governor General in Council was supposed to make the decisions, in practice they were often made, as in England, by individual ministers.

Supplements to the Executive Council

During the pre-Confederation period, the problem of improving the cabinet's methods of handling business was explored in several other ways. Although it is impossible to speak of a cabinet secretariat at this time, there were several agencies actually dividing up some of the responsibilities of a secretariat. In the first place, there was the small staff employed in the Executive Council Office. This group was supposed to receive and register all departmental applications which had to be referred for decision to His Excellency in Council.[39] The clerks prepared a statement of each case for the attention of Council and after the Council had deliberated and approved the necessary orders, these were transcribed by the office for the information of the departments concerned. Judging from the difficulty already noted of inducing departments to follow the rules, the Executive Council Office

---

[38]State Book Y, April 7, 1863, p. 401; April 13, 1863, p. 404.

[39]For a description of duties in the Office see "Return to an address etc. for Statements of Financial Affairs of the Province and a List of the Clerks and Other Employees in the Public Departments . . . ," *J.L.A.C.*, 1852–3, Appendix F.F.F.F.

played a purely passive role in the process. That is, it had no power to take the initiative in order to ensure that the Council would have the necessary papers and at the proper time. The menial tasks of registration and transcribing were its major preoccupations.

Another office, that of the Provincial Secretary, also provided some secretarial assistance to the cabinet. It gradually took over from the Governor General's Secretary his original function as a centre of reference on all issues raised by the colonists. All applications for public office and complaints against officialdom were channelled through the office of the Provincial Secretary.[40] In practice, of course, most of this business was transacted directly between the ministerial head and his public. The Provincial Secretary also served as an office of registration for land warrants, patents, and other business matters which frequently occupied the time of Council. The Office played a somewhat passive role in the complicated process then employed for releasing appropriations to the separate departments; it issued all warrants for payment of public money. Finally, the Provincial Secretary's Office early assumed full charge of departmental returns to questions asked in the legislature—a responsibility which its successor, the Secretary of State, still retains. These somewhat routine duties probably contributed very little to easing the burdens placed on the cabinet.

The other official who perhaps contributed most to the improvement of the procedure of cabinet was the President of Council, or, more accurately, the President of the Committees of Council. Nowadays, the Prime Minister makes a practice of assuming the mantle of President of Council. Consequently, we have come to attach a prestige and authority to the title which it has not always carried.[41] The notion of creating a co-ordinating head or a sort of business manager for Council appears to have originated with the Royal Commission on the Public Departments which reported in 1839.[42] The Commissioners proposed that a President of the Council be appointed

[40]A concise description of the manifold duties of this office is given in McGee's "Report," section on the Provincial Secretaryship.

[41]For example, when a scandal forced the Commissioner of Public Works to resign from the cabinet in 1850, Merritt was moved from President of Council to this "working department," while the Assistant Commissioner of Public Works assumed the vacated Presidency of Council along with his other portfolio.

[42]See *Journals*, Legislative Assembly, Upper Canada, 1839–40, Appendix, vol. II, "Report of Committee no. 3 on the Executive Council," p. 12: "We think that, without distributing all the business among the Departments, or necessarily subdividing the Council itself into Committees or Bureaus, the efficiency of the Board might be promoted, through the appointment of a President of the Council, with an adequate salary, to rank next to the Chief Justice. . . ."

"whose first and principal duty it should be to attend to the details of the Council Office, in all their branches; and who should have it peculiarly in charge to examine and report upon all matters submitted to the Board." This official, they thought, ought to possess "high legal attainments."

In his reorganization of the executive branch of government in 1841, Lord Sydenham, obviously relying on the recommendations of the Royal Commissioners, gave special attention to this official. "Your Lordship is aware," he wrote to Russell, "that a very large portion of the business of that body [the Executive Council] has consisted in advising the Governor on applications or claims for land and cases of that description—or in reporting on the accounts of the several public offices or departments. I have for these services constituted a committee to be presided over by a President . . . and I have conferred that appointment on the Hon. R. B. Sullivan, who was for several years Presiding Councillor of the Executive Council of Upper Canada."[43] Since Sydenham looked upon himself and acted as Prime Minister, there was no reason to suppose that the President of the Committees of Council was to be superior in status or prestige to his other cabinet colleagues. Later, when the Governor's personal command over the cabinet dwindled, leadership of the cabinet went not to the President of the Council but to the informal, although fully acknowledged heads of the party factions making up the governing coalition from Upper and Lower Canada. Normally, the two Prime Ministers, as has been noted, preferred to operate from some other office—usually the Attorney General's Department.

That the role of the President of Council was not fully understood even by those well acquainted with government is revealed in the personal diaries of Merritt. "Having been offered the situation of President of the Council yesterday [Sept. 13, 1848]," Merritt notes, "took until this day to consider of it—having no knowledge of the duties, and no inclination to confine myself to mere official routine determined to decline it, but Messrs. Lafontaine, Sullivan and Baldwin assuring me it was a situation which would give me the best opportunity of bringing my views before the Government and in which I could render more essential service than having the immediate charge of any single department [I accepted]."[44] Both Merritt and his colleagues were to regret his decision: Merritt because the job proved frustrating; his colleagues because the position left Merritt

[43]Sydenham to Russell, no. 92, July 18, 1841, Public Archives of Canada, R.G. 7, G. 12, vol. 57, pp. 289–94.
[44]Merritt Papers, Note Books, vol. 3, 1849.

with too much time to look about and raise those embarrassing direct questions which a businessman-turned-politician is so adept at raising.[45] Merritt's diary continues: "This day [Oct. 16, 1848] assumed the duties of my office as President of the Committee of the Executive Council of the Province of Canada, not President of Council, as generally supposed, inasmuch as on the final passage of measure the governor presides." Merritt's diary then records how the President spent his time. Before each Council meeting he went over the various documents filed with the Executive Council Office and examined the applications for land patents with the clerk of the Office. This paper work appears, from Merritt's comments, to have been accompanied by numerous interruptions for personal interviews with various applicants. At the Council table the following day, His Excellency presided and referred to the President, very much as a chairman would refer to the secretary, for information on any given point. Apparently, the Council's procedures proved very annoying to Merritt, the methodical, conscientious businessman. The "Ordinary Business of Council" which was transacted on Wednesdays and Saturdays involved the approval in much detail of "all monied transactions" of the government. These, according to Merritt, were passed

without proper investigation or the possibility of any effective check, as an instance—
A claim of Hewit and Schram for some £800—was reported on by Mr. Gzowsky—Engineer—asking no claim under the Contract, but recommended to be paid, on the ground that it would be allowed if referred to arbitration—On investigation it appears this claim had been twice examined, reported upon and paid over in 1847—and again in November 1848.

The minute book of Council provides much evidence to support Merritt's criticisms. There seems to be no question that of all the business coming before Council, that involving the expenditure of public funds (for which the Act of Union held the executive solely responsible) was the most difficult to handle. The largest spending department—Public Works—and the auditing of departmental expenditures provided the two major sources of irritation. Both problems were met in the same fashion by creating special committees of cabinet which were expected to provide a detailed supervision and report to the full Council. In 1849 Council recorded that "with a view

[45]Elgin was inclined to be suspicious of Merritt's "Yankee" leanings and he referred to him as the "speculative Mr. Merritt"; he had to admit, however, that he enjoyed a wide popular following because of his "retrenchment" policies. For the results of his "speculations" see his evidence and memoranda presented to the Select Committee on Public Income and Expenditure, *J.L.A.C.*, 1850.

of making a more equal division of labour, a saving of time, and of gaining a more thorough knowledge of each separate transaction on which the Council is called upon to decide from the Department of Public Works, it is considered advisable to appoint a committee to meet once in a month to examine those separate claims."[46] The committee, consisting of the two Commissioners of the Board of Works, the Receiver General, Inspector General, and President of Council, was to meet at 10 o'clock on the first Tuesday of the month at the office of Public Works, and here it was to obtain "such reports and information from the several departments as will at one view show the amount expended, the cost of management and the amount received from month to month or quarter to quarter."

Apparently even this careful arrangement was not entirely effective for in 1856 Council recommended that the Department of Public Works submit a *weekly* statement of works under contract, appropriations or estimated cost, rate of monthly progress, and probable period of completion.[47] No matter how elaborate the precautions, however, the ingenuity of Public Works in evading all controls (as later chapters will show) proved too much for the cabinet. Possibly the most important advance in official thinking on this matter of cabinet control of departmental expenditures is recorded in the minutes of Council on August 19, 1858.[48] The Inspector General, Cayley, considering that revenues were low and that there was a corresponding need for economy, recommended to Council "that each Head of Department do lay before your Excellency in Council at the earliest possible day an estimate of the proposed outlay till 31st December next—distinguishing between those items which do not admit of reductions and such as might admit of reconsideration." Here in embryo and presumably only in temporary form, we find the modern system according to which each department submits its estimated needs for the coming year through Treasury Board to cabinet.

The cabinet had greater success with the committee which it set up to audit the expenditures of the public departments. Essentially this was a continuation of a function for which the Council always had some responsibility. This responsibility was never properly carried out until after 1855, when a permanent auditor was appointed and a Board of Audit created. Fortunately, the man first appointed to the position of Auditor was John Langton, an able, forthright, and courageous official. He needed to be. Teamed up with certain ad-

[46]State Book J, June 6, 1849, p. 165.
[47]State Book Q, Nov. 8, 1856, p. 605—on memorandum of Inspector General.
[48]A more detailed treatment of this point appears in the following chapter.

ministrative reformers who also had considerable experience in business—the most notable being Alexander Galt—he laid the basis for the modern system of budgeting. In the last five or six years before Confederation cabinet became less concerned with the detailed audit of expenditures and more concerned with the process of co-ordinating the estimates and revenue-raising proposals now channelled through a vigorous Minister of Finance. As was noted above, the Inspector General's recommendations to Council in 1858 foreshadowed the development of such a permanent system. The stage was thus set for what has now become the most complicated and crucial process in administration—modern budget making. In this task, today, the cabinet relies heavily on a specially staffed cabinet committee—the Treasury Board. Indeed, by Order in Council this organ was attached to the Department of Finance on the second day following Confederation. But even before Confederation, especially in the cabinet committee set up to deal with the heavy expenditures on public works, we find early recognition of the need to create special machinery for close consideration of departmental finances.

The Deputy Minister

The developments traced above gradually converted the cabinet into a real co-ordinating centre for the entire public service. At the same time, within each department, the top command was being strengthened and consolidated by subordinating all the branches to one official—the permanent deputy minister. The evolution of this official and his relations with the political head of the department comprise a necessary part of this analysis of overhead direction and control.

The idea of having in each department a permanent co-ordinating head was not new. As has already been noted, the Colonial Office viewed the Governor's Secretary in this light. Moreover, most of the public departments employed a chief clerk or a secretary who tended at least to be a centre of reference for the public, and who enjoyed some superiority of status and salary. Formal recognition of the need for, and actual development of, a permanent head in each department did not come, however, until the comprehensive Civil Service Act of 1857.[49] Here, for the first time in any statute, the expression

---

[49]20 Vic., c. 24, s. vii–viii (1857). In the brief biography of J. C. Taché, Deputy Minister of Agriculture from 1864 to 1888, in G. M. Rose, *A Cyclopedia of Canadian Biography*, p. 68, it is stated that he was the "first to bear the title of deputy minister now given to all the chief permanent officers of the Departments of the Canadian public service."

"deputy Minister" was used and here, too, provision for such an official in every department was made obligatory.

The genesis of the term "deputy minister" is not clear. It certainly does not follow equivalent British terminology, for there the official was early known as the "permanent secretary" or "permanent undersecretary." Nor was American terminology influential, for to this day no such official exists in the hierarchy of the American civil service. The term, it is suggested, actually took its origin from the period of Imperial domination of the colonial civil service. The Postmaster General at Whitehall, for example, appointed a Deputy Postmaster General for British North America. That official, unlike his political chief, by custom enjoyed permanent tenure. Similarly, the Receiver General and Inspector General had deputies who were regarded as permanent. It is likely that the Civil Service Act simply borrowed this term from the colonial past—although it is interesting to observe that prior to 1857 the official literature never uses the term in referring generally to the permanent heads of departments. Whatever the origins of the title it has now become a familiar and accepted term. Technically, however, it is misleading, because it suggests that the permanent head has complete power to act in the place of the Minister. As several deputy ministers pointed out to a royal commission in 1890 the deputy does not have such powers and public misunderstanding of this fact has often embarrassed the permanent official.[50]

Whatever the reasons for using the title and whatever the ambiguities in its use, the important fact is that by 1857 the law could recognize that such an official was essential to each department. Seven years before this Act, in fact, Robert Baldwin, testifying before a parliamentary committee, made the following far-sighted observation:

... in my opinion, with a view to the efficient working of the Government, there should be, to every department of it, two subordinate officers, call them Assistants, Deputies, or whatever else may be deemed most appropriate according to the nature of the Department. One of these should be a non-political and permanent officer,—and the other a Political Officer, either in Parliament or not, according to circumstances, but one in whom his Principal, and the Administration generally, should have full political confidence, and who should of course come in and out with them. Without such assistance, it will, I think, be found, that the Heads of the different Departments will not be able to attend to the higher duties of Ministers of the Crown. . . .[51]

[50]See "Report of the Royal Commission Appointed to Enquire into Certain Matters Relating to the Civil Service of Canada," *Sessional Papers*, Canada, 1892, no. 16c, evidence of A. M. Burgess, Q. 523, and of J. Johnson, Q. 2457.

[51]See his evidence before Select Committee on Public Income and Expenditure, *J.L.A.C.*, 1850.

Thus did Baldwin envisage not only the development of the Deputy Minister's office but, some seventy-five years ahead of his time, the need for the political position now familiar to us as "parliamentary assistant."

About the same time as Baldwin presented these views, the Department of Public Works—one of the largest of the pre-Confederation departments—was informally acknowledging the existence of a permanent head. This evolution came about in a fashion rather different from that which occurred in most of the other departments. Instead of the senior clerk or secretary of the department becoming the acknowledged "deputy minister"—as was the case in the other departments—an official, the Assistant Commissioner, hitherto regarded as a political, temporary appointee ultimately became the permanent deputy head. That both a Chief Commissioner and an Assistant Commissioner of Public Works were required was attributable to the forces of dualism already mentioned. Until 1851 both these officials were political—one French speaking, the other English speaking. After 1851 a quiet metamorphosis took place, and during the next eight years the Assistant Commissioner in effect became permanent head of the Department, no longer holding a seat in the legislature.[52] Not until 1859, however, did legislation finally acknowledge the presence of a "deputy commissioner of public works."[53]

In the Crown Lands Department, the other large pre-Confederation department, there was also a Commissioner and Assistant Commissioner. But in this case, the Assistant was never a political officer. In fact the first Commissioner of Crown Lands was omitted from Sydenham's Council and from the pay schedule appended to the Civil List. Some observers, in fact, argued that the Department should be treated on a strictly business basis and separated entirely from politics. As one pamphleteer argued in 1847, the "practical attention of business matters" of the Crown Lands Department necessitated "the whole time and undivided attention . . . of an active, enlightened industrious head" who should have no seat in the legislature.[54] This businessman's instinctive dislike of mingling politics with a business

---

[52]Dent, *The Last Forty Years*, pp. 235 f., describes this change apparently in conformity with the belief that there were certain departments where long-range programmes could be implemented only by having permanent "working heads." This attitude as noted in the next paragraph was also expressed in connection with appointments to the Department of Crown Lands.

[53]22 Vic., c. 3, s. 6 (1859).

[54]See C. Rankin, *A Letter to His Excellency the Governor General on the Subject of the Crown Lands Department* (Toronto, May 20, 1847, Public Archives of Canada, Pamphlet no. 2084).

concern did not keep the Commissioner of Crown Lands out of the legislature or the cabinet—or out of politics. The Assistant Commissioner at first, however, did not operate as an effective permanent deputy—even though he was "out of politics." His function until about 1850 was to superintend the administration of the branches of the Crown Lands Department in Lower Canada.[55] At what date the Assistant Commissioner became the real permanent focal point of administration in the Department cannot be exactly determined. However, the Civil Service Act of 1857 formally established the Assistant Commissioner as permanent Deputy Minister. That the other departments all complied with the obligatory requirement to appoint a permanent head and that, in fact, this official did remain permanent is shown by the Departmental Blue Book at Confederation. Here we find a list of the deputies appointed for the eight departments. With two exceptions the deputies were all officials who had come up through the departments and had been employed for times ranging from the 43 years of William Henry Lee, Clerk of the Executive Council, to the 13 years of W. H. Griffin, Deputy Postmaster General. Only one deputy, Dr. J. C. Taché, newly appointed to the Bureau of Agriculture and Statistics, arrived via a political career.

In considering this description of the development of methods and instruments to control and co-ordinate the public service, we get the clear impression that the separate departments created by Sydenham were still, at Confederation, far from operating in a neatly integrated system. Colonial administrators should not be condemned on that account. For at this same period the British civil service was still a loose assemblage of autonomously minded departments scarcely emerged from its confining chrysalis of feudalism.[56]

Viewed from this perspective, we can deduce that Canadian administrators had made a fair start on the task confronting them when the colonial Governor and his Secretary lost their personal powers of direction and co-ordination. Sydenham had formed and handed down a number of separate departments whose co-ordination was expected to take place through the Governor and his office. He had created, in the remodelled Executive Council, a potential focal point for the

---

[55]For example, the "Report of the Commissioner of Public Works in 1848," *J.L.A.C.*, 1848, Appendix N, notes how the death of Casgrain, the Assistant Commissioner, has created a real gap in the Department's knowledge of the roads in Lower Canada and of the public works below Quebec.

[56]See J. E. Hodgetts, "Unifying the British Civil Service: Some Trends and Problems," *Canadian Journal of Economics and Political Science*, vol. XIV, no. 1 (1948), pp. 1–19.

public services, but until fully responsible government had arrived the cabinet could not assume this function. With the advent of responsible government the cabinet had to work out several problems. First, it had to learn to act as a single entity in order to impart unity of direction in policy as well as administration. This development could occur only over time and as a result of a painful maturing process. Secondly, the cabinet had to undertake all those duties which had hitherto been handled by the Governor and his Secretary. As was noted, the business arrangements in Council up to Confederation were still being remodelled so that the cabinet could satisfactorily serve as the vital centre of the public service. In the most important and difficult task of managing departmental finances, the cabinet had also begun to pave the way for the ultimate creation of a Treasury Board.

By Confederation the cabinet had prepared itself for the task of examining and approving departmental budgets and the general revenue proposals put up by the Minister of Finance. Meanwhile, in the evolution of the office of permanent deputy minister the colonial politicians had made a really important technical improvement in the administrative apparatus of each department. That this official did not fully solve the problem of imparting unity at the top of the larger departments was not surprising, since this problem is still one of the most persistent and intricate confronting modern administrators.

CHAPTER VII

TIGHTENING THE PURSE STRINGS

WILLIAM LYON MACKENZIE is, perhaps, better known to Canadians for his exploits as a political rebel than for his practical contributions as an economic reformer. Nevertheless, he played a major part in laying the foundations for that supervision of the public service which the popular assembly maintains because of its control over the purse. His contribution came at the end of a career whose earlier dramatic stages tended to obliterate the constructive contributions of his declining years. Mackenzie began his agitation in 1835 when he dominated the famous Committee on Grievances.[1] Twenty years later —a rebellion and embittering exile having intervened—Mackenzie once again returned to his programme of financial reform. From his position as chairman of the Select Committee on Public Accounts, Mackenzie initiated a series of reforms without which parliamentary control of the purse would have remained entirely ineffectual.[2] The nation thereby received the delayed dividends from Mackenzie's earlier, ardent reading of the British "economists," Huskisson, Parnell, Hume, and Bowring.[3]

While Mackenzie was instrumental in rousing the legislature to a sense of its duties as guardian of the public purse, his efforts would have proved abortive had they not been accompanied or even preceded by certain adjustments to the machinery of financial control within the bureaucracy. Most of these alterations were initiated by the first Auditor General, John Langton.[4] In the long run his contribution was the greater because he possessed the advantages of

---

[1]See "Seventh Report from the Select Committee of the House of Assembly of Upper Canada on Grievances," *Journals*, Legislative Assembly, Upper Canada, 1835, Appendix 21.

[2]See "Second Report of the Standing Committee on Public Accounts," *Journals*, Legislative Assembly, Canada (*J.L.A.C.*), 1854–5, Appendix J.J.

[3]The findings of the Parnell Commission on Financial Reform in Britain are quoted with approval by the Committees of 1835 (pp. 75–6) and of 1854–5 (Second Report). For Mackenzie's reading habits see list provided by his biographer Charles Lindsey, *The Life and Times of Wm. Lyon Mackenzie* (2 vols, Toronto, 1862), vol. II, Appendix A.

[4]See the excellent review of Langton's work in Herbert R. Balls, "John Langton and the Canadian Audit Office," *Canadian Historical Review*, vol. XXI (1940), pp. 150–76.

permanency not vouchsafed Mackenzie, the politician. Coaching from the wings, Langton exerted a continuous influence on several prominent Ministers of Finance including Alexander Galt, William Cayley, and J. P. Howland. Improvements in the format of the public accounts and in departmental accounting practices which were announced as triumphs of the Minister of the day were, in fact, largely the product of Langton's exertions.

Mackenzie the politician and Langton the permanent public servant never worked together as a team. Probably no single harness could have held them. Langton, Tory in politics, rather aristocratic in social outlook, retiring by preference (though dogmatic and assertive in private), was the antithesis of Mackenzie—even the chastened post-rebellion Mackenzie. None the less, the interests of the two men happily complemented one another when applied to the great task of establishing legislative control over public expenditures. Mackenzie's interest stemmed from political and constitutional motives: attaining responsible government would be a hollow victory if the local executive could not be held responsible to the legislature for its annual outlay on the public services. For Langton, who spoke for the business community (represented in public office by men like Merritt, Hincks, Young, and Galt), the issue was more a matter of applying business-like methods to governmental affairs. Mackenzie sponsored the claims of parliamentary or "external" control over the executive's financial operations; Langton spoke for those who understood the intricacies of double-entry bookkeeping, reconversion of the debt, cash statements, balance sheets, and capital accounts. Langton's task was to translate the complexity of governmental financing into terms that could be readily understood by the layman in Parliament.

Parliamentary control of the purse was by no means an automatic outgrowth of the winning of responsible government. A long, painstaking series of reforms had to be undertaken before that control was firmly established. It is the purpose of this chapter to trace the main features of this development.

Internal Control

Within the Canadian public service after 1840 four important changes connected with the handling of public money took place. (1) The issue of public money allocated to the use of each department was gradually brought under central control. This type of control is now generally termed the *comptrol* function. (2) The audit of public expenditures was centralized. (3) The public accounts containing a record of the year's transactions were amplified and made more intelligible to Parliament. (4) Finally, there was introduced the process of estimating in advance the financial needs of each department for the coming year. Each of these aspects of internal financial control—the issue, audit, accounting, and estimating phases—had to be satisfactorily developed if Parliament was to become the watchdog of the executive.

The issue phase. At the time of Union, the process of releasing funds to the public departments followed no system. Indeed, until Confederation, the issue and audit phases were not properly distinguished. Today the Comptroller General, located in the Department of Finance, is responsible for the issue phase of fiscal control.[5] His duty is to ascertain that when a department makes a requisition for funds there is money available and the department has legal authority to spend it for the purposes stated in the application. The Auditor, then, is able to confine his attention primarily to the examination of expenditures which have already been made. This clear separation of the issue and audit phases was not attained in the pre-Confederation public service.

At first the issue of public money was controlled by the Executive Council working with the Offices of the Receiver General and Inspector General.[6] The audit was vested in the Deputy Inspector General.[7] In principle, a department applied to the Inspector General's Office for money. On a favourable report from that Office, the Executive Council Office approved a warrant which was the authority upon which the Receiver General's Office issued a cheque to the spending department. The Inspector General was required to countersign all such cheques. Even more elaborate procedures were used in the case of expenditures for public works.[8]

In addition to the obviously unwieldy apparatus just noted, there were several other weaknesses in the system of controlling the issue of funds. Theoretically the controls seemed to be excessive for there were really two departments set up to watch one another, the Offices

[5]R.S.C. (1952), c. 116 (The Financial Administration Act), ss. 11–15, and part II. The Comptroller General, however, did not make his appearance until 1931.

[6]For a description of the early workings of financial control see "Report on the Public Departments," *Journals*, Legislative Assembly, Upper Canada, 1839–40, vol. II, "Fifth Report on the Executive Council Office."

[7]*Ibid.*, "Second Report of Committee No. 2 on Receiver General's Office" and "Report of Committee No. 3 on Inspector General's Office."

[8]For a criticism of the complex procedures used for public works, see Merritt's second memorandum to the Select Committee re State of the Public Income and Expenditure of the Province, "First Report," *J.L.A.C.*, 1850, Appendix B.B.

of Inspector General and Receiver General maintaining duplicate accounts of all expenditures. In fact, the two sets of books were kept in such different ways that they could not be compared: they did not "assimilate," as one official body remarked.[9] The only possible value of dual finance offices whose records could not be checked against each other was that, with the perpetual threat from fire in stove-heated offices, there was a better chance of preserving at least one set of records. In 1856, with that objective in mind, a committee of the legislature recommended that the two offices be located in separate buildings.[10] With the passing of time, the Receiver General's Office became more and more an agency for managing the debenture issues of the province and the Inspector General's Office acquired full control over the issue phase. Duplicate records were still maintained but the books kept by the Deputy Inspector General were now gradually made comparable with the books which, after 1855, the newly appointed Auditor was compelled to set up.

Another weakness in the control of the issue of public funds was that many departments were able to evade the formal requirements described above. This could be done in two ways.[11] Departmental spending agents could borrow from the banks in anticipation of future revenue or subsequent appropriations. Since many departmental accountants held the money in their own name, the bank advances were to all intents and purposes equivalent to personal loans. Headquarters had to take the local spending agents' word that the money had been spent legitimately for the projects under their jurisdiction. In 1858 this practice was terminated by Order in Council. Henceforth, every local agent had to issue a cheque on an account opened in the department's name rather than his own. Each cheque had to state the purpose for which the money was to be spent. The banks made their contribution to the cause of internal expenditure control by sending monthly statements to departmental headquarters and to the Auditor.

The other method of evading formal internal controls was open to those departments, such as Crown Lands, the Post Office, and Customs,

[9]"Second Report of Standing Committee on Public Accounts," *J.L.A.C.*, 1854–5.
[10]"First Report of Select Committee on Public Accounts," *J.L.A.C.*, 1856, Appendix 30.
[11]The details of departmental evasions are scattered through the reports of the inquisitive Public Accounts Committee. The Report of the Committee in 1858 shows how the strings of central control were gradually being tightened: *J.L.A.C.*, 1858, Appendix 4, Report of Committee appended to "Public Accounts for the Province of Canada, 1857."

which collected large revenues. These departments were entitled to pay all "costs of management" from gross revenues, neither Parliament nor the central financial agencies having any control over the money thus drained off at the source. Even after 1858 when, as will be noted later, an attempt was made to force the revenue departments to turn over their gross revenues to the treasury, a system of so-called "accountable advances" was used which had the effect of leaving with departmental accountants or sub-accountants large unspent balances.[12] These balances were recorded as part of the year's expenditures, thus distorting the accounts. Moreover, unspent balances did not, as now, lapse but remained at the disposal of the department for the next year.[13]

Where the system of accountable advances was used, the departmental accountant would apply to the Provincial Secretary for a warrant. This application was transferred either to the Minister of Finance, the Auditor, or, in the case of expenses on the administration of justice, to the Deputy Inspector General.[14] One of these officials reported whether an appropriation existed to cover the expenditure. If there was no appropriation—a not unlikely situation—the Auditor made a note to this effect on the back of the application. These applications, with their official sponsoring signatures, then went to the Executive Council Office where a warrant was issued. This warrant constituted the department's authority to spend, subject to a quarterly or monthly "progress report" from the department to the Auditor. In 1864 a "letter of credit" system replaced the accountable warrants, thus eliminating the possibility of large balances hanging over from one year to the next in the hands of subordinate "accounting" offices.[15] From that time, the accounts more accurately portrayed the expenditures actually made during the year.

One of the major problems associated with the issue phase of

[12]See "Public Accounts of the Province of Canada for the half-year ended June 30, 1864," *Sessional Papers*, Canada, 1865, no. 1, Report of Board of Audit prefacing the accounts.

[13]See "Report of Special Committee to which were referred the Public Accounts," *J.L.A.C.*, 1844–5, Appendix M.M. "The balances of course remain in the Treasury, and are available at the vote of the Legislature, to the public purposes of the Province, as part of the Consolidated Revenue Fund thereof." But in 1858 the modern practice was officially approved by Council. See State Book T, Public Archives of Canada, Sept. 18, 1858, pp. 164–5.

[14]See "Report of Select Standing Committee on Public Accounts," *J.L.A.C.*, 1861, Appendix 2.

[15]"Report of Minister of Finance for the Year 1864," *Sessional Papers*, Canada, 1865, no. 1.

expenditure control was that all the expenditures took place on the authority of the executive *before* Parliament was given a chance to sanction them. Under these peculiar circumstances, of course, it was quite impossible to check a departmental request for money against a legal document which declared that Parliament had voted money for that purpose. The important amendment to the Audit Act in 1864 provided for the system which is the basis of our present method of issuing money to the public departments.[16] The new legislation required a vote of supply for each department for a financial period which had not yet commenced. Both the issue and audit phases of expenditure control were enormously improved by this change. There was now a legal authority against which the agencies of control (at that time the Auditor) could assess the financial claims and ultimate actions of each department. Since this particular innovation had widespread implications, it will be examined more fully below.

The audit phase. It has already been emphasized that, throughout the period of Union, the issue and audit phases of expenditure control tended to be combined. Prior to 1855, the Deputy Inspector General—acting under instructions issued in 1845 by Lord Metcalfe—audited the accounts of the departments.[17] His instructions required him to keep the auditing activities separate from his other duties. In practice, this proved easy because the audit was extremely casual. In 1855, the new Audit Act brought John Langton on the scene as the first Auditor General, his office being attached to the Inspector General's.

From the outset both Langton and other leading public officials treated the audit function as something more than an *ex post facto* check on departmental expenditures. Writing to his brother in England during November 1856, Langton revealed how he had informally become what today might be described as a one-man Treasury Board, Comptroller of the Treasury, and Auditor.

A man who is willing to work generally gets plenty to do and they have commenced referring all sorts of things to me which do not strictly belong to my department. Amongst other things they have gradually got into the way of sending down applications for warrants to me for report which Caylay [the Inspector General] always objected to at first. I think it is more correct that I should report whether a payment is authorized before it is made than afterwards but there are difficulties. [Langton is speaking of a comptrol activity here which is not now regarded as the Auditor's proper

[16] 27–28 Vic., c. 6 (1864).
[17] See State Book D, Aug. 27, 1845, p. 515.

function.] An order in Council must necessarily be authority enough for me and precludes my inquiring whether the O.C. is founded on just grounds but if I report upon a claim for money it is evidently not very easy for them to pass an order contrary to my report. Sometimes too an application is referred to me *after* the O.C. has passed when I have to interpret it, no very easy thing sometimes. In both cases it occasionally happens that my report is not what they want it to be altogether and it comes back to me with an unofficial intimation they want the report altered. It is treading on ticklish ground sometimes and I have refused to alter it, but I generally get out of the difficulty by submitting to Council whether it should be so or so, or submitting whether they meant so or so, and in almost all these cases I have found that they decide according to my original report. It is one thing to do a questionable act at once without any explanation and another to decide between two courses pointed out to you.[18]

Langton might well speak of "treading on ticklish ground" when called upon to pass judgment on departmental requests for money which really raised policy issues. A permanent, politically irresponsible official ought not to have been called on to make such decisions, for the future independence of the Audit Office was endangered. Nevertheless Langton was the kind of person who thrives on responsibility. He rapidly became the hub of the whole financial universe, taking up in 1870 the position of Deputy Minister of Finance and Secretary to the Treasury Board while retaining his original position as Auditor.[19] Thus the legal forms were shaped to fit the large capacities of one man, but they did not coincide with our present-day view of the status or duties of the Auditor General. Not until Langton's retirement in 1878 was the Auditor properly separated from the Deputy Minister of Finance.[20]

Even had Langton been content to confine his attentions to the audit of past expenditures, he still faced a difficult task. He inherited a haphazard system of bringing departmental accountants to book. They did not take kindly to the new régime which Langton's immediate vigorous actions indicated he would attempt to impose. Unfortunately, Langton's political chief was not prepared to back him

[18]Letter to his brother William Langton (a businessman in England) dated November 9, 1856. The original which was kindly supplied by the late H. H. Langton is now in the Ontario Archives. Extracts are to be found in W. A. Langton, ed., *Early Days in Upper Canada* (Toronto, 1926), pp. 271-2.

[19]32–33 Vic., c. 4 (1869), formally created the Treasury Board, although Order in Council P.C. 3 (1867) creating the Board was passed on the second day of the new Dominion's career. By 33 Vic., c. 7 (1870), the Auditor was also made Deputy Minister of Finance.

[20]41 Vic., c. 7 (1878).

up or sustain his rulings. Since he had no independent powers of compulsion—apart from his own informal lobbying with key politicians—Langton made slow progress.

The exasperated account he has left us of his attempts to deal with one of the greatest offenders, the Department of Public Works, illustrates the problem he faced on first assuming office.

> Lemieux [the Chief Commissioner] receives you with the greatest suavity (and he really is a very pleasant man), he asserts to the justness of everything you say, but he does not profess to know anything about details and refers you to Killaly [the Assistant Commissioner]. Killaly is also a most agreeable man, he is quite shocked at the irregularity in the department but he is only an engineer, he never meddles with anything, also he knows no more about accounts than he does of politics and refers you to Mr. Begley [the Secretary]. Mr. Begley is not an agreeable man, his situation is a very unpleasant one, he is only a servant, he writes letters as he is instructed and if he is instructed to send accounts he will do so, but he is only a servant and you must speak to Mr. Lemieux or Killaly. So they wisely determined to dismiss the bookkeeper who came into office about 6 months ago and inherited books which they never tried to balance for a great many years and naturally have failed to accomplish now. . . . It is pretty clear that we must have a fight before long and I am preparing for it.[21]

Langton's tactics involved the use of first-class financial ability and, at a lower level, adroit political lobbying. "Finding Cayley (the Inspector General) too timid and John Macdonald too easy I have," so he informed his brother, "latterly tried to work upon another member of the Ministry . . . Joe Morrison."[22] During the next two or three years Langton managed to win grudging recognition from the departments and all submitted their accounts to be audited. Only a partial victory was won, however, for many of the accounts—as later chapters will show—were so incomplete that Langton's audit was virtually a formal ritual. This was the conclusion of a royal commission which reported in May 1863 on "the prevailing mode of keeping the Public Accounts."[23] The recommendations of the Commission produced the important amendments to the Audit Act in 1864. Langton was instrumental in forcing the appointment of the Commission and his influence was also apparent in its final recommendations.

The new legislation, unfortunately, still left the Audit Office as a

---

[21]Letter to brother, Nov. 9, 1856.
[22]*Ibid.*
[23]*First Report of the Financial and Departmental Commission* (Quebec, 1863), pp. 6 f.

branch of the Department of Finance. However, one change did improve the Auditor's status and, to some extent, assured a more independent audit. The Act of 1855 had created a three-man Audit Board on which the Auditor participated as a member and over which the Deputy Inspector General presided as chairman. Thomas D'Arcy McGee in his comprehensive report on the public service in 1863 had pointed out the weakness of this arrangement, for it made the three permanent officials in the Finance Department—the Deputy Inspector General, the Auditor, and the Commissioner of Customs—responsible for the audit.[24] The new act of 1864 established a seven-man board and made the Auditor chairman. Not only did this raise the status of the Auditor but the final examination of departmental expenditures was no longer a family affair in which three permanent officials in the Finance Department placed their imprimateur on the accounts submitted by other departments. Moreover, the Auditor was now authorized to report any illegal money warrants—a procedure made possible, as previously mentioned, by the introduction of a system of voting all appropriations one year in advance. The Auditor now possessed a standard against which to test the legality of the issue and expenditure of public funds.

The public accounts. Of all the blue books published today by the government, the Public Accounts and the Auditor's commentary on them enjoy the largest reading public. From these documents the opposition normally finds enough ammunition to keep sniping at the government during the session. The press also finds them newsworthy items. That these records are now so ample, clear, and informative must be attributed to the labours of a succession of able Auditors General of whom John Langton was the diligent precursor.

When Langton first assumed office in 1855 he found great difficulty in making any sense out of the accounts submitted by the departments. If Langton found difficulty in understanding the accounts, we may assume that Parliament must have been even more perplexed. Consequently, in so far as he succeeded in forcing improvements in departmental accounting practices and in the format of the full accounts he was able to make a real contribution to the cause of parliamentary control of the purse.

Enough has already been said about his struggle with the departments to suggest that he was not nearly as successful as he would have wished or as Parliament required in obtaining good accounts.

[24]See his "Report on the Origin and Organization of the Public Departments" in Public Archives of Canada, M. 837, 1863, section on the financial departments.

Nevertheless, his presence had a salutary influence upon the casual book-keeping methods employed by most departments. His signature at the bottom of an account, as the Royal Commission testified in 1863, gave "a certain degree of confidence in the correctness of statements and accounts."[25] Moreover, in the first five years after his appointment as Auditor Langton did much to improve the form in which the accounts were presented to Parliament. In 1855, for example, a committee on public accounts, after lengthy examination of the records, was forced to conclude: "It is scarcely possible to imagine a more imperfect financial system than we are describing."[26] Five years later, a similar committee prefaced its report with a vote of thanks to those who had framed the accounts: its task of detailed scrutiny, it claimed, had been greatly eased by the improvements in the presentation of the accounts.[27]

The technical details of these revisions need not detain us. That Langton, with the enthusiastic support of Alexander Galt, laboured to good purpose may be surmised from the previouly cited reactions of the public accounts committees. One essential feature of the revision may be noted from Galt's own criticism of the accounts for the year 1858: "The statements are not complete under the several heads ... items of similar character are so distributed throughout the volume that there is very great difficulty in effecting any analysis of outlay."[28] A re-ordering of the accounts to eliminate this criticism was subsequently attempted. Although improvements were made, to this day no ready solution to this particular problem has been discovered. Items scattered under departmental headings may still have to be assembled by researchers interested, for example, in the total cost of social services in Canada.

Galt was also anxious to have the accounts show the cash position of the government at the end of the year. Without this statement of total income and expenditure, Galt contended, "it is absolutely out of their [the public accounts committee's] power properly to audit the accounts, and to report that the Cash Balances and Debt are as stated."[29] Between 1858 and 1860 the accounts were much improved along these lines. Langton, with Galt's approval, also grappled with

[25]*First Report of Financial and Departmental Commission*, 1863, p. 6.
[26]"Second Report of Standing Committee on Public Accounts," *J.L.A.C.*, 1854–5.
[27]"Report of Select Standing Committee on Public Accounts," *J.L.A.C.*, 1860, Appendix 11.
[28]*Ibid.*, 1858, Appendix 4.
[29]*Ibid.*

the accountant's nightmare—the proper allocation of items to capital and income accounts. In the case of public works, where this problem was raised most acutely, the traditional practice had been to charge major public projects against income rather than capital account. In 1860 the Auditor provided an improved classification of expenditures on public works which transferred many items to capital account.[30]

In this highly necessary work of technical revision Langton appears to have received little help from departmental accountants. On the other hand he received the cordial and skilled help of Galt and a number of men with business training who were zealous workers on an extremely active public accounts committee.

The estimates. The modern procedure of presenting Parliament with detailed estimates of the financial needs of each department for the coming year was not introduced until after 1864. In that year the important amendment to the original Audit Act of 1855 provided that Parliament should, for the first time, approve all the financial requirements of the public services for a fiscal year which had not yet commenced. This procedure we now recognize to be essential to successful internal, as well as external, expenditure control. Internally, each department is thereby compelled to assess its needs for the coming year and to submit these for the approval of cabinet. Treasury Board, which here acts as agent for cabinet, is thus able to assemble a budget which allocates estimated revenues in accord with a general policy, giving priorities where required. Moreover, when departments apply to the Treasury for money to pay their accounts, those responsible for the issue may find in the estimates (transformed into votes of supply) the required legal authorization.[31] The Auditor, at a later stage, also finds in the estimates a legal standard against which he may measure the financial rectitude of the spending departments. Externally, the estimates provide Parliament with a means of focusing criticism on contemplated departmental expenditures which raise either major policy issues or detailed administrative considerations.

Prior to the amendment of 1864 the estimates used by the province provided few of the benefits just described. The estimates did not refer to the financial requirements for a fiscal year not yet commenced. Instead, they were regarded as a method of informing Parliament that the executive had spent so much money during the current year for which as yet no appropriations had been made. In

[30]*Ibid.*, 1860, Appendix 11.
[31]A. E. Buck, *Financing Canadian Government* (Chicago, 1949), chaps. II–VI, has an up-to-date analysis of the machinery of fiscal control.

short, as the Board of Audit reported in 1864, the system was open to the "objection that all the expenditure had already taken place on the authority of the Executive before Parliament had been asked to sanction it by a vote."[32] As a result, each spending department was encouraged to live a hand-to-mouth existence, taking little forethought for the financial morrow. It is precisely this compulsion to plan for the future which makes the modern process of estimating so valuable. The large block of "supplementary estimates" attached to the accounts for each year was strong evidence of the lack of planning under the old system.

The Department of Finance, similarily, was not able to assemble an omnibus financial programme for the whole public service in which total departmental needs could be related to total estimated revenues for the ensuing year. Moreover, the various agencies responsible for the issue of public funds (the offices of Deputy Inspector General, of Receiver General, and of the Executive Council) were unable to refer to prior parliamentary votes as legal authority for releasing funds to departments. This authority had to rest on Orders in Council which often had to be improvised hastily in order to cope with a sudden call on the Treasury. The difficulty of interpreting these authorizations has been noted in Langton's previously quoted comments. The Auditor, too, was incapable of providing a legal audit when Parliament had not given its sanction to expenditures. Over and above all these internal difficulties was the fact that external control by Parliament was almost entirely *ex post facto*. Members of Parliament who today tend to feel that their scrutiny of the executive's financial transactions is negligible might take some comfort from the plight of their predecessors in the era before 1864.

It would appear, therefore, that the amendment of 1864 marked a revolution in the methods of internal and external financial control. Certainly, the adjustments required to implement the new principle of estimating in advance were not made all at once or with immediate success. The Auditor, reporting on the new scheme, admitted that the departments had not been given sufficient time to prepare their estimates and that "it is not surprising that the first attempt to provide for everything by a vote was not entirely successful."[33] In the years that followed, the large number of "unprovided items" listed in the

---

[32]"Public Accounts of the Province of Canada for the half-year ended June 30, 1864," *Sessional Papers*, Canada, 1865, no. 1, prefaced by Report of Board of Audit.
[33]*Ibid.*

accounts gives some indication of the practical difficulties of "providing for everything by a vote."

Perhaps the most important institutional change connected with the new system of estimating was the appearance of Treasury Board. Although this important subcommittee of cabinet did not receive statutory recognition until 1869, it was brought into being by Order in Council in July 1867. It was not the first subcommittee to deal with financial matters, but it was certainly the first to be assigned the grave responsibility for collecting, collating, and adjusting all departmental estimates. Elsewhere it has been pointed out that as early as 1858 Cayley had recommended to cabinet that the departments present to Council their proposed outlay for the coming year, distinguishing the fixed commitments from those items which might be adjusted for purposes of economy.[34] This recommendation could have had little effect, for six years later in 1864 the Auditor reported: "the estimates were submitted as prepared by the several Departments having charge of those services, and the Finance Department had no knowledge of the sums actually expended until the accounts of the other Departments came in, long after the Supply Bill had been passed."[35]

Clearly, new machinery was required if all departmental financial needs for one year in advance were to be made ready for Parliament's early scrutiny and approval. Immediately after the reform of 1864 Langton, acting now in his capacity as Chairman of the Board of Audit, appeared to assume this central position. After Confederation, his new office of Deputy Minister of Finance (coupled with his old role of Auditor) made him the obvious choice as Secretary to the newly formed Treasury Board. It was Treasury Board that then undertook the co-ordination of departmental estimates contemplated in the legislation of 1864.

External Control

Money, we are told, is the root of all evil. Certainly in the period prior to Union, it provided one of the most persistent sources of disagreement between the legislature and the Governor. The Civil List controversy of the 1820's and 1830's in the colonies paralleled the debate in England during the last quarter of the eighteenth century between George III and the House of Commons. In both cases the

[34]State Book T, Aug. 10, 1858, p. 62.
[35]Report of Board of Audit in "Public Accounts for half-year ended June 30, 1864," *Sessional Papers*, Canada, 1865, no. 1.

legislature sought to limit the executive's access to funds which could be raised and spent without the approval of the legislature. Canadian historians have explained the details of this dispute in the course of describing the evolution of responsible government in the colonies.[36] As will have already become apparent from the previous analysis of internal expenditure control, the settlement of the Civil List controversy was only a necessary preliminary to the Assembly's attainment of real control over executive expenditures. The later stages in the evolution of parliamentary control of the purse need further elaboration.

The Act of Union in 1841 achieved a fixed settlement of the Civil List which, in principle, left the representative of the Crown dependent on the Assembly.[37] The "Civil List" arrangements appear in section 52 of the Act where a sum amounting to £75,000 was allocated in accordance with two Schedules (A and B) appended to the Act. Under Schedule A, £45,000 was devoted to the salaries of the Governor and Lieutenant-Governor, the judiciary, some pensions, and a large miscellaneous item. In Schedule B, to which £30,000 was allocated, the salaries and office expenses of the departmental heads appeared. The Governor was empowered to abolish any of the offices under Schedule B or to vary the sums appropriated to any of the services or purposes named in that Schedule. In 1846 the Civil List was amended to reduce the fixed charges under Schedule A by about £10,000 and to increase the charges under Schedule B by about the same amount. This measure, after being reserved by the Governor, was approved by the Queen in 1847.[38]

The Civil List by no means covered all the expenses of civil government in the province. The money for these was expected to be provided out of the territorial and other hereditary revenues of the Crown which by the Act of Union (section 54) were now transferred to the control of the legislature.[39] The Act also established (section 56) an

---

[36]See, for example, D. G. Creighton, "The Struggle for Financial Control in Lower Canada, 1818–1831," *Canadian Historical Review*, vol. XII (1931), pp. 120–44; D. C. Harvey, "The Civil List and Responsible Government in Nova Scotia," *ibid.*, vol. XXVIII (1947), pp. 365–82; W. G. Ormsby "The Civil List Question in the Province of Canada," *ibid.*, vol. XXXV (1954), pp. 93–118. See also Hincks, "Memorandum on the Civil List," *J.L.A.C.*, 1843, Appendix U.

[37]*Imperial Statutes*, 3 & 4 Vic., c. 35 (1841).

[38]10 Vic., c. 114 (1846), and *Public General Acts* (Great Britain), 10 & 11 Vic., c. 71 (1847). Ormsby, "The Civil List Question in the Province of Canada," has a good explanation of the political manœuvres behind the change.

[39]The original transfer had been made by the Imperial government in 1831 when the proceeds from the Quebec Revenue Act 1778 had been turned over to the province.

order of precedence for each charge against the Consolidated Revenue Fund. One is reminded of a similar technique which Edmund Burke incorporated into his famous "Economical Reform Bill" of 1782. Burke, with an unexpected Machiavellian instinct, arranged his order of payments so that the officers in charge of the money-spending departments were the last to receive their salaries—a real stimulus to be economical.[40] In Canada, oddly enough, the expenses of collecting and managing the public revenues constituted the first charge against the Consolidated Fund. The subsequent history of uncontrolled spending departments in Canada suggests that we might have done well to have followed Burke's precedent. Other charges against the fund were to be paid off in the following order: first, the allocations provided under Schedules A and B, and finally all "other charges." Subject to this order of payment, the Legislative Assembly was to originate all bills for appropriating any part of the surplus in the Consolidated Revenue Fund or any new tax. However, an important proviso borrowed from British practice was introduced (section 57) requiring all money bills or tax measures to be sponsored by a message of the Governor. In practice this came to mean that only responsible ministers of the Crown were entitled to originate such measures.

Thus, the Act of Union provided the framework within which the popular assembly could emulate the efforts of the Mother of Parliaments to control the financial operations of the executive. The Assembly soon discovered, however, that its victory over the financially independent representative of the Crown had merely shifted the battle ground. Charges of irresponsibility formerly levelled at the colonial Governor and his distant superiors were now transferred to the colonists' own ministerial heads. Between 1841 and 1864 scarcely a session passed without one motion of censure against "unsanctioned Executive expenditure."[41] While the government always managed to deflect the motions, their indignant tone was unmistakable— "it is the undoubted privilege of this House that no expenditure of Public Moneys be made without the express sanction of Parliament."

That Parliament was justified in feeling dissatisfied with its role as guardian of the public purse will already have become apparent from the previous comments under the heading "internal controls." It was noted there that at least three prerequisites to efficient parlia-

[40]See *Parliamentary History* (London, T. C. Hansard), vol. XX (1778–80), cols. 1298 f.

[41]See, for example, *J.L.A.C.*, 1854–5, pp. 506, 509; 1856, p. 246; 1857, pp. 521, 701; 1859, p. 329; 1860, p. 274.

mentary scrutiny had to be provided within the bureaucracy. First, all the operating costs of the public service ought to have been provided in annual votes of supply. Second (closely related to the first condition) gross revenues ought to have been returned to the Treasury. Third, informative accurate public accounts of income and expenditure were needed. Aside from these three prerequisites associated with internal control, Parliament needed to take one important step on its own behalf: it had to develop a business-like method of scrutinizing public expenditures. A comment on each of these four prerequisites to successful legislative control over finance will round off this discussion.

Voting "supplies." One of the major obstacles to parliamentary control over the purse was that, as we have seen, until 1864 Parliament confronted "dead" expenditures. It was invited annually to approve "payments for which a supply is required"—a polite formula suggesting that the executive had spent so much money and would thank the Parliament to fill up the purse again. The situation described by the Public Accounts Committee of 1854-5 exemplifies the problem confronting Parliament.[42] "Estimates" to cover a financial period ending December 31, 1852, were voted in June 1853. Between June 1853 and September 1854 no estimates were submitted and no vote of supply was requested by the executive. "The Government," the Committee reported, "has gone on, taking the public treasure, during three quarters of a year, and a part of a fourth quarter as if the usual votes had been given."

Even had the modern system existed of submitting the estimates in advance of expenditure, the legislature would still not have been in a strong position to exercise proper control. The Minister of Finance explained the reason for this situation in his report for 1862:

> Over the great proportion of the expenditure, Ministers exercise little or no control. Speaking generally, more than one-half of the whole is in fulfilment of obligations already incurred. Other large amounts are expended in pursuance of engagements which cannot be summarily terminated. And yet another large expenditure takes place under annual grants of the Legislature to which the Government of the day simply gives effect.[43]

Debt payments, for example, usually amounted to about one-third of the total annual expenditures and were beyond the range of parliamentary control, as were also the fixed appropriations for the Civil

---
[42]See Second Report of Committee, *J.L.A.C.*, 1854-5.
[43]See Report of Minister of Finance prefacing "Public Accounts for 1862," *Sessional Papers*, Canada, 1863, no. 10.

List. In other words, there were many fixed annual commitments for which no special supply vote needed to be taken. Over the remaining expenditures, parliamentary control, as noted, came after rather than before the event.

Returning gross revenues. Possibly the most serious obstacle to parliamentary control over departmental finances was the steady refusal to force revenue-collecting agencies to pay their gross collections into the Treasury. Mackenzie's Committee on Grievances in 1835 recommended this reform, echoing the wise words of the Parnell Commission on Financial Reform, which in 1828 had deplored the same situation in England.[44] As chairman of the Public Accounts Committee, 1854–5, Mackenzie returned to the same recommendation. The Committee discovered that over £125,000 was being "arrested on its way to the public treasury, not voted by the Legislature" but spent on a great assortment of objects. "This unconstitutional practice requires a remedy," the Committee concluded, "else the Assembly will degenerate into a body convened at the pleasure of the Executive, only for form's sake."[45]

The Committee estimated "that nearly one-eighth of the gross revenues of the nation are disposed of without the interference of Parliament to sanction their application." This situation posed an interesting legal paradox. The Civil List arrangements provided that the costs of collecting the revenues should be a first charge on the public funds. This could be (and apparently was) interpreted as permitting the revenue-collecting departments to return only net receipts to the Treasury. On the other hand, if the Assembly's control over expenditures was to be complete, no department ought to have had the privilege of disposing freely of its own collections. In fact, the House had prohibited this practice in adopting as its 46th Rule the regulation that all aids and supplies were gifts of the Assembly and that it should "direct, limit, and appoint in all such bills, the ends, purposes, considerations, conditions and qualifications of such grants. . . ."[46]

Succeeding public accounts committees after 1855 recommended that the revenue departments come to Parliament for an annual supply vote to cover administrative costs. The Committee of 1858 recorded that the victory had been won and that henceforth gross revenues would be turned over to the exchequer.[47] However, in 1862 the

---

[44]See "Seventh Report of Committee on Grievances," 1835, p. 1.
[45]Second Report of Committee, *J.L.A.C.*, 1854–5.
[46]Quoted in *ibid.*
[47]*J.L.A.C.*, 1858, Appendix 4.

Minister of Finance was compelled to report: "The true system appears to be one that will bring into the Treasury the whole of the receipts, from whatsoever source derived, and that will confer on Parliament the power, and impose upon it the duty of determining specifically the sums that shall be expended under departmental authorization and supervision."[48] Apparently the revenue departments after 1858 had paid in their gross revenues but then had asked for such extended "accountable warrants" that Parliament still did not have complete control over the "expenses of management." Until Confederation the public accounts continued to list the costs of collecting the revenue as if they were deductions from gross revenues, rather than votes of supply from Parliament. Consequently, we must assume that this large sector of departmental expenditure still remained partly independent of parliamentary control.

Accounts. The third prerequisite to successful parliamentary control of the purse was the provision of accurate, meaningful accounts. Possibly the earlier unreliable accounts of the province can be traced back to the period when the Imperial authorities had to cover deficits in colonial budgets.[49] If the British taxpayer was to be kept in ignorance of the fact that colonies cost money then accounts were best designed to conceal rather than reveal. Whether or not this is an adequate explanation of the unsystematic fiscal reports of pre-Confederation times, by the 1850's they obviously required the skilful attention lavished on them by Langton, a succession of Finance Ministers, and the Public Accounts Committee. The improvements effected by their labours during the years 1858 to 1860 have already been mentioned in the discussion of "internal controls."

Even with improved accounts certain difficulties still stood in the way of effective parliamenary control. One of these was described in the report of a legislative committee in 1855: "It is remarkable," [the Committee commented], "that while . . . [seven] pages of the Public Accounts are occupied with a very minute record of exceedingly small sums, and [two] pages . . . nearly all filled with items of five shillings and upwards (the total being £531 11s.) between fifty and sixty thousand pounds were crowded into one item because . . . 'it is feared to swell the Public Accounts by needless detailed enumerations'!"[50] The Committee was properly critical of this tendency to conceal important expenditures in large lump-sum votes. However, its

[48]Report of Minister of Finance in "Public Accounts for 1862," *Sessional Papers,* Canada, 1863, no. 10.
[49]This suggestion is found in H. T. Manning, "The Civil List of Lower Canada," *Canadian Historical Review,* vol. XXIV (1943), pp. 24–47 at p. 28.
[50]Second Report of Committee, *J.L.A.C.,* 1854–5.

observations on this common practice overlooked a fundamental problem which still perplexes the modern public service. Those responsible for dividing up the appropriations into separate votes confront a difficult choice. Members of Parliament, on the whole, prefer rather detailed estimates for they are often more interested in scrutinizing the minutiae than in checking the larger expenditures. The Auditor General, on the other hand, has recently argued that too many separate "votes" encourage inaccurate estimates of expenditures. That is, the chances of misjudging financial needs for a year in advance are multiplied as the number of separate items is increased. As a result there will be either more unspent ("lapsed") money or more demands for supplementary appropriations at the end of the year. In either case the accounts will either overstate or understate the actual amounts spent.[51] In the 1850's when the Committee called attention to the importance of a proper breakdown of the larger items, the full implications of their proposal were not appreciated.

A special instance of the block-sum appropriation was to be found in the departmental "contingencies" funds. These items covered a host of unspecified "miscellaneous expenditures" in each department. It was like a petty cash drawer designed on a liberal scale, reserved for such office essentials as pen, paper, printing, ink, and postage. However, when amounts approximating $100,000 were drained out of several petty cash drawers in unidentifiable lump sums, parliamentary suspicions were roused. On several occasions, Parliament sent search parties to explore the darker corners of these convenient but much-abused "contingency funds."[52]

The original method of controlling the departmental "contingencies" was to appoint an "accountant of contingencies" in the Department of Finance through whom all departmental orders had to be cleared. This special officer was unable to exercise any effective control over the departments and in the 1860's each deputy head was made responsible for these expenditures. At the same time, Parliament was provided, through detailed accounts, with a more satisfactory assurance that the money would be properly spent.

One final technical problem connected with Parliament's scrutiny of the public accounts warrants brief mention. Much of the value of the accounts is lost if they refer to expenditures that have taken place

[51]See Standing Committee on Public Accounts, 1947, *Minutes of Proceedings and Evidence*, pp. 443 f.

[52]For example, most of the *Second Report of the Financial and Departmental Commission*, Feb. 1864, was devoted to the problem of departmental contingencies; the Select Committee on Public Accounts, *J.L.A.C.*, 1862, Appendix 7, also concentrated on these large miscellaneous uncontrolled expenditures.

too far back in the past. On the other hand, those responsible for making up the accounts are anxious to have them record as completely as possible the major transactions of the year. Obviously the date selected for closing the government's books for the year will have a direct bearing on the timing and the completeness of the accounts. A date that may enable the Auditor to present Parliament early in the session with up-to-date reports may not satisfy the other requirement of complete coverage of the relevant transactions.

Until 1864 the fiscal year coincided with the calendar year. The Auditor considered this date failed to meet the first requirement noted above, for he seldom could audit the year's accounts in time to have Parliament consider them at its next session. The members' preference for winter sessions, starting as early in the new year as possible, made his task all the more difficult.[53]

The Auditor's persistent pleas for alteration of the fiscal year were finally recognized in the amending act of 1864. A new terminal date, June 30, was set. It would appear from subsequent developments, however, that this date was established more with a view to providing complete accounts than with easing the task of the Auditor and Parliament. The decisive factor was the harvest period, June 30 marking the end of one year's harvesting and marketing activities and preceding the opening of the next period. In addition nearly the whole of one navigation season could be covered, so that complete trade statistics could be reported. Since public revenues depended on prosperous harvests and buoyant trade, full coverage of these statistics enabled the government to make more accurate estimates of revenues for the coming year.

Unfortunately, with the legislation of 1864 the fiscal year was forced to meet a third requirement. The fiscal year was expected now not only to satisfy the demands for complete coverage and the necessities of parliamentary audit but also to meet the new system of estimating departmental expenditures one year in advance. This was and still is too much to ask of one terminal date. While the date selected might meet Parliament's need for approving estimates of expenditure for the coming year, it was not likely that the same date could equally meet Parliament's responsibility for auditing expenses of the year just past. And, clearly, the same date could not provide the ideal coverage of the whole year's transactions.

The selection of practically any terminal date had its hazards. The

---

[53]See Reports of Minister of Finance in "Public Accounts," *Sessional Papers*, Canada, 1862, no. 4; 1863, no. 10. See also Auditor's comments as early as 1856 before Public Accounts Committee, Third Report, *J.L.A.C.*, 1856, Appendix 30.

date June 30 was regarded as generally satisfactory until 1877 when the House approved a bill setting March 31 as the terminal date. Amongst the reasons presented for the change in 1877 was that this date was better fitted to both the Auditor's abilities and Parliament's time-table. At the same time, it provided a reasonably comprehensive coverage of navigation returns and the main flow of expenditures and revenues for the year. In short, as one Member said, it conformed closely to the country's "natural year."[54] This measure failed to reach the Senate and it was not until 1906 that this "natural year" was officially recognized.[55]

The Public Accounts Committee. Setting up a system for voting supplies, insisting on the gross payment of all revenues collected, and establishing clear public accounts were all reforms to which the permanent civil servants made real contributions. Parliament, however, had to take one important step for itself—the creation of appropriate machinery for scrutinizing the detailed financial returns submitted to it. The Select Standing Committee on Public Accounts was Parliament's extremely effective response to this demand. As early as 1841 a special committee was set up to examine the accounts. Five similar committees continued this work between 1844 and 1851. Finally in the session 1852–3, the Public Accounts Committee emerged as one of the eight (later seven) standing committees of the House. Between that date and Confederation there were only two years when the Committee failed to make a valuable series of reports.[56]

William Lyon Mackenzie, as chairman of the Committee in 1854, set the tone for subsequent investigations and reports. Leading members of the opposition were normally in the chair, the Minister of Finance merely occupying a seat as one of the members. The Committee, considering its glorious opportunities, exercised singular restraint in its exploration of partisan "jobs," although occasionally

[54]*Debates,* House of Commons, Canada, 1877, pp. 1765 f., 1823 f.
[55]6 Ed. VII, c. 12.
[56]Reports from Public Accounts Committees appeared in the *Journals* as follows: 1841, Appendix F.F.; 1844–5, Appendix M.M.; 1847, Appendix K.K.K.; 1849, Appendix F.F.F.; 1850, Appendix Y.Y.; 1851, Appendix M.M.M.; 1854–5, Appendix J.J. (five informative reports); 1856, Appendix 30 (four excellent reports); 1858, Appendix 4 (a model report including public accounts and reports of Inspector General and Board of Audit, followed by Committee's own report); 1859, Appendix 5 (similar in form); 1860, Appendix 11 (includes only the Committee's own report, that of the Inspector General being merged with separate Public Accounts); 1861, Appendix 2 (similar form); 1862, Appendix 7; 1863, Appendix 6 (the Committee uses subcommittees for first time); 1865, Appendix 1; 1866, Appendix 5.

temptation and the "jobs" were simply too large to be resisted. The evidence taken at these sessions and the flood of vigorous reports submitted by the Committee places the administrative historian deeply in its debt.

At the time the Auditor probably felt most indebted to the Committee for it provided him with a forum for promoting many of the internal reforms which have already been examined. It also compensated for the relatively dependent status of the Auditor: in the Committee he found a vigorous, sceptical champion who spoke out boldly against the financial laxity which he deplored. Even Ministers of Finance, like Galt and Howland, found it to their advantage to work through and with the Accounts Committee. One can find no better evidence for proving the claim that ordinary members of Parliament, equipped with the proper instrument and powers, can be counted on to do a competent job of sustaining the ancient and cherished privilege of the House of Commons in controlling the purse. Looking at the subsequent history of this Committee one can only deplore the decline that has, for a number of reasons, been allowed to set in.

CHAPTER VIII

THE CROWN LANDS DEPARTMENT: "A FAIR SUBJECT OF DISCUSSION"

THE PHRASE in this chapter heading belongs in the remarkable report which Thomas D'Arcy McGee made to Council in 1863. Setting down his conclusions on the Department of Crown Lands, he wrote: "Whether any one political chief, however energetic, or any one 'deputy head' however indefatigable and systematic, can judiciously direct and control this extensive accumulation of offices, is . . . a fair subject of discussion."[1]

A fair subject of discussion; so, too, thought the Honourable Joseph Cauchon, Commissioner of Crown Lands. In his office near the Toronto waterfront in the year 1857 he had just appended his signature to a large map of Canada which had been drawn by Thomas Devine, his chief surveyor, to accompany his comprehensive report on the affairs of the Department. Although he did not yet know it, the report was to be his swan song as Commissioner, for he was soon to break with his cabinet colleagues on the subject of the North Shore Railway. His report, however, has come down to us as a masterpiece of administrative analysis, a permanent testimonial to the logical and penetrating mind of its author.[2]

A native of Quebec, Cauchon had trained for the bar and at the age of twenty-six had eagerly embraced political journalism.[3] In the custom of the day, he used his newspaper as a means of winning a seat in the legislature. When he attained this goal in 1844, according

[1]"Report on the Origin and Organization of the Public Departments," Public Archives of Canada, M. 837, 1863.

[2]See "Annual Report of the Commissioner of Crown Lands for the Year 1856," *Journals*, Legislative Assembly, Canada (*J.L.A.C.*), 1857, Appendix 25. This brilliant, comprehensive report is a starting point for any student interested in the administration of this great "holding company" department.

[3]See H. J. Morgan, *Biographies of Celebrated Canadians* (Quebec, 1862), pp. 609 f., for a revealing brief biography. "M. Cauchon possesses a great power of concentration; whenever he takes up a question for discussion, all the faculties of his mind are called to his assistance. He pertinaceously studies his subject until thoroughly acquainted with all its details, and then his pen glides with decision and earnestness." An equally perceptive commentary which tallies very closely with the previous estimate is to be found in W. Notman and F. Taylor, *Portraits of British Americans* (2 vols., Montreal, 1865), vol. I, pp. 403–18. For a brief account of his later career see W. Stewart Wallace, *The Dictionary of Canadian Biography* (2 vols., Toronto, 1945), vol. I, p. 158.

to one of his contemporaries, Cauchon's "bump of combativeness [was] very largely developed." Cauchon shrank from no personal encounters and as a result was soon "known the length and breadth of Canada—not altogether favourably." An impetuous tongue and a sarcastic pen earned him many enemies, but he had an undeniable capacity for work, an incisive yet far-ranging mind equally at home in the realms of literature, science, and philosophy. He brought an analytical approach and a breadth of vision sorely needed in the Department. During a later brief association with the Department of Public Works he made yet another contribution to an administrative structure whose reorganization was long over-due.[4] After Confederation he was destined to preside over the vast area to the west of Lake Superior as the second Lieutenant-Governor of Manitoba.

Cauchon's report and its accompanying map provide us with a convenient vantage point from which to view the far-ranging activities of his Department. Commencing at the western portion of the province our eyes first fall on that great stretch of country lying north of Lakes Superior and Huron. The Surveyor-General's map of Canada described this area in 1838 as a "Great Tract of Wilderness." Cauchon's map twenty years later could scarcely improve on this description. A few mining locations had been carved out of the northern shorelines of both lakes—the Wellington and Bruce Mines being the only active claims. In addition, about a dozen Indian Reserves had been scattered through the region. Here, the responsibilities of the Crown Lands Department were slight. One clerk was enough to look after the claims to mining locations, and since most claims remained quiescent for the first twenty years after Union, he was not overworked. In the sixties, however, this area witnessed more activity. The surveyor arrived to block in townships for settlement out of the wild lands, and a trunk road began to snake its way through rock and bush, stretching slowly along the north shore of Lake Huron and thrusting out towards the Lake Superior area. By 1860, also, the Indians in this area had become the wards of the Commissioner of Crown Lands.[5] At Confederation the vast mineral wealth of this area still lay locked away in the great Shield; but the land and settlements bordering the lakes were serviced by roads, and numerous lots—including portions of the Indian Reserves—had been surveyed and sold to settlers. Land, timber,

---

[4]While Cauchon's intervention was vigorous it was not altogether fortunate in its results as a later chapter describing the construction of the Parliament Buildings will reveal.

[5]The detailed discussion of Indian affairs has been reserved for a separate chapter.

and Indian agents, as well as fisheries overseers, were all at work here and all came under the direction of the Crown Lands Department.

Moving eastward and to the south, we come next to the area known as the Huron-Ottawa Tract. On the Surveyor-General's map of 1838 this Tract is marked "Immense Forests." A frustrated cartographer, trying to depict a river flowing from the east into Lake Simcoe was forced to record his ignorance of the terrain thus: "Black River flows a great way into the country." By 1857 the scene had changed, for this had now become one of the most active portions of the Commissioner's domain. "The immense forests" of the region were now being exploited by lumbermen who obtained their timber berths and cutting licences from the Woods and Forests Branch of the Department. The Ottawa region was the hub of this lumbering universe and A. J. Russell, Crown Timber Agent, was responsible for granting timber concessions whose total area was half that of Ireland. Other agents of the Department were guarding the timber slides on the Ottawa River, keeping track of the squared timber and saw logs passing through, so that the owners could be assessed a "slidage toll." At other strategic points on the long river route to Quebec City similar operations were being performed.[6]

Even while the lumbermen, under the surveillance of the Woods and Forests Branch, were exploiting their concessions, another branch of the Department was trying to promote a programme for settling this somewhat forbidding territory. At this period the surveyors' frontier had been pushed north to Parry Sound on Georgian Bay, but as late as the mid-fifties a German tourist was informed, as he threaded his way through the stumps lining the main street of Orillia, that "there is no European town or village from Orillia to the North Pole."[7] Although the surveyed townships extended back from Lake Ontario in considerable depth, the frontier of settlement ran pretty well on a line extending from the northern tip of Lake Simcoe across to the Ottawa River. The plan to attract settlers beyond this frontier was based on a free land grant system—the lands to be strung out along the routes of "colonization roads."[8] Grants appropriated by the

[6]The Department of Public Works built and maintained the slides and the toll collectors were responsible to the Deputy Inspector General's Office.

[7]The observant German traveller was J. G. Kohl. See his *Travels in Canada and through the States of New York and Pennsylvania*, trans. by Mrs. Percy Sinnett (2 vols., London, 1861), vol. II, p. 66.

[8]More will be said about this plan in the chapter dealing with immigration and settlement. The Bureau of Agriculture, between 1854 and 1862, had charge of the colonization roads scheme in the Upper Province, but Crown Lands retained an active interest in the programme.

legislature for the construction of these roads were administered by agents of the Department. The "colonization roads agents" kept a parental eye on the general progress of the settlers, and pressed headquarters for the extension of postal services, larger grants for branch roads, seeds, and supplies, or the amelioration of settlement conditions where they proved too burdensome.

As Cauchon surveyed his map in 1857 the outlines of this plan were visible, although ten years later the network of colonization roads was much more complete. In its final stages, five roads running roughly north and south intersected by three running east and west were projected for this vast area. The settlements slowly seeping along these arteries of communication actually threatened the Department with an administrative civil war. The clash of interests represented by the large-scale lumberman and the struggling settler was awkwardly reflected within the very walls of Cauchon's Department. Woods and Forests stood staunchly behind its clients and the Colonization Roads Branch angrily defended the interests of its lowly constituents. The compromise between these interests usually reached in other regions— a lucrative part-time winter employment of the farmer-settler as a timber-cutter—was not feasible in a region where lumbering had to be undertaken on a large-scale, full-time basis.[9]

Leaving this dispute as an item of unfinished business for the Department we move next to the older settlements of the province, embracing, in Upper Canada, the western peninsula and all the surveyed land bordering the shores of Lake Ontario. Now that sales were no longer booming in these regions one would have expected the real estate business of the Department to have fallen off greatly. Against all expectations, most of the staff at headquarters were occupied on work connected with this area. Lands had been so badly surveyed at the start and the system of perfecting titles to land so labyrinthian that the Department was constantly plagued by awkward contested claims. The sins of their administrative predecessors rested heavily on the shoulders of Cauchon's staff. As the pressure of settlers became heavier on these older lands, legal actions seemed to increase rather than diminish. So-called "final settlements" made by the Department could always be reversed by the final court of appeal—the local

---

[9]The rumblings of this internal conflict are distinctly heard in the evidence presented by the heads of the branches before the Select Committee on the Present System of Management of the Public Lands, *J.L.A.C.*, 1854–5, Appendix M.M. Cauchon's report for the year 1856 also examines the arguments of the timber cutters and settlers.

Member. Cauchon, for all his administrative insight, was unable to unravel this tangled skein, although one of his successors, P. M. Vankoughnet, had moderate success in clearing up some old claims which had been outstanding for twenty years.[10]

The real estate business of the Department also gave rise to one of its most intractable administrative problems: how to control the host of local land agents spread across its vast domain.[11] At one time these agents absorbed over one-quarter of the revenues obtained from land. It was for this reason that Cauchon could glance with legitimate pride at the new, consolidated district boundaries which he had outlined on his map of 1857. His hopes of reducing the number of local agents were never realized, however, for this expensive, somewhat unreliable group of satellites steadfastly resisted the pruning operations of successive political heads.[12]

As the duties of the land agent in the older settled parts of the province dwindled, the work of his logical successor—the immigration agent—expanded. Since these agents were of no concern to the Crown Lands Department we need not examine their functions here.[13] Even as the land agents' duties dwindled, so too the timber agents became redundant. By 1857, only one timber agent was required for the whole western peninsula and his responsibilities must have been extremely light when compared with those of his fellow agents employed on the Ottawa River and in the northern area we have just traversed. While the Ottawa agent was issuing 534 timber licences in 1857, his counterpart in the older settled area issued only 9 licences. The cut of logs and white pine had been reduced to insignificance when contrasted with the tremendous operations in the Ottawa region.[14]

Still, Commissioner Cauchon could not look with any feeling of relief at the declining labours of his local agents in the settled portions of Canada West. For, scanning the watery vastness of the Great Lakes and their tributary rivers, he could see a new cloud on his administrative horizon—the inland fisheries. During that very year (1857)

[10]See "Annual Report of the Commissioner of Crown Lands for the Year 1861," *Sessional Papers*, Canada, 1862, no. 11.

[11]See chap. x for full discussion of this important problem.

[12]While the Commissioner boasted of having closed up twenty-two land agencies in the older settled areas during the year 1862, at Confederation the Department still employed a force of 57 local land agents as compared with 71 agents in 1857.

[13]See below chap. xv on immigration and colonization.

[14]In the western peninsula in 1857, for example, 2,590 saw logs and 2,945 pieces of pine timber were recorded as against a cut in the Ottawa District of 230,498 logs and 180,600 pieces of white pine.

Cauchon had steered through the legislature the first comprehensive fisheries bill.[15] This new measure gave birth to yet another branch in his already crowded Department. Henceforth, a force of thirty "fisheries overseers," distributed throughout the two Canadas, was to engage the ruggedly independent fishermen in spasmodic guerilla warfare. Previous regulations long in force had been so mild that the fishermen had come to view the waters and their teeming bounty as a strictly personal matter. Now the heavy hand of the state had descended and, judging from the drastic decline in catches, it had descended neither too soon nor, as experience soon showed, heavily enough.

Accompanying Cauchon into his native province of Canada East, we find the Department's work following much the same pattern as that already described for the Upper Province. Settlements straggled down a ribbon-like trail on the east side of the Ottawa River, broadened at Montreal, and thence huddled close to both shores of the St. Lawrence, growing sparser as they reached the Gulf region and the Gaspé peninsula. The land business of the Department was complicated by the existence of special tracts of land in Lower Canada —the Jesuits' Estates, the Seigneury of Lauzon, and the King's Domain.[16] Most of these lands were not for sale but were leased by the Department. The functions of landlord and rentier were performed by a special small branch of the Department. With the exception of a strip of settlement running up the Saguenay and circling Lake St. John, the timberland north of the St. Lawrence was too formidable a barrier to such settlement programmes as those being launched in the Huron-Ottawa Tract of Canada West. However, on the south shore, after 1860, a great trunk road—the Taché Road—was built parallel to the St. Lawrence but some distance inland. Subsequently, a number of short "feeder" cross roads helped open up this section, even extending to Gaspé and Metapedia. This programme was the

[15]*Statutes of Canada, 1857*, 20 Vic., c. 21 (June 10, 1857).
[16]The area of the King's Domain or King's Post, about 72,000 square miles, extended 300 miles along the north shore of the St. Lawrence roughly from Quebec City to the Gulf. Until the 1860's, according to one irate seal fisherman, the Hudson's Bay Company had "locked up and held desert . . . half the sea coast of the Province of Quebec and its chief harbours . . . for the only object of enabling a few adventurers to cheat the miserable aborigines living on this tract. . . ." The Company paid £600 per year for the exclusive right over this vast domain. See E. T. D. Chambers, *The Fisheries of the Province of Quebec: Part I, Historical Introduction* (Quebec, Department of Colonization, Mines and Fisheries of the Province of Quebec, 1912), pp. 125 f.

counterpart of the colonization roads project developed in Upper Canada but was operated by Public Works rather than Crown Lands.

The responsibilities of the Department for mining claims did not develop until gold was discovered in the Chaudière region in 1860. A little later, oil lands in Gaspé were blocked out in very large alternating sections of 5,000 acres, selling at fifty cents an acre. By Confederation, this part of the Department's operations was just beginning to come to life and the mining branch was expanding. Local timber agents, as in Canada West, were stationed at strategic points throughout the Lower Province—the main locations being in the St. Maurice, Saguenay, and St. Francis areas. Since Quebec City was the chief marketing centre for the timber floated down out of the hinterland of the United Provinces, a special responsibility devolved upon the Department at this point. Straddling the entire export trade in timber was the Supervisor of Cullers' Office. Assisted by deputies stationed at Lachine and Sorel, this official was responsible for counting, measuring, and grading all the many types of timber moving into the export trade. Over sixty cullers employed on a seasonal basis—usually from May 1 to the end of December—specialized in the task of measuring square timber, spars, oars, staves, lathwood deals, and boards. While the Cullers' Office had, in earlier days, been privately operated under the jurisdiction of timber merchants, by Cauchon's time it had become an official member of his motley administrative family.

The regulation of the watery domain of the Crown Lands Department in Canada East was a much more difficult undertaking than in Canada West. In addition to the stream fisheries, the prolific and variegated fisheries of the Gulf required attention. In fact, it was this area which called forth the first organized efforts of the government to cope with the problems of the fisheries. The history of this operation, which after 1852 was fitted out annually like a military expedition, contains some of the most fascinating episodes in our administrative history. The tireless, dedicated virtuoso who was officially entitled "Magistrate in Charge of Her Majesty's Expedition to Protect the Fisheries" was Pierre Fortin, doctor, sailor, Justice of the Peace, member of Parliament, Speaker of the Quebec Legislative Assembly, Commissioner of Crown Lands for the Province of Quebec, and Senator.[17]

---

[17]See *ibid.*, pp. 157 f., for an excellent account of Pierre Fortin's remarkable career. His annual reports to the legislature from 1853 to Confederation make fascinating, often exciting, reading.

Even this sketchy survey of the far-flung domain of the Crown Lands Department will have revealed the enormous scope, variety and complexity of the administrative responsibilities vested in the Department. It is equally clear that the major operations of the Department had to be performed by local agents, often compelled to work in lonely isolation from headquarters, often open to many temptations because of the natural resources which they controlled and because of the inadequate supervision of their operations. Supervision at times was so lax that a land agent like a certain Mr. Baines could build up a bank account of $130,238.89! On the surveying side of his operations the Commissioner could maintain friendly relations with the various members of Parliament by finding jobs for "friends" in the Surveys Branch. If the departmental inspectors were lax in their inspection of survey lines only posterity would discover the inefficiences of the patronage system. If a survey was discontinued, the disappointed provisioner could always be placated by the grant of a sum to cover his costs up to three or four times the real value of the supplies. The Commissioner, in his discretion, might also be induced to forget the statutory requirement that claims concerning errors in surveys must be made within five years. He could also be prevailed upon to compensate for such errors. He might even be willing to go against any number of Orders in Council which stated that settlements of claims were to be final. He could be brought to open up a case settled over twenty years previously.[18]

In the handling of land sales there were many opportunities for exercising discretion both at headquarters and amongst the local agents. During the period when scrip was accepted by the government in payment for lands, duplicate scrip could be fraudulently issued; when proper checks were finally instituted some undiscoverable group was found to have netted $23,036. Collusion with speculative purchasers of land was possible in the face of legislation designed to protect the small settler. Departmental survey records could be made available to such speculators, at a price, so that all the best land could be monopolized by the few. The renting of beach lots and deep water lots in Canada East was supposed to be done at public auction, but

[18]These illustrations and the ones that follow have been taken at random from the evidence which various officers of the Department presented to the Royal Commission on the financial administration of the province in 1862–3. See *First Report of the Financial and Departmental Commission* (Quebec, 1863) and the appended evidence.

the Commissioner had discretion to dispose of these properties in any manner he saw fit. Mining lands were supposed to be sold only to persons genuinely interested in immediate exploitation and prepared to comply with the full purchase provisions after a preliminary survey; In practice a few speculators were allowed to hold the locations unworked and unpaid for throughout most of this period. In the management of timber lands local agents were able to relax rigorous regulations governing the matter of trespass on squatters' preserves. The Commissioner could bargain with timber interests over the matter of dues to be charged on unused timber berths; he could postpone payment of dues in arrears or could "compound" such payments. Special rates might be levied on lumbermen, presumably to be spent on road building, in fact to be pocketed by the local agents. Timber dues on a floating piece of cut timber could easily be overlooked, as could "slidage tolls." In the Fisheries Branch the allocation of fish bounties after 1860 was a ready source of patronage. The Department could also make friends in high places by easing the statutory provisions for the making of fishways by dam-builders or in checking water pollution by mills.

An extremely unattractive picture of maladministration in the Department might in this way be built up. Yet a fairer estimate suggests that such arrangements were marginal and that the state of public morality was not so low as to condone instances of dishonesty and administrative intrigue brought to light by investigating committees. Nor was the record of the local agent as negative and disastrous as the previous assessment might indicate. Not by their fruits shall ye know them but only by their misdemeanors. The real test is to ask how the country could possibly have expanded without them. First in order came the surveyors—and there were many honest and able ones—trekking and portaging through the Canadian hinterland, locating possible areas of settlement or likely sites for minerals, or estimating the timber prospects. And preceding the departmental survey parties, one must also mention the pioneer work of the Geological Survey, a glorified land detective created in 1842 on the insistence of that polished dilettante, Sir Charles Bagot.[19] Then came the land agent with a convenient local office containing the records

---

[19]Until Confederation the head of the Geological Survey reported directly to the Governor General, and even after Confederation the office was treated as a temporary one, subject to five-year renewals. A brief biography of the first two directors appears in C. L. Fenton and M. A. Fenton, *Giants of Geology* (New York, 1952), chap. xv.

of available locations, with his knowledge of the best lands, coupling admonitions to over-anxious and generally ignorant settlers with a glowing sales talk on "his" country. To these agents we must add the colonization road agents employed along their isolated routes. In the reports submitted by these agents, one senses a real paternal interest, an anxiety for the success of their small flock of settlers. Nor could we complete the story of the labours of the local agents without mentioning the timber agent and the timber culler, presiding at the point where Canada's most valuable staple of the period moved into world trade. Finally, there were the fisheries with a tradition of unregulated self-reliance. Here again underpaid minions of the Department are found at work, tearing up brush nets that would obstruct the upstream movement of spawning salmon; fining torchlight spearmen; prevailing on fishermen to accept the leasing system for beaches instead of engaging in bloody pirating expeditions against one another; attempting to enforce close seasons, and generally acting as the public's conscience even against the public's feeble will.

The body of a fisherman might require disinterment for autopsy because of death in Gaspé under suspicious circumstances; a stranded and starved lighthouse-keeper must be rescued from his lonely outpost in Lake Huron; at the Sault, the testimony of an ancient Indian must be taken to prove the vicious effects of American firewater; a special report on the government of the Islands of St. Pierre and Miquelon is submitted as part of a report on fisheries in the Gulf: so the local agents send back their factual reports to headquarters.[20] There is a meticulous attention to detail in these reports, sometimes brightened by philosophical passages or glowing descriptions of nature which help explain the willingness of some men to lose themselves in far-away places in humble service. These administrative pioneers deserve better of us than oblivion.

This, then, is the domain and the tasks of the Department with whose policies and administrative problems the next two chapters propose to deal.

[20]These are actual illustrations selected from the reports of agents scattered across the province. Pierre Fortin's annual report for the year 1859 contains a model synopsis of the administration and of the economic and social life on the French islands of St. Pierre and Miquelon, together with notes on trade possibilities for Canadian merchants. Indeed, the eventful voyage of that particular year would in itself make an interesting social history of the Gulf region.

CHAPTER IX

NATURE PROVIDES, MAN DIVIDES

WHAT WAS the "public interest" which the Crown Lands Department attempted to define and protect in administering the natural resources of the province? While the question was never posed in just this modern form, in fact, throughout the period of Union, the Department was gradually evolving distinguishable concepts of the public interest. Modern administrative counterparts of the old Department of Crown Lands have built on these foundations. Since the policy issues facing the Department were entirely different for each natural resource a separate analysis of each general area will be necessary.

Land

Two somewhat contradictory policies struggled for dominance within the various branches concerned with the disposal of the public lands. The primary policy, which had been inherited at the time of Union, was to treat the public lands as a commodity, the proceeds from their sale being earmarked for special purposes such as education or road building. The secondary policy, which one might have assumed to have deserved the main emphasis, was to dispose of the lands in such a way as to foster settlement. While it is true that administrators were unable to neglect either policy, they unquestionably did concentrate on the revenue-raising aspects of the Crown lands, often to the disadvantage of settlement.

The reasons for this emphasis on land as a commodity can be traced originally to the economical policy of the Imperial government: colonies should not be a financial burden on the mother country.[1] This reasoning led Imperial authorities to treat such agencies as the Post Office less as service agencies and more as tax-gatherers for the home government. It also led them to exploit any local revenue source to the full and apply the proceeds to the costs of colonial administration. The lands set aside as an endowment for the "protestant clergy" (the Clergy Reserves) were the most famous examples of this policy. In a colony short of cash and with a low credit rating, one can easily

[1]Throughout the 1840's, British officials and colonial governors were deeply impressed by the dogmatic theories of the Buller-Wakefield colonization group who asserted that the price of land should be kept high as a means of preserving a "balance" between land, immigrant labour, and capital. See below, chap. xv.

appreciate this temptation to use the major capital asset as a means of endowing various public projects. Nor is it surprising that some colonial statesmen—particularly those drawn from the business community—shared the same attitude toward the lands.

In 1850, as was previously noted, Merritt developed an optimistic plan for relieving the colony for all time of any taxation by using the proceeds from the sale of the "wild lands" and tolls on the public canals.[2] Indeed, throughout this whole period the "territorial revenues" were burdened with many large items of expenditure. Not only were the administrative costs of the Department itself made a charge against gross revenues, but also the revenues from special parcels of Crown lands were used to endow grammar and common schools in Upper Canada.[3] After secularization of the Clergy Reserves in 1854, the revenues from these lands were turned over to Municipal Investment Funds set up to provide finacial backing for local government enterprises in both Canada East and Canada West. In Lower Canada the Jesuits' Estates served as a support for the Superior Education Fund.[4]

Why the decisions were taken to allocate parts of the territorial revenue to certain public purposes is not our concern here, nor do we need to review the tangled history of the secularization of the Clergy Reserves and the commutation of seignorial tenure.[5] The

[2] See chap. v above. Merritt prepared this plan while serving as President of Council, and when he presented it to a select committee of the Legislative Assembly his cabinet colleagues publicly disowned him as an overly zealous busybody. See "First and Second Reports of the Select Committee re State of the Public Income and Expenditure of the Province," *Journals*, Legislative Assembly, Canada (J.L.A.C.), 1850, Appendix B.B. Note especially the memorandum accompanying Merritt's evidence.

[3] For example, see 4 & 5 Vic., c. 18 (1841).

[4] See 18 Vic., c. 2 (1854) for the Municipal Fund arrangements and 19 Vic., c. 54 (1856), for the Superior Education Fund provision. In the year ending December 31, 1866, the following amounts were made available from the sale of these various parcels of land:

Clergy Reserves—U.C.	$ 78,933
Clergy Reserves—L.C.	6,785
Common school lands	5,896
Grammar school lands	1,781
Jesuits Estates (L.C. Superior Education Investment and Income Funds)	14,719
Total	$108,115

An additional $71,480 was taken out of the gross proceeds from the Crown Lands Department to pay for various administrative charges.

[5] Sir Francis Hincks in his *Reminiscences of His Public Life* (Montreal, 1884) has a good account of the Clergy Reserves question at pp. 288 f.

general point has already been made: both Imperial and local authorities shared the conviction that, to keep the costs of government low, the public lands offered the readiest source of funds. When governments first began to interest themselves in railways, they relied once again on the public domain as a means of financing such works. There was one important difference, however, which greatly reduced the direct responsibilities of government for land sales. In all previous cases the Department of Crown Lands had been retained as real estate broker for the government, only the proceeds of land sales going to the particular public project. In the case of the railway companies the government donated the land and then left each company to realize as best it could on the potential value of the land. In the post-Confederation period, the land sales branches of the big railway companies began to suffer from the administrative problems which had hitherto perplexed the Crown Lands Department.[6]

The early stress placed on the revenue aspects of the public lands restricted the Department's efforts to sponsor a land sales programme directed to settlement. Land disposal policies in the United States also started with a bias in favour of revenue prospects but then moved much more quickly than in the Canadas toward policies favouring settlement. This shift in American emphasis was marked in its early stages by the pre-emption laws and reached a climax with the Free Homestead Act of 1862. In Canada, the public lands were expected to provide cash endowments for so many public services that the revenue bias always remained more prominent. On the other hand, the claims of the settlement policy could not be dismissed, for only in so far as the province developed well-settled communities could the land be made attractive to potential purchasers. The Department constantly sought a satisfactory compromise between these two policies but always the desire for revenue seemed to predominate. William Spragge, a forthright permanent official in the Lands Branch, argued as early as 1845 that a great mistake had been made in converting the Crown Lands Department solely into a real estate agency, concerned only with revenue.[7] Ten years later he reiterated this

[6]See the problems raised in James B. Hedges, *The Building of the Canadian West* (Toronto, 1939), *passim*.

[7]"Report of the Commissioners Appointed to Enquire into the State and Organization of the Crown Land Department," *J.L.A.C.*, 1846, Appendix E.E., evidence of William Spragge. Blaming the first Commissioner, J. Davidson, for what he considered to have been an unfortunate twist in policy, Spragge argued that the business of selling land ought never to have been associated with the other responsibilities of the Department which were connected with the encouragement of settlement.

complaint before a legislative committee, contending that not enough attention had been devoted to encouraging agriculture and immigration.[8] The state of the administrative system itself offered a proof for Spragge's thesis. The Bureau of Agriculture was hurriedly thrown together in the mid-fifties and up to Confederation never enjoyed very great prestige. Administration of immigration matters, for example, was not effectively co-ordinated by the Bureau until as late as 1860. A mild concession to the settlers' interests was made in 1852 when, by legislation and regulation, the Department arranged for cash sales of small holdings to *bona fide* settlers and went even further in offering free lands along colonization roads—an extremely stunted homestead plan.[9]

Giving evidence before a legislative committee in 1855, Mr. Justice Morin, a former Commissioner of Crown Lands, neatly summarized the nature of the conflict created by the two policies of the Department. His sympathies clearly lay with that policy which thus far had received insufficient support: "I think the public lands of this country," he testified, "ought to be disposed of with a view to their speedy settlement by actual farmers, being proprietors of the soil, and not with the view of making money by the sale." Morin then admitted that complications existed. Even though settlement should come before revenue, he agreed that the land could not be given away. If a purely nominal price only were charged speculators would be encouraged to move in, buy up large tracts, and wait for land prices to rise. "Besides," he continued, "Government has also to dispose of lands in trust for Education, for the Indians, for Clergy Reserve Fund, etc., and too great a disproportion in price between them and the Crown Lands, would make the former unsaleable, while a mere nominal price for them would annihilate the trusts."[10] Since sale of lands could not be avoided, Morin argued that at least the conditions of sale ought to favour the settler. "Then, two opposite systems present themselves for consideration," he concluded, "one, to consider the public lands as an article of trade, sell them to any applicant and in any quantity, and for the best price which can be got, leaving the purchasers to dispose of them in retail afterwards, as they may be

[8]"Report of Select Committee on the Present System of Management of the Public Lands," *J.L.A.C.*, 1854–5, Appendix M.M., evidence of Spragge. This Committee produced a short report and a bulky, rather jumbled file of evidence from experienced administrators.

[9]See chap. xv below for further details concerning the free grant system which appears to have been tried first in the early forties in the Owen Sound district.

[10]See Morin's letter (dated March 28, 1855) to the Committee on Land Management, *J.L.A.C.*, 1854–5.

able; the other, to sell them out in lots of a small extent to actual settlers, with such regulations as may best attain the object of having a proprietary and independent population." He added: "I prefer the second system, even if it could be partially evaded for . . . a speedy improvement of forest lands is congenial to the consideration of a country receiving constant immigration, for which no great manufacturing occupation is to be found; because a proprietary population not over-burthened with ground rents, is a guarantee of peace and order for the future."

In such phrases did Morin honestly and far-sightedly set out the alternatives and his own view of where the true public interest lay in disposing of the Crown lands. In retrospect, it now seems clear that the Department vacillated between the two alternatives, never wholly satisfying either the revenue-raising potential of the lands or the demand for an attractive settlement programme. This uncertainty and vagueness as to ultimate objectives had repercussions in certain detailed aspects of land management which merit further comment.

Up to Confederation the Crown Lands Department tried to combine three different systems for disposing of the public lands. Alexander Galt assessed the nature and merits of each system in his evidence before a legislative committee in 1855.[11] First, the land could be given away to settlers—their *bona fides* being checked by attaching certain conditions to the grant such as clearing, improving, and building on the land. Second, the land could be sold at a low price—again as a means of attracting settlers and again the sale would be made conditional on the fulfilment of certain settlement provisions. Or, thirdly, unrestricted sale of land for cash could be instituted.

In considering the merits of these three systems of land disposal, one must assess their impact on three interested parties: the settler, the speculator, and the administration. Superficially, the free grant system with settlement conditions attached would appear to have been most attractive to *bona fide* settlers. There was always the danger, of course, that such settlers, having no personal pecuniary interest in their grants, would be careless in meeting the settlement conditions. Land speculators might then be able to move in and take the land for a small sum or else the whole location would have to be abandoned.

Apart from the early grants of land awarded to Loyalists and

[11]See his letter (dated March 7, 1855) to the same Committee on Land Management. Galt was the chairman and obvious guiding spirit of this Committee.

militia men, the only instance of free land grants was that developed in the colonization road programme of the 1850's. The Department experimented with this plan for more than twenty years. According to the glowing reports submitted annually by the agents in charge, this project fulfilled all the hopes held out for it. On the other hand, the annual reports of the Commissioners of Crown Lands—particularly in the closing years of the period—speak of a disappointing response to the settlement programme.[12] Nevertheless, the period closes with the Commissioner introducing a measure designed to permit the Governor General in Council to use his discretion in extending the free grants system beyond the colonization roads. While this measure was defeated in the Assembly, its approval by Council suggests growing support for some kind of limited homestead plan.[13]

Galt's conditional cash sale plan, the second of the three methods of disposing of the public lands, had many advantages. It was straightforward and promised immediate issuance of the title to land, thereby reducing the possibility of contested claims. Furthermore, as land salesmen in the United States argued, the real interests of the settler were better served by forcing him to pay cash.[14] With any instalment plan the poor settler might be led to dissipate his small savings and then have no cash left to meet his instalments. Thus he might be forced to forfeit his land. This line of reasoning became more popular in Canada during the last few years before Confederation. But by then, long experience with a flexible instalment purchase plan had made the strict cash policy extremely difficult to inaugurate.

Indeed, the unconditional "cash and carry" plan which Galt, with his own experience as administrator of the British North American Land Company, had most favoured in 1854 was never pressed with any enthusiasm. After 1859, it is true, new regulations provided, in special cases, for a public auction of lands for cash. But these regulations were used mainly as a threat to induce purchasers to keep up with their instalments and to force squatters to pay up or clear out.[15]

In practice the conflicting needs of the Canadian community were

[12]See especially, "Annual Report of the Commissioner of Crown Lands of Canada for the Year 1863," *Sessional Papers*, Canada, 1864, no. 5.

[13]*Ibid.*, for the year ending June 30, 1865, *Sessional Papers*, Canada, 1866, no. 3.

[14]See Galt's letters and evidence submitted to the Committee on Land Management, *J.L.A.C.*, 1854–5.

[15]Although evidence that they were used on occasion with considerable effect is provided in the Commissioners' annual reports for the years 1859, 1860, and 1861 contained in *Sessional Papers*, Canada, 1860, no. 12; 1861, no. 15; and 1862, no. 11.

met by a plan which, throughout most of the period, combined a free grant system and a direct cash sale on the instalment plan. Settlers were to be lured by easy payments, while territorial revenues were to be maintained by large sales at a fair price. This compromise solution, however, as Galt emphasized in 1854, was the worst of all possible schemes to administer; ineffective administration in turn could impair the territorial revenues and obstruct settlement. Galt's gloomy prognostications proved to be correct.

The major indictment against the system of instalment purchase was that it made many colonists far too dependent on the discretion of the government. Until Confederation practically every page of the records reveals this state of dependency. Local land agents, for example, could wield enormous power over the local electorate on behalf of a favoured political candidate simply by threatening to foreclose on those settlers who had failed to comply with settlement requirements or who were behind in their instalments.[16] Indeed, this was the essence of the power conferred on the government: the discretion to ease up on all the regulations or, if pressure needed to be applied as in a closely contested election, to threaten the settlers with a more rigorous application of the regulations. Astonishing laxness in application was the rule. For example, when the instalment plan was inaugurated in Lower Canada in 1849, with the first instalment required five years after the date of sale, only one-tenth of the purchasers complied with the conditions.[17] The reason was that most of the purchasers were interested in the timber, not the land. In five years' time these bogus settlers could have cut all the timber they wanted and could have then departed without paying a single instalment! But even more disastrous were the delays which the instalment plan necessarily created for the final perfecting of title to the land. One experienced official testifying before a legislative committee in 1855 said: "I have known many instances where references for the same lots have been withdrawn from the Secretary's Office three or four times in consequence of the land being assigned several times subsequent to the issue first of references and previous to the payment of the Patent fees. These assignments have to be examined and registered in the Crown Lands Office every time the

---

[16]Galt, in his evidence before the Committee on Land Management, *J.L.A.C.*, 1854–5, clearly pointed out this particular danger.

[17]The royal commissioners investigating the finances of the government departments in 1862 pointed out all the opportunities for the exercise of discretionary powers by the political head. See *First Report of the Financial and Departmental Commission* (Quebec, 1863), pp. 18–33.

title changes, until the final issue of Patent. . . ."[18] Additional evidence was provided by Mr. Hector, another employee of the Department, before the Financial and Departmental Commission in 1862.

Question 777. Have cases formerly disposed of on their merits been revived on subsequent application, and adjudicated upon afresh?
Answer: Again and again. Decisions of the Department have been repeatedly revised in Council and by the Department itself.
Question 778. In regard to the period within which the revival of cases may occur, what is the rule of the Department?
Answer: There is no rule in force limiting time for the reconsideration of a case on application of parties concerned. Decisions rendered by the Department twenty years ago have been reversed by the Department within the last few weeks.

The same official quoted from a typical Order in Council dated November 17, 1847, which said that claims to land were to be treated as final unless there was "clearest evidence that such Orders had worked positive injustice." Such Orders in Council were completely disregarded.[19]

The annual reports of the Commissioner of Crown Lands, beginning with Cauchon's great narrative covering the year 1856 and extending to Confederation, reiterate this theme. The comments of Commissioner William McDougall in 1864, in particular, reveal the disastrous impact of the instalment plan.[20] The past leniency of the government toward land purchasers, according to McDougall, had "induced a very general feeling of security against forfeiture or loss on account of non-performance of their engagements, so that mere threats by the Department produce little effect." Flooded by applications to be relieved of debts, to have the interest on overdue instalments reduced, or to reduce the original price, the Department unhappily grappled with the administrative sins of a loose-handed past. "The applications," McDougall lugubriously continued, "are often supported by affidavits, petitions of municipalities, recommendations of Members of Parliament, clergymen, etc., causing much labor to the subordinate officers of the department, and no little trouble to its head." Even the far stricter regulations of 1859 failed to change the picture. As McDougall remarked in his report: "These

[18]Evidence of Mr. Collins, clerk in charge of land returns, before the Committee on Land Management, *J.L.A.C.*, 1854–5.
[19]*First Report of Financial and Departmental Commission*, evidence, Qs. 777–800.
[20]"Annual Report of the Commissioner of Crown Lands for the Year 1863," *Sessional Papers*, Canada, 1864, no. 5.

regulations have not been rigidly enforced, nor indeed would it be possible to enforce them without creating a general panic in the new settlements, and much alarm and distress in many of the older ones."

The endless appeals, the constant litigation, and the complications of the instalment plan coupled with settlement provisions produced chaos in the land branches of the Department. In order to discover whether settlement conditions were being fulfilled, whether speculators were being kept in their place, and whether instalment payments were being met, a large number of local agents had to be employed throughout the province. Headquarters' staff spent their time assembling and checking the accounts and reports of these agents or conducting the correspondence with the many aggrieved parties.[21] Much of the legal bickering in which headquarters got embroiled was attributable to the inefficiency or outright dishonesty of the local agents. The next chapter will deal with the administrative problems created by the necessary presence of the local agent; it is sufficient here to note that slipshod methods of checking on these officials often meant that inaccuracies, embezzlement, and fraudulent connivance between speculators and local agents remained undiscovered for years. Later, court action or political pressure was required to rectify the damage done. Indeed, Cauchon's report for the year 1856 tended to attribute all the evils noted above to the local agents. Concerned only in those aspects of their work which were remunerative, the local agents failed to fulfil their function as the eyes and ears of headquarters. Through the lack of necessary local information headquarters made unwise decisions which were quickly appealed. Still lacking the necessary information and confronted by a contested claim, headquarters deferred a decision. These deferred cases became "the great curse of the Department."[22]

Had it been possible to wipe the slate clean and institute a system of cash sales, in accord with Galt's earlier views, all these administrative ills might have been avoided. The local agents would have been redundant, the complex system of accounting required

---

[21]For every official employed at headquarters there were three agents of the Department in the field or "outside service."

[22]This was Cauchon's summary of the situation he inherited in 1855–6. The report for 1863 found the situation much the same: "I cannot flatter myself that my adjudications will be treated with more respect than those of my predecessors, or that the masses of documents I have laboriously examined will not remain on file to torment my successors. A Government Department is, in this respect, as well as others, unlike a Court of Justice. In the former, the right of appeal is never completely extinguished."

for recording instalment payments could have been simplified, and, best of all, the myriad complaints and appeals, the endless delaying tactics of the Department would not have arisen. It would still be a legitimate query whether or not such a cash system would have discouraged settlement any more than did the instalment plan. However, in the nature of things, the government was never really able to make a fresh start and, once committed to the instalment purchase plan, was under great public pressure to continue it. Certainly this uneasy compromise solution produced neither the revenue nor the settlers expected of it. Furthermore, it opened the door to easy speculation, endless regulations—respected mainly in their breach and subject to unhealthy discretionary interpretations by local agents—and left the true settler always uncertain about his legal title. Politics rather than administration must receive the major portion of blame for this situation, for the administrators were constantly frustrated by outside pressures when they tried to make the regulations work. Nevertheless, as the next chapter will show, administrative immaturity contributed to the endless problem of the land sales division of the Department.

Timber

The public interest with regard to the regulation of this important natural resource has always betrayed a struggle between the short-run exploiter's interest and the long-run view of the forests as a slow-growing crop requiring protection and conservation from wood borers and wood cutters.[23] The official record reveals that the Woods and Forests Branch considered its main task as that of balancing the two major competing interest groups connected with the exploitation of this resource: the timber cutters and the timber merchants. This definition of the public interest was obviously directed to maximizing production for the benefit both of provincial revenues and of those private interests directly connected with the trade. In fact, these interests were localized so that the economic struggle became a regional struggle: Ottawa Valley "timber makers" *versus* Quebec timber merchants. As will be shown, the timber makers felt the direct impact of the Department's regulatory powers but, since the regulations affected the supply of timber, the merchants at Quebec were almost as directly involved. Only in the last few years before Con-

[23]The overwhelming evidence of the depredations of the indiscriminate timbermen is to be found in both the title and text of A. R. M. Lower's *The North American Assault on the Canadian Forest* (Toronto, 1938).

federation are there signs that the long-run objective of conservation is beginning to take shape in the administrator's minds. And, as with most conservation measures, the decision had not been taken soon enough to save much of this valuable resource.

Prior to 1852, there was (to quote Commissioner Cauchon) "no special surveillance over the [timber] trade, though it must be evident that no branch of the public service required it more."[24] Even after 1852, when a Woods and Forests Branch within the Department of Crown Lands gave greater coherence to the administration, the protection of the public interest was seldom satisfactory. The major concern of the department was in the production rather than the marketing of timber. And it was precisely at the timber-leasing and timber-cutting stage that the main administrative problems arose. Since most of the easily cultivated land was taken up by settlers the bulk of the surveyed land coming on the market after 1850 tended to be located in the regions of heavy forests. As Joseph Cauchon clearly realized in his report for 1856, regulating the timber lands was even more difficult than handling land for settlers. At least with land, one had an immovable security which could be held until the client had complied with all the settlement requirements and paid the full purchase price; whereas, once timber was cut and floated away on the long route to the sea it was extremely difficult to keep track of it or hold it as a lien against failure of the lumberers to comply with departmental regulations.

With the increasing pressure of settlement on the old lands, the settler's interest now began to compete with that of the lumberman on forested lands. The settler and the genuine licensed timber cutter often clashed. Settlers who had not yet perfected title to their lands wanted to be given, nevertheless, the rights of a full owner to protect themselves against trespassers. On the other hand, experience showed that the settler was often a speculator in disguise. In this case, to grant him the right to take action against a trespasser would have been disastrous. The timber cutter, acting in good faith, might obtain timber rights from one of these unscrupulous "settlers" only to find his cuttings seized by the bogus owner on the grounds of "trespass." Or even worse, the regulations required licensed timber operators to build all the slides and roads necessary to haul their cuttings off the public land. If such land were sold the purchaser acquired rights over these works and could charge the lumberman for using roads or slides

---

[24]See "Annual Report of the Commissioner of Crown Lands for the Year 1856," J.L.A.C., 1857, Appendix 25, section on Woods and Forests Branch.

which had, in fact, been built at the lumberman's own expense. The lumbermen were ultimately protected against this eventuality by a modification of the old system of setting apart 5 per cent of the public lands for road allowances. The traditional method had been to take this 5 per cent in a straight line, but now it served the lumberman's interests to make the road allowance flexible, following his timber hauling requirements.

But the problem of trespass remained unsolved up to the end of the period. The Superintendent of Woods and Forests revealed to the Financial and Departmental Commission in 1862 that a semi-official method of dealing with trespassers "had grown up into a system."[25] These so-called official "compromises" enabled trespassers to retain their illegal cut if they paid double timber duties. In 1858 and again in 1860 the Department circularized the local timber agents and advised them that the compromises had been made for the last time, and that henceforth the full penalty of seizure and sale would have to be invoked. But the compromises continued to be made, the terms largely left to the arrangement of local agents. The compromises were made "with a distinct knowledge that they [were] contrary to law" and the Superintendent testified that this was why he had "urged the suppression of trespass on the ground of public morality, as well as in justice to the revenue, and to the lumberers who respect the law."

The lumberers who respected the law could, of course, complain that there was no reason for them to pay licence fees and ground rents when others could evade them with the semi-official blessing of a seemingly helpless Department. But even for the law-abiding there were many escape hatches in a watertight system of regulations. These regulations are worth considering for they indicate how the Department attempted to define the public interest purely in terms of the interested parties. During the 1840's the regulations were designed to promote the maximum exploitation of the forest resources. Timber dues were charged on the lumber cut and slidage tolls on the river transport of timber through government-built slides. Large production meant high revenue for the province and this was deemed an appropriate version of the public interest.[26] At the same time,

[25]See evidence of P. M. Partridge, *First Report of Financial and Departmental Commission*, evidence, Qs. 707–12.
[26]In 1866, for example, the revenue from timber licences and ground rents together with the toll charges on the timber slides approached half a million dollars—about two-thirds of the revenue obtained by the Department from the sale of public lands.

the regulations aimed at preventing lumbermen from taking up large tracts of forests and leaving them uncut. A high quota of production was the main requirement, coupled with a threat to subdivide the berths if, at the end of three years, they remained unworked. These severe regulations probably marked the ascendancy of the Quebec timber merchants who complained that a few lumbermen monopolized the largest berths and thereby restricted supply in order to keep prices up. Until 1859, too, the local departmental timber agent had the power to hand out timber berths to the first comers at a privately agreed price. Not until 1859 were licences to timber berths publicly auctioned and an important protection to the public revenues thereby obtained.[27]

In accord with the first regulations, then, a lumberman maintained his cutting rights by paying timber dues and meeting a standard of output established by the government. In 1846, when the trade was badly hit by a depression which could be attributed to the reduction of the Imperial preferential tariff, departmental regulations were blamed for the situation.[28] The depression was attributed to the overstocking of the Quebec market, where domestic prices to the lumbermen seriously declined. In turn, over-production was traced to the government's policy of establishing a high level of annual output as a basis for renewing the timber licences. Since overseas (English) demand remained relatively unchanged and the export price fairly stable, the Quebec merchants enjoyed prosperity at the expense of the Ottawa Valley producers. Whether or not the critics were correct in their analysis of the causes of the depression, the department rescinded all regulations during the last few years of the forties. In 1850 a new scheme of regulation was developed which remained unchanged until Confederation. A ground rent of fifty cents per square mile of leased timber berth was levied against each

[27]See evidence of Partridge, *op. cit.*, Q. 688. That the public auction was not a perfect safeguard may be discovered by reading the next few questions and answers.

[28]See "Annual Report of Commissioner of Crown Lands for the Year 1856," *J.L.A.C.*, 1857, where Cauchon summarizes the timbermen's explanations for the depressed state of the trade. Oddly, the timber interests seem to have placed more blame on departmental regulations which they alleged encouraged over-production, than on changes in the Imperial tariff laws which governed the demand. Certainly by 1860, when the Imperial timber preference was completely abolished, neither the trade nor the Department were under any illusions about the effect of Imperial policy. Nevertheless, the Canadian Supervisor of Cullers while inspecting the prospects in European timber markets took care to warn against flooding these markets by rash exploitation of timber berths in Canada.

licensee. If the berth remained unoccupied the ground rent was increased in geometric progression. By 1856 the mathematics of this scheme had increased the rents eightfold at a moment when a new depression confronted the trade. The producers pressed the Department to drop the system of ground rents, while the Quebec timber dealers, fearful as ever of an up-river monopoly by a few timber-cutting firms, urged the government to retain its regulations. The memorial of the Quebec merchants was pressed with great urgency because in this depression, unlike that of 1846, they too were caught by falling prices.[29]

Retention of the existing regulations, with their emphasis on maintaining production, obviously would contribute to the depression. The alternative adopted by the Department was to reduce the burden on the producers by setting a ceiling on the accumulation of ground rents. In practice, another alternative developed. Testifying before the royal commission in 1862 the permanent head of the Crown Lands Department revealed that the arrears in timber and slidage dues then amounted to $229,545 and $24,987 respectively.[30] Once again a liberal interpretation of superficially rigorous regulations was used to protect the large producers—even though the public revenues suffered. Perhaps, in retrospect, one's judgment on the official policy adopted towards the forests can be too harsh. The forests, after all, seemed such an inexhaustible resource that in many instances they were viewed not as an asset but a liability—something to be cleared away to make room for civilized settlement. Moreover, the government's desperate search for local sources of revenue contributed to the short-run view of the forests as something to be exploited for the immediate revenues which could be obtained from rents and timber dues. When the rigour of the regulations or the state of the trade were such that private interests balked in the performance of their obligations, the government had to give way to that pressure which was immediate and powerful. The fable of the goose and its golden egg taught that too much pressure on the producer did not pay the expected dividends. However, as a result of the reluctance of the government to enforce its regulations not only the public revenues suffered but the larger conception of the public interest also remained in abeyance.

[29]Cauchon has a masterful summary of the regulations and of their estimated impact on the trade in his report for the year 1856, *J.L.A.C.*, 1857, Appendix 25.
[30]Evidence of A. J. Russell before Financial and Department Commission, Q. 562.

It seems clear from the record of the administration of the forests that the Crown Lands Department had been forced into a position where it had to perform more than the referee functions implicit in *laissez-faire* philosophy. If departmental regulations affected the supply situation in the trade, then it was impossible to avoid the pressures which opposing interests felt they might appropriately apply against the administration. Policy was then contrived in the knowledge that a balance must be preserved between the major direct interests concerned with the trade. This notion of the public interest is popular today but it has one inevitable accompaniment: the balance is never satisfactory and the pressure of private interests never slackens. Thus the state wedges itself deeper into a cleft of its own contriving. Upholding the public interest is interpreted as a complicated adjustment of policies to conform with competing claims of private interests. Clearly, until Confederation, this was the situation in the Woods and Forests Branch.

However, just at the close of the period two slight indications of a new orientation were displayed in the Department. In 1860, the Imperial authorities dropped the remnants of their preferential tariff on Canadian timber and, at the same time, the United States market for sawed lumber was constricted by the Civil War. Accordingly, the problem of discovering new markets was raised in an acute form. In this search for markets the Department seized the initiative and thereby added another dimension to the hitherto restricted conception of the public interest. The Superintendent of Cullers, acting on behalf of the Woods and Forests Branch, in 1861 and 1862 made an extended tour of the United Kingdom and Europe in search of markets, the whole trade watching his efforts with interest and expectation.[31] However, it was in post-Confederation times, particularly in the twentieth century, that governmental concern for the marketing as well as the production of timber came to be expected as a routine operation appropriately forming part of the administrator's domain. In addition to this rising interest in markets, we find in the last few reports of the Commissioner of Crown Lands a growing concern for conservation accompanied by a growing fear of the purely "extractive" approach thus far applied to the forests.[32] How-

[31]See special report of Supervisor of Cullers, William Quinn, on the lumber trade, Sept. 10, 1861, appended to Commissioner's "Annual Report for the Year 1861," *Sessional Papers*, Canada, 1862, no. 11.
[32]The annual report for 1866 recommended, for example, that the practice of cutting trees in rotation used in Norway and Sweden ought to be adopted in Canada. Not only did indiscriminate cutting waste the forest resources; it tended, by flooding the markets abroad, to depress the overseas prices.

ever, such comments remained only pious expressions of goodwill on the part of enlightened public officers. Prior to Confederation no legislation had reached the statute books to record the maturity of thought which a conservation programme implies.

Fisheries

The fisheries of the province really divided into two separate parts: the inland stream and lake fisheries and the infinitely more varied and potentially more lucrative fisheries in the Gulf. So far as the internal fisheries were concerned, conservation soon became a dominating principle. The Gulf fisheries, however, required policing and regulatory operations which were different in scope and character from those employed in the interior. The Gulf was a vast stretch of relatively unknown waters whose wealth in fish must have been regarded with the same optimism as that with which the lumberman scanned his seemingly inexhaustible forest wealth. Consequently, conservation was not a dominant theme in the policy relating to this area.

The supervision of the fisheries was added to the tasks of the Crown Lands Department just ten years before Confederation. Prior to 1857 the fisheries were spasmodically and indifferently regulated by justices of the peace and other local authorities. A number of statutes theoretically conferred large magisterial powers to convict and fine persons caught violating the regulations.[33] In practice this legislation was important only in so far as it established a precedent for the subsequent delegation of powers of a judicial nature to administrative officials of the department—the so-called "fisheries overseers." Indeed, fisheries legislation is outstanding for its elaborate descriptions of the judicial procedures to be followed by the administrative branch.[34]

The principles which governed the regulation of the inland fisheries differed greatly from those which we have already seen applied to the forests. Timber, as was noted, was recognized by the government as a valuable asset to be exploited by private interests who in turn would bolster the province's revenues by paying timber dues, ground rents, and licence and slidage tolls. The government's interest in revenue and the private producers' interest in rapid exploitation apparently coincided so that the government leaned over backwards

---

[33]See, for example, 8 Vic., c. 47 (1845).
[34]The basic fisheries legislation is that approved June 10, 1857, in 20 Vic., c. 21. Regulations made by the Governor in Council covered nearly every aspect of the fisheries and every regulation when printed in the *Canadian Gazette* was to be "prima facie evidence . . . that it is in force as Law."

in its efforts to protect the private interest. By Confederation, conservation is still a rather foreign word in the vocabulary of departmental officials. The inland fisheries, however, were on a different footing. The natural and known habits of the fish early made clear to the concerned few—especially ardent anglers like the Governor, Sir Edmund Head—that conservation measures were necessary to maintain the supply. Furthermore, the government did not look to these fisheries as a source of revenue, as was the case with timber. Consequently, from the government's point of view, conservation rather than exploitation seemed a more logical approach. Nevertheless, the principle of conservation never enjoyed widespread popularity, becoming largely the rallying cry of two or three dedicated officials in the Department, aided by the indignation of sport fishermen.

Another distinction between forests and fisheries was that there were not the concentrated organized pressures of powerful interest groups in the administration of the latter. The possible exception was the Hudson's Bay Company which monopolized most of the stream salmon fisheries along the north shore of the St. Lawrence River—an area known as the King's Posts. But even this powerful company bowed before the determination of departmental officials in the 1860's. The absence of any concentrated pressures coupled with the general ignorance or apathy of the legislature left more than the usual area of freedom for permanent departmental officials to develop what seemed to them an appropriate conception of the public interest. There is no question that the comprehensive fisheries legislation of 1857, 1858, and 1865 was entirely the work of a few officials concerned directly with this branch of the Department's activities.

The principle of conservation was apparently first recognized in 1822 by the legislature of Upper Canada. In that year the idea of a closed season to protect the breeding period of game fish was incorporated in a statute. It is not altogether certain, however, that the legislature was not more concerned with protecting millowners from the incendiarism of torchlight fishermen, for the statute prohibited this type of nocturnal fishing within 100 yards of any mill. In Lower Canada conservation measures were introduced more slowly. In 1843 the salmon, trout, and 'lunge in Lake Memphramagog and in the Eastern Counties were given the protection of a closed season.[35] But not until 1855 was legislation passed to cover the whole of Lower Canada.[36] In addition to a closed season, specific prohibitions against the use of certain types of nets and torchlight fishing were to be in-

[35] 7 Vic., c. 13 (1843).   [36] 18 Vic., c. 114 (1855).

voked. Reinforcing this legislation at a later stage came the decision in 1857 to experiment with artificial propagation. That this more positive measure was necessary to revive the supply of fish was adequately revealed in the drastic falling off in the annual salmon catch of Lower Canada.[37] It was also in the legislation of 1857 that the positive policy of encouraging the fisheries by paying bounties was introduced.

Conservation measures were readily devised and written into statutes but they remained virtually dead letters until their administration was transferred from local authorities and the J.P.'s. The violent opposition to the officers of the Department who sought after 1857 to enforce regulations which had long been on the statute books clearly suggests that early conservation measures had never been enforced. The ardent trout fisherman may read in anguish of how speckled trout were used as bait for catching coarse fish. The salmon angler who stalks his prey with dry fly and a twelve-foot rod will also bring his sporting blood to the boil as he reads of the killing of salmon by means of stake and barrier nets, torchlight spearing expeditions, and other forms of mass execution. One can readily appreciate the holy zeal with which the acting head of the Fisheries Branch, himself an ardent fly fisherman, personally undertook the destruction of illegal salmon traps against strong physical opposition.[38] There was surely much to justify the view of the Commissioner of Crown Lands who wrote in 1857: "For the preservation of our fisheries of every kind it is desirable that such superintendence should be established and organized in such a manner as to ensure the law being carried into effect in all parts of the Province."[39] The administrative organization designed to give effect to this policy involved the appointment, for each section of the province, of one fishing superintendent and about fifteen overseers vested with magisterial powers. The overseers, in effect, took over from the local authorities, the expectation being that centrally promulgated regulations would now be uniformly enforced. At the same time the restoration of the fisheries depleted by the incursions of uncontrolled fishermen could

[37]On the River St. Paul on the coast of Labrador, where 1,400 barrels of salmon per year had been a normal yield, in 1856 there was produced only 90 barrels. See E. T. D. Chambers, *The Fisheries of the Province of Quebec* (Quebec, 1912), pp. 162 f.

[38]See report of W. F. Whitcher, clerk in charge of the Fisheries Branch, appended to reports from Superintendents of Fisheries in the "Annual Report of the Commissioners of Crown Lands for 1859," *J.L.A.C.*, 1859, Appendix 17.

[39]See "Annual Report of the Commissioner of Crown Lands for the Year 1856," *J.L.A.C.*, 1857, section on Fisheries.

be attained by artificial propagation undertaken by the Department. The comprehensive enactments of 1857, 1858, and 1865 provided the statutory basis for this programme.[40] The legislation and the outcry it provoked are reminiscent of the similar situation created by early factory legislation in England a generation before. Indeed, the centrally appointed and supervised fishery overseer with his quasi-judicial power of seizure and search was not unlike the first factory inspector with his power of entry and search.

Apart from the efforts to foster conservation the Fisheries Branch also faced the difficult task of licensing the operators of fishing stations located on sedentary shore or stream fisheries. This problem was particularly acute in Lower Canada where the Hudson's Bay Company had been awarded the monopoly of salmon fishing in the extensive area of the King's Posts.[41] Between 1855 and 1860 the leasing system was tightened up, the Hudson's Bay Company and other privileged lessees dispossessed, and the salmon fisheries rights put up to public competition.[42] (This programme was consistent with the public auctioning of timber berths and of certain public lands introduced in 1859.) Several practical benefits flowed from these measures. In the first place, the pressure on the salmon streams was relieved, thereby checking their threatened exhaustion. Secondly, the attention of fishermen was directed towards the varied sea fisheries of the Gulf which had been exploited mainly by outsiders. Finally, the licensing system by defining the boundaries of each sedentary fishing station promised to eliminate a major cause of unrest and litigation—the constant dispute over fishing rights.

Over and above these aspects of fishery administration, Lower Canada was faced with regulatory problems of a different nature. The aspects just dealt with related primarily to inland fisheries on lake or stream. The regulatory activities of the Department were devoted to conservation or the grant of fishing concessions through licensing and leasing powers. In addition, the most important and varied fisheries of Lower Canada were carried on in the Gulf of St. Lawrence. The measures required in this area were reminiscent of the legislation passed by the Imperial Parliament several centuries

[40]20 Vic., c. 21 (1857); 21 & 22 Vic., c. 86 (1858); 29 Vic., c. 11 (1865).

[41]The terms of this grant, which was approved by the Governor and local Executive Council in 1842 for a period of 21 years, are set out in a supplementary return to the Legislative Assembly, "Copies of all Titles, Leases, Concessions etc. . . with Hudson's Bay Company," *J.L.A.C.*, 1851, Appendix J.J.J.

[42]See the excellent review of these measures in Chambers, *The Fisheries of the Province of Quebec*, pp. 174 f.

before to regulate the fisheries of Newfoundland. Here questions of landing privileges arose, the right to a beach, the right to build curing flakes, cut wood, collect bait. Here also the clash of international interests appeared and with it the need to police waters, protect fishing rights of different groups, and generally keep the peace of the port.[43]

Given the commercial importance of these fisheries and the extensive problems emerging from them, it is not surprising that attention was directed much sooner to this sector of the fisheries than to the internal aspect which has just been considered. The semi-military nature of this venture is revealed in the title conferred on Captain Pierre Fortin when in 1852 Canadian authorities decided to intervene on behalf of their own fishermen. Captain Fortin reported to the government as "the magistrate in command of the expedition to protect the fisheries in the Gulf." Until 1858 this astonishing official was employed on *La Canadienne*, a government vessel owned by the Public Works Department. He reported to the Provincial Secretary because of his position as stipendiary magistrate and because there was no other ministerial official available. On the whole he was a solitary worker and his reports show what can be done by a rugged individualist with a strong sense of public duty when he is left to his own resources. His reports on such exotic topics as seal or whale fisheries in the Gulf or the French administration of St. Pierre and Miquelon, as well as his careful record of the state of the fisheries in the Gulf, along its shores, and around its islands must have been a constant source of revelation to the "landlubbers" whose knowledge of their country generally stopped at Kingston or, at the farthest, Quebec.

Fortin maintained a well-drilled crew on board which he disciplined along naval lines. The frequent intervention of these civilian "marines" made life tolerable for isolated officials of other departments who often required a show of force to prove that public authority really existed. The Magdalen Islands were the key to the Gulf fisheries, as many as 100 vessels crowding Amherst Harbour during the height of the mackerel season. Fortin's assistance here as a police patrol was invaluable. The collector of customs frequently called upon him to take smugglers under arrest (a power he enjoyed as stipendiary magistrate). Maintaining the peace of the port when "600 men of all characters" and "the scum of the sea port towns" roved loose

[43]The annual reports of Pierre Fortin which accompanied the report of the Crown Lands Department often contained exciting accounts of international rowdyism in the Gulf.

and lawless in these remote areas was largely his responsibility. The preservation of law and order during elections in remote constituencies fell not infrequently to his lot, and salvaging wrecks, saving crews, chasing smugglers or timber poachers, patrolling harbours to prevent water pollution by careless fishermen, and keeping rowdies subdued were all part of the day's operations. The saga of the Canadian fisheries seen through the reports of this loyal official would form a notable addition to the literature of our country's development.[44]

While Captain Fortin's activities in themselves were purely of a police character his astute observations frequently raised matters of policy. On the whole he was concerned with fostering positive measures to build up the commercial value of the varied fisheries of the Gulf. This was not so much a matter of conservation—although in the case of whale and seal, conservation was becoming increasingly important; it was more a matter of stimulating Canadian fishermen to take advantage of their natural riches before strangers better organized and equipped got too deeply entrenched. He was constantly bemoaning the lack of interest in the herring fisheries which had produced for the New England States and Maritime Provinces that famous and valuable triangular trade with the West Indies. The complete failure of Canadian fishermen to exploit the mackerel fisheries was another sore point. It was a constant complaint of Fortin that, while we built boats and had valuable goods to carry in them, we let others come in to sail them for us across the seas and reap the real rewards. One of his proposals was a training school for sea captains on board his beloved *La Canadienne*.[45] His desire to see positive measures taken to encourage the fisheries was fulfilled in 1858 when a system of fishing bounties was introduced.[46] Later in 1865 bounties were also granted to encourage oyster planting in the Gulf.[47]

Fortin's activities also carried him to both shores of the Gulf where he undertook the collection of dues for fishing leases and exercised his powers as magistrate in punishing offenders against the conservation regulations. Altogether, the fisheries of the Gulf with their multitudinous problems—almost always connected with some other department like Customs or Public Works or some other country like the United States—stand apart from the fisheries of the rest of

[44]The career of this remarkable public servant is summarized in Chambers, pp. 157 f.
[45]See his annual report, *J.L.A.C.*, 1858, Appendix 31.
[46]21 & 22 Vic., c. 86, s. 62 and s. 68 (1858).
[47]29 Vic., c. 11, s. 19, subs. 5 (1865).

the province. The man who almost single handed reigned over this vast watery territory also stands out as a romantic figure, too vigorous and unique to fit into the frame of a staid government department. Nevertheless, after 1858, Fortin, the rugged individualist, was forced into the departmental mould, his reports and activities losing much of their former exuberance.

At Confederation the Fisheries Branch had settled upon several operative principles which were to guide it through the wider policy area opened to it by the new union. At the same time there were a number of unsettled issues which were carried over to perplex the federal Department of Fisheries after 1867. The "settled" items included, first, the establishment of the basic principle of conservation. This had been elaborated in many statutes and covered the major fisheries at Confederation. Post-Confederation records reveal a persistent *laissez-faire* philosophy in the Department when it came to pressing conservation restrictions to the point where they greatly interfered with private rights—for example, in the matter of stream pollution by sawdust from sawmill operators.[48] On the positive side, the Department had also committed itself to the policy of artificial propagation in order to make up for deficiencies in the conservation programme. After Confederation doubts were at times voiced concerning the efficacy of artificial propagation but the Department wisely continued its experiments. Another policy established during the later stages of the pre-Confederation period was that of leasing fishing rights by auction and of licensing fishermen. Thus did the Department protect private rights from trespass and at the same time provide a means of witholding such privileges if departmental regulations were not properly recognized. This policy, however, was based on the statutory powers conferred on the Governor in Council to make regulations having the force of law. It was this element of discretion accorded in practice to officials of the Department that became a source of criticism in the post-Confederation period.[49] A third development which had reached the embryo stage, at least, prior to Confederation was the Department's tendency to view the fishermen as its clients whose interests it must represent in government circles. This side of the Department's activities has expanded greatly since Confederation but we find early traces of this development after

[48]See "Annual Report of the Department of Marine and Fisheries," *Sessional Papers*, Canada, 1872, no. 5; *ibid.*, 1874, no. 4.
[49]See, for example, *ibid.*, 1874, no. 4, p. lxxx; 1876, no. 5, pp. lxxiii f.; 1891, no. 8, p. li.

1858 in the adoption of bounties to foster various branches of the fisheries.

The fishing interests had come to accept the benefits to themselves of a regulatory system which involved licences. But they were not prepared to countenance government tampering with the product itself. Consequently, legislation providing for compulsory inspection of fish and fish oil, which was strongly recommended by the permanent staff of the Department, was defeated in the 1860's.[50] The new Department of Fisheries had to renew the attack after Confederation. In the meantime, the conception of the public interest was not held to involve the interest of the wider consuming public. Secondly, the problem of conflicting jurisdictions both domestically and internationally had barely made its appearance before 1867. The Reciprocity Treaty of 1854 had, it is true, introduced a large element of international competition in the Gulf. And, where Lower Canada bordered on New Brunswick, the necessity of joint legislative provisions for mutually safeguarding their fisheries had developed. However, in 1862 the Imperial authorities had disallowed the measure designed by both provinces to assimilate their fisheries laws.[51] After Confederation both international and domestic problems of jurisdiction loomed large in the Department's records. The device of international joint commissions ultimately proved a satisfactory means of resolving the first set of problems. But the issue of Dominion-provincial control remained a disturbing administrative factor, ultimately necessitating, in 1897, a reference of the disputed points to the Judicial Committee of the Privy Council.[52]

Mining

In principle, the administration of mineral lands was supposed to foster the development of a pioneer enterprise which had to be carried on under difficult physical and financial conditions. An effective policy ought to have been sufficiently restrictive to prevent speculators from taking over lands which they had no intention of

[50]See "Report of the Select Committee on the Working of the Fishery Act," *J.L.A.C.*, 1864, Appendix 5, evidence of Richard Nettle. An early Act passed in 1828 by the Assembly of Lower Canada provided for the inspection of fish and fish oil exported from the colony, but it apparently remained a dead letter.

[51]See "Annual Report of Commissioner of Crown Lands for the Year 1863," *Sessional Papers*, Canada, **1864, no. 5.**

[52]The text of the Judicial Committee's decision is printed in full in the Toronto *Globe*, June 11, 1898, p. 12. For the administrative repercussions see "Annual Report of the Minister of Marine and Fisheries," Report of Fisheries Branch, pp. xxxiv f., *Sessional Papers*, Canada, 1899, no. 11 A.

exploring and working themselves. At the same time, policy ought also to have protected the legitimate entrepreneur spirit and encouraged the venturing of capital in the unknown wilderness. In practice, the administration of mining locations—particularly in Upper Canada where the major mineral finds had turned up—notoriously failed to implement these principles. Mr. Gibbard, the official who almost single handed carried out the responsibilities of the Department for the mineral lands, was amazingly outspoken in his criticism of the lackadaisical attitude adopted by most of his political superiors and vociferous in appealing for a more positive interpretation of the public interest.[53] His successors in the provincial agencies that took over after Confederation fought the same battle for many years.[54]

The general situation prevailing almost up to Confederation was that a few monopolists too cautious to invest capital in working their locations persistently prevented more enterprising prospectors from opening up the claims. The most notorious example was provided by the Montreal Mining Company which held sixteen locations, each consisting of a block of land five miles by two miles on the north shore of Lake Superior. These blocks had been granted between 1845 and 1846 to prominent businessmen and leading politicians.[55] The separate holdings had been consolidated in the Montreal Mining Company and after 1847 the locations had been allowed to lie idle, despite the widely held view that rich copper ore was readily available. A criticism heard much later by a royal commission on the mineral resources of Ontario was that "capital will not explore."[56] The criticism was certainly valid in the pre-Confederation period.

Mr. Gibbard, the Crown Lands' official in charge of mining locations, wrote quite bluntly in his report of 1863, "they [the Montreal Mining Company] will neither work nor sell, and under the present

[53]See reports of Mr. Gibbard, Mining Inspector for Lakes Huron and Superior, appended to "Annual Report of Commissioner of Crown Lands for 1860," *Sessional Papers*, 1861, no. 15, Appendix 11; for 1861, *Sessional Papers*, 1862, no. 11, Appendix 32; for 1862, *Sessional Papers*, 1863, no. 5, Appendix 43.

[54]Both the pre-Confederation and post-Confederation history of mining regulations in Ontario is covered in the "Report of the Royal Commission on the Mineral Resources of Ontario," *Sessional Papers*, Ontario, 1889, no. 67. See especially the evidence of E. B. Borron, manager of the Bruce Mines, 1852-7, at pp. 92 f.; also section IV, "Mining Laws and Regulations."

[55]See *J.L.A.C.*, 1847, Appendix A.A.A., "Papers etc. re Grant of Land in Certain Parts of Upper Canada for Mining Purposes . . ."; also in *ibid.*, 1851, Appendix U, "A Tabular Return of the Persons who have Received Licenses for Opening and Working Mines etc. . . ."

[56]"Report of the Royal Commission on the Mineral Resources of Ontario," p. 259.

system may hold the same for 15 years more unimproved, without incurring any extra expense."[57] While this was an outstanding example of monopolistic greed it was by no means unique. The Hudson's Bay Company along with numerous mining companies incorporated in Quebec and Montreal persisted in asserting their rights to old mining locations even though many of them had never been properly paid for. "The last portion of our mineral lands are locked up," Mr. Gibbard complained in language surprisingly strong coming from a permanent official of the Crown Lands Department. Genuine explorers were discouraged because they could not obtain accurate information about the availability of mineral lands or the validity of the rights of these ancient claimants to them.

Before Confederation there was surprisingly little legislation dealing with mining problems. Most regulations were made in Orders in Council and these clearly determined the progress of mining in Upper Canada.[58] Private bills to incorporate mining companies serve as a criterion of public interest in the mineral wealth of the country. Such bills came in sudden spurts, always associated with an alteration in governmental policy, or, of course, the discovery of new riches. The first forward surge came in the years 1846 to 1848 when the mining locations around Lakes Superior and Huron were granted and then consolidated in the Montreal Mining Company—presumably on the strength of the findings of copper reported by Sir William Logan, the head of the recently created Geological Survey. By 1850 the government had issued 23 licences to exploit the minerals located around Lake Huron and 43 licences for the north shore of Lake Superior. These were all issued under regulations published by the Crown Lands Department in November 1846 but based on a Minute of Council dated November 2, 1846. Every applicant on payment of £150, which was to cover the cost of surveying the land, was to be granted a certificate of exploration. Every licence holder had an option of buying a maximum bloc 2 miles by 5 miles at 4 shillings per acre within two years. If he bought the land, the original £150 was applied to the purchase price. If he failed to purchase he forfeited the £150. Actually, these regulations do not appear to have been enforced, for over half the licence holders in the late 1850's had not completed the formalities or bought their locations.[59]

[57]See his report appended to "Annual Report of the Commissioner of Crown Lands for the Year 1862," *Sessional Papers*, Canada, 1863, no. 5, Appendix 43.

[58]Indeed, there was no statutory regulation of mining until the new gold discoveries in 1864. See 27 & 28 Vic., c. 9 (1864).

[59]See Gibbard's first report as mining inspector for the year 1860, *Sessional Papers*, Canada, 1861, no. 15, Appendix 29.

There was another mild spurt of mining company formation in the mid-fifties reflecting the stimulus provided by an easing of the regulations governing the right to explore. In 1853 an Order in Council provided merely for a £25 licence fee to explore at will and, within a period of two years, to purchase a tract of land of 400 acres at 7/6 an acre. The Commissioner of Crown Lands in his report for 1857 favoured the elimination of the £25 fee in order to encourage free-lance exploration by individual prospectors. By this time it was realized that governmental policy had encouraged the "sitting hen" approach to the mineral wealth of the north and that it was necessary to take positive steps to encourage intensive exploitation. A new regulation of the Department in 1861 sought to give effect to the policy by penalizing those holders of locations who failed to work their claims. The regulation withheld the full patent of ownership to the licensee for two years after his purchase of the land and at the same time insisted on proof of one year's genuine exploitation of the claim. A year later, however, there was a change of heart and a new order was issued which permitted the purchaser to obtain his patent for the land after payment and without the previous requirement of having worked his claim. At the same time a royalty of 2½ per cent was charged on the value of the ore prepared for the market at the minehead. With the imposition of royalties a long debate was started which was still inconclusive in the late 1880's when a royal commission on mining heard further testimony on the subject.[60] Certainly, in 1863, Mr. Gibbard had no doubts about the inadvisability of the royalty plan. He frankly reported that the royalty "is universally condemned ... and, I may say, is a quietus on all fresh operations. It is generally supposed to have been passed so as to enable the Montreal Mining Company to stand in a more favourable position than those who may hereafter purchase mineral lands." Commissioner McDougall must have shared his subordinate's opinion for during his short régime in 1864 a tax of one dollar a ton on all ore extracted replaced the 2½ per cent royalty. A year later, under a new régime, both tax and royalty disappeared. However, in post-Confederation times, Ontario returned to the royalty system.

The discovery in 1860 of gold on the Chaudière River and in 1863–4 of oil in various parts of the province touched off another flurry of incorporations and enlarged the administrative responsibilities of the Department. Between 1863 and 1866 nearly one hundred mining companies applied for statutory incorporation, and in 1864 for the

[60]See "Report of Royal Commission on the Mineral Resources of Ontario," pp. 259, 311–12, and 314.

first time special mining legislation was deemed necessary to regulate the gold fields.[61]

One feature of the earlier Orders dealing with mining locations was that they made no effort to instruct the operators in the proper method of working their claims or handling their employees. The agent in charge of mining locations in the Crown Lands Department held little more than a watching brief, reporting on the actual operations—although always in such a way as to suggest to the private operators the need for revising their methods. For example, Mr. Gibbard, the official in question, reported in great detail on the methods in vogue at the two main mining locations—the Bruce and Wellington mines.[62] As for the Company itself, as the Department's report claimed, "the whole business of the Company appears to be selling goods, meat and wood and preventing all others from doing so except under their immediate control."

This was the typical situation which pained Mr. Gibbard as he compared the amazing development of mining on the Michigan side with Canada's "fur trading wilderness." Yet the Department until about 1864 seemed to find no stronger regulatory programme than the one just described. In the last few years before Confederation we find the Department prodding the speculators to act or suffer the consequences of dispossession; but even here the timidity of the government towards the larger vested interests did not lend much vigour to the campaign. However, in the legislation regulating gold mining, beginning in 1864, there is at last official recognition of the need for the state to define more precisely the conditions under which mining could be undertaken. Indeed, the new province of Ontario in 1868 adopted it as a model for the next twenty years.[63] By this legislation, officers of the Department were given magisterial

---

[61]27 & 28 Vic., c. 9 (1864); amended 1865 by 29 Vic., c. 9. Again we find, as in the fisheries Acts, power conferred on the Governor in Council to make regulations with the force of law on a wide range of subjects.

[62]At the Wellington Mine he reported on the nefarious activities of imported Cornish miners who "have regular meetings and organizations, and in cases of this kind, take a vote, are sworn to secrecy, act as one man, and terrify all others working about the mines." At the Bruce Mine he found operations conducted on a system known as Tribute. The company was responsible for supplies, equipment, and shipping; the miners were to do all the work and assume all expenses below ground to bring the ore to the top. As a result only the richest veins were followed, as little time as possible was wasted on making proper passages, dirt from new workings was thrown back over unused parts of the mine, and in general chaotic, wasteful exploitation was the result.

[63]See "Report of Royal Commission on the Mineral Resources of Ontario," p. 268.

powers in districts declared by the Governor in Council to be mining divisions. These powers entitled the officer to settle summarily all disputes over boundaries of claims, use of water, forfeiture of licences, and so on. All decisions were final. Full publication of the work and extractions had to be made to the Department; there were regulations governing taverns and provisions for constables, police force, and the invoking of the Riot Act which had applied in the past only where public works were endangered. In the concluding section the Governor in Council was awarded that discretionary power which today has become more familiar to us, namely, the power to "make regulations with the force of law" covering a wide variety of mining matters.

In summary, it appears that the administration of mineral lands was viewed, prior to Confederation, as one of the less important duties entrusted to the Crown Lands Department. Essentially, the administrative problem was a licensing one. But behind the issuance of the licences lay important policy considerations which could only be determined by balancing several conflicting interests against one another. The public interest obviously lay in a policy which would encourage vigorous exploration of unknown territory and an efficient working of the locations which had been found to contain valuable ores. But the Department never really came to grips with the operative or extractive side of mining until the legislation of 1864. As a consequence such inefficient systems as the Tribute system of mining were permitted to continue unchecked. Even the preliminary stages of exploration and confirming of grants of mineral lands were not effectively regulated. Here the "inside" information possessed by various men in public office led to a rapid leasing of copper mining lands from 1845 to 1846, and, with the partial amalgamation of these separate interests in 1847, to a conservative monopoly of speculators which in turn retarded the exploration of mineral lands by less privileged persons. Departmental regulations, with few exceptions, seem to have been devised in the interests of those people who had moved in on potentially valuable land at the early stages. In the effort to confirm the shaky rights of such immobile licensees the Department would appear to have retarded the growth of a vital industry more than seems warranted by the obvious difficulties of finding the necessary capital and transportation.

CHAPTER X

ADMINISTERING THE NATURAL RESOURCES: THREE PROBLEMS

LIKE THE NUMEROUS ANCIENT CITIES constructed upon the ruins of their predecessors, the Department of Crown Lands at Confederation consisted of a number of branches superimposed on each other in a bewildering fashion. A detailed description of the organization and operation of each of these branches would be as tedious as it would be unrewarding. The chart in the Appendix shows the six main functions ultimately embraced by the Department in 1867. The main concern here is to ascertain how the Department responded to three persistent administrative problems which confronted it throughout its whole history.

Briefly, the three problems were these. First, how could the Department best be organized to cope with the sprawling area over which its jurisdiction extended? Modern administrators still confront this fundamental issue: how much administrative decentralization can be achieved without devitalizing headquarters? Second, at the centre of the problem was a governmental agency with a vast natural treasure at its disposal. How could the staff be kept honest in the face of enormous temptations and how could unscrupulous pressure from special interests be resisted on behalf of the public? Third, how could unified control and administrative co-ordination at the top be attained when the Department was so heterogeneous? A consideration of each of these three problems and of the responses to them will provide a sufficiently comprehensive view of the main features of the administrative history of the Department.

The Problem of Decentralization

The activities of the Crown Lands Department not only were carried on by a number of relatively small sub-divisions at headquarters but also involved an extensive field service. The existence of a large number of local agents created the most important immediate problems for headquarters. Could the use of local agents have been avoided? If not, how much discretion could safely be conferred on them either in the handling of public money or in making final decisions in the application of policy? What were the most satisfactory controls? These were not academic questions then, nor are they now.

They are questions which are universal wherever administration must be conducted over a large area and whenever it is important to maintain intimate contact with the public or adapt general rules to meet peculiar local conditions.

The extension of the welfare state undoubtedly explains much of the contemporary proliferation of the central bureaucracy. For every official required at Ottawa today, for instance, there are at least three working in the field.[1] But it is important to realize that in the pre-Confederation public service, long before the advent of the welfare state, the same ratio of field to headquarters staff prevailed.[2] Without intermediate levels of government and without an extensive network of properly functioning local authorities, the widespread field service of the central departments at that period seemed inescapable. There were three additional reasons for decentralizing the operations of the Crown Lands Department. In the first place the policy of regulation adopted by the central authorities could only be carried out, as in the Fisheries Branch or Colonization Roads Branch, by employing a field force to police the local areas. Secondly, where the execution of policy required the settlement on the spot of contested claims to land titles and where adequate knowledge of the local situation could best be provided by the man in the field, decentralization was imperative. Here, obviously, the departmental decision to maintain local agents was guided by the well-intentioned belief that this system best served the convenience of widely scattered and often isolated settlers. The third consideration weighing heavily in favour of decentralization was the inadequacy of communications and the number of references to the Department by its numerous clients. These two factors taken together would have swamped the Department with correspondence had there been no local agents to handle the requests.[3] Clearly, spiriting the seat of government from one end of the United Provinces to the other must have contributed to the desire to decentralize operations rather than have the bulky records at head-

[1] In 1952, there were 32,689 federal civil servants at Ottawa, as against 98,957 in the "outside service." See DBS Memo, prepared in the Public Finance and Transportation Division, *Federal Civil Service Employment and Payroll, Fiscal Year Ended Mar. 31, 1952*.

[2] At Confederation there were 69 officials at the headquarters of the Crown Lands Department and 221 departmental agents in the field; roughly the same ratio of 1:3 now prevailing.

[3] These three considerations were developed by officers of the Department who appeared before the royal commissioners investigating the Department in 1845–6. See "Report of the Commissioners Appointed to Enquire into the State and Organization of the Crown Land Department," *Journals*, Legislative Assembly, Canada (*J.L.A.C.*), 1846, Appendix E.E.

quarters shifted back and forth. Alexander Galt, in fact, recommended that, for this very reason, Crown Lands ought to be excused from the quadrennial move and located permanently at Montreal.[4] It is significant that this suggestion was coupled with his recommendation to centralize the operations of the Department. His views apparently did not find general support.

Most of the points in favour of a decentralized administrative system were brought out in 1845 by a royal commission which considered especially the excessive cost of managing the public lands.[5] Subsequent investigators continued to elicit evidence from departmental officials in support of the system of local agencies but the record reveals increasing dissatisfaction with the scheme. It gave rise, despite earlier optimism, to much delay in rendering final decisions, it was expensive, and periodically investigators brought to light cases of dishonesty, graft, and connivance with speculative pressures which reduced public faith in the system.

The evidence suggests, then, that despite the strong arguments in favour of decentralization there were other conditions which blocked its successful functioning. Most of these conditions could have been remedied by taking appropriate measures, but in most cases these seemed to be either beyond the inventiveness of contemporary officialdom or else had to await the maturing of a new sense of morality in public office and the development of more adequate means of communication. It is possible, indeed, that this early unsatisfactory experience with decentralization produced after Confederation an unnecessarily strong reaction in the opposite direction, with the result that today a few officials at headquarters have developed ulcers simply because proper devolution of authority has not been worked out. In any event, towards the end of the pre-Confederation period there are indications of this centralizing trend having set in.[6]

[4]See "Report of Select Committee on the Present System of Management of the Public Lands," *J.L.A.C.*, 1854–5, Appendix M.M. Galt contended that "in the case of the Crown Lands Office, removal is attended with such great interruption to the public business, that it should at least be made an exception."

[5]See "Report of Commissioners on Crown Land Department," *J.L.A.C.*, 1846. The Commissioners themselves were not impressed with the arguments in favour of decentralization but as the Assistant Commissioner, T. Boutillier, argued, "it would be [im]possible to manage efficiently the business of the Department, the details of which extend from Gaspé to Sault Ste. Marie, without the employment of paid external agents of some description."

[6]Cauchon, in his report for the year 1856 (*J.L.A.C.*, 1857, Appendix 25), attempted a reduction of the local agencies and the Commissioner reported in 1862 (Sessional Papers, Canada, 1862, no. 11) that the abolition of twenty-two local agencies had been a progressive measure even though more work had been thrust upon the staff at headquarters.

What factors obstructed the successful operation of the local agency system? First, the common economical approach to the public service, which was discussed in chapter v, can be blamed for much of the difficulty. Most of the local agents were paid on a commission basis presumably because this would relate the costs of administration to the "business" done by each agent. Here again the businessman's instinct proved a false economy, for two evil consequences followed. The agents—even the most energetic—could scarcely make a decent living from their commissions. Naturally, they were the more readily tempted to abuse the trust and discretion conferred on them to supplement their meagre pay. Further, where they were responsible for regulatory operations and where reporting the local situation to headquarters was perhaps the most important part of their labours, the commission system proved disastrous. Commissions were received only on the direct business operations of their agencies, and no salary was received for these other duties. The obvious response of many agents was to neglect all but the paying portion of their duties.[7] Unfortunately the solution most commonly proposed for this situation was not the correct or most obvious one. Those who criticized the system seldom objected to the commission form of payment. Their answer to inadequate commissions was to propose a drastic pruning of the local agencies: more business could then be distributed amongst fewer agents and their commissions raised to a point where dishonesty could be discouraged. However, such reductions proved impossible, the Department having a larger field force at Confederation than ever before. The obvious remedy, but one which was adopted only in isolated cases and mainly for supervisory officials, was to put all agents on a salary. But the businessman's view that each agency should have enough business to pay all its own costs tended to discourage the full adoption of this plan.

Successful decentralization requires, secondly, the provision of adequate central control. Such control normally involves periodic reports to headquarters, strict accounting for all money taken in or spent, independent audit of accounts, and periodic regular inspection by headquarters staff. Until the appointment of an Auditor General in 1855 there was no effective, independent examination of the accounts of any department.[8] The new Auditor General, John Langton, was a most energetic individual, but nevertheless it took him

---

[7]See Cauchon's observations in his oft-cited report for the year 1856, under the heading "Administration."

[8]See *supra*, chap. vii, for the general financial setting and the problems of instituting central controls.

three or four years to bring the Crown Lands Department to book, mainly because of the sorry state of the local agencies' finances and their free-and-easy book-keeping practices. Quarterly, sometimes monthly, reports were required of the agents but most of them were sufficiently imaginative to be capable of "doctoring" their books if the game seemed worth while. Until 1857 local agents handled all the revenues received in their offices, deducted "expenses of management," and then returned (usually after considerable delay) the remainder to the Receiver General. This open invitation to dishonesty was finally removed, first by having the agents send in gross receipts every month and later by requiring the public to make payments directly to the banks.[9] In Lower Canada, however, the local agent continued unmolested almost until Confederation. Inspection, one of the most obvious devices for preserving central authority, was early viewed as the effective solution to the problem. But again, penny-pinching resulted in the loss of many pounds. Such inspectors as were appointed generally had to undertake other responsibilities, either in the field or at headquarters. The testimony of various senior officials before the Financial and Departmental Commission in 1862 contains all the documentation necessary for the conclusion that central inspection as well as central accounting practices as then applied were entirely inadequate.[10]

The third prerequisite to successful decentralization is the conferring of sufficient authority and discretion on the local agent. If the local agent is to be an extension of the personality of headquarters, he must be given at least some of the discretion conferred on the central staff. Otherwise local agents will simply be a burden, contributing delay and confusion to the process of decision-making, and piling up correspondence at headquarters. This, in fact, was the major criticism of the investigating commission which examined the agency system in 1845. Its report cut through to the very heart of the universal administrative issue posed by decentralization:

> It will be seen . . . how limited their [local agents'] powers are, and in how trifling a degree they can, in reality, give information or assistance to parties applying for the purchase or grants of Public Lands . . . far from diminishing the labour and expense of the Chief Office, they have, to a

[9]The detailed measures are described by the permanent head of the Department appearing before the Financial and Departmental Commission in 1862. See *First Report* (Quebec, 1863), evidence, Qs. 416–17.

[10]*Ibid.*, evidence of William Ford, accountant of the Department; John Langton, Auditor of Public Accounts; Andrew Russell, Assistant Commissioner; John C. Tarbutt, Upper Canada Sales Branch.

great extent, increased both; and the large increase in the correspondence and other business of the Department further show that they have in no degree decreased its labours; it is evident indeed, that without powers equal to those of the Commissioner of Crown Lands himself, they cannot diminish the labour, because in every case where the mode of proceeding must necessarily differ from that laid down in their letter of general instructions, they are compelled to refer to the Chief Office; and it is sufficiently obvious that such a power can never be given to so great a number of small Agents.[11]

Part of the difficulty mentioned by the investigators could have been removed by keeping the local agencies properly informed of new policies and well supplied with detailed maps and records of surveys. Some of the headquarters staff were quite aware of this need, as when the Deputy Minister Andrew Russell differed with his political chief Joseph Cauchon on the subject of a large expensive map. Russell rightly claimed that a single map—however complete and detailed—would be of no immediate value to local agents. And yet, not until the report of the Department for the year 1863 does the Commissioner mention that survey notes were to be provided for the local agents, as well as good regional maps.[12]

In practice, the local agents, with or without the necessary information, tended to go beyond the powers conferred on them, mainly because headquarters' supervision was so inadequate. However, as has already been noted, one of the great problems confronting the Department was its inability to make final settlement of disputed claims. Certainly, decisions of the local agents did little to reduce the complaints, indeed their presence aggravated the situation. At any rate, this became the opinion at headquarters shortly before Confederation. Reporting on the operation of the fisheries overseers in 1864, the Commissioner of Crown Lands claimed that much unnecessary expense had arisen because of the discretion conferred on these local agents. "Waiting legislation," he reported, "these faults are partially remedied by concentrating in my Department authority for each outlay, and by denying every expense that does not appear to be indispensably necessary."[13] In the annual report for 1861, his predecessor had taken an even stronger centralizing stand. Commending the policy of auctioning public lands and the firmer, more arbitrary application

[11]"Report of Commissioners on Crown Land Department," *J.L.A.C.*, 1846.
[12]"Annual Report of the Commissioner of Crown Lands for the Year 1863," *Sessional Papers*, Canada, 1864, no. 5.
[13]*Ibid.*; William McDougall, the Commissioner, was most conscientious on behalf of the taxpayer.

of rules with no exceptions allowed, he then went on to explain why he had dispensed with a number of local agencies. Admitting that this had meant more work for headquarters he nevertheless believed "that the Government, as well as individuals having claims to land, will profit by the change. Brought into direct contact with the Department, they will feel the necessity for an immediate arrangement of some kind, and where they have had disputes with the local agents, their cases will, perhaps, for the first time, occupy the attention of the Commissioner."[14]

Thus at Confederation we find the Department moving gradually against the local agency system. Unable to dispense with it altogether, however, the Department was also evolving methods of bringing the situation under central control. The most effective solutions appeared to be enlargement of the regions, full-time travelling inspectors—especially for surveys—and a more rigorous accounting and auditing system, both in the field and at headquarters.

The Problem of Integrity

In Canada, the Crown Lands Department assumed the burden of administering an enormous store of potential wealth. The public domain, timber, mineral, and fisheries resources, not to mention one group of God's creatures—the Indians—were all placed at the Department's disposal. Here was the real capital of the colonies, locked up in Nature's warehouse to which officers of the Department alone held the keys. What wealthy prizes for the speculator who could cajole his way into the administrative sanctum and emerge with vast tracts of fertile land or monopolize a string of mining concessions or press for new arrangements with the Indian tribes which would open up new lands! What favours could be rendered by adjusting a survey line or overlooking a stiff regulation!

Only one other department could compare with the Department of Crown Lands in its power to dispose of so much, namely the Department of Public Works. But Public Works was a spending Department and the favours at its disposal were mainly in the form of the direct cash benefits which could be obtained by contractors and suppliers. Such benefits were received by capturing a portion of that great flood of public money that was being poured into the construction of public works. It was difficult to conceal this fact from the taxpayer. Not so with the Crown Lands Department. Concessions to

[14]*Sessional Papers*, Canada, 1862, no. 11; P. M. Vankoughnet, like McDougall, was clearly a strong-minded minister with a positive approach toward the reform of departmental practices.

speculators in lands, timber, mines, and fisheries could be made without any immediate impact on the general interest. As the Royal Commissioners pointed out in 1845, "Few or no complaints have been made regarding the expenditure in the management of the Public Lands, the burden falling on no one personally...."[15] As long as the revenues from the sale of land, timber, and other concessions could be used to defray the charges of management, few people really knew how much the administrative services were costing the country. Only after a significant portion of the public domain and its resources had been squandered or captured by speculators did it become generally apparent that Nature's purse was not bottomless.

Beginning with Lord Durham's scathing indictment of the lands management system and carrying on through to the remarkable testimony presented to the Financial and Departmental Commission in 1862, we find a trail of profusion, favouritism, political "deals," inaccurate surveys, tardy handling of legitimate claims, laxness in checking up on defaulters, and a steady deflection of revenues away from the public treasury. While the administration of Crown lands under the Family Compact had been severely criticized before the Union of 1841, twenty years later, under less aristocratic and presumably more responsible officials, the administrative situation had not greatly improved. Tristram Shandy's wise observations concerning man as a creature of habit seem to apply with peculiar relevance to administrative organs: "When they are once set a-going, whether right or wrong, 'tis not a halfpenny matter, away they go cluttering like hey-go mad, and by treading the same steps over and over again, they presently make a road of it, as plain and as smooth as a garden-walk, which, when they are once used to, the Devil himself sometimes shall not be able to drive them off it."

Commissioner Cauchon, shocked at the scene in his own offices in 1857, would have appended a hearty "Amen" to Tristam's homely philosophy. Here is his astonished report on the situation in the Lands Branch: "[The custom had been established] of allowing everyone who pleased to enter the office and communicate directly with anyone employed in it." This not only took up the time of the staff but, as Cauchon put it,

While these speculators were enjoying this undue advantage, the necessary communications of persons residing at a distance (who form the majority of those having business with this office) had to remain unanswered to the annoyance and injury of the parties. Also from the facilities afforded

---

[15]"Report of Commissioners on Crown Land Department," *J.L.A.C.*, 1846.

by indiscriminate access to them, important documents, such as field notes, were sometimes torn and parts of them taken away, evidently from interested motives.

The records of the office being thus accessible to them, such land speculators . . . were enabled to acquire the most valuable vacant lands.[16]

An earlier chapter has already referred to the implications of a land sales policy which involved instalment purchases. As Galt pointed out to a legislative committee in 1854: "Apart from the vast labor of collecting a series of small instalments, it is a very serious objection to the credit system that it places so large a number of the population in the position of debtors to the Government, thereby engendering a desire for relief by other means than payment. . . ."[17]

Nor was the situation in the Surveys Branch any better, partly because surveyors were appointed, as the Financial and Departmental Commission put it, "on the recommendation of members of Parliament without consulting the officers who are supposed to be responsible." Errors in surveys, as the Commission noted, were "more than a matter of inconvenience to the settlers and waste to the Province" for they led to endless wrangling: ". . . decisions passed in full view of the facts, and in accordance with the law as existing at the time, are reversed when the Commissioner chooses so to exercise the great discretionary power vested in him." The Commission concluded: "This want of finality is a fruitful source of intrigue, of bargaining, of injustice and corruption. It affords scope to the exercise of individual and political influence to which no Commissioner should be exposed: and further, in numberless cases the public interests have suffered."[18] While this final judgment of the Commission was intended to apply to all activities of the Department, it held with special force in the Surveys Branch.

The Woods and Forests Branch was open to similar pressures. "There is perhaps no other Department of Government," Commissioner Cauchon remarked of this branch, "through which such persevering efforts have been made to secure special advantage to particular interests."[19] In 1862, the Financial and Departmental Com-

---

[16] "Annual Report of the Commissioner of Crown Lands for the Year 1856," *J.L.A.C.*, 1857, last section of this long and able report.

[17] "Report of Committee on Land Management," *J.L.A.C.*, 1854–5, Galt's letter to the Committee.

[18] These strictures on the Department were expressed in the *First Report of the Financial and Departmental Commission*, pp. 19–22.

[19] "Annual Report for 1856," *J.L.A.C.*, 1857, section on Woods and Forests Branch.

mission put the following question to the Superintendent of the Woods and Forests Branch: "Are agents in the habit of consulting the convenience or wishes of lumberers, without specific authority from the Department?" He answered: "In some instances I have had occasion to observe the agents appear to consider themselves as acting in the interest of the lumberers as well as of the Department."[20]

That the temptations were great and the opportunities for succumbing to them were much too available is evidenced by the famous defalcation (over $130,000) of Thomas Baines, local land agent at Toronto.[21] Returns had been falsified by him since at least 1847 and yet when clear-cut evidence of his dishonesty was provided in 1852 by the Accountant of the Department this was the action taken:

> Baines was about that time written to, not once, but several times [so Mr. Ford, the Accountant, testified in 1862]. I think that he evaded enquiry by bringing counter claims for services and commission. Some of these claims were allowed; the greater part were not entertained. Nothing decisive was done by the Department until the Government removed to Toronto in 1855, when Mr. Baines was suspended under suspicion of being a defaulter. Having taken possession of his books and papers, we ascertained that he was in default, and that he had been so eight or ten years. . . . I am under the impression that in bringing actions against defaulting agents, prompt measures have not generally been adopted. The cause of the delay I am unable to explain.[22]

Even as late as 1862 the Deputy Minister was compelled to admit that the Department had "no means of checking the truthfulness of the agents' returns."[23] Constant defaults—on a much smaller scale than that of Thomas Baines—revealed that the local agents were unable to withstand the temptations so easily put in their way. The situation was similar throughout the local agencies connected with other branches of the Department.

This purely negative tale had some positive and more hopeful aspects. As the previous section has indicated, one of the obvious solutions was for the Department to evolve central financial and auditing controls which would make it dangerous to yield to temptation. By the 1860's such controls were clearly producing results; indeed, the number of defaulters turned up and the official indictment

[20]*First Report of the Financial and Departmental Commission*, evidence, Q. 686.
[21]See "A Return re Proceedings against Agent for Public Lands in Huron, etc. . . . ," *J.L.A.C.*, 1858, Appendix 22.
[22]*First Report of the Financial and Departmental Commission*, evidence, Q. 923.
[23]*Ibid.*, Q. 518; see also Q. 685.

of speculative pressure groups on the Department testify to the improvements made.

For the longer term, an equally important reform was slowly making its difficult way in certain branches of the Department. In the Surveys Branch and in the Supervisor of Cullers' Office attached to the Woods and Forests Branch efforts were early made to initiate professional standards. These efforts antedated the first Civil Service Act of 1857 by many years. This particular development has been noted in an earlier chapter and does not need to be repeated here.[24] Admittedly, the impact of political patronage coupled with the low standards of supervision tended to negate this movement of reform. But it was at least a slight glimmer on the distant horizon of the slowly maturing Canadian bureaucracy. The province, it ought to be emphasized, was, in this respect, not far behind the senior democracies of the United States and Britain at this time and it is important to maintain proper perspective in considering the subject of public (and even private) morality.

The Problem of Ministerial Co-ordination

In an earlier chapter the subject of unity and overhead direction of the public service was treated in a general way. The Crown Lands Department offers the most interesting case study of this problem at the departmental level, for in terms used by modern administrative analysts the department was of the "holding company" type.[25] That is, to employ the language of Thomas D'Arcy McGee in 1863, "by a natural attraction that which was in 1841, simply a public land office, . . . has become an aggregation of offices, perhaps the most extensive and important of any in our system."[26]

"An aggregation of offices" accurately described this loose confederacy of semi-sovereign administrative entities. The political head never really enjoyed complete control over the managers of his subordinate branches. The peculiar instability of colonial politics resulted in a wasteful turnover of Commissioners—seventeen in twenty-seven years. No political chieftain remained in office long enough to bring all the feudal barons of his administrative domain into proper attitudes

---

[24]*Supra*, chap IV.

[25]See, for example, S. C. Wallace, *Federal Departmentalization: A Critique of Theories of Organization* (New York, 1941), pp. 76 f.

[26]"Report on Public Departments," Public Archives of Canada, M. 837, 1863, section on "Crown Lands Department."

of obedience and subordination. Nor, until 1857, was the political head able to call upon a permanent deputy to assist him in his task of overhead co-ordination and control. Even after this official's position was established, the traditional isolationism of branch heads continued to assert itself.

The comments of various political heads provide ample evidence of the chaotic conditions at headquarters. Commissioner Cauchon had this to say of the situation in 1857:

This Department had not long been under my charge before it became apparent to me that, owing no doubt to the successive changes of Ministers holding the office of Commissioner of Crown Lands, and the circumstances of much of their attention being occupied by their Legislative and Executive duties, leaving little to devote to the internal organization and management of the Crown Lands Office, a degree of irregularity had arisen and practices had grown up which greatly impaired the efficiency of the Department.

The head of the Department embracing so many duties and comprising various branches, having previously a separate existence, with functions peculiar to each—on assuming charge of this office, is necessarily, to a certain degree, dependent on the leading subordinates of the office, so much so as, under the pressure of political duties, to render it much the easier course to make no important change in the existing routine of the Department.

The natural consequence of which is, that the authority of the head of the Department, does not practically bear, in a sufficient degree, on the government of the office under his charge; the direction of the business of it falls to the heads of branches, each of whom conducts the duties of his branch according to his own views, while their inferiors feeling the absence of general control, become indifferent and inattentive to their duties and irregular in their attendance. In this manner there arises not only a want of co-operation, common principle and systematic action, but sometimes even antagonism, and an undue share of labor falls to the diligent and zealous from the remissness of the indolent.

. . . The consequence was that when there was more such work to be done than the few individuals could perform, it accumulated. . . .

From the same cause also, and from the want of systematic control and direction it had become the practice for the heads of branches or leading subordinates to transact business with the public independently of the head of the Department and of each other, certain official documents being signed by them and issued without the cognizance of the Commissioner, clashing occasionally with each others duties and involving serious errors.[27]

This lengthy comment tells the whole story as far as the political head could read it. Needless to say Cauchon's ability to remedy the

[27]Annual report for 1856, *J.L.A.C.*, 1857, last section.

evils fell far short of his skill in assessing their true character. In 1866, for example, the last Commissioner to hold the position was still complaining "that the administration of the Department does not rest with a permanent officer and less with its political head."[28] He ruefully admitted "that the practical administration of the Department should [not] be subject to the vacillations and delays, and the lack of permanent policy and rules of decision, which the present system entails."

The reference to the lack of any effective permanent head of the Department at first glance appears to be at odds with the actual appointment of a permanent deputy in 1857. But the testimony of the Deputy presented to the Financial and Departmental Commission in 1862 reveals how constricted were his powers over the whole Department.

Question 405. The Civil Service Act . . . assigning to each Department a Deputy Head, prescribes that he "shall have the oversight of the other officers, clerks, and messengers or servants, and the general control of the business of the Department"; did you exercise this general control . . .?

The oversight I exercise consists in my seeing that the officers and clerks attend to their duties. For this purpose I visit their rooms between 9 and 10 o'clock in the morning, and occasionally (when my other duties permit) during the day. I exercise the general control of the business of the Department, with the exception of that part which the Commissioner reserves to himself.

406. Are we to understand that you have been relieved from some portion of the oversight prescribed by the Civil Service Act, and that a portion of the prescribed general control has been withdrawn from you?

I have not been relieved from any portion of the oversight of the other officers, clerks, and messengers or servants. If "general control" means the decision of important cases, involving the general policy of the Government, that was never conferred upon me. No power or duty I ever exercised has been withdrawn.

407. Do you consider that the settlement of ordinary land claims involves the general policy of the Government?

Certain classes of land claims do involve the policy of the Government. Ordinary claims do not.

408. Special or peculiar claims being referred to the Commissioner, are ordinary claims referred to or decided by you?

Yes, excepting those in the Counties of Bruce, Huron, Grey, Perth, and Wellington, which were never under my control.

409. Do not the five counties named contribute the great bulk of the claims? Yes, the greater part. I have no idea of the exact proportion.[29]

[28]See *ibid.*, for the year 1865, *Sessional Papers*, Canada, 1866, no. 3.
[29]*First Report of Financial and Departmental Commission*, evidence, Qs. 406–9.

This exchange suggests the lowly conception of his office entertained by the first permanent Deputy Minister. With this attitude one could not expect the permanent head to become the administrative focal point or the chief co-ordinator; he was apparently little more than a glorified office manager at headquarters.

Flabby control at the top was enhanced by the attitude of independence adopted by the heads of the separate branches. Some of these, like Surveys, Ordnance Lands, Geological Survey, and Indian Affairs, had all been adjuncts of some Imperial government department at Whitehall. Each entered the Crown Lands Department an unwilling captive of the departmental system, determined to retain old traditions and with an inflated view of its own peculiar importance to the public service of the province. For example, when the Ordnance Lands passed out of the Imperial government's hands in 1856, the officer in charge, Colonel Coffin, between the years 1856–60, reported directly to the Governor General. When he was at last caught in the drag-net of the Crown Lands Department, he continued to make separate reports in which he was always careful to point out that his peculiar status in the hierarchy distinguished him from the ordinary land agents.[30]

This independent attitude was not merely found in the old agencies which had lived a separate administrative life outside the Department; it was also highly developed in the new "Canadian" branches of the Department. The Fisheries Branch provided an excellent example, for the struggle for independence was fought not only between its head and the rest of the Department but between various rugged individualists within the Branch. Mr. Whitcher, second class clerk in charge of the Branch at headquarters, did his best, before a parliamentary committee in 1864, to stress his sovereign control.[31] "The Fisheries business has been *ab initio* almost organized . . . through my office and out-door labours, and its administration has been put into official shape and practical operations under my hands. . . ." But this was only one man's opinion and rather difficult to stomach for men like Captain Pierre Fortin who had inaugurated the regulatory system in 1852. Adopting the superior air justified by his pioneer experience Fortin testified that he could easily have handled the whole branch without the help of a clerk like Whitcher whose closest contact with

[30]See "Annual Report of Commissioner of Crown Lands for the Year 1862," *Sessional Papers*, Canada, 1863 no. 5, Appendix 38(a).
[31]See "Report of the Select Committee on the Working of the Fishery Act," *J.L.A.C.*, 1864, Appendix 5, evidence of W. F. Whitcher.

fisheries had been as an amateur fly-fisherman.[32] Richard Nettle, Superintendent of Fisheries for Lower Canada, also had his innings, expressing his distrust of the efforts to harness the overseers to an inexperienced headquarters staff.[33] This group of prima donnas could get along without directors and supporting cast to share the spotlight.

Perhaps the most astonishing display of forthright independence came from the veteran official William Spragge. He had entered the Surveys Branch in 1829 and its amalgamation with the Crown Lands Department in 1845 rankled deeply. Testifying before a royal commission in 1846 he bluntly disagreed with the views already expressed by his departmental overlords on the subject of employing local agents.[34] He also inserted a gratuitous criticism of the policies inaugurated by his former Commissioner which, according to him, had incorrectly emphasized the revenue aspects of land sales, thus overlooking the settlers' interests. Ten years later, Spragge testified even more boldly against the redoubtable Joseph Cauchon.[35] On this occasion his strong Upper Canadian prejudices were brought to the boil by what he felt to be the excessive costs of managing the public lands in Lower Canada. Since he was in charge of the parallel branch in Upper Canada, even Spragge realized that the subject was a bit touchy. "I feel," he commented sententiously, "that I should not be justified were I to allow myself to be withheld by departmental etiquette from giving expression to views and opinions which may have some effect in arousing to energetic action some of those who are deeply interested in the welfare and progress of Lower Canada. . . ." Then followed his biting criticism. But even this did not exhaust Spragge's critical faculties. He could not resist the following jibe at his political chief, Cauchon: "Political changes," he said, "entail changes of the head of the Department. . . . Political heads of Departments must hold their political levees, and the opportunities for becoming acquainted with details of business, and with the system of management . . . in such a department as that of the Public Lands [are] exceedingly limited even when decided business ability is brought to the task; and as to the political heads of the Department supervising its working, it is simply an impossibility. . . ." It was quite

[32]*Ibid.*, evidence of Pierre Fortin.
[33]*Ibid.*, evidence of Richard Nettle.
[34]"Report of Commissioners on Crown Land Department," *J.L.A.C.*, evidence of William Spragge. Saint Peter is reported to have publicly denied his Lord thrice; Spragge just as openly defied his political chieftains at least twice.
[35]"Report of Committee on Land Management," *J.L.A.C.*, 1854–5, evidence and supplementary memorandum of Spragge.

proper, of course, for Cauchon to reach almost the same conclusions himself in his report for 1856 (quoted above) but when it came from one of his subordinates a strong defence was required. Appended to the main report of the Committee of 1854-5 is Cauchon's rebuttal, couched in violent language.[36] But Spragge, persistent and undaunted, is permitted to incorporate a rebuttal of his own. Strange as this episode sounds today, perhaps the strangest part is that neither the official investigators nor Cauchon—not to mention Spragge himself—seemed to think of questioning the propriety of a permanent official disagreeing publicly in such violent terms with his political chief. The change in departmental etiquette that occurred after Confederation can be illustrated by a comment drawn from the report of the Royal Commission on the Civil Service in 1881: "In presenting the evidence . . . some of the Deputy Heads and Chief Officers exercised a degree of reticence in their answers, which however natural in view of the relation they bear to the Ministers on one hand and their Clerks on the other, rendered their statements somewhat imperfect. . . ."[37]

The story of Mr. Spragge may be concluded by noting that he was made the first Canadian Deputy Superintendent General of Indian Affairs in 1862, ostensibly under the Commissioner of Crown Lands. The degree of co-ordination accompanying this move may be readily surmised from what has already been said about Spragge's earlier record.

A Commentary

The previous analysis of the special administrative problems confronting the Crown Lands Department suggests that it would be a good testing ground for the hypothesis that major policy decisions are really made by the permanent officials and that the political head is a mere façade for their underhand exercise of effective power. Looking back on the record of the Department we certainly find ideal conditions for promoting "rule by the bureaucracy": amateur political heads, chosen for their "connexions"—their ability to attract support to a shaky ministry—for their forensic skill, or because they represented a certain section of the country;[38] politicians who, even if they had ability, seldom held office long enough to grasp the complexities of this sprawling department. Then there is the long history of separately

[36]*Ibid.*, Cauchon's special memorandum in answer to Spragge.
[37]See "First Report of the Civil Service Commission," *Sessional Papers*, Canada, 1881, no. 113, p. 15.
[38]Sir Francis Hincks in his *Reminiscences* (Montreal, 1884) gives an excellent inside view of the process of cabinet-making, pp. 255 f.

developing administrative agencies reluctantly succumbing to the indiscriminate embrace of this catch-all Department. Next, as we have seen, there is the collection of isolationist permanent administrators, sometimes openly revolting against their political head. Finally, we find the government itself groping in the unknown for policies which will adequately safeguard the public interest, realizing all too well that powerful antagonistic pressures will be roused by any successful regulatory programme. Surely all the circumstances point to rule by the permanent experts—a cry which is common enough today but was not so common a century ago. Indeed, it was in the earlier *laissez-faire* climate that Britain evolved the concept of the neutral public officer—a sort of administrative eunuch. Yet civil servants have always influenced policy-makers and the contemporary outcry is louder only because the sphere of state action has enlarged opportunities for the permanent expert to formulate policy and press it on his political masters.

While it is true, then, that conditions within and around the Department of Crown Lands seemed to favour the ascendency of the permanent bureaucrats, the available evidence does not altogether support this hypothesis. The nucleus of the Department—the Lands Branch—for all the independent attitudes assumed by its officers, exerted little influence on wider policy decisions. From what has already been said in the previous chapter, it is clear that, had the permanent officials been influential, the settler's interest rather than revenue would have predominated as the major objective of the Branch. The determination to apply certain of the revenues derived from the sale of lands to specific purposes really established the frame of reference within which the permanent staff operated; such decisions were taken in the political arena. The numerous regulations designed to implement land management policies also appear to have been the work of legislative committees, royal commissions, or even individual Commissioners of Crown Lands. The bureaucrat acquired effective power because overhead direction was weak and he was often left in isolation to exercise his own discretion in the application of the rules. In practice, of course, this made the local agent a real power in the community.

However, it is the Fisheries Branch which undoubtedly provides the clearest illustration of the permanent official's contribution to policy-making. As one reads the record of crass spoliation of our great fisheries resources, it is with relief and much sympathy that one turns to those few civil servants who devoted themselves to blocking the pressure of the greedy or thoughtless. There are times, it would appear, when the Canadian public needs to be told where its true interest lies. To be sure, we hear much today on this point: the state —or more precisely, its servants—order us about too much. But when the expert can see what the general public cannot or is unwilling to see, when he can prove that the public is being robbed of its patrimony, should he stand by or should he attempt to awaken the public to its danger? The situation confronting the new Fisheries Branch after 1857 raised this question in an acute form: the public— primarily "land-lubbers"—were apathetic or ignorant and the fishermen, especially those drawn to the fisheries from foreign shores, were lawless and vigorous; facing this ignorance, apathy, and vested interest were a few permanent officials with a strong personal conviction and a professional pride in seeing that something was done to regulate the fisheries.

Whatever one's views may be on the subject of "bureaucratic dictation," a reading of the evidence here suggests that successful regulation and conservation of the Gulf and inland fisheries of the Canadas was founded on the work of two or three bureaucrats, assisted by two cabinet ministers who sponsored their experts' draft legislation through Parliament. Richard Nettle must take first place in this record, for not only did he draft the basic fishery Acts of 1857 and 1858, but he was probably the first person in Canada to propagate fish successfully under artificial conditions.[39] A room adjoining his office in the Crown Lands Department was Canada's first fish hatchery. His writings—especially a book on the salmon fisheries of the St. Lawrence published in 1857 and dedicated to Sir Edmund Head, himself an ardent fisherman—influenced many citizens. In 1859, Nettle recommended cancelling the monopoly of the Hudson's Bay Company over the fishing streams traversing that large tract on the north shore of the St. Lawrence known as the King's Post. Five hundred miles of coast, hitherto locked against proper development, was thereby opened up and Nettle's scheme of publicly auctioned fishing leases introduced.

Among the other permanent officials of the Branch who had a marked influence on policy was Captain (or Doctor) Pierre Fortin whose name and deeds have already received mention. His reports on the potential value of the Gulf fisheries were an eye-opener to the land-conscious Upper Canadians. His searching, inquisitive mind

[39]See the interesting account in E. T. D. Chambers, *The Fisheries of the Province of Quebec* (Quebec, 1912), pp. 166 f. Dr. Theodotus Garlick is described as "the first successful hatcher of fish fry in the United States," his experiments having been attempted four years before Nettle's.

turned up a vast array of problems requiring treatment and many of his recommendations he had the pleasure of administering himself as they appeared in departmental regulations.

Credit for early fishing legislation must also be conferred on two successive Commissioners of Crown Lands, Joseph Cauchon and J. V. Sicotte. They apparently recognized the need for regulation and assumed the political burden of pushing it through the sessions of 1857 and 1858. During the session of 1857, petitions from various parts of the province helped to reinforce Cauchon's arguments in support of the new Fisheries Act. But certainly the pioneer conservation and protection policies enshrined in this legislation would never have reached the draft stage without the persistent, knowledgeable agitation of men like Nettle and Fortin. In passing, it may be noted that a generation or so later the Department of Fisheries and the public as a whole once more fell back on the resources of the expert. Long after Confederation, Dr. Tupper, then Minister of Fisheries, brought over from Scotland a quiet-spoken professor, A. E. Prince.[40] His scientific reports on varied aspects of the fisheries—notably on oyster culture—led inescapably to policy decisions modelled after his recommendations.

It is clear that the early regulatory programme adopted by the Fisheries Branch owed much to the influence of the permanent experts. But to call this bureaucratic dictation would be to misconstrue the process of policy-making. For permanent officials, the task of recommending decisions of a policy nature must ever be a lesson based on the ancient cautionary adage "know thy place." In the final analysis the decision can only be taken by the political head and the influence of the permanent official is only one of the precipitating factors. However, if there is a situation where public opinion is weak or silent—as appears to have been the case in the area of fisheries regulation—the views of the permanent experts will undoubtedly carry much weight with the Minister. Our protection against bureaucratic dictation in such instances arises from the inability of the permanent officials to conduct an open debate against those who oppose their policies. If they cannot persuade their political chief of the value of the policy they cannot stage on their own a campaign for its adoption. Nor is any political head likely to be willing to risk his political fortunes merely to satisfy the strong convictions of permanent advisers.

[40]See "Report of the Minister of Marine and Fisheries for the Year 1892," *Sessional Papers*, Canada, 1893, no. 10, p. vi.

Approval of the basic fisheries legislation of 1857 and 1858 seems to have been one instance where the political heads (Cauchon and Sicotte) were completely convinced by the case for a regulatory programme submitted by their permanent advisers. Since there was no large body of opinion urging them forward, the Ministers might well have taken the view that their advisers could safely be disregarded. It is an indication of their statesmanship that, having no short-run political dividends to earn from sponsoring these measures, they nevertheless took up the cause which their permanent officials had so insistently urged upon them.

Today, the permanent official—with few exceptions—must leave to his political head the task of pushing "his" proposals. Presumably his function ends when he has convinced his political chief. Perhaps the major difference dividing contemporary administration from that of the pre-Confederation period is that the state has now moved into many activities where policy lies beyond the public's direct interest or comprehension. Indeed, policy-making lies beyond the capacity of isolated experts. Accordingly, teams of permanent officials—often without waiting for public opinion of any sort, perhaps in defiance of the limited opinion already present—proceed within the administrative branch itself to formulate policies. The whole field of taxation would be a fair contemporary example of this situation. The outcry against "bureaucracy" heard today comes, however, not because of this situation—most thinking people agree it is an indispensable part of modern state operations. The complaint really arises because Parliament's capacity to pass judgment on these decisions as presented by a well-briefed Minister is now much in question. It may be added, also, that members of the higher civil service themselves tend to let their minds move in the same channels as their political chiefs. It is true that the permanent official is no help to his chief if he persists in presenting him with proposals which are obviously politically impracticable. On the other hand, the permanent official should not attempt to do the political thinking for his chief. It is not wasting his chief's time to confront him with the known alternative and then leave the politician to assess the "politics" of the issue. This matter, however, raises general problems which already have produced a lengthy digression from the main narrative. The digression is defensible in so far as it suggests that even in the pre-Confederation bureaucracy problems were being raised which are still very much with us.

CHAPTER XI

PUBLIC WORKS: DEPARTMENT OF TRANSPORT AND HOUSEKEEPER EXTRAORDINARY

AFTER THE UNION of the two provinces the bizarre figure of Hamilton Killaly became a familiar sight to the citizens of Kingston. This burly, jovial Irishman often strolled the streets attired in tight satin breeches and patent leather dancing pumps, his upper man bearing a gaudy outdoors shirt bared at the throat, exposing a hairy chest, the ensemble topped by a hat so dilapidated that it looked, as one chronicler described it, as if he had tumbled into the mud of a nearby ditch returning from an Irish fair.[1] This was the man whom Sydenham had selected in 1840 to serve as the head of his newly created Board of Works.[2] His association with Public Works continued, with a few brief interruptions, until Confederation.

The new agency over which Killaly was to preside—first as political head and later as permanent head—was Sydenham's most prized project. The Union of 1841, like the larger union of 1867, was cemented by an Imperial loan. The proceeds were destined to be spent mainly on public works. Consequently, the new Board was a necessary administrative adjunct to the loan. Sydenham was jubilant after successfully piloting the measure through the local legislature but his triumph was short-lived. The operations of the Board soon proved that there were serious defects in its organization. Within five years, as will be seen, the "extensive powers" delegated to his Board were severely trimmed and its whole mode of operation substantially modified.

[1]A remarkable portrait of Killaly is painted by the Reverend Agar Adamson, Lord Sydenham's chaplain, who shared with the Commissioner and a later Governor General (Head) an ardent love of fishing. See *Salmon-Fishing in Canada*, by a Resident, edited by Colonel J. E. Alexander (London, 1860), pp. 152–3.

[2]See letter to Colonial Secretary Lord Stanley from Sir Charles Bagot, April 28, 1842, contained in Private Letter Book of Sir Charles Bagot, Public Archives of Canada. Also letter of John Langton to his brother where he describes Killaly as "a jolly fellow brought out by Lord Sydenham and about as double dealing and corrupt a scoundrel as you will meet anywhere" (letter dated Nov. 9, 1856).

W. A. Langton in his *Early Days in Upper Canada* (Toronto, 1926), p. 270, exercises an editor's careful pen in suppressing the last revealing phrase from the original letter.

A more appropriate title for the Board of Works (or Department of Public Works as it became in 1846)[3] would have been Department of Transport, for the main function of the agency was to superintend the construction and maintenance of a vast canal project. In this respect it differed from its post-Confederation namesake whose duties were (and have remained) largely of a housekeeping nature, i.e., the provision of buildings and services for the other government departments. Prior to Confederation the Works Department was also made responsible for these housekeeping activities but they were definitely a side-line when compared to the concern over transportation problems. On the other hand, the government's housekeeper had to contend with a domestic situation which has never bothered its modern counterpart: rotation of the seat of government—as we have seen—involved the Department in perpetual negotiations for accommodation and confronted it every four years with the enormous task of transferring the staff at headquarters up or down the St. Lawrence.

Building and repairing the aquatic life-line of the Canadas constituted the greatest challenge to the Department and to Killaly, the Keefer brothers, Benjamin Gzowski, Merritt, and a few other devoted public officers. Nature is deceptive, and nowhere has this been more apparent than in the optimism with which Canadians have looked on the St. Lawrence waterway. It was obvious to the colonists that Nature had intended man to use the great stretch of water highway extending 2,400 miles from the Strait of Belle Isle half way into the continent to the head of Lake Superior. Politicians of the day never failed to burst into florid poetic passages in dealing with this great natural asset which was so obviously placed there to serve as the central ganglia of the whole communications system. And yet Nature, when one faced the situation dispassionately, had not been so generous after all. Canadians were either mesmerized by the geographic simplifications produced by maps or else they were excessively optimistic. That wonderful stretch of 2,400 watery miles was not continuous according to Nature's plan and the Department of Public Works would have been the first to throw this fantasy back in the teeth of the unthinking patriots. Nature was a demanding wench as the Department of Works learned to its sorrow and at the expense of the colonists. This "natural" life-line, it soon discovered, contained the following obstacles: (1) Lake Superior is over 600 feet above high tide in the St. Lawrence at Three Rivers; (2) between

[3] 9 Vic., c. 37 (1846).

Montreal and Duluth there are six major natural blockades—at Lachine, Beauharnois, Cornwall, Williamsburg, Niagara, and Sault Ste Marie. In order to overcome these manifestations of Nature's malevolence, man had to construct 73 miles of "artificial navigation," requiring 56 locks and constant dredging operations to deepen other stretches of the route.

In 1840, however, Sydenham's Board of Works contemplated the following situation. At Lachine, the first canal link with the sea, only a vessel drawing 4½ feet could proceed (14 feet is the present depth); the Beauharnois Canal connecting Lake St. Louis and Lake St. Francis was an ancient out-moded structure built between 1779 and 1783 by British engineers; the Cornwall Canal circumventing the tumultuous white water of the Long Saulte was not completed and the bateau or even the Durham boat piloted by the picturesque French-Canadian boatmen still monopolized this section of the route; a further stretch of 26 miles of narrow, treacherous water giving access to Lake Ontario still awaited the construction of three canals. Beyond Lake Ontario the flank of the Niagara escarpment had been turned by the twenty-seven primitive locks of the first Welland Canal. During the lifetime of the Department of Public Works this Canal was the pivotal point in the whole system, the source of most of the revenue obtained from canal tolls but also the most costly of all the projects of the Department. The last important link in the chain of inland waterways, the St. Mary Canal connecting Lakes Huron and Superior, had been destroyed in the war of 1812 and was not reopened on the Canadian side until 1895.[4]

The Canadians were justifiably jubilant when, in 1847, the whole canal route was opened to uninterrupted navigation by vessels drawing up to 9 feet of water. But opening the system, as will be shown, was merely the beginning of a long-drawn-out struggle for survival in which the Department of Works strove valiantly to protect its vested interest and the province's vast capital outlay in the canals.

While the St. Lawrence was the central artery of water communication, four other canal systems also came under the jurisdiction of Public Works. Only two of these, the routes connecting Ottawa with Montreal and New York with Montreal, could lay claim to commercial importance. The Ottawa-Montreal route depended upon the Lachine Canal, St. Anne Lock, and the Carillon and Grenville canals. British engineers had constructed these canals between 1825

[4]Material on the canals has been obtained from annual reports of Commissioners of Public Works and articles in the *Encyclopedia of Canada*, ed. by W. S. Wallace (Toronto, 1935).

and 1833, and the St. Anne Lock was built by the new Board of Works between 1840 and 1843. The Montreal–New York route commenced at Sorel where the St. Ours Lock connected Sorel with Chambly. The twelve-mile Chambly Canal with its nine locks carried the route as far as St. John's at the head of Lake Champlain. From there, Public Works passed on the torch to the United States to see that the waterway was taken as far as New York. In 1840, the Board of Works found the canals in this system had been started but the St. Ours Lock had to be constructed. By 1858 small vessels with a 6½ foot draft were able to traverse the 457 miles of waterway to New York.

The other two canal systems, the Rideau and the Trent, were commercially less important. The Rideau system which weaves its way up and down 47 locks between Ottawa and Kingston had been built as a military project by the British government between 1826 and 1832. Although the Rideau system theoretically provided an alternative route between Montreal and Kingston, its existence was dictated by military considerations. Consequently, when the Imperial Ordnance pulled out of Canada in 1856 this expensive white elephant was bestowed on the Department. The Trent Canal system was expected to connect Georgian Bay and Lake Ontario, thereby cutting off the longer journey via Lake Erie. The project was never completed, although it was pushed sporadically by business interests from Canada West and some of the mid-western states. Today the Trent Canal system is known mainly to tourists interested in a scenic cruise and it has also been developed as a source of electric power. Before Confederation it saw considerable traffic in timber passing down into Lake Ontario. Several local canals which were not part of any major communication system were also supervised by Public Works after Union. But as municipal authorities grew stronger these works were turned over to them by the Department.

Canal building activities of the Department had to be supplemented by provision of navigational aids along the vast stretch of inland waterways. Construction and servicing of lighthouses, beacons, and buoys were soon added to the Department's responsibilities. Scattered appropriations going back to 1809 had produced the first lighthouses, mainly in the Gulf. After Union the stretch of water between Kingston and Montreal received the most attention from the Department and by the late 1840's a regular lighthouse service had been established for the Upper Lakes.[5] Below Montreal, the long

---

[5]See "Annual Report of Commissioner of Public Works for the Year 1847," *Journals*, Legislative Assembly, Canada (*J.L.A.C.*), 1848, Appendix N.; *ibid.*, 1849, Appendix B.B.; *ibid.*, 1850, Appendix H.H.

reach of the St. Lawrence was serviced, following an ancient British pattern, by two semi-private agencies, the Trinity Boards of Quebec and Montreal, which were expected to provide all the necessary navigational aids for their respective stretches of the river from tonnage dues. This revenue was far from adequate, and the inability of the Trinity Boards to provide all the necessary navigational aids was emphasized by increased traffic in the fifties. In 1853 the first contract providing for regular steamship connection between Liverpool and Quebec–Montreal was signed and in 1858 regular steamers also began to ply the route between the Maritimes and these two great river ports. Nevertheless, at Confederation a curious mixture of public and private enterprise still supplied and maintained the lighthouses, beacons, and buoys from Montreal to the Gulf. The Montreal Trinity House had charge of the river between Montreal and Quebec, furnishing all supplies, carrying out repairs, and appointing the keepers. The Department here merely acted as the construction agency for the Board. The Quebec Trinity House had lesser powers in the Gulf, where the Department controlled all construction, provided its own steamer service, and appointed all the keepers, who, however, were paid by the Board.[6]

A final subordinate aspect of the Department's responsibilities for maintaining the inland waterways was its supervision of nine harbours. By 1851, only two of these, at Port Stanley and Burlington Bay, remained in the Department's hands, the rest having been sold to local authorities. The up-and-down history of these harbours was paralleled by the similar precarious position of a number of local roads. In both cases the Department obviously tried to free itself of the incubus of what were considered local works. But frequent default on payments and failure to maintain the works in a decent state of repair forced the Department, from time to time, to resume control over them.

The Department's responsibilities for land communication were not nearly so important as those relating to water communication. Lord Sydenham's basic statute had handed over to the original Board of Works all "provincial roads," but, unfortunately, had failed to define these roads.[7] The important amending Act of 1846 clarified the situation by listing seven roads, title to which was now vested in

[6]A concise review of the Department's jurisdiction in this area is provided in the "Annual Report of the Department of Marine and Fisheries," Canada, *Sessional Papers*, 1869, no. 12, pp. 2 f.

[7]For criticisms of this omission see "Report of Board of Works," *J.L.A.C.*, 1844–5, Appendix A.A.

the Crown, with the new Department of Public Works given jurisdiction.[8] Most of these were toll roads and the Department farmed out the task of collecting tolls to private contractors. At the time of Union, District Councils in Upper Canada had been given charge of road building, while in Lower Canada before the Board of Works was appointed in 1839, a grand voyer with several deputies, all appointed by the province, superintended what little local road building there was. Accordingly, the new Department made constant efforts to sell back to local authorities or private toll companies, roads which it could declare "productive." Although the annual report of the Department for 1853 announced with relief that all these roads had been sold, they kept coming back on the hands of the Department.

The Hamilton–Port Dover Road and the Toronto Roads, two of the most important "productive" roads, typified the problems facing the Department in its efforts to shift the responsibility to private or local interests. The first, completed by the Department about 1846, was sold to a private company in 1850, but by 1863 the government had to resume control and bring it back to usable condition. It was then sold to another private company on the understanding that repairs would be kept up. The Toronto Roads went through precisely the same changes in ownership, eventually being sold to the Counties of York and Peel in 1865.[9] In Lower Canada, the absence of sound local government left the Department no choice but to continue its control over the main roads it had constructed—particularly the Metapedia and Temiscouata Roads which were designed to connect the lower province with New Brunswick. Apart from the road building activities of the Department of Public Works, two private turnpike companies —at Montreal and Quebec—undertook responsibility for road upkeep in their respective sections. In addition, as was noted in an earlier chapter, some road building was being undertaken in frontier areas by the Colonization Roads Branch of the Crown Lands Department. Public Works apparently had no connection with this programme, although the main artery of the scheme in Lower Canada—the Taché Road—was constructed by the Department.

While dealing with land transportation it is interesting to observe how little railway affairs figured in the operations of the Department. In 1815, it is true, a Board of Railway Examiners was formed,

[8] 9 Vic., c. 37 (1846), Schedule A.
[9] See "Annual Report of the Commissioner of Public Works for the Year Ending June 30, 1865," *Sessional Papers*, Canada, 1866, no. 1, where the financial history of the various roads is related.

to which both the Commissioner and Assistant Commissioner of Public Works were appointed. The operations of this Board were tied up with the intricate arrangements for financing railways in which the government gradually became enmeshed during the 1850's.[10] The Department itself, however, had no share in this advisory work, although several of its best engineers, lured by the glitter of steel rails, turned their backs on the great canals which had first commanded their talents. Perhaps the official reports of the Department remain oblivious to the railways because of the vested interest in the competitive system of canals. In any event, the first piece of general legislation touching on the subject of railways appeared in 1849, following closely upon the formal opening of the canal system over its whole length.[11] The energies, interest, and capital of the province were now to be turned in a new direction and yet the Department of Works knew full well that too much had already been committed to the canal system over which it presided to permit any talk of its abandonment.

Thus far the record of the Department's activities has been that of an agency interested only in transportation. Its other main responsibilities have been previously classified as servicing or housekeeping duties. In the pre-Confederation period they were of secondary concern to the Department when compared with its responsibilities for providing transportation facilities. One of the most important of its special services was the construction and maintenance of timber slides for the Woods and Forests Branch of the Crown Lands Department.[12] Just before Confederation, an estimate of the totals spent on various works showed that over one million dollars had been allocated to building works for the timber trade as compared with less than half a million spent on road construction. Indeed, during the height of the trade in square timber the demand for timber slides was equivalent

[10]The *Second Report of the Financial and Departmental Commission,* February 1864 (Quebec, 1864) contains in the evidence a wealth of material on this politically charged subject.

[11]12 Vic., c. 29 (1849), provided provincial guarantees for the bonds of railway companies and assistance to the Halifax and Quebec Railway.

[12]Timber slides were, apparently, first introduced into Canada in 1829, by a Mr. Ruggles Wright who borrowed the idea from Sweden and Norway. Consisting of a long inclined plane on one side of the falls or rapids in a river, these slides permitted whole cribs of logs—first detached from the original rafts—to be floated intact down the rivers. The growing population and prosperity of Bytown (Ottawa) was partly based on the congregation of rivermen around the first government slide on the Ottawa which had been built to circumvent the picturesque Chaudière. See, for a colourful account, Lucien Brault, *Ottawa Old and New* (Ottawa, 1946), pp. 182 f.

to the demand, fifty years later, for branch railway lines. It appears to have been equally difficult to resist. The major works thus serviced by the Department were located on the Ottawa, Saguenay, and St. Maurice Rivers, as well as the Trent River system. At Confederation they were retained by the new central government.

The basic servicing operations of the Department were related to its role as governmental housekeeper and real estate agent. Provision of office accommodation as has already been noted was an unenviable task so long as the seat of government kept shifting. It is not altogether clear, however, why the Department was forced to assume this unpleasant task. Perhaps the quadrennial movement up and down the St. Lawrence helped to give the rest of the civil service an opportunity to see how well the Department was performing its duties as canal builder! Presumably its housekeeping role was derived from the power, conferred by the amending Act of 1846, to manage any works undertaken at public expense for which no other provision had been made.[13] In any event, as early as 1847, the Department was undertaking the construction and repair of jails and court houses in Lower Canada, a task which received legislative sanction ten years later[14] and remained with the Department until Confederation. Construction of customs houses and post offices in the larger centres became a growing concern of the Department as these facilities were expanded in the 1850's. The upkeep and repair of the Marine Hospital at Quebec and of the Quarantine Station on Grosse Isle were also charges upon the Department. The real housing problems however were connected with the provision of parliament buildings, official residences for the Governor General, and office accommodation for the civil service. At Confederation the Department owned buildings suitable for parliamentary gatherings in Ottawa, Quebec, and Toronto, while the viceregal needs could be met either at Ottawa, Quebec, Toronto, or Montreal. The task of supervising the construction of a large project such as the new parliament and departmental buildings at Ottawa over-taxed the administrative resources of the Department. The following chapter presents this particular episode in the life of the Department as a startling illustration of certain basic administrative weaknesses which seemingly defied all the efforts made to remove them.

At the close of the period, Public Works still impressively combined

[13] 9 Vic., c. 37: a general clause attached to Schedule A which listed the specific works vested in the Crown and placed under the jurisdiction of the Department.
[14] 20 Vic., c. 44, s. 109 (1857); the Judicature Act.

the labours of a Department of Transport with those of a central housekeeping agency. It was responsible for the construction and upkeep of three major canal systems which had cost the province about $12 million; nearly 120 lighthouses came under its management; four steamers were operated in the St. Lawrence and the Gulf, supplying the lights, repairings buoys and carrying mail. It was still the reluctant owner of several roads and bridges valued at half a million dollars. Certain harbours and piers were also in its hands. On the Saguenay, St. Maurice, Ottawa, and Trent river systems nearly eighty stations equipped with slides and booms for the timber trade stood as memorials to the construction work of the Department. Finally, spread out across the Canadas were customs houses, post offices, county court houses, jails, all testifying to the servicing operations of Public Works. Under more immediate control were other public buildings such as the various vice-regal residences and the parliamentary and public buildings located in those cities which had once served as the seat of government.[15]

After Confederation, the federal Department of Public Works inherited only the housekeeping responsibilities of its namesake. A new Department of Railways and Canals soon took over the main transportation duties of the Department. Harbours, piers, lighthouses, beacons, and buoys, although still constructed by Public Works, were placed under a new Department of Marine and Fisheries. Slides and booms were still serviced by the Department, but their importance declined with the falling off in the timber trade. Stripped down to the basic task of housing and furnishing other departments, the post-Confederation Department faced a restricted future in which it confronted the antagonism and impatience of the departments it was supposed to service. This is the fate of other such central servicing agencies as the Civil Service Commission and Public Printing and Stationery. If they perform their functions well, departments criticize them for their overbearing interference or finicky attention to "the rules." Centralizing responsibility for meeting the housekeeping needs of the departments appears, inevitably, to open the door to circumlocution. While the pre-Confederation Department of Public Works faced its fair share of antagonism, it was not until it was confined strictly to these servicing operations after Confederation that friction with other departments became serious.

[15]See the "Report of the Commissioner of Public Works for the Year 1866," *Sessional Papers*, Canada, 1867–8, no. 8.

The Canals: Policy or Predicament?

The activities of the Department of Public Works tangled it in politics of the loaves and fishes variety rather than in larger issues of policy. However, in relation to the great canal building projects a policy issue of real substance was involved. Urged on by a determined optimism, the Department became deeply mired in a programme which rapidly deteriorated into a predicament. Either the government must write off the vast capital outlay on the canals as a dead loss or else it must continue spending money on improvements which the experts always hoped would turn the tide. The Department constantly faced a situation where too much money had to be spent too late on a system of transportation that was plagued by more successful rival canals and outmoded almost from the start by rail transport. Finally, the canals were particularly vulnerable to economic forces. Shifts in trade and tariff policies of the Imperial government or the United States had a direct impact on traffic. Similarly, depressions brought on by external forces could produce a drastic decline in traffic and tolls.[16] Internally, the reduction in revenue encouraged economizers to postpone improvements which might have helped the canals attract more traffic away from their competitors.

On the eve of the completion of the system, the Commissioner of Public Works sounded what was to become the familiar note of mingled pride and anxiety in all subsequent reports of the Department:

There are no works in the Province to be compared to them in point of importance; and the Commissioners are of opinion, that an absolute impossibility, from a want of pecuniary resources, could alone justify any delay, in giving the finishing stroke, to the accomplishment of an enterprise, from which the country has powerful reasons to expect, at a later period, a revenue more proportionate to the immense sacrifices which that enterprise has cost.

Then followed the usual plea: unless the canals were deepened throughout to a depth of nine feet "it is impossible for them to attain that degree of undoubted superiority to which they are destined by nature, for the transport of the greater part of the produce, derived from that always increasing source, the Far West."[17]

[16]Gross revenue from canal tolls in 1857 was $341,280; in 1859, $222,603; in 1861, $419,385; in 1863, $385,220; in 1865, $282,257; in 1867, $317,643.
[17]"Annual Report of the Commissioner of Public Works for the Year 1848," *J.L.A.C.*, 1849, Appendix B.B.

At the beginning, then, officials considered that the manifest destiny of the Western produce was to follow the God-given Canadian route —provided the awkward obstacles of Nature could be satisfactorily conquered. With this programme completed in 1849, it was taken for granted that the Erie Canal could not possibly compete. In 1849, a barrel of flour paid 77 cents in tolls and freight charges on the Erie route from Buffalo to Albany whereas from Port Maitland on Lake Erie to Montreal, the charge was 35 cents. The time factor was also on the Canadians' side. From Chicago to either Quebec or New York was 1,600 miles by water. Travelling the Canadian route a 300-ton vessel would encounter only 70 miles of canals and could go the whole distance in ten days. On the American route, the same vessel would encounter 364 miles of canals and would have to divide its cargo into five parts at Buffalo in order to reach New York. In all, eighteen days would be spent on this route, twelve of them in the canals. The obvious conclusion to be drawn from these figures was triumphantly reported by the Commissioner of Public Works in 1849: the fortunate ship using the Canadian route, on arriving at Quebec and transferring its cargo to a vessel sailing for Europe, "with a fair wind, will have reached the banks of Newfoundland before the cargo passing through the Erie Canal, will have landed at New York."[18]

It happened that W. H. Merritt, promoter of the Welland Canal and the foremost exponent of the St. Lawrence system, came to preside over the Department of Public Works at this moment of great optimism. He became Chief Commissioner in 1850 and from this vantage point pressed on his cabinet colleagues as well as on a special legislative committee a vast plan of civil service reform. Part of this plan called for a renovated Department of Works and (the inevitable rider) a deepening of the canal system which would repay posterity a thousandfold by producing sufficient tolls to relieve the taxpayer for all time of the costs of government.[19] It was significant that Merritt played a leading part in the movement to introduce reciprocity between the United States and Canada. Freer trade would mean greater traffic on the canals and larger revenues from the tolls. Merritt's plans received scant enthusiasm from his colleagues, some of whom spoke against him publicly in terms scarcely compatible with our present understanding of the rules of cabinet solidarity.

[18]*Ibid.*
[19]See his memorandum No. 2 attached to "Annual Report of the Commissioner of Public Works, 1850," *J.L.A.C.*, 1851, Appendix T. This is the same memorandum, forming part of the longer report on government reorganization, which Merritt presented to a legislative committee in 1850.

The success of his plan required even larger expenditures on the canals but, since his colleagues were rendered economy-minded by a depression, the necessary funds were temporarily refused. Merritt resigned but continued his agitations from his position as chairman of the legislature's Standing Committee on Trade and Commerce.[20]

None of Merritt's successors in the Department of Public Works ever quite shared his optimistic estimate of the revenue-producing potential of the canals. Nevertheless, during the next decade the Department was always able to find a reason for the continued disappointing showing of the Canadian route. Unquestionably, all the natural advantages were still with the St. Lawrence as against the Erie-New York route. And yet, the Erie traffic continued to expand, following the rapid development of the West. What was the explanation and what should be done?

The standard explanation given by the Department during the decade 1852–62 was that the system needed still further deepening in order to eliminate the breaking of bulk and transshipment at the natural bottlenecks. Further, it was contended that the route would remain incomplete until a connecting link had been constructed between the St. Lawrence and Lake Champlain.[21] There were two possible implications underlying this second plan, one of which was never stated by the Department and the other admitted publicly but with great reluctance only in the 1860's. The unstated implication was that Quebec had lost the struggle with Montreal for dominance of the "Commercial Empire of the St. Lawrence." The Lake Champlain route would have re-directed the traffic southward away from Quebec. The other implication of this Champlain "cut-off" (which was finally admitted) was that the port of New York was the key to the whole scheme of inland water transport. The up-river port of Montreal had won the battle against the down-river port of Quebec, whereas New York, the port at the mouth of the Hudson, had easily defeated Albany at the head of the river, and (incidentally) Montreal beyond. By the same token the Erie Canal, which led to New York, won the lion's share of the Western traffic away from the St. Lawrence.[22] This was the sobering thought which the Commissioner of Public Works was finally bold enough to state in his 1862 report:

[20]See "Annual Report of the Commissioner of Public Works," 1850, *J.L.A.C.*, 1851, Appendix T., and *ibid.*, 1855, *J.L.A.C.*, 1856, Appendix 31.
[21]*Ibid.*, 1851, *J.L.A.C.*, 1852, Appendix Q.
[22]See A. R. M. Lower, *Colony to Nation* (Toronto, 1946), pp. 202 f., for development of this interesting theme of "metropolitan rivalry" which was based primarily on rivers.

In the early settlement of the Province, and, indeed until the opening of the Erie Canal in 1825, the trade of the country bordering upon the river and the upper lakes found its way to the sea by Montreal and Quebec. But upon the opening of that canal, the products of the West were at once diverted to the other side of the boundary line, and taken to New York, and notwithstanding the noble efforts which have since been made by Canada to regain a fair share of this trade, by the construction of canals of more than double the tonnage capacity of the Erie Canal, and by the formation of a more direct and cheaper channel of inland navigation, still, such has been the commanding influence of that commercial metropolis in drawing trade to itself and in keeping down the price of ocean transport, that these efforts, though not fruitless, have not been so successful as at first anticipated.[23]

This was indeed a bitter disappointment, rendered the more difficult to accept by one last unsuccessful attempt to defeat the Erie Canal. In 1860, all toll charges on the St. Lawrence canals were dropped and a 90 per cent drawback granted on tolls paid by vessels using the Welland Canal, provided they proceeded via the St. Lawrence system. Even before this desperate experiment, tolls on the Canadian side were only about one-quarter the tariff charged on the Erie system. And yet only about 4 per cent of the gross tonnage plying the St. Lawrence was of American origin. The abolition of tolls had not the slightest effect on traffic, and at the same time deprived the government of tolls averaging over $350,000 annually. There was also the question of making the taxpayer bear the costs of passing vessels through the system. The estimated cost to the Department of moving a vessel through the Welland and St. Lawrence canals was nearly $120. Tolls had originally been set so as to cover this cost. After 1860, in the absence of tolls, the general public was called upon to pay these charges. But not for long.[24] Within two years the experiment was a proven failure and the tolls were restored. The Erie Canal with an important assist from the port of New York had won its battle against Canadian manifest destiny and the St. Lawrence. In the event, however, the victory lost some of its sting for the vanquished because the new union of 1867 was to be strung together on double steel rails rather than—as in 1841—on a water highway. The new Department of Railways and Canals inherited the difficulties created by the politics of transportation and the post-Confederation Department of Public Works subsided into the background as general housekeeper to the government.

[23]See "Annual Report of the Commissioner of Public Works for the Year 1862," *Sessional Papers*, Canada, 1863, no. 3.
[24]See *ibid.*; and *Sessional Papers*, Canada 1864, no. 4.

CHAPTER XII

A "ONE MAN POWER" VERSUS THE ENGINEERS' EMPIRE

Two INTERMINGLED THEMES dominated the early administrative history of the Department of Public Works. As a great spending department it proved constantly incapable of balancing its budget; as a department staffed almost entirely by engineers it never found a satisfactory balance between the rival claims and interests of these experts and the laymen who sporadically discharged the duties of Chief Commissioner of Public Works.

In the pre-Confederation civil service, the Department held undisputed title as champion public spendthrift, more than one-third of the annual budget of the province vanishing into its insatiable craw.[1] Its major problem, therefore, was precisely the domestic issue which perpetually harassed Mr. Micawber. As with Mr. Micawber, intimate living with the problem did not bring its solution any nearer. Having borrowed a shilling, that blithe gentleman put away his pocket handkerchief and became all smiles: the Department of Public Works had the same insouciant attitude towards its financial obligations.

While over-expenditure was superficially the most impressive evidence of administrative weakness in the Department, it was the second unique feature—the preponderance of technically trained experts on its directing staff—that posed the basic problems for the Department. Throughout the pre-Confederation period there appears to have been an unresolved tension between these experts and the various political heads. The law conferred on the Commissioner of Public Works almost unlimited discretion to make the final decisions on a host of subjects—even including such technical decisions as those relating to surveys, contracts, building specifications, allowances for "extras" and so on. However, as a standard practice, the engineering staff tended to assume the Commissioner's discretion in settling these matters, often failing to keep the political head sufficiently informed of the decisions taken in his name. As a consequence, while D'Arcy

[1]See G. N. Tucker, *The Canadian Commercial Revolution 1845–1851* (New Haven, 1936), pp. 69 f. Tucker notes (p. 72) that interest payments on the public debt (in the main attributable to the construction of public works) averaged 40 per cent of provincial expenditures.

McGee writing in 1863 could describe the Department as an exceptional example of "a one man power,"[2] in fact it was a power that was exercised informally by engineers with scant respect for the broader claims of Parliament upon their politically responsible chief. The conflict produced by the efforts, on the one hand, of temporary Commissioners of Public Works to live up to the vast discretion accorded them by law, and the inevitable tendency, on the other hand, for experts in charge of isolated public works to make the decisions themselves, seems to provide the significant clue to the administrative defects of this agency.

The original impetus toward this unique centralization of power was provided by Sydenham's statute of 1841. His Board of Works, as has been previously noted, was designed to direct the execution of a vast public works programme made possible by the Imperial loan of one and a half million pounds. This five-man Board, like some boards already operating in England, was essentially a working committee of the cabinet.[3]

During the short period of the Board's existence, 1841 to 1846, three factors conspired to transform it into a "one man power" and, in turn, to confide that power to the skilled engineer. First, Sydenham's Act conferred corporate status on the Board—a forecast of the now familiar device of the public corporation.[4] Wide powers were granted to this corporation to hold and sell properties and to enter into contracts in its own name rather than in the name of the Crown. In practice, the chairman of the Board, exercising his statutory right to make decisions on behalf of the corporation, quickly came to dominate the Board. Indeed, the chief criticism of a royal commission in 1846 was that the Board "armed with immense power, and acting as though irresponsible in its operations . . . plunged into heavy engagements

[2] See his "Report on the Origin and Organization of the Public Departments," Public Archives of Canada, M. 837, section on Department of Public Works.

[3] All members of the Board held seats in the legislature and were also Executive Councillors. The statute even permitted the Secretary to the Board to sit in the legislature, but in fact he always remained a permanent, non-political official. Only the Chairman and Secretary were full-time, salaried appointments. See 4 & 5 Vic., c. 38 (1841).

[4] This appears to have been the first experiment with the device of the semi-independent public corporation. Perhaps Sydenham was trying to imitate the private land companies which were incorporated to do business in the province. His previous experience in private business may have inclined him to the typical businessman's distrust of the regular civil service when called upon to conduct a business venture. The operations of the Board—negotiating contracts, buying and selling property, and handling the large revenues expected from the public works—were of the type that have encouraged resort to the corporate form today.

with contractors, which at once committed it on every work for which an appropriation had been made, without any regard to the wholesome checks imposed by Legislative enactment."[5] The resulting overexpenditure on every appropriation necessitated continuous resort to the cabinet to authorize "extraordinary" payments to cover commitments made by the chairman.

Further contributing to the seizure of power by the chairman was the provision that gave the Governor a veto over any decisions made by the Board. As long as Sydenham was on hand exercising his vigorous role of administrator-in-chief, this veto power might have been expected to counteract irresponsible decisions taken by the chairman on behalf of the corporation. But with Sydenham's sudden death and the arrival of a less interested Governor (Bagot), the chairman was allowed a free hand.[6]

The centralizing tendencies were exaggerated by a third factor which led also to the dominance of the technically trained expert. At the outset the Chairman, Hamilton Killaly, undertook as well the duties of Chief Engineer—a position for which he possessed the necessary expert knowledge.[7] This doubling-up process set off a chain reaction that had disastrous consequences. The Chairman was a member of the cabinet and consequently he contented himself with communicating all decisions of the Board verbally rather than in writing. There also seemed to be no particular reason why he, as Chief Engineer, should write letters to himself in his other capacity as Chairman telling what decisions had been made at the technical level. As a result the Engineer spent public money on his authority as Chairman and was able to have his decisions ratified by defending

---

[5]See "Preliminary Report of the Commissioners of Enquiry into Management of the Board of Works," *Journals*, Legislative Assembly, Canada (J.L.A.C.), 1846, vol. II, Appendix O.

[6]Nevertheless, Bagot shared Sydenham's view that the Governor had a special responsibility to see that the funds from the Imperial loan were properly spent. In 1842 he criticized Merritt because "His primary object is to establish the principle that all decisions upon the public works to be undertaken in the Country shall be left to the Provincial legislature—a somewhat dangerous principle to lay down in any case. . . . "

[7]When the question arose of appointing an engineer to supervise the expenditures on the loan, Bagot write to Stanley at the Colonial Office to say that a British engineer was needed but preferably a civilian rather than one connected with the Army. He hoped, by such an appointment, to prevent jealousy on the part of the legislature "or what is perhaps quite as important, on the part of Mr. Killaly, the President of the Board." Whether Killaly objected or whether another civilian engineer could not be found, in any event Killaly assumed both positions.

the expenditures before Council (where he was already certain of the four votes held by his other Board members).[8] That the first incumbent, Hamilton Killaly, was a strong personality, with an engineer's "direct action" approach to the task of advancing the public works with all possible speed, added but the crowning piece to this whole administrative structure.

With Killaly in full and irresponsible charge, spending vast public funds with the abandon of the zealot anxious to get things done whatever the cost, the inevitable reaction set in. In 1845, responding to a rising clamour of indignation over optimistic estimates that were soon left far behind in the wake of unforeseen charges, Governor Metcalfe appointed a royal commission to enquire into the management of the Board of Works.[9] Killaly had forged ahead with construction projects but he had badly overreached his own powers and the province's resources. The conclusion reached by the investigators established a pattern for the subsequent chequered career of this agency. It was obvious to them that between 1841 and 1845 the balance of power had swung too far over in favour of the expert. It was necessary, now, to reassert the authority of the politically responsible Ministers by severing the positions of Chief Commissioner and Chief Engineer and subordinating the latter to the political head. This alteration was accomplished through legislation passed in 1846 which deprived the agency of its corporate status, insisted on written records of all decisions made, substituted a Chief Commissioner and an Assistant Commissioner for the five-man Board, and converted the Board into a Department of Public Works.[10] Reviewing the intention of this statute before a special committee of the legislature in 1850, Sir Etienne Taché, who held the office of Chief Commissioner from 1848 to 1849, remarked:

---

[8]The details of this evolution are carefully developed by the royal commissioners in their "Report on Management of the Board of Works," *J.L.A.C.*, 1846. They concluded, in part: "Had the two offices of Chairman and Engineer been kept in distinct hands from the first establishment of the Board, the decision of the Council must have been communicated officially in writing, either to the one officer or the other, as his authority and guide in proceeding with the works. And those official communications would have now been a matter of record in the Department."
[9]The Commission was appointed on Sept. 5, 1845, and the report was dated April 6, 1846.
[10]9 Vic., c. 37 (1846). The provision of two political heads was in line with the powerful forces of dualism, the two positions being rotated between English- and French-speaking Commissioners.

I am of the opinion that after the difficulties which raised the whole Province from one end to another against the Department, when it was under the exclusive control of Engineers, it would not be expedient again to place the Public Works under their direction, the Commissioners . . . having, if I may judge by the small number of complaints against them, given infinitely greater satisfaction to the public.[11]

The report of the royal commissioners and the amending statute of 1846 were obviously designed to emphasize the proper subordinate role of the permanent expert. However, within five years the old pattern began to reappear and the technical specialist (to borrow the phrase of a British administrator) once more began to appear on top rather than on tap. By 1859 administrative history had repeated itself; the political head angrily requested the dismissal of his two key technical specialists and new legislation sought once again to guarantee the necessary pre-eminence of the Chief Commissioner.[12] Mainly as a result of a series of scandals associated with the construction of the new parliament buildings at Ottawa, a similar administrative cycle was disclosed in the early 1860's. In 1864, once again, we confront the unusual spectacle of the political head of the Department angrily dismissing Samuel Keefer, his expert permanent head.[13]

This persistent appropriation of effective discretionary power by the engineer, despite the measures taken to keep him in a subordinate position, may be partly explained by examining the place accorded the two key permanent officers, the Secretary and, after 1851, the Assistant Commissioner, in the departmental hierarchy. Sydenham's original Board of Works had been given a permanent salaried secretary and the amending Act of 1846 left this position intact. T. A. Begley, Secretary of the Department from 1841 to 1859, became an indispensible part of the administrative apparatus, his responsibilities including the keeping of separate accounts for each major work, filing all plans and surveys, and preparing the preliminary reports

[11]See his evidence before the Select Committee on Public Income and Expenditure, "First Report," *J.L.A.C.*, 1850, Appendix B.B.
    Killaly was also made aware that his services could no longer be retained. In a letter to his friend Merritt he complained that Robinson, the new political head, "can do all by himself—he is actually making a fool of himself running up and down with Bourret [the Assistant Commissioner] to the total neglect of the Lachine." He was now "a gentleman at large," he lamented. See Merritt Papers, Public Archives of Canada, Killaly to Merritt, Sept. 19, 1846.
[12]The antagonism between the key performers in this episode can be detected in the Merritt Papers, Killaly to Merritt, Dec. 19, 1859 and in State Book T, Public Archives of Canada, Oct. 29, 1858, p. 263.
[13]See the case study at the end of this chapter for fuller details.

on proposed work for cabinet consideration. An amending Act of 1847 enabled the Secretary acting with the Assistant Commissioner to sign all contracts and make decisions in the name of the Chief Commissioner.[14] In 1850, Malcolm Cameron, then Assistant Commissioner, testified that "practically the Secretary does all the work."[15]

At the time Cameron made this statement he also admitted that his own duties as Assistant Commissioner were negligible and that the position was a sinecure. This situation changed almost overnight in February 1851 with the reappointment of the Department's hardy perennial, Hamilton Killaly, to the post.[16] The Assistant Commissioner now ceased to be a political figure and became in fact, if not yet in law, the permanent deputy head of the Department. When, in 1853, Killaly also took on the duties of Directing Engineer of the Welland Canal—the most important public work in the province—the old pattern of the years 1841 to 1845 was almost fully restored, with the technical expert once again in the ascendancy. This situation persisted until 1859, with the peculiar anomaly that Killaly as informal permanent head had equal and co-ordinate powers with the political head. This anomaly was forcibly called to the attention of the cabinet in 1858 by L. V. Sicotte, then Chief Commissioner of Public Works. In a careful memorandum, Sicotte pointed out how incompatible this situation was with the requirements of ministerial responsibility. He concluded: "It is obvious that the organization of the Department is vicious and will either retard action . . . or . . . allow action by one of the Commissioners uncontrolled by the other contrary to the law, and leaving the responsibility upon neither of the Commissioners."[17]

[14]10–11 Vic., c. 24 (1847).
[15]See his evidence before Select Committee on Public Income and Expenditure, *J.L.A.C.*, 1850. Showing a businessman's preference for leaving technical details to the expert, Cameron contended that the statutory duty imposed upon the Commissioners to visit all public works and report on them was useless "inasmuch as the Commissioners are not scientific men; they have resident Engineers, perfectly competent, whose duty it is to perform that service." On the other hand Taché, the Chief Commissioner, felt that only the politically responsible officials could be entrusted with this special surveillance. "I am not aware," he told the same Committee, "of what can be got through in the course of two hours by a man of the Honourable Mr. Cameron's talents, but for my part, I must in all humility admit, that mine were barely sufficient, when I was not too frequently called away from the business of the office, to enable me to get through the day's work in less than six hours. . . . " But, then, Taché had no notion of leaving vital decisions to the engineers.
[16]Killaly was appointed by letters patent in the same fashion as any regular political head of a department, but in fact he never took a seat in the legislature or at the Council table.
[17]See State Book T, pp. 263 ff.

Sicotte's memorandum produced two immediate results. First, the informal compact between Begley, the Secretary, and Killaly, the Assistant Commissioner, was destroyed. Begley was the first to go, dismissed as "inefficient, unfit and utterly incapable for the duties assigned to him." Killaly thought "poor Begley" had been sacrificed to the politicians, but perhaps his acid observations were attuned to the almost certain knowledge that his head would be the next to fall before the axe of the Chief Commissioner, as indeed it shortly did.[18]

The second result of Sicotte's memorandum was an amendment in 1859 to the Public Works Act.[19] The position of Assistant Commissioner which, since 1851, had become a permanent office, was now finally recognized as equivalent to the permanent Deputy Head properly subordinated to a single political chief. The duties of the Secretary were left unchanged but the terms of the Act made it clear that the holder of this position was to keep to his own subordinate place in the hierarchy. Once again, as in 1846, the politician had sought remedial legislation to help him reassert his authority over his technical aides. But again, as in the previous situation, legislative amendments appeared incapable of restoring harmony between the politician and the experts. Samuel Keefer, who had enjoyed a long career with the Department as an engineer, was elevated in 1859 to the new permanent post of Deputy Commissioner. In less than five years he suffered the same fate as Killaly, the Commissioner recording his opinion "that it is not advantageous to the public interest that Mr. Keefer should be continued in office"—an opinion in which cabinet concurred.[20] The episode which gave rise to this drastic action has been appended to this chapter as a case study which illustrates the major defects of the Department, particularly the failure to establish effective working relations between the permanent expert and the politically responsible layman.

Failure to harmonize the different interests sponsored by layman

---

[18]See his long lament to Merritt in Merritt Papers, letter dated Dec. 11, 1859. "[Begley] has been most cruelly treated—after 20 years faithful service he has been kicked off like an old shoe—He asked upon what charges he was dismissed, Sicotte answered 'none whatever'. He then asked the grounds of his dismissal 'total incompetency'!!! Now my dear Sir you know well that for the last 6 months since Sicotte came in, we *are literally doing nothing*—Begley has served under a number of Chief Commissioners, when the expenditure of millions was going on . . . and I never heard a word of complaint. . . . For my part I have had more opportunity than any other of knowing the extent of his labours, and the indefatiguable attention he gave to them, *night and day.*"
[19]22 Vic., c. 3 (1859, 2nd session).
[20]State Book Z, March 7, 1864, pp. 517 ff.

and expert was responsible in large measure for the other prominent departmental defect noted at the beginning of this chapter, namely, constant over-expenditure. Was the political head primarily responsible for this situation or could the fault be laid at the door of the permanent expert? A commission investigating the financial administration of the public departments in 1862 argued that the Chief Commissioner of Public Works—"the one man power"—was to blame. The investigators discovered that in the absence of proper accounts and in the presence of constant local political pressure, the Commissioner of the moment was always tempted to use his discretion at the expense of the country. Toussaint Trudeau, the Secretary of the Department, testified in 1862 that "the will of the Commissioner forms the system for the time being. There is no absolute rule."[21] As a consequence, some of the more strong-willed incumbents, such as Joseph Cauchon, went ahead on their own discretion without proper technical advice and altered contracts, dispensed with public advertising of tenders, authorized the issue of payments to contractors without seeing that the work had been checked by experts, and granted "extras" beyond the terms of the contracts. The oral order of the Commissioner was accepted by all senior officials as sufficient authority for any action.[22] To the investigators of 1862, therefore, it appeared as if the permanent experts in the Department were abused innocents who, despite their professional skill and efficiency, were constantly thwarted by the prodigal exercise of the Commissioner's vast discretionary powers. If their interpretation was correct, then clearly the repeated efforts to reassert the authority of the political head over his permanent technicians had been ill-advised.

The alternative view which appears to be more consistent with the sporadic eruptions already noted was that responsibility for the Department's financial difficulties rested on the shoulders of the engineers. In the first place they apparently refused to pay any attention to the Department's budgetary allocations. F. P. Rubridge, Assistant Engineer to the Department for over 22 years, was asked by the Financial and Departmental Commission in 1862: "In exam-

[21]See his evidence before the Financial and Departmental Commission, *First Report* (Quebec, 1863), Q. 132.
[22]*Ibid.*, Q. 239. The Commission recorded one instance where the expenditures on a new house for the Governor General at Quebec were incurred "without contracts, without the sanction of Parliament, without any specific appropriation, without any authority whatever beyond that of the Government of the day, and without any check upon the items beyond the will of the Commissioner of Public Works."

ining estimates [on the cost of public works] do you take into consideration the appropriation made by Parliament for the work?" He replied: "This is a matter which concerns the Commissioner more than the Engineering Branch." Asked how the engineers kept track of the amount of appropriation available or still to be spent he replied: "We are aware of this amount, but we have no record of it, except by reference to the Accountant. I cannot say in what form the Accountant's record is kept." Asked if he would "refuse to give [his] certificate if the account were in excess of the appropriation," the reply was "I think not . . . we should direct attention to the fact of excess, leaving responsibility to rest upon the head of the Department."[23]

Even had the engineers been interested in the accounts of the Department they would have derived little enlightenment from them. The Commission of 1862 reported that "The looseness and irregularity which are visible in the Public Works Department extend far beyond its book-keeping. Its records of account are defective; its checks upon expenditure worthless; its paucity of information on points essential to a correct understanding of its transactions in their progress is, confessedly, deplorable."[24]

Admittedly the experts had some justification for their woeful ignorance of the state of the accounts relating to the works upon which they were engaged. Nevertheless, the record clearly suggests that their disregard of financial matters extended to an excessively independent point of view which induced them to be careless of the claims of ministerial responsibility. It was a matter of constant complaint by several investigating bodies that there was no settled channel of communication between the Chief Commissioner and his technical advisers. The want of system aided and abetted the independent engineers who could get ahead with their own specialized tasks without bothering to keep in touch with their politically responsible chief. Even when matters were referred to the Commissioner for a decision he could never be certain that his senior permanent experts had been fully informed by the subordinate technicians. Indeed, he could not even count on senior officials bothering to keep him posted on issues of a technical nature. It was this independent attitude of the professional man toward the untrained political head that occasioned the sudden violent revolts of the politician, often finding expression in an unnecessarily dramatic discharge of the key permanent officials

[23] *Ibid.*, Qs. 240–6.
[24] *Ibid.*, p. 14.

as untrustworthy and lacking in judgment. Certainly the best illustration of this defect in the professional engineer's attitude toward his political chief is to be found in the long-drawn-out controversy occasioned by the construction of the parliament buildings. The essential features of this controversy seem to indicate that both the "one man power" and the proclivity of the engineer to dominate the situation were at fault. However, on the whole, it would appear that the engineer was most to blame for disregarding the obligations imposed upon him by his special position in the hierarchy to keep his chief sufficiently informed on all major decisions of a technical nature.

Constructing the Ottawa Buildings: A Case Study[25]

Listening to the silver bells of the carillon pealing out over Parliament Hill on a bright Sunday afternoon, it would be difficult to visualize the hubbub occasioned by the construction of those massive Gothic buildings that crouch beneath the soaring Peace Tower. Scarcely had excavations been made for the original parliament building and the two flanking departmental buildings than the bickering started. For months a flood of reports came from special investigators, arbitration boards, and royal commissioners, while the air over Parliament Hill was filled with the angry shouts and denials of contractors, architects, engineers, and political officials. The plans had been badly devised, the contracts had been carelessly drawn up, appropriations had long been exhausted and supplementary appropriations swallowed up, the construction work was slipshod, and no one had provided proper supervision or maintained adequate progress reports. In 1861, two years after the contracts had been let, the situation had become so serious that the government had for a time to call a halt to construction. It appeared that the government and the bureaucracy, then stationed at Quebec, would never be able to move to Ottawa. However, despite these vicissitudes the buildings once more got under way and groped towards completion. Late in the year 1865—over four years after construction had started—the government finally moved into its new permanent residences.

[25]This case history has been pieced together from the following documents: "Report of the Commission appointed to Inquire into Matters Connected with the Public Buildings at Ottawa," *Sessional Papers*, Canada, 1863, no. 3; *First Report of the Financial and Departmental Commission*," especially the evidence of Toussaint Trudeau; annual reports of the Commissioner of Public Works from 1860 to 1868; State Book Z.

From the viewpoint of the administrative historian the affair of the Ottawa Buildings epitomized the failure of the Public Works Department to solve the two basic problems which have formed the theme of the foregoing analysis: over-expenditure and the conflict between the layman and the technician.

Preliminaries. When a plan for a work as large as the Ottawa buildings was presented to the Department, its statutory duty was to have its own engineers estimate whether the design would prove too costly for the amount of money appropriated for the project. On May 7, 1859, the Department called publicly for plans to be submitted, announcing that the cost of the parliament building was to be limited to $300,000 and of both the departmental buildings to $240,000. The design selected was described as "civil Gothic" and both the architects and the Deputy Minister (an engineer by profession) later admitted that this style of architecture was far too costly for the appropriations announced. At the time, however, no officer tested the plans for cost. Worse still, no preliminary examination of the site was made; the Deputy Minister, whose expert advice on this important point ought to have been given, apparently never bothered with this trifling detail. As a result, the architects had to work with hypothetical ground lines and had to guess at the nature of the rock on Parliament Hill. Their guesses on both points proved to be far too optimistic as the sequel will show.

The plans having been drawn up in the dark and one design accepted without anyone troubling to see if it could be constructed with the money available, the Department moved on to the task of letting tenders. The law required the Department to advertise publicly for tenders and to accept the lowest competitive secret bid. Each contractor submitting a tender was supposed to include a detailed schedule of prices to enable the Department to make "progress estimates" on work completed and to assess the value of "extra" or "additional" work. But, as noted previously, the Department followed no regular system and this was quite apparent in the present situation. The tender of a Mr. McGreevey was accepted, despite the fact that it included no schedule of prices, while a competitor, Mr. Peters, tendered for the same amount and included a proper schedule. Mr. McGreevey obviously had friends at court for he was permitted to supply the required schedule some time after his tender had been accepted. It even appears that officials of the Department accommodatingly made up the missing schedule by using prices taken from tenders that had been rejected. The peculiar aspect of this schedule was that had progress estimates been paid on the prices listed there, Mr. McGreevey "would have received the whole contract sum before the work was half finished." Nor did this exhaust Mr. McGreevey's ingenuity, for we find that after the contract had been drawn up by the Law Officers, he asked that the work be split up—the firm of Jones, Haycock & Company to undertake the construction of the departmental buildings. In the process of redrawing the contract, somehow the schedule of prices was left out and no reference at all made to what should constitute "extra" or "additional" work. Mr. McGreevey even arranged to have his contract exclude the clause that would have given him no claim for compensation had he exhausted the appropriations.

Who was privy to this arrangement which allowed Mr. McGreevey to make his own terms with the government? The deputy head, Samuel Keefer, contended that John Rose, the Commissioner of Public Works, had agreed to the arrangement. Rose denied the existence of any agreement and testified that his deputy had not kept him properly posted on any of the major problems connected with the Ottawa buildings. This disagreement was the first of many indications of the tension existing between the lay and the professional heads of the Department. Whoever was party to the connivance with McGreevey, the Department emphasized its adherence to regulations by announcing that it had scrupulously refrained from opening nine tenders that had been handed in late.

Construction. Plans, tenders, and contracts having been arranged, excavation for the buildings was commenced in 1860. Immediately Mr. McGreevey's loosely drawn contract began to pay dividends. It was suddenly remembered that buildings in Canada required heat and that no contract had been let for heating, nor indeed had the original plans provided for heating and ventilating arrangements. Quickly the Department rectified this omission by awarding a contract to Mr. Garth for $61,285. The extra digging required to instal this plant and provide ventilating ducts was performed of course by Mr. McGreevey who submitted a bill ultimately amounting to $333,000 for "extra work." Obviously he was overcharging, but how could this be proven when there was no price schedule in his contract?

The bills submitted for "extra" work were the main reasons for the enormous over-expenditure. The law required the Commissioner of Public Works to give his approval to all "extra" work, but naturally, if his subordinates failed to call his attention to the existence of such work, the Commissioner could not properly fulfil his statutory obligations. The evidences of mismanagement in this vital matter all point to the deputy head as the culprit. The royal commissioner who investigated the whole fiasco in 1862-3 reported:

> The gravest feature in the whole mismanagement was that the works connected with the heating and ventilating system were allowed by the Deputy Commissioner to be undertaken, proceeded with, and paid for, without estimate being made or called for, without a contract, without any check, any schedule of prices, or any arrangement whatever as to terms or price of work.... Considering the extent of the work required ... and the complications it was likely to produce, it was the duty of the practical head of the Department of Public Works, not to have allowed plans for the building to be exhibited to tenderers, until that for heating and ventilation had been maturely adopted, and incorporated.... This was not done.

John Rose, political head of the Department, testified to the commission: "I was not aware till towards the end of the year 1860, that extra work to any unusual or extraordinary amount, had been done. My attention had not been specially called to it. I was but the political head of the Department. It was the duty of the Deputy Commissioner, and the Assistant Engineer [in charge of buildings] and Architect to see that nothing was done but what the contract orders of the Department warranted."

However, the Deputy was not the only person at fault. The architects hired to superintend the construction were to be paid 5 per cent on progress estimates up to an authorized maximum of $33,000. The architects considered that they were entitled to 5 per cent on all payments—including "extras." Consequently, while they were not supposed to permit any extra work to be done without the written approval of the Commissioner of Public Works, in fact they never kept track of the work done and their clerk of works "assumed the right and power to give instructions to do work, which neither the contract nor the circumstances warranted." For example, he ordered the unnecessary but very costly deep rock excavation for foundations, he kept no accurate measure of this work, but the contractors charged it as extras. Having unnecessarily dug out this hard pan at an extra price, they then sold the diggings back to the Department as gravel. In concluding their report, the royal commissioners on the parliament buildings were unable to restrain their annoyance with the attitude assumed by the head of the firm of architects responsible for this work of supervision—as the following astringent comment reveals: "The high tone of professional duty and etiquette which Mr. Fuller [the architect] assumed as due to his position in the first instance, would have been detracted from in no way, by his using or at least superintending the use of the tape line in testing the laying out of the foundation walls, or by figuring the plans for those less skilful than himself in the execution of a work from which he expected renown rather than reflection. . . . "

By the end of 1860 it had become apparent that gross mismanagement had occurred. During that year over $423,000 (a good part of the whole appropriation) had been paid out and the buildings were not even above ground. Indeed when Mr. Page, the Department's competent Chief Engineer, was sent to inspect the situation, he could make no report because the works were covered with snow.

During the year 1861 matters came to a head. Commissioner Rose, caught up in the tangle of "extras" which his own Deputy's carelessness had created, helplessly watched the appropriations dwindle. He resigned in June and his place was taken by the opinionated but competent Joseph Cauchon. The new Commissioner, feeling strongly that Deputy Commissioner Keefer had really brought about the resignation of Rose, simply refused to consult him. He stormed ahead, using to the full the "one man powers" conferred by statute on the Chief Commissioner. However, having inherited an impossible situation, Cauchon's own personal intervention only made matters worse. Refusing all expert advice he proceeded in four months to pay out nearly $300,000 to Mr. McGreevey, without calling for vouchers. At the end of September the appropriations were exhausted and all work was brought to a halt.

At this point the ubiquitous Mr. Killaly was called back by the Department as special investigator. Killaly's own lengthy experience with departmental practices apparently had left him with an extremely lenient attitude toward the contracting profession. In effect, he was required to take such measurements and make such estimate of "extra" work as ought to have been performed from the outset. His findings indicated that the government was still deeply in debt to the contractors—nearly half a million dollars, in fact. This estimate satisfied the contractors who were prepared to resume construction on the basis of Killaly's findings. The government was less happy about the matter and finally in 1862 appointed a royal commission to investigate the entire series of transactions and to make a new estimate of the balance due the contractors. The commissioners reported that the contractors, far from being creditors of the government, had been overpaid about $40,000! They estimated that another million and a quarter dollars would be required to complete the buildings.

While their whole report was a vote of want of confidence in the deputy minister of the Department, the contractors, and the architects, they merely proposed that new contracts with proper schedules of prices be offered to the old contractors. The new contracts were signed in April 1863 and work was resumed. A year later, the Department's Chief Engineer assumed direct supervision of the works in order to avoid the delays occasioned by having to refer matters to headquarters at Quebec. Obviously a new spirit permeated the Department. Certainly a new deputy minister had come to preside over the Department in the place of the disgraced Keefer. During the same year, in October, the persistent claims of the contractors were submitted to arbitration and the two firms settled for amounts totalling less than $150,000. The final settlement of these claims came in 1866, a year after the government had moved in.

Conclusions. Between May 1859 and Dominion Day 1867 a total of $2,572,193.24 had been spent on buildings whose original bulk contracts called for the expenditure of $688,595. At Confederation part of the library, all the roads, and the main tower roof still were incomplete. After this harrowing experience one could readily accept the recommendation of the Chief Engineer which urged "that buildings of this extent and character will require a considerable annual outlay for maintenance which could be more judiciously applied by a person whose sole business it would be to keep the Buildings and works connected with them in a thorough state of repair, and the grounds (when finished) in proper order than if this service were intrusted to various parties who have other duties to perform."

We learn by our mistakes but it required a myriad of small mistakes and one gross blunder over the Ottawa buildings to teach the Department of Public Works better administrative habits. The lessons learned from this fiasco were, first, that the political head should never be forced into a position where in making his decisions he had nothing to fall back on but his own discretion and vast ignorance of technical matters. The second lesson was that unless close liaison was maintained between the responsible politician and the expert technicians, the Department would always suffer from over-expenditure of appropriations. Third, the Department learned the value of fixed routines so that the views of the experts could be channelled through to the political head, so that the discretionary element in loosely drawn contracts could be avoided, and so that the technicians could never make vital decisions without referring them to the head. This last lesson was one of the most important, for it is a tendency that readily emerges in a department like Public Works. The foregoing pages have revealed how often the permanent technician simply took matters in his own hands, apparently assuming that the political head was too ignorant of the technicalities involved. The *débâcle* of the Ottawa buildings was clearly a product of this autonomous spirit. But for decisions involving large expenditures only the political head can be held responsible; the Department therefore had to learn that, above all, the expert must pocket his pride and clear matters with the layman, for only on this condition could the political head be prepared to take full responsibility before Parliament. Killaly and Keefer, the first two deputy heads, refused to recognize this maxim and they paid the price in ignominious discharge.

CHAPTER XIII

INDIAN AFFAIRS: THE WHITE MAN'S ALBATROSS

THE HISTORY of the Indian Department affords rather convincing evidence for the cynical view that where there are no votes administrative services are bound to be neglected or starved for funds. The affairs of the aborigines were of paramount importance in 1763 when the Proclamation which transferred control from French to British hands was issued. About one-third of that document was devoted to the future arrangements to be made for the Indians.[1] Eighty years later, Indian affairs had been pushed so much into the back eddies of provincial politics that the Act of Union of 1841 forgot to provide for the annuities to which the Indians were entitled.[2] The omission was discovered and remedied only in 1844. As late as 1850 Lord Grey observed to Elgin that he felt "that less has been accomplished towards the civilization and improvement of Indians in Canada in proportion to the expense incurred than has been done for the native tribes in any of our other Colonies."[3] From highly useful military assistants they had become expensive impediments to the white man's search for *Lebensraum*. Their degenerate and sometimes depraved state of existence bore embarrassing testimony to the neglect by the Great White Father who operated out of Whitehall.

The Department of Indian Affairs—which until seven years before Confederation led such a shadowy existence in Canada that it scarcely warranted the title—is of interest to us here for three reasons. First, it was called upon to nurse a new policy of managing the Indians which had been developed by the Imperial authorities. Second, it provides a good example of administration at arm's length by the

[1] See D. C. Scott, "Indian Affairs 1763–1841," in *Canada and Its Provinces*, ed. by Adam Shortt and Arthur G. Doughty, vol. IV (Toronto, 1913), p. 703.
[2] This omission is recorded by investigating commissioners in a report published in 1858. The neglected annuities were covered by proceeds from Crown revenues or by special vote of the provincial legislature. See "Report of the Special Commissioners to Investigate Indian Affairs in Canada," *Sessional Papers*, Canada, 1858, Appendix 21, part I, "Relations with the Government." See also Lord Elgin's comments to Lord Grey, letter dated Oct. 25, 1850, in *The Elgin-Grey Papers, 1846–1852*, ed. by Sir Arthur Doughty (4 vols., Ottawa, 1937), vol. II, p. 1227.
[3] *Elgin-Grey Papers*, vol. II, p. 703, Grey to Elgin, Aug. 2, 1850.

home government, the provincial authorities assuming full charge only in 1860. Finally, it was and remains one of the few administrative agencies organized on a clientele basis.

Protection and Instruction versus "Necessary Generosity"

Until 1830, the policy governing administration of Indian affairs reflected clearly the original military use to which the native population had been put by the occupying powers on the continent. True, the Proclamation of 1763 had envisaged a programme of protected settlement and progressive "civilization" of the aborigines, but under military administrators this programme remained only an unrealized ideal; pacification, through a judicious distribution of presents and an accompanying glittering display of military pomp, seemed to be the major purpose of Indian policy. "The presents," as Elgin explained to Grey in 1850, "have always been given and received as Royal Bounty in acknowledgement of the fidelity with which the tribes stood by their Great Father the King of Great Britain in various wars."[4] At the same time, as settlement progressed, various tracts of land were surrendered by the Indians in return for annuities. The annuities were normally paid out in the same form as the presents: clothing, blankets, guns, anything that would help the natives survive.

The first significant effort to bring a more enlightened policy to the fore was made in the late 1820's by Major General Darling, Superintendent of Indian Affairs.[5] In a report to Governor Dalhousie he recommended that active steps be taken to civilize and educate the Indians and that gifts of agricultural goods be substituted for the presents. Succeeding Governors spiritedly took up the cause of the Indians. In 1829 Sir John Kempt reported that the new policy could operate only if the scattered Indians were brought together in settlements. As an essential element in civilizing the Indians, Sir John emphasized the need for religious training as well as instruction in "husbandry." An interesting nationalistic note is struck in his request to the home government for "active and zealous missionaries for the Indians . . . and . . . Wesleyan Missionaries from England to counteract the antipathy to the Established Church, and other

[4]*Ibid.*, p. 727, Elgin to Grey, Oct. 25, 1850.
[5]An excellent résumé of changes in Imperial policy towards the Indians is presented in "Report on the Affairs of the Indians in Canada," *Journals*, Legislative Assembly, Canada (J.L.A.C.) 1844–5, Appendix E.E.E., Section I, "History of the Relations between the Government and the Indians." This Commission was appointed in 1842 and reported in 1844. The report was published in instalments between 1844 and 1847.

objectionable principles which the Methodist Missionaries from the United States are supposed to instil into the minds of their Indian converts."[6] Sir John Colborne, Lieutenant-Governor of Upper Canada, also pursued the same objective by making arrangements to have the Indian annuities applied to house building and the purchase of agricultural implements and stock.

In 1830, under the vigorous direction of Lord Glenelg, the Colonial Secretary, the new policy of civilizing the Indians got underway. It proved popular, particularly because it sounded well in official records and because there were few to register complaints at the slow progress of the programme. A long tradition of neglect had to be overcome and a completely new administrative apparatus—as will be shown later—had to be designed. "Civilizing" the natives implied a long-range policy of "raising" them to the moral and intellectual level of the white man and preparing them to undertake the offices and duties of citizens. Assimilation into the white community was looked upon as the ultimate natural goal. The two instruments of civilization were the church and the school. Christianity would introduce the stabilizing influence of morality, while education—only in trade and manual practices, of course—would fit the Indian for the new sedentary life required of the civilized. He would drop his allegiance to Nimrod and kneel before the plough and the machine.

The policy seemed clear enough, as were the instruments for implementing it, but there were many obstacles to the attainment of the final goal of assimilation. One of the most persistent and controversial issues was that provided by the system of annual presents. Since these were charged against the Imperial Treasury, British authorities were inclined to agree with some experts who claimed that the bestowal of presents was bad for the Indians. It encouraged all those characteristics which, it was alleged, came naturally to the natives: sloth, unwillingness to assume responsibility, a perpetual pauper's attitude. The first requisite to civilizing the Indians was a programme that would encourage rather than stifle their ability to stand on their own feet. Bestowal of presents such as gunpowder merely encouraged the hunting and nomadic instincts which had to be suppressed if a policy of settlement was to be successful. Whether, in fact, all these criticisms of the system of bestowing presents were true seems never to have been thoroughly proved. Colonial politicians, interested in keeping the costs of government down, continued to argue that presents were necessary—as long as the Imperial government

[6]*Ibid.*

would foot the bill. In 1846 the Legislative Assembly forwarded an address to Her Majesty (in which the Governor concurred) requesting that the presents to the Indians be continued.[7] But in the same year the Colonial Secretary, Lord Grey, reiterated the Imperial government's intention of discontinuing the dole.[8] Grey, in giving reasons for this policy, denied that the Imperial government was breaking a pledge with the Indians (an argument emphasized by colonial statesmen); he reasoned that the presents were no longer needed to ensure loyalty from the Indians as potential allies in wartime, and that they counteracted the measures designed to make self-sufficient citizens of the Indians. Despite this impressive reasoning, the arguments for and against this special form of out-door relief for the Indians continued through the fifties. In the end the colonial politicians agreed to the policy of ending the system of presents, but the Imperial government had to accept the view that they had to be tapered off very slowly, commencing with the wealthier and well-established tribes.[9]

While the annual presents complicated the problem of civilizing the natives, the real difficulty was created by the decision to settle the Indians on reserves. This decision was presumably reached by the military personnel still in command of Indian affairs in the 1820's; it was strongly supported by the colonial governors—both in Upper and Lower Canada—and the Imperial authorities gave approval to it in a Treasury Minute in the dying days of 1829.[10] It was a policy which once begun has been followed unswervingly to this day by the Department.

Two pressing issues were raised by the system of reserves. The Indians' corporate rights to the land, timber, fish, and game had to be protected against "villians" (to use Lord Elgin's term) who surrounded them. According to the very exhaustive inquiry conducted by the royal commission in 1857, protection against poachers and squatters on Indian lands had been entirely inadequate.[11] Although strong provisions had been inserted in legislation passed in 1850 vesting officials of the Indian Department with magisterial powers to punish

[7]"Report of the Special Commission," *Sessional Papers*, 1858, part I. Lord Cathcart was then acting Governor General.

[8]*Ibid.*, part I. On July 30, 1846, the Secretary of State formally endorsed his earlier view that the presents ought to be discontinued.

[9]In 1851 the Imperial authorities were still requesting a speedy end to the presents, but had to settle for a terminal date of 1858. See the detailed history in *ibid.*, part I.

[10]See the detailed account in "Report on the Affairs of the Indians in Canada," *J.L.A.C.*, 1844–5, section I.

[11]"Report of the Special Commissioners," *Sessional Papers*, 1858, part III.

such offenders, apparently these provisions went unheeded. The commission recommended that a strengthening of the administrative machinery for guarding the Indians' property was the least that could be done by the government, since it had been Imperial policy at the outset which had fostered this undesirable state of helplessness and dependency.

The easiest way of protecting the Indians against encroachers appeared to be that of setting them apart in isolated reserves. And yet if the ultimate aim was civilization and assimilation, this isolation was undesirable. The curious paradox seems never to have struck the white administrators: the Indian must obviously be forced to embrace the superior culture of the white man and yet contact with that culture and with the bearers of that culture seemed to render the plight of the natives even worse. Consequently, the programme of isolated reserves was designed to protect the natives against the worst feature of that civilization which it was also the policy to foist on the Indians. An interesting working commentary on this problem is provided by the attempts to settle Indians on a reserve on Manitoulin Island. This settlement programme, which was begun in 1835 on the ambitious scale that was possible during the first flush of enthusiasm for the new civilizing policy, was Lord Glenelg's special project.[12] The elaborate provision for schoolteachers, missionaries, artisans, and trade schools suggested the original ideal was to lure as many Indians as possible into one isolated place where their rights would be protected while they acquired civilization in mild doses. The scheme was never a success because the establishment created for this Shangri-la was too pretentious and expensive for the small number of Indians who volunteered to enter it.

Probably as a result of this costly failure, a compromise solution was adopted. This consisted in establishing what the royal commissioners of 1857 called "compact Reservations surrounded by whites." Separation without isolation, it was hoped, would still provide sufficient protection for the Indian and yet not check the progress toward ultimate assimilation. The commissioners in recommending a continuation of this policy pointed out that the State of Michigan had found that reservations in close proximity to the whiteman had not increased immorality among the Indians or endangered their rights. Indeed, the commissioners had discovered greater signs of immorality amongst the Indians living on remote reservations.[13]

[12]The history of this venture is told in *ibid.*, part II, "Present Condition of the Indians in Canada," section on Manitoulin Island; also Report of 1844–5, section II.
[13]"Report of the Special Commissioners," 1858, part III.

As a result of the commissioners' findings a comprehensive statute passed in 1857 reiterated in its preamble the basic policy of encouraging "the progress of civilization among the Indian Tribes." The Act also made the long-range intention of assimilating the natives perfectly clear: there must be a "gradual removal of all legal distinctions between them and their Canadian subjects to facilitate acquisition of property by individual Indians." A procedure for enfranchising the Indians and a definition of the rights and liabilities of such enfranchised Indians were also incorporated in the Act.[14] Yet still the basic paradox remained: how was it possible to assimilate the Indian when he had been quite deliberately singled out as a class apart by being placed on a reserve and given only the corporate rights enjoyed by his tribe? As will appear in dealing with the third feature of the Indian Department (its clientele basis of organization), the very existence of a special administrative agency to service the Indians—and only the Indians—also resulted in setting them apart. Only one official investigating body was sufficiently farsighted to visualize this peculiar consequence of a clientele administrative agency.[15] Possibly the system of reserves was the only practicable solution to the problems of the defeated, demoralized, impoverished, and bewildered native population; perhaps, too, a clientele organization was the most satisfactory administrative arrangement for servicing the various needs of the Indians on these reserves. But if this was so, then surely it followed that assimilation and transformation into "first-class" citizens were really not compatible with the special administrative machinery which had been created.

Nevertheless, in the legislation by which the Canadian government took over complete control of Indian affairs from the Imperial government in 1860,[16] the basic objectives of civilization and enfranchisement (or assimilation) were restated, and at the same time the administrative forms which inevitably isolated the Indian from the Canadian community—the reserve and the clientele department—were continued and have been continued to the present. The more obvious forms of paternalism which earlier took the shape of presents have been replaced by a subtler form of guardianship and for this change in policy the early administrators must receive credit. As Duncan Campbell Scott, the gifted deputy head of the Department, stated the ideal: "Protection from vices which were not his own, and

[14]20 Vic., c. 26 (1857).
[15]See "Report on the Affairs of the Indians in Canada," *J.L.A.C.*, 1847, Appendix T.; this is section III of the voluminous report, the first two sections having been published in 1845. See under heading V, "Indian Department."
[16]23 Vic., c. 151 (1860).

instruction in peaceful occupations, foreign to his natural bent, were to be substituted for necessary generosity."[17] Yet still the paternal note is struck and still the Indian is treated as an outsider in his former kingdom. Thus a policy devised in the 1830's was reiterated, elaborated, and carried forward to Confederation. Almost intact it has served up to this day as the guiding star for administrators of Indian affairs.[18] Probably in no other sphere has such continuity or consistency or clarity of policy prevailed; probably in no other area has there been such a marked failure to realize ultimate objectives. The fault cannot be laid at the feet of willing, concerned administrators: the fault is partly that of public neglect and mainly that of the antipathy traced above between means and ends.

The Imperial Connection

Administration of Indian affairs was one of the last of the Imperial government's responsibilities to be transferred to the United Provinces. The official transfer took place in 1860, when the Commissioner of Crown Lands received this uncherished legacy. Long before this time, however, the Imperial authorities had been seeking a convenient way of effecting the transfer, while colonial officials were using their ingenuity to keep the situation unchanged.[19] This transfer of power clearly formed no part of the Canadians' demand for autonomous control over all their administrative services, comparable, for instance, with the very positive local desire to attain control over the Post Office and Customs. This point was strongly emphasized by Lord Elgin during an exchange with the Colonial Secretary on the British government's decision to drop the annual presents to the Indians.

> I shall feel myself obliged . . . to protest most strongly against the attempt . . . to saddle me and through me the Canadian Gov't . . . with the responsibility of the opinion that the Indians have no claim to continuance of their presents. . . . Measures of economy of this class are very popular at home and very much the reverse here; their adoption in any shape will be attended with hazard, and I am sure that it is safer and often better that they should appear to be forced on the local authorities than to be recommended by them.[20]

[17]See his excellent section "Indian Affairs 1840–1867," in *Canada and Its Provinces*, vol. V., pp. 329–62.
[18]For a recent criticism of departmental policy see Diamond Jenness, "Canada's Indians Yesterday: What of Today?" *Canadian Journal of Economics and Political Science*, vol. XX (Feb. 1954), pp. 95–100.
[19]For the Imperial pressures see "Report of the Special Commissioners," 1858, part I.
[20]*Elgin-Grey Papers*, vol. II, pp. 724–5, Elgin to Grey, Oct. 11, 1850.

As early as the 1820's some British officials had contemplated tapering off the Indian Department so that the Imperial government could ultimately drop its responsibility for the aborigines. This idea was submerged during the 1830's by the enthusiastic pursuit of the policy of civilizing the Indians. In 1837 a Select Committee of the British House of Commons argued that the colonists were not fit persons to control their own native tribes: ". . . the settlers in almost every colony," the report concluded "having either disputes to adjust with the native Tribes, or claims to urge against them, the Representative body is virtually a party, and, therefore, ought not to be the judge in such controversies."[21] The Executive Council of Lower Canada hastened to endorse this view, adding that only the mother country was capable of providing the proper parental protection for the Indians. Again in 1844 a special investigating commission in the province also recommended "That as long as the Indian Tribes continue to require the special protection of the Government, they should remain under the immediate control of the Representative of the Crown within the Province, and not under that of the Provincial Authorities."[22]

Even as the commissioners framed their report in 1844, the British government was experiencing a rapid change of mind. By 1846 Lord Grey, the Colonial Secretary, was vigorously opposing the colonists' efforts to have the Imperial government continue the system of issuing (and paying for) annual presents to the Indians. But it was not until 1851 that the Imperial government delivered its ultimatum to the province, insisting that it would pay for no more presents after 1858.[23] The Imperial authorities were so eager to relieve themselves of the incubus of the Indians and the colonial politicians were so anxious to avoid this responsibility that neither group gave much consideration to the needs of the Indians themselves. Indeed, when Colonel Bruce, Superintendent General of Indian Affairs, recommended in 1851 the methods by which he thought the Imperial government could dispose of Indian affairs, he failed to recommend any provision for a local department to take over. Not until 1854 did Colonel Bruce rectify this omission by arguing that, in so far as the Imperial government dropped the Indians, to that extent the need for a local department would grow.[24] During the next six years, as colonial officials realized

[21]Quoted in "Report on the Affairs of the Indians in Canada," *J.L.A.C.*, 1847, heading I, "General Views as to the System of Management and General Recommendations."
[22]*Ibid.*, first "General Recommendation."
[23]See "Report of the Special Commissioners," 1858, part I.
[24]*Ibid.*

that Imperial withdrawal was inevitable, a growing local concern was displayed for the Indians. As has been noted, in 1857 the local legislature approved the statute which set forth the basic objectives of Indian policy. Three years later the necessary local administrative machinery for giving effect to this policy was created by statute of the local legislature. The Commissioner of Crown Lands became Superintendent General of Indians Affairs on July 1, 1860, and broad discretion was conferred on the Governor in Council to determine how the revenues of the Indians would be spent, how their moneys and lands would be managed, and other details of administrative policy. In 1862, William Spragge, veteran employee of the Crown Lands Department, was raised to the status of permanent head, reporting directly to the Commissioner of Crown Lands as Deputy Superintendent General of Indian Affairs.

The administrative machine handed over to the United Provinces in 1860 had had a complex history. Prior to the Union, Indian affairs were managed by several Imperial authorities, the representative of the Crown in the colony acting as the co-ordinating force. Special instructions issued in 1796 and 1800 to the Lieutenant-Governors of Upper Canada and Lower Canada gave them direct control of Indian Affairs.[25] In practice this meant that they transferred to local Indian authorities any instructions issued by the home government or special orders from the Governor General. The executive officers were closely tied to the Imperial military establishment in the colonies, of which the Governors were the heads. Indian agents wore military uniforms—especially to make an impressive display on the occasion of the annual distribution of presents to the various tribes. A military representative always attended at these pompous annual affairs. Part of their pay was in rations, also a military practice. Military men, without exception, occupied the highest administrative positions such as Superintendent and Deputy Superintendent General, Chief Superintendent, and Superintendent of Indian Affairs. In 1830, for example, Indian affairs in Lower Canada were directed by a Superintendent who was a Lieutenant-Colonel of Militia, reporting to the military Secretary of the Governor General; in Upper Canada, the Lieutenant-Governor (the military leader) was in charge of the Chief Superintendent, also a Lieutenant-Colonel.

In the mother country three major departments shared in the direction of Indian Affairs in the colonies. The Colonial Secretary

[25]See "Report of the Deputy Superintendent General of Indian Affairs" (D. C. Scott), *Sessional Papers*, Canada, 1922, no. 27.

appears to have been the most concerned with major policy issues, as, for instance, authorizing the General Order of 1828 which carried out an important reorganization of the Department or in the introduction of the new policy of civilizing the Indians. He also approved the appointment of Indian agents recommended by the Lieutenant-Governors and channelled through to the Treasury the requisition for the annual presents to the Indians.[26] The Treasury also appears to have worked in conjunction with the Colonial Secretary right through the whole period of Imperial control, settling such personnel questions as the kind of tenure to be enjoyed by a newly appointed Chief Superintendent.[27] The third Imperial Department concerned with managing the Indians was the Army Commissariat, for it was through the local agents of this Department that the annual supply of presents was issued. For this purpose—the major administrative purpose so long as military views predominated—an extremely devious procedure had been worked out. The Superintendents of Indian affairs estimated their needs eighteen months to two years in advance. The Governor General transferred these estimates to the Commissariat Department in England, which ordered the necessary supplies. These supplies were then transferred to local depots of the Commissariat in Canada. The chief Indian officer requisitioned the presents from the stores of the depots and the Indian Department was debited with the cost when the goods were forwarded to the local Indian agent. The Imperial Treasury received these accounts which it then transferred to the Audit Office, at that time one of its subordinate branches.[28] This bewildering arrangement presumably continued until 1860 when the Imperial government stopped issuing presents. As an investigating commission reported in 1840, the commissariat machinery might have been "admirable in relation to the Army, and to the contracts connected with so vast an establishment and expenditure, but [it was]

[26]For suggestive indication of relationships see "Despatches on Indian Affairs," *Journals*, Legislative Assembly, Upper Canada, 1837-8, Appendix, pp. 180 f.

[27]See the action taken in 1844-5 when S. P. Jarvis, the Chief Superintendent of Indian Affairs, was on the carpet for having exceeded his powers and was ultimately discharged. Before this business was cleared up the Colonial Office, the Chancellor of the Exchequer, the Audit Board, and the Commissary General in England were all involved as were also the local Receiver General's Office, the Crown Lands Office, the Governor General, the Civil Secretary, and the Inspector General of Public Accounts! See "Return re correspondence with S. P. Jarvis etc. . . . ," *J.L.A.C.*, 1847, Appendix V.V.

[28]The arrangements are described and criticized in the "Report on the Affairs of the Indians in Canada," *J.L.A.C.*, 1847, heading II, "Presents."

productive only of delay and expense, when applied in all its rigid details to the little purchases of the Indians. . . ."29

While it was customary to refer to the "Indian Department" in the colonies and while permanent directing heads were early appointed in each province, in fact so many Imperial departments shared responsibility for making vital decisions that the local administrative machinery remained shadowy and almost completely unorganized. Reporting just before the Union in 1840, an official investigating commission remarked " . . . with regard to this Department, it was not so much a reforming, as an organization of the office *ab initio* that is wanting."30 At another point in their report the commissioners concluded:

Had, indeed, an effective protecting power over the Indians' property been, many years since, given to a properly organized Department, . . . your Committee should not now have to lament the injudicious disposal of much valuable property, and the disappearance of unaccounted funds. . . . With regard to the Indian Office itself, nothing can be less proportioned to the extensive and varied duties which it ought to perform. The Chief Superintendent is himself the only Officer in it. There is not even a permanently appointed Clerk. . . . This total inadequacy of the office to the growing interests of the various Indian communities, has been probably one cause of the business which properly belongs to it, being conducted by other Departments.31

A longer view than the commissioners then possessed suggests that the conclusion in the last sentence ought to have been reversed: *because* so many departments had undertaken various responsibilities for the Indians, they had crowded out the Indian Department. Even where authority had been conferred on the Department, its chief officer, as the same commissioners complained, had "to trouble the Lieutenant Governor on the most trivial occasions for his signature."32

And yet the permanent officers derived advantages from the hit-and-miss organization of the Department. The Governors and Lieutenant-Governors, who were technically supposed to provide detailed supervision over Indian Affairs, found that they lacked both the information and the time to perform the task. By default the Superintendent General was allowed to go his own way. Lieutenant-Governor Arthur

---

29*Ibid.*
30See "Report of Committee No. 4 on Indian Department" in "Report on the Public Departments," *Journals*, Legislative Assembly, Upper Canada, 1839–40, vol. II.
31*Ibid.*   32*Ibid.*

and Governors Sydenham and Bagot all felt their inadequacies and in 1842 Bagot was finally induced to appoint a special commission to recommend improvements. The commission, after reiterating the view that only the Imperial authorities were fit to govern the native tribes, proposed that the Governor's responsibilities could be effectively exercised by placing them in the hands of his Civil Secretary.[33] This recommendation was accepted in 1844 by the home authorities, the Civil Secretary becoming *ex officio* Superintendent General of Indian Affairs, a post which he held until the transfer to the Crown Lands Department was completed in 1860.

This reorganization coincided with a criticism of the Chief Superintendent for having abused his powers; accordingly, this post was abolished in 1845 and the Department was left without an experienced permanent head.[34] A chief clerk and an accountant between them handled the correspondence from the resident superintendents, kept up the files in a desultory fashion, and maintained a loose record of the finances of the tribes. The Deputy Receiver General was paid an allowance of $400 out of the Indian funds for his services in receiving the payments made for Indian lands. In short, at the end of nearly one hundred years of Imperial control, the local administrative arrangements still revealed a startling absence of any permanent central nucleus. The special investigating commission of 1857 was forced to repeat the criticism made twenty years before by another royal commission: the Department still lacked a central focus. True, the Governor's Secretary had undertaken this task after 1845, but as the commission of 1857 remarked:

The Governor's Secretary is necessarily partly engaged by his other duties; he is, in all probability a stranger not only to the Indians, but to the country at large, and from the nature of his appointment, vacates the office of Superintendent General soon after he has mastered the intricate details of the business, leaving his successor to go through the same apprenticeship.[35]

This comment is all the more significant when it is noted that the Governor's Secretary was a member of the commission which came to this conclusion.

The closer the time came for the Imperial government to cast off

---

[33]See "Report on the Affairs of the Indians in Canada," *J.L.A.C.*, 1847, heading V, "Indian Department, Recommendations."
[34]"Report of Special Commissioners," *Sessional Papers*, 1858, part III.
[35]*Ibid.*, part III.

the Indians the more apparent to the colonists became the administrative vacuum that would be left. Hence the commission of 1857 reported strongly in favour of a permanent deputy head for the Department—a recommendation that the Canadian authorities implemented in 1862, two years after they accepted their new charges.

Perhaps the clearest indication of the hit-and-miss attitude of both Imperial and colonial authorities towards the Indians is revealed in the complex process by which the costs of administration were met. Indeed, as has already been noted, it was the consideration of expense which induced the Imperial government to seek to free itself of the responsibilities for the Indians. Between 1840 and 1860, while the Imperial government still retained control over Indian affairs, administrative costs were covered from five different sources.[36] An annual grant voted by the Imperial parliament provided the largest amount for the Indians. The fact that the sum varied and, after the mid-1840's, was a popular target for criticism by economy-conscious members of the British House of Commons, left a perpetual sense of uneasiness in the colony. The Imperial grant was used to pay the salaries of the Indian agents, the pensions of certain former officers in the Department, and the expenses of maintaining a few selected officials such as missionaries and teachers. When the time came to break the Imperial connection with Indian affairs, the pensions were the only charges which the home government were willing to continue to meet.

The General Fund provided a second but much smaller source of revenue for the Indians. This Fund was made up from the sale of Indian lands, the sale of timber seized after it had been unlawfully cut off these lands and interest on money held by the provincial Receiver General to the account of the Indians. The salaries of the small headquarters' staff of the department (e.g., the accountant, chief clerk, and messenger), the special allowance to the Deputy Receiver General (who received the funds from the sale of Indian lands), and some contingencies for the office in Upper Canada not covered by the Imperial grant were paid from this Fund.

The third source of revenue was the Land Fund which was derived from the sale of Indian lands made by the Crown Lands Department. According to a complicated formula worked out by Lord Sydenham, the expenses connected with the management of all lands—including

[36]Excellent details on the financing of the Indian Department are to be found in *ibid.*, part III.

Indian lands—were lumped together and then an arbitrary percentage of the costs of management charged against the revenues derived from the sale of each type of land. In practice 10 per cent of all costs of management were assessed against the Indian lands, 50 per cent against Crown lands, and 40 per cent against Clergy Reserves. If it happened that the lands owned by one tribe enjoyed heavy sales during the year then that tribe would bear most of the 10 per cent assessment for the general costs of management. This obvious injustice was noted by various investigators but apparently remained unchanged as long as Imperial control continued.

A fourth special source of funds was provided by the estate of the Six Nations located in the area around Galt. The money from this source was used to defray the salaries of the trustees who helped the Indians manage the estate. When the provincial government took over in 1860 the charges of managing the Six Nations' property were merged with the general charges of managing all Indian lands. Finally, each tribe had its own local funds—mainly the annuities paid in perpetuity out of provincial revenues—which were used to pay the tribal chiefs, interpreters, missionaries, surgeons, and schoolmasters. The ultimate complication in this fantastic scheme of financing Indian affairs was the payment out of the Commissariat funds for the annual presents of blankets, ammunition, clothing, and so forth. The decision of the Imperial authorities to cut off the distribution of presents was not acted on until the end of the period of Imperial control, so that this item of administrative expense properly formed part of the whole budget for Indian affairs.

The complicated method of financing the administration of Indian affairs afforded unlimited opportunities for petty wrangling between Imperial and colonial authorities when the time came to effect the transfer. The protracted negotiations leading up to the transfer can be attributed almost entirely to these complications. When the commission in 1857 made a careful assessment of the financial situation confronting the Department they discovered that, if the Imperial authorities withdrew, existing local sources of funds would fall short of current administrative costs by over $8,000 (about half the total budget). It was the attempt to find a satisfactory method of bridging this financial gap that was the occasion for prolonged bickering and compromises between colonial and Imperial authorities. The sum, even in those days was not large; "it was the principle of the thing." The royal commissioners bluntly stated the principle in their report of 1857. The Imperial authorities might continue the grant for another ten years, hoping in the interval that the sale of Indian lands would be stepped up enough to close the gap. But if this was the solution, the Imperial government must be expected to retain its control over patronage and policy. However, the commissioners hastened to add, "If the aid hitherto afforded by the Imperial Government be withdrawn, it is but equitable that its control over the Department should cease likewise." This was the advice which the colonial authorities ultimately accepted in 1860. The extra price they had to pay for acquiring complete authority over their own native population seems at this distance to have been so paltry that neither set of authorities could take any credit for the prolonged bickering which preceded the transfer. The explanation was surely not in the $8,000 involved but in the fact that this was one responsibility that the colonial government would have been happy to have evaded. By the same token it was a responsibility which Imperial authorities were glad to shrug off, since their own administrative performance had not enhanced their reputations as bearers of the white man's burden.

A Clientele Department

The third conspicuous feature of the Indian Department was closely related to the long experience with Imperial control which has just been examined. Was it possible to administer the affairs of the Indians in bits and pieces, conferring responsibility on several departments for various interrelated aspects of Indian management? Or was it preferable to assemble the various agencies into one department and make it solely responsible for all matters pertaining to the native population? The record of neglect and unsystematic administration under the former arrangement (which characterized the period of Imperial control) spoke strongly in favour of the second alternative. And yet if this alternative were adopted—as in fact it ultimately was—would this not perpetuate the isolation of the Indians from the white population and thereby frustrate the efforts to civilize and ultimately assimilate the natives? Between the years 1840 and 1857 this problem was discussed by several official investigating bodies, with the weight of evidence gradually tending toward the policy of centralization in one "clientele" department. When centralization was ultimately achieved after 1862, it was marked, as will be noted, by a practical compromise which made the decision palatable.

As might be expected, the desire to bring together in one department the scattered agencies responsible for Indian affairs was first expressed by a senior permanent official in the Indian Department.

In 1839, Colonel Samuel Jarvis, Superintendent General of Indian Affairs, strongly urged an investigating committee to report in favour of such a plan.[37] In particular he objected to the Crown Lands Department managing Indian lands and charging against the revenues derived from their sale a fixed percentage of the total cost of administering the whole Crown Lands Department. Neither Department, as a result of this divided responsibility, maintained a proper record of the sales or any clear accounts for the Indians' business affairs. Furthermore, as has already been explained, several Imperial authorities also shared important responsibilities for Indian affairs. The investigators in 1839 finally agreed with Jarvis that the Indian Department ought to assume fuller control of all matters pertaining to their special charges.

However, the commission appointed in 1842 carefully assessed the arguments for and against centralization and ultimately rejected the verdict favourable to centralization which had been reached by the previous investigators.[38] Four strong arguments could be made in support of the plan for focusing all responsibility for Indian affairs in the one agency. First, a department organized on a strict clientele basis would be less likely to become indifferent to its public. If responsibility for Indians affairs—the sale of their land, education, welfare, health, finances—was dispersed in a number of departments whose chief concerns lay elsewhere, then the interests of the Indians might easily be overlooked. Second, agents who had to work only with Indians could acquire the necessary special information and insight to deal effectively with their charges in their own localities. This would not be so if the responsibility were dispersed. Third, a closer adaptation of policy to special needs of the Indians could be effected if the Department had only the Indians to consider. The Crown Lands Department, for example, would not need to adapt its general land policy to the special requirements of the Indian lands. Finally, all books and accounts relating to the Indians could be brought together in one Department rather than scattered in the several offices which dealt with separate aspects of Indian administration.

[37]See "Report of Committee No. 4," *Journals*, 1839–40, and the criticisms of that committee for the acceptance of Jarvis' views by the Commissioners appointed in 1842, "Report on the Affairs of the Indians in Canada," *J.L.A.C.*, 1847, heading V, "Indian Department."

[38]"Report on the Affairs of the Indians in Canada," *J.L.A.C.*, 1847, heading V, "Indian Department."

On the whole these benefits of the clientele basis of organization seem most convincing. And yet the royal commissioners, reporting in 1844 concluded that it would be wrong to create a department vested with full responsibility for managing every aspect of Indian Affairs. One of their criticisms was predicated on the Imperial government's view that the Indian Department was an "expiring" one. Accepting this assumption, the commissioners argued that a clientele department would only expand an administrative entity which it was thought would eventually be abolished. This argument lost its validity as colonial statesmen became increasingly aware that administrative arrangements for managing the Indians' affairs would have to be continued and even expanded. However, the commissioners were on firmer ground when they developed two additional criticisms. Unquestionably a clientele department would increase administrative costs. Instead of allowing the technical specialists employed in subdivisions of other departments to handle the Indians it would be necessary to employ the same kind of specialists in the Indian Department. Branches for the sale, management, and surveying of Indian lands, timber agents for the Indian forests, special accountants for managing the Indian funds and annuities, an office to supplant the Commissariat in handling the ordering and supplying of presents, and so on, would be required. A duplication of skills and special knowledge is inevitable when a clientele basis of organization is employed. That is perhaps one reason why it is seldom found today—even the Department of Veterans Affairs, the closest approximation to a clientele organization, relies on other specialist departments for certain services. The final criticism of the clientele arrangement was that it would serve only to foster the isolation of the Indian population and perpetuate the sense of tutelage. Both of these tendencies would certainly negate the efforts to develop and then assimilate the Indian as a first-class citizen. In this observation the commissioners proved themselves true prophets, for there was no better way of preserving the corporate and distinct character of the Indians than by setting up a special department to deal only with their needs.

While opposing a clientele organization, the commissioners nevertheless realized that the existing arrangement lacked coherence and proper central direction. Accordingly, they proposed that the Governor General's Secretary become the co-ordinator and that all the records be amalgamated, kept at the seat of government, and maintained in an up-to-date form by a permanent clerk. With the Governor's Secretary as the new head of the Department the permanent Superintendent General became at first advisory and then superfluous; in 1846 his office was abolished. Thus from about 1846 to 1860 Imperial management of Indian affairs was directed theoretically by the Governor General with the assistance of his Secretary who acted as the channel of communication between the Indian agents of the Department and the Governor. In fact, the clerk and accountant of the Department were the only active members of the staff at headquarters. They, in turn, were surrounded by the Commissariat, the Colonial Secretary, the Imperial Treasury, and Audit Office, while Crown Lands continued to act as the selling agency for the Department.

Unfortunately, as the commission of 1857 discovered, this dispersion of administrative responsibility for the Indians proved disastrous. The benefits of the clientele arrangement were lost and, despite the good will shown by the Imperial government and successive Governors, "interests of greater magnitude had sprung up and the Indian has been lost sight of and has sunk to a state of comparative neglect." This was the commissioners' verdict in 1857, after over a decade's experience with the system of dispersed piecemeal administration. Moreover, far from confirming the Imperial government's view that the need for the department would "expire," a strong administrative agency seemed now to be even more insistently required by the Indians. Unfortunately, too, the dispersed system had not fostered the desired assimilation of the Indians; indeed, the gap between the tribes and the white settlers seemed to have widened, while the Indians' sense of helplessness, isolation, and dependency had deepened.

The royal commissioners in their report of 1857 did not directly assess the merits and liabilities of the piecemeal system of administering Indian affairs; nor did they argue the claims of the clientele or centralized system of administration. However, their whole report reflects dissatisfaction with the previous ten years' experience of the piecemeal system. At the same time, their recommendations pointed the way toward the creation of a centralized, properly co-ordinated Department of Indian Affairs. They denied absolutely the popular Imperial belief that the Department was an "expiring one." They appealed to the colonial government to recognize its responsibility to the Indians and recommended that this could best be done by appointing a permanent head for the Department. They considered that the appointment of the Governor's Secretary to act as Superintendent General of Indian Affairs (following the recommendation from the earlier royal commission) had been a mistake. Finally, they made clear their preference for colonial control of the Indians with the consequent elimination of the confusing and overlapping jurisdiction of various Imperial Departments. In short, the commissioners appeared to favour the centralization of all responsibility for Indian affairs in the hands of one local administrative agency. The decision to transfer control from the Imperial to colonial authorities provided a real opportunity to make this break with the past administrative arrangements. As a necessary adjunct to this proposal the commissioners recommended appointment of a senior permanent official to lend strength and co-ordinative power to the centre.

When the colonial authorities assumed full control over the Indians in 1860 nearly two years passed before the local arrangements for their management were completed.[39] These arrangements more or less confirmed the recommendations of the royal commission of 1857 but juggled with the issue of the clientele department. The desire to consolidate responsibility for all matters relating to the Indians was displayed in two administrative reforms. A single agency was created to administer Indian affairs and a permanent head, with the status of a deputy minister, was appointed to that agency. But still it could not be said that a truly clientele department had been established, for the new agency was set up as one of the many branches within Crown Lands. Nevertheless, a great improvement had been made, for at least all the major concerns of the Indians—land, timber, fish, and business records—were now under one political head, the Commissioner of Crown Lands. Furthermore, judging from the independent character of each of the main branches in Crown Lands (examined in a previous chapter) the new Indian Affairs Office would have enjoyed virtually the full autonomy of a department in its own right. Certainly in the few years remaining before Confederation the records and financial accounts of Indian affairs were greatly clarified and presented in consolidated form.[40] This was made possible because of a strengthened central office and the ability of that office to work with the surveys, sales, and timber branches of the Crown Lands Department.

It is interesting to note that until 1936 this organizational arrange-

[39]See Appendix for organization of Department of Crown Lands at Confederation.

[40]See, for example, the detailed statistics and accounts (lack of which had been a common complaint of all early investigators) provided by William Spragge after 1862, as appendices to the Annual Report of the Commissioner of Crown Lands.

ment for Indian affairs remained unchanged. After Confederation it became the practice—with a few scattered exceptions—to place Indian affairs under the Department of the Interior, the federal government's successor to the Crown Lands Department. But Indian affairs always enjoyed a rather special independence—indeed after 1880 it was given the legal status of a department,[41] but always had a ministerial head who doubled both as Superintendent General and as Minister (usually) of the Interior Department. During this whole period, too, the permanent head of Indian Affairs had the rank of a full deputy minister. Moreover, the department's basic organizational form remained that of a clientele department. Today, it has its own Field Administration Service to which the local Indian agencies report; there is a Medical Service and a Welfare Service to which the doctors and welfare workers to the Indians report; and its own Reserves and Trusts Service to handle the special historic accounts of the tribes. There is scarcely a feature of Indian life which specialists of the Department do not serve: health, welfare, education, special supplies, annuities, protection, and management of the Indians' estate, all are encompassed by the one Department.

The record of the period during which dispersed control characterized the management of Indian Affairs suggests that the centralized arrangement in a clientele department was the more appropriate organizational basis. Nevertheless, it is probably true to argue, as did the commissioners who reported in 1844, that the clientele arrangement reinforced the public view of the Indians as a group apart. This attitude, in turn, was in opposition to the long-run goal set for the Department in the 1830's, that of civilizing and assimilating the native population.

Was the original decision to create a clientele department in 1860 the best answer to the problem of managing the Indians? Probably no certain answer can be given to this question, for the authorities faced an unpleasant predicament. Under military rule and after the first impact with the white man, there seemed little alternative to the policy of treating the Indians as wards. Yet, if the Indians could not be neglected, no more should they be pampered, for that was no way to raise them to the level of individual self-respect and responsibility which was required of potential citizens. Primarily, the short-run problem was the danger of neglect, and the history of the Department suggests that the clientele basis of organization

[41]See D. C. Scott's historical sketch in his report for 1921, *Sessional Papers*, Canada, 1922, no. 27.

was best designed to prevent neglect and indifference. On the other hand, the long-run problem was (and remains) that of assimilating the Indian into the white community. In the administrative machinery designed to protect and educate the Indian there lay the danger of frustrating the attainment of the larger objective of assimilation. The clientele arrangement necessarily and deliberately singled out the Indians from the rest of the community, while the system of Indian reserves only reinforced this process.[42]

Perhaps it is significant of the special status conferred on both the Indians and the Department erected to manage their affairs that until 1913 the major expenses of administration were borne by the funds derived from the Indians' own estate. The eccentric Secretary of State Labouchere had argued in the 1850's that he "was convinced that if those entrusted with the care of the Indians were made sensible that their establishment must be self-supporting, they would not fail to find the requisite means of accomplishing the object."[43] His comments apparently were taken to heart by the colonial officials who replaced the Imperial authorities. Certainly under the new management of a centralized department the interests of the Indians received better attention. But one might query the adequacy of the budget thus made available. Further, one might ask whether placing the costs of managing Indian affairs directly on the taxpayer might not have aroused a more general critical interest in their administration. As it was, the Department operated mainly in a quiet backwater, isolated from parliamentary interest and by the same token unable to stir up any interest in expanding the services to the Indians. Periodically, the white man feels the weight of the albatross and institutes a full-scale inquiry, amends the Indian Act, and sits back again, his conscience partially salved. This being the situation perhaps it has been for the best that the Indians had a single Department wholeheartedly concerned with their affairs, if not always able to attract the funds or efficient personnel required for its work.

[42]The conclusions reached by the legislative committee which recently (1955) studied the affairs of the Indians in Ontario appear to confirm the general thesis sustained throughout this chapter. See *Civil Liberties and Rights of Indians in Ontario*, Report of the Select Committee of Legislative Assembly, March 19, 1954, section 1.

[43]Quoted in "Report of Special Commissioners," *Sessional Papers*, 1858, part I.

CHAPTER XIV

AGRICULTURE: DEPARTMENTAL POTTING-SHED

"Government," wrote Tom Paine, "is no further necessary than to supply the few cases to which society and civilization are not conveniently competent; and instances are not wanting to show that everything which government can usefully add thereto, has been performed by the common consent of society, without government." A pioneer community like the United Provinces devoted to agricultural pursuits could readily embrace this *laissez-faire* doctrine. It was soon forced to realize, however, that the "common consent of society" on which Paine relied could no more be expected to sprout full grown from colonial soil than its own grain. Before the period of Union had expired, the agricultural interests of the community had been literally organized to death through the creation of an elaborate maze of privately run agricultural associations. Ensnarled in their own cumbersome machinery, these agencies groped with varying success for "the common consent" of the agrarian element of the community. In this exploratory operation they were assisted, after 1853, by a rather formless governmental agency which ten years later was to become the nucleus of the present-day Department of Agriculture. The tardy and extremely hesitant occupancy of this important sector of the colonial economy by the state, coupled with the elaborate apparatus of private associations, testify to the strength of the *laissez-faire* tradition in agricultural affairs.

Laissez-faire doctrines obviously influenced another feature of the administrative machinery which was slowly set up by the state to supervise agriculture. As the machinery was expanded a curious assortment of seemingly unrelated matters was attached to it. When the government is uncertain about the appropriateness of undertaking particular functions it is common to find them grouped uncomfortably and somewhat illogically in an "oddments" Department. In Britain, during this same period, the Home Office mothered an administrative motley which shared no common ancestors and which, as time confirmed their necessity, grew to independent departmental stature.[1]

[1] K. B. Smellie, *A Hundred Years of English Government* (London, 1937), pp. 252 f., describes the agencies under the nominal tutelage of the Home Office. He also indicates (p. 251) how "the Ministry of Agriculture and Fisheries reveals the furtive and often infertile commerce of science with politics which our Constitution compels."

In the Canadas, the original Department of Agriculture served the same purpose—what Professor Smellie has called "potting house" function. Amongst the exotics "potted out" in the Department of Agriculture were a statistics branch, a branch for administering patents and copyrights, a branch to handle immigration and colonization, and, finally, without any special executive machinery, ministerial oversight of an astonishing array of cultural, artistic, scientific, educational, horticultural, and agricultural societies. In the post-Confederation period, these seedlings matured and were transplanted into such separate Departments as Trade and Commerce, Dominion Bureau of Statistics, Agriculture, Immigration and Colonization.

The most telling complaint continuously registered against the pre-Confederation Department of Agriculture was that it directed its limited resources almost exclusively to all these peripheral subjects and maintained only the most limited—even casual—contacts with agricultural affairs. (As late as the 1870's, similar complaints were still heard.[2]) If there was a connecting thread it could only be detected in the Jeffersonian belief in the power of education and the capacity of the rank and file to benefit from it. The practical instrument of education, in turn, was the collector and disseminator of facts and figures—the statistician and the publicist. Given these underlying presuppositions, it is perhaps not surprising to discover that, up to Confederation, Thomas D'Arcy McGee, visionary publicist and democratic, inspirational orator, proved to be the most vigorous and successful Minister of Agriculture.[3]

To McGee, there was nothing odd in the juxtaposition of these varied activities under the generous roof of the Department of Agriculture. Indeed, he was quite prepared to add fisheries, mines, and minerals to the group, contending that "this would give the Department, in all, seven branches, including the chief subjects of our internal economy and Social Science, which classify naturally together."[4] While McGee's proposal was never adopted, there was

[2]This admission appears, for example, in the "Annual Report of the Minister of Agriculture for the Year 1862," *Sessional Papers*, Canada, 1863, no. 4. For a later reiteration of the complaint in even stronger terms see "Annual Report of the Minister of Agriculture for the Year 1871," *ibid.*, 1872, no. 2A, p. 2.

[3]See the estimate of McGee in Josephine Phelan, *The Ardent Exile: The Life and Times of D'Arcy McGee* (Toronto, 1951), p. 267, and also in Isabel Skelton, *The Life of Thomas D'Arcy McGee* (Gardenvale, 1925) pp. 425 f. McGee's interest in improving the methods of gathering statistical material and increasing the accuracy of the census stands out both in his reports as Minister of Agriculture and in his special Report on the Origin and Organization of the Public Departments," 1863, Public Archives of Canada, M. 837.

[4]See McGee's "Report on the . . . Public Departments," 1863, section on Department of Agriculture and Statistics.

more logic in the existing arrangements than would appear at first glance. After all, statistics of agriculture took precedence over all other types of information; much of the census was also devoted to agriculture. Some system of crop reporting and some central agency for assembling these statistics were obviously indispensable to an agrarian community. Hence, it was quite logical to place the responsibility for statistics in the hands of the Department of Agriculture and, at the same time, to make the Minister chairman of the Board of Registration and Statistics—the agency which arranged the decennial census of the province.[5] Then again, since the most important inventions coming on the market consisted of improved agricultural implements or machines designed to transform the products of the farm, it seemed equally legitimate to place Patents and Copyrights under the Department.[6] Furthermore, at this period, promotion of immigration and colonization required information services which could best be supplied by the Department already engaged in collecting statistics.[7] Finally, the Department's paternal supervision of a host of grant-aided private societies—agricultural societies, mechanics' institutes, boards of arts and manufactures, and horticultural societies—was all part of the optimistic belief, previously mentioned, that ordinary men and women if given the opportunity and the facts could be made to absorb culture and think deeply. The government was to provide financial support and paternal inspiration, the private associations were to distribute the funds in accordance with the Benthamite theory of practical incentives for good work and high thinking.[8]

When the social history of Canada comes to be written, one of the most interesting chapters will be the one dealing with this astonishing optimistic vision which in the 1850's and 60's appeared to guide official policy. Amongst the farm population a rural utopia was envisaged: farmers well briefed on the latest mechanical services,

[5]16 Vic., c. 11 (1853). Hitherto the Inspector General had been chairman of the Board.

[6]For some account of these inventions—e.g., tile digging machines and new types of seeds—see the informative report of William McDougall to Dr. Rolph, Minister of Agriculture, included with "Documents Submitted by the Bureau of Agriculture to the Legislature," *Journals*, Legislative Assembly, Canada (*J.L.A.C.*), 1854–5, Appendix I.I.

[7]Indeed, after immigration affairs were placed under the Bureau of Agriculture in 1853, the officials in charge assumed that their responsibilities extended only to compiling and making available to immigrants statistics of labour conditions, food prices, and so on. See remarks of William Hutton, Secretary to the Bureau, before the Select Committee on Emigration in 1860, *J.L.A.C.*, 1860, Appendix 4, pp. 43 f.

[8]Hence the emphasis on fairs and exhibitions with lengthy prize lists.

the best types of seeds and breeds, the most efficient farming practices; their interest perpetually titivated by prizes, fairs, exhibitions; a select few returning from agricultural colleges with sound theoretical and practical training; the many, listening avidly to occasional authoritative lectures delivered by travelling experts. In the towns, no less than on the farms, a similar vision emerges: libraries sponsored by mechanics' institutes; science museums filled with models and specimens of the new manufacturing enterprises; lectures and even adult education courses, sponsored by the boards of arts and manufactures, crowded with vigorous artisans thirsting for knowledge and culture. Here, surely, on the harsh Canadian soil, we see the last full-flowering of the Age of Enlightenment. It was a bright, naïve, generous vision, destined to produce a mushroom harvest of local societies and then to wither sadly in the years ahead. At the full flood of optimism the Department of Agriculture presided over this development—presided, it must be emphasized, for it neither inspired its inception nor actively directed its course. In return for its annual grants, the government hoped that the private organizations would feed a constant flow of factual information into the central statistical section.

We must look to the hierarchy of private associations if we are to understand why the government took such a restricted view of its obligations to agriculture—so restricted, in fact, that, as McGee admitted toward the end of the period, the Department was unable to render "any considerable service to the agricultural interest."[9]

Clearly, even the limited services provided by the Department of Agriculture depended upon the initiative and vigour with which the hierarchy of private agricultural organizations was run. In turn, this hierarchy could only function fruitfully if the members in its broad base of local associations remained enthusiastic and active, and only if all parts of the structure could maintain contact for mutual stimulation of effort. Unfortunately, in all these respects both public and private administration revealed many deficiencies. There was far too much machinery for the available man power and for the tasks to be performed. Between 1841 and 1867 the statute books indicate that the colonial legislature took a continuous and intimate interest in improving the organization for advancing agriculture in the province. On the whole, this interest resulted in the accumulation of an unwieldy, uncontrollable structure which, by Confederation, had little to show for its laboured efforts.

[9]See his remarks in his "Report on the . . . Public Departments," 1863.

Constructed on the currently familiar "grass roots" principle, the basic organizational unit was the local agricultural society—generally one, occasionally two, in each county. Any person subscribing the annual five-shilling fee could become a member of the local society and the members elected their own officers. As early as 1818, legislation in Lower Canada had made available to these local societies annual public grants ranging between £700 and £1,000.[10] Similar legislation was approved for Upper Canada in 1830.[11] After the Union, new legislation in 1845 systematized the grant-in-aid procedure. The government's contribution, based on the paid-up membership of each local society, amounted to three times the fees paid into the society. The grant was a vaguely conditional one, for the legislation specified the purposes to which the money could be devoted: holding exhibitions, sponsoring publications, encouraging stock breeding, and donating prizes. Annual reports were to be presented to the local legislature.[12]

Superimposed on these local societies after 1847 were two provincial bodies, one for each section of the province—the Lower Canada and the Upper Canada Agricultural Societies.[13] The governing body of the Lower Canada Society was made up of thirty-three directors elected by the dues-paying members. In Upper Canada the local societies each appointed two members to serve on the governing body. Ostensibly, these two bodies were introduced to co-ordinate and supervise the efforts of the local societies. While they were clearly self-managing, they were required to transmit annual reports to the legislature. The grants to the local societies were now to be channelled through the two provincial societies, and in turn the reports from local societies were to be sent through the central societies to the provincial legislature. The objects of the provincial societies were much the same as those outlined for the local

[10]58 Geo. III, c. 6 (1818). A most useful outline of the early legislation is to be found in an unpublished manuscript in the Library of the Department of Agriculture, Ottawa: R. P. Gorham, "The Development of Agricultural Administration in Upper Canada during the Period before Confederation."

[11]11 Geo. IV, c. 10 (1830).

[12]8 Vic., c. 53 (Lower Canada), c. 54 (Upper Canada). These acts also provided that expenditures of the societies were "to be accounted for to Her Majesty . . . through the Lord Commissioners of Her Majesty's Treasury, in such manner and form as Her Majesty . . . shall be pleased to direct." This provision which is found in other statutes even after 1845 may have been only a formality, but superficially it clearly implied the subservience of colonial administration at the time.

[13]10 & 11 Vic., c. 61 (1847).

societies, except that the encouragement of domestic manufactures and inventions was added to the task of improving stock, produce, tillage methods, and agricultural implements. Until 1850, then, the entire administration of agricultural affairs was vested in privately operated societies. This complex structure was founded on provincial enactments which outlined both the organization and powers of each association. Inevitably the forces of dualism found expression in the structure, for Upper Canada and Lower Canada each possessed its own entirely separate complement of associations. The government remained in the background, providing small grants and calling for annual reports from the private societies.

At this time (1850) there were twenty-seven county societies reporting to the legislature from Lower Canada and twenty-one from Upper Canada.[14] Superficially, these figures give the impression that there was a widespread interest in the work of the associations. A closer scrutiny of their operations reveals that the societies had a high overhead for the small amount of money they disbursed. Moreover, their practical encouragement to agricultural interests seems to have been confined to a small clique of well-to-do farmers who least needed the support, and most of the prizes to have been distributed for prime beef cattle. The limited government grants obviously were not being directed to the proper persons nor encouraging that reform in agricultural methods which was contemplated. Actually, the local societies were working in isolation, with scant support from the provincial associations, and their slender financial resources tended to be dissipated on petty projects.

While these weaknesses were displayed at the "grass roots" the central Agricultural Societies for Upper and Lower Canada during their brief existence (1847-53) appear to have made valuable contributions.[15] They neglected their main duty of co-ordinating and invigorating the operations of the local societies, but, on the other hand, for the first time the government was provided with expert information about the state and progress of agriculture in the province. Employing

[14]In 1844 just two societies reported; in 1846 there were thirty-one and by 1850 there were forty-six. See *J.L.A.C.*, 1844-5, Appendix V; 1846, Appendix J; 1851, Appendix J. The critical comments that follow in the text are drawn from a "Report of a Special Committee on Agricultural Improvement of Lower Canada," *ibid.*, 1850, Appendix T.T.

[15]See "Report of the Special Committee on Agricultural Instruction," *J.L.A.C.*, 1864, Appendix 3; Gorham, "The Development of Agricultural Administration"; and "Reports of Agricultural Societies in Lower Canada" and "First Annual Report of the Board of Agriculture of Upper Canada," *J.L.A.C.*, 1852-3, Appendix S.

questionnaires with considerable success, the provincial associations were able to obtain limited information upon which new legislation was quickly erected. In Upper Canada, for example, the Agricultural Society was instrumental in formulating the Act of 1850 which created the Board of Agriculture, thereby sponsoring the first governmental influence in the councils of the private associations. In Lower Canada, the Society was the sole source of information from which a special legislative committee, sitting during 1850 and 1851, produced a comprehensive statute in 1853 dealing with the reorganization of the administration of agricultural matters.

From the early 1850's on, one can observe a progressive increase in the government's participation in the administration of agricultural affairs. The first timid step was taken in 1850 when the Board of Agriculture for Upper Canada was created.[16] It was a ten-member board, and for the first time two public officials—the Inspector General and the Professor of Agriculture at the University of Toronto—were made *ex officio* members. Like the Agricultural Society it replaced, the new Board was to collect information and report to the legislature. In 1851 it also became the co-ordinator and grant-disbursing agency for the local societies. With the legislation approved in 1853, we discover a much bolder assertion of governmental influence.[17] The new legislation created a Bureau of Agriculture "to be connected with one of the Public Departments." A Minister of Agriculture was also introduced, although until 1862 this portfolio was undertaken as part of the duties of the President of the Executive Council.[18] It was with this legislation, too, that Agriculture began to gather unto itself that host of somewhat unrelated activities mentioned above. In particular, the statute specifically directed the Minister of Agriculture to collect statistics of agriculture, and appointed him chairman of the Board of Registration and Statistics. The significance of this change will be noted below. The same legislation of 1853 reshuffled the existing private associations, but obviously expected them to carry the main burden of missionary to the agricultural interests. At the provincial level there were now to be two Boards of Agriculture and two Agricultural Associations, one of each for both sections of the province. Both Boards approved the grants for the local societies and operated experimental farms; the Lower

[16]13 & 14 Vic., c. 73 (1850).
[17]16 Vic., c. 11 (1853).
[18]In his *Reminiscences,* Sir Francis Hincks suggests that the portfolio was devised to meet political rather than administrative necessities; see Francis Hincks, *Reminiscences of His Public Life* (Montreal, 1884), pp. 256 f.

Canada Board also operated an agricultural college. The Associations, working under the Boards of Agriculture, were responsible for provincial fairs and exhibits. The county and township agricultural societies continued as before.

It might be noted, to complete the picture, that legislation of 1857 contemplated similar boards for arts and manufactures, for trade, for mechanics' institutes, and for horticultural societies, the Minister of Agriculture being *ex officio* on each board.[19] The state's share in these semi-private agencies was to provide several *ex officio* members and to pay their expenses. The record reveals, however, that the Minister of Agriculture made little effort to push the rival financial claims of any of these other associations. While the grants to agricultural societies remained surprisingly large, the other societies rightly complained that they were starved. Indeed, in the annual reports of the Boards of Arts and Manufactures we hear the familiar lament: the new interests of the labouring artisan and small tradesmen are being sacrificed to the pampered agricultural interests. While the mechanics' institutes in both sections of the province were struggling with an annual grant of $4,000, the agricultural societies received from the state over $90,000 per annum.[20] On the other hand, the number and vitality of the local associations in the field of agriculture, as contrasted with the few isolated cases of successful mechanics' institutes, suggested that the state was showering its favours only on those who had given indications that they were prepared to help themselves. In 1865, for example, the members of 63 county agricultural societies and 252 branch societies in Upper Canada had paid-up subscriptions amounting to $32,000, while in Lower Canada 19,317 members of 72 local societies had contributed over $20,000.[21]

By Confederation, then, the Department of Agriculture is mothering a mixed flock of private societies concerned with agricultural improvement, technical innovations, the development of trade, adult education, dissemination of culture and scientific knowledge, and the advancement of domestic arts and crafts: all this, in addition to

[19]20 Vic., c. 32 (1857). This legislation was the outcome of a special report prepared for Council by William Hutton, Secretary to the Bureau. See his evidence before the Select Committee on Emigration in 1860, *J.L.A.C.*, 1860, Appendix 4, p. 44. For his memorandum see State Book O, 1885, Feb. 20, p. 668.

[20]See "Report of Boards of Arts and Manufacturers of Upper and Lower Canada," appended annually to main "Report of Minister of Agriculture." Note especially reports for 1864 in *Sessional Papers*, Canada, 1865, no. 6, and *ibid.*, 1866, no. 5.

[21]See "Reports of Agricultural Societies for Upper and Lower Canada for the Year 1865," appended to "Report of Minister of Agriculture," *ibid.*, 1866, no. 5.

the other responsibilities for statistics (including the census), registration of patents and copyrights, and, after 1862, immigration and colonization.

As has been mentioned, this curious collection of responsibilities —most of which were to develop ultimately as separate departments— can best be explained in terms of the Department's interest in educating or, at least, informing the Canadian people. Indeed this information service, after immigration affairs were handed over by Imperial authorities, had to be extended abroad. Basic to this informational service was the collection of statistics. And yet in the estimation of McGee, certainly the most zealous supporter of the state's duty to collect and collate statistics, this part of the Department's work was conducted with singular lack of success. Writing as late as 1863, McGee offered these observations on the work of the Board of Registration and Statistics which was directly under the Minister of Agriculture:

Whether from some inherent defect in the present Constitution of the Board of Statistics from the absence of a properly qualified Secretary to that Board to classify, collate, digest, tabulate and index even such returns as are made, the large annual outlay on reports, is, in a great degree thrown away; is a loss to the Provinces and a source of humiliation to every advocate of judicious progress.[22]

McGee then went on to recount the experience of Holland which had been cited at a recent session of the International Statistical Congress meeting in London. Here it was revealed that a Statistical Commission had been given the authority to go direct to the source for its figures and compel their production, rather than trying fruitlessly to extract the figures through an "intermediary." In this reference to an "intermediary," obviously McGee was striking out against the practice of relying on the private associations to channel facts and figures through from the localities to the Department. McGee's observations emphasized the two basic weaknesses of the whole *laissez-faire* approach which had characterized the management of agricultural affairs in the province. The government's own central agency was neither properly organized nor properly manned; there had never been sufficient agreement that there were important tasks which could be performed only by such an agency. The other weakness was related to the overly elaborate organization of private associations which not only dissipated the energies of the members

[22] See his "Report on the ... Public Departments," 1863, section on Department of Agriculture and Statistics.

but blocked adequate communication with the government agency. A weak central agency having little official or public support, and a weak, because inchoate, structure of private associations having little contact with one another or with the government's co-ordinating agency, combined to render impossible any constructive, positive action.

The annual reports of successive Ministers of Agriculture amply support McGee's analysis of the flaws in administration which have here been associated with the *laissez-faire* milieu in which agricultural matters were handled. The weakness of the private portion of the structure has already been noted. The first Minister of Agriculture, the Honourable Malcolm Cameron, on retiring from his post in 1853 summarized the difficulties in the somewhat pompous style which characterized most official reports to the Governor General:

Our Government, regarding labor as the source of wealth, has adopted a policy—as wise as it is enlightened. We now possess a system almost as complete in its naked arrangements without reference to action in any of its divisions, as the theorist can devise. It is only desirable to discover if possible, the proper adjustment of the parts to the whole, and the amount of tension each part is capable of sustaining without hazard to the movements of the machine. I allude to the Township and County Societies, the Provincial Associations, the Boards of Agriculture, and the Public Department designated the Bureau of Agriculture. . . .[23]

Ten years later, another Minister of Agriculture, having investigated the comparable organization for handling agricultural affairs in Britain, France, and the United States, concluded:

We have our Board of Agriculture, constituting a superior council charged with the management of all the County agricultural societies. Unfortunately, there is not sufficiently close connection between the local societies and the Boards of Agriculture, any more than between the latter and the Department of Agriculture. Thus each society is left to take its own course without being under the control of any superior authority.[24]

Two years later his successor, Thomas D'Arcy McGee, also admitted that Cameron's "proper adjustment of the parts to the whole" still awaited completion. "It is to be regretted," McGee remarked, "that the relations between the Department and the two Boards of Agriculture for Upper and Lower Canada, if they ever were intimate,

[23]See his report included in "Documents Submitted by Bureau of Agriculture," *J.L.A.C.*, 1852–3.
[24]"Annual Report of Minister of Agriculture and Statistics for the Year 1862," *Sessional Papers*, Canada, 1863, no. 4.

have ceased to be so."[25] The same observation, he continued, also applied with respect to the relations between the Department and the Boards of Arts and Manufactures. In the years between Cameron's first report and McGee's report we find steady complaints recorded against the unresponsiveness of the private agencies who were expected to act as the eyes and ears of the governmental agency. In 1861, for example, out of 1,300 questionnaires circulated by the Department to agricultural interests, only 50 were returned.[26] McGee was so disheartened by the whole process of assembling statistics that he reported in 1864 that the last two Censuses "are not to be relied upon."[27] There is also reason to believe that despite the number of local societies some were organized not by enthusiastic interested members, but merely as a means of qualifying for government grants.[28]

All the evidence indicates that the local societies were generally ineffectual and that the provincial boards did not maintain contact either with these subordinate associations or the Department of Agriculture. This state of affairs can be attributed as much to the refusal to strengthen the governmental administrative apparatus as to the weaknesses of the private associations. Here again successive Ministers of Agriculture reported on the administrative weaknesses of the governmental machine and offered solutions. All the political heads of the Department agreed that nothing could be done without a permanent deputy minister. Unfortunately, in the early stages of its development the Bureau of Agriculture lost its energetic secretary, Mr. Hutton.[29] It was this key official who pointed out

[25]"Annual Report of the Minister of Agriculture for the Year 1864," *ibid.*, 1865, no. 6, p. 4.
[26]"Annual Report of the Minister of Agriculture and Statistics for the Year 1861," *ibid.*, 1862, no. 32.
[27]"Annual Report of the Minister of Agriculture for the Year 1864," *ibid.*, 1865, no. 6, p. 14.
[28]Although in the annual report of the agricultural societies in Lower Canada for the year 1865, a different view is taken: "An unequivocal mark of progress is exhibited by the simple fact that most of the agricultural societies have made efforts always to subscribe sufficient to entitle them to the whole amount of the government grant. . . . Thus the whole government grant is drawn and subsequently offered in high premiums for improvements of all kinds . . . ," *Sessional Papers*, Canada, 1866, no. 5, p. 160.
[29]Hutton became secretary in 1855 when by Order in Council the two branches of agriculture and statistics were amalgamated—presumably on the basis of his recommendation to Council. He continued to provide the dynamic force in the Department until his death in 1861—a loss which paralysed a department most of whose employees were temporary and whose duties, as has been emphasized, were so varied as to constitute the nuclei of several post-Confederation departments.

in a special report to Council in 1856 that the government's responsibility for agricultural affairs was "if not wholly neglected, very imperfectly carried out."[30] His report, proposing a full-scale reorganization of the Bureau, was implemented by the statute of 1857. In this legislation the responsibility of the Department was broadened to include the Boards of Arts and Manufactures and the mechanics' institutes. Unfortunately, Mr. Hutton did not live to direct the reorganization he had planned, and in 1863 McGee regretted that "except in the increase of its [the Department's] patronage, it is to be feared, that the new powers thus conferred by law, have not enabled successive administrations to render any considerable service to the agricultural interest."[31]

While Hutton's efforts to invigorate the administration of agricultural matters produced no immediate results, the last three Ministers of Agriculture before Confederation did much to prepare the Department for the kind of duties envisaged by Hutton. In a penetrating analysis of the Department's operations for the year 1862, the Minister of Agriculture, F. Evantural, admitted:

The Department of Agriculture and Statistics has unfortunately been, perhaps more than any other, subjected to neglect. Its organization and internal discipline had been left in a condition so little efficient that the public had begun to doubt the necessity or the importance of keeping it up, under the special management of a member of the Executive Government. The lengthened absence of certain of my predecessors, and the consequent want of any responsible superintendence and direction, the small number of permanent officers attached to the Department, the too ready admission and dismissal of temporary employees, whose interest in the public weal is of a passing nature, and to crown all, the death of the secretary, Mr. Hutton, have with several other circumstances, contributed to reduce the Department to a state of disorganization which is much to be regretted. . . .[32]

Evantural's solution was to reduce the number of temporary employees and to place a responsible official in charge of each of the separate branches. The secretary was to serve not only as branch head for agricultural affairs but also to assume general direction of all branches in the Department. Evantural's successor, Mr. Letellier, apparently discovered that these reforms still left the political head

[30]Quoted by McGee in his "Report on the . . . Public Departments," 1863, section on the Department of Agriculture and Statistics.
[31]*Ibid.*
[32]See "Annual Report of the Minister of Agriculture and Statistics for the Year 1862," *Sessional Papers*, Canada, 1863, no. 4.

of the Department with insufficient permanent assistance, for he concluded: "the surest remedy for the defects still existing in its management, would be the appointment of a permanent deputy head."[33] This change was finally effected by McGee in 1864 when he succeeded in luring J. C. Taché away from the Board of Prison Inspectors to serve as Deputy Minister of the Department of Agriculture. Taché, as a former member of parliament and chairman of the important special committee on agricultural improvement in Lower Canada (1850–1), proved himself an experienced, vigorous administrator who carried on as Deputy Minister of the new Dominion Department of Agriculture, retiring as late as 1888.[34]

Two immediate reforms were effected under McGee and Taché. First, departmental discipline and lines of authority were asserted probably for the first time in the Department's life. "The want of direction and permanent influence," according to McGee, "was such that official letters were received and answered under the names and sole responsibility of several of the clerks, in one word the authority being so dispersed and underrated, was in fact nowhere."[35] The second reform required the classification and rearrangement of the documents and records—particularly those pertaining to the Census. Since, as has been noted, the chief responsibility of the Department was to collect, compile, and disseminate information about agricultural, technical, and cultural affairs in the province, the slipshod handling of this material accounted for most of the Department's failures as a centre of information, if not inspiration, to the individuals and the private associations with which it was supposed to be in intimate contact.

Under McGee and his two predecessors, Evantural and Letellier, the statistical and recording work of the Department was gradually developed. Evantural had found "no executive machinery in the Department for the collection of statistical information." A Board of Registration and Statistics, consisting of the Minister of Agriculture (prior to 1853, the Inspector General), the Receiver General, and the Provincial Secretary, had met sporadically about a dozen times

[33]*Ibid.*, 1864, no. 32.

[34]J. C. Taché, physician, editor, member of Parliament, professor of physiology, chairman of Board of Prison Inspectors, and from 1864 to 1888 Deputy Minister of Agriculture, was "one of the most distinguished gentlemen of which Canada can boast." G. M. Rose, *A Cyclopaedia of Canadian Biography* (Toronto, 1886), pp. 68–9. Taché died in 1894 leaving "the Dominion, especially the scientific medical portion of it, under such obligation as it never will be able to repay him."

[35]See "Annual Report of the Minister of Agriculture for the year 1864," *Sessional Papers*, Canada, 1865, no. 6, p. 2.

since its creation in 1847. No minutes or records of these meetings had been kept, its chief concern having been to supervise the arrangements for the Census of 1851 and 1861. Evantural, stressing the value of statistics for public administration and the "furtherance of political science," contended that the state should not leave this important function to private means "since the machinery of executive business enables a Government readily to collect statistical facts, and it has, moreover, the right to demand information. . . . " The Board was, accordingly, resuscitated by Evantural and an extra clerk was placed in charge of making statistical abstracts of the figures then available.[36] In these somewhat unpromising circumstances, Evantural optimistically declared his intention of producing a handbook of the statistical history of the country. McGee enthusiastically endorsed this objective when he took over the Department. As a beginning, the Department undertook the compilation and publication of "The Blue Book," a useful compendium of statistics on departmental personnel which had its origin in the blank forms originally filled out in each colony for the information of the Colonial Office. Until 1864 this material had been entered by hand on the standardized forms provided by the Colonial Office.[37] After 1864, it was published as part of the Department's annual report. McGee envisaged the expansion of the Blue Book into a printed volume, full of historically valuable statistical material and information which might well forestall the need for questions asked in Parliament or by special committees of investigation. This early enthusiasm and foresight eventually bore fruit in 1886 when the first issue of the *Statistical Abstract & Record* was published. This was the predecessor of the now well-known and much-valued *Canada Year Book*. In the meantime, the forerunner of our Dominion Bureau of Statistics (which today employs many hundreds of officials) consisted at Confederation of a scarcely defined organization within the cluttered Department of Agriculture and Statistics, employing less than half a dozen clerks. As McGee remarked in one of his able annual reports,[38] the Department had reached the stage where it needed a few men "of thorough education, and more than ordinary aptitudes, among its permanent staff," if its multifarious responsibilities were to be properly undertaken.

[36]See *ibid.*, 1863, no. 4.
[37]The Public Archives of Canada holds a complete file of this predecessor of the "Blue Book" and the present Canada Year Book. This annual publication constitutes a neglected source of valuable statistical information not only on the public departments but about social and economic conditions generally.
[38]For the year 1864, *Sessional Papers*, Canada, no. 6, p. 4.

CHAPTER XV

IMMIGRANTS OR ITINERANTS

THROUGHOUT THE GREATER part of the period of Union the administrative agency responsible for dealing with the flow of newcomers to Canada bore the title "Emigration Office." The title was significant for it revealed the British origin and orientation of the agency. From the British point of view the office located at Quebec City was simply a useful adjunct to the Imperial Emigration Service. As far as Canadians were concerned, however, *emigrants* were *immigrants*—potential settlers who had to be made to feel at home in a strange new world. The Colonial Office found such difficulty in recognizing the distinction that it was reluctant to co-operate with Canadian efforts to cope with the immigrants.

In the early 1860's, the Emigration Office became in name what, in fact, it always ought to have been, an Immigration and Colonization Department. By this time, moreover, the emigration from the British Isles had tapered off, while more and more newcomers were arriving from North Europe. The Quebec agency could no longer be viewed as a forwarding post for the surplus population of the mother country. The shift in the sources of immigration to Canada emphasized a situation which had gradually been forcing itself on the attention of Canadian authorities. Most of those who landed on Canadian shores were simply using the St. Lawrence route as a cheap means of gaining access to the American West. Canadian officials might well have wondered whether a more appropriate title for the Department of Agriculture and Immigration which had been reorganized in 1863 ought not to have been the Department for Colonizing the United States.

It is clear, of course, that immigration cannot be divorced from the problems associated with colonization. Generally speaking, until 1848, the Imperial authorities showed themselves unwilling to permit the United Provinces to take any initiative in the matter of regulating immigration. At the same time they continually pressed the colonies to embark on elaborate schemes of systematic settlement of the immigrants. These proposals the Canadian authorities stubbornly repelled. The Imperial government, for its part, would not admit the Canadian claim that the flow of emigrants from British ports was not being properly regulated. When, after 1848, Canadian authorities were permitted to take the initiative and sought to regulate immigration, they were still unable to co-ordinate immigration and settlement programmes. As a result, many potential settlers flitted like birds of passage (often at Canadian expense) quickly over Canadian territory, making towards the nearest exit to the American West.

Successful settlement of the Canadian hinterland obviously demanded close co-operation between the administrative agencies responsible for surveys, land sales, natural resources, transportation services, and the immigrants. Until Confederation, as will be shown, the Canadian authorities concerned with these matters operated in watertight, jealously guarded compartments and co-operation—to say nothing of co-ordination—was almost non-existent. The administrative divorce between the immigration service and the settlement programme is reflected in the twofold division of material adopted in this chapter. The first part examines the arrangements made for the flow of immigrants; the second part deals with the efforts to make *bona fide* settlers out of the immigrants who constantly threatened to become itinerants.

Immigration

The administrative apparatus for looking after immigrants evolved first under British direction and carried with it until Confederation the marks of its Imperial sponsor. In 1828 a Chief Emigration Officer (more frequently termed Chief Emigrant Agent), appointed by the Imperial government but paid by Lower Canada, was stationed at Quebec and left, without either funds or clear-cut instructions, to check on the shipmasters' compliance with the regulations imposed by the Imperial Passenger Act.[1] Only in 1832, when the legislature of Lower Canada approved a capitation or head tax of one dollar for each immigrant landed at Quebec, was the agent provided with a small fund with which to carry out his duties. In practice half the fund was divided between two voluntary emigration societies operating in Quebec and Montreal and the other half was turned over to the Marine Hospital at Quebec and the General Hospital at Montreal. A. C. Buchanan, who occupied the position of Chief Emigrant Agent

[1]For this early history see the excellent review of the organization and operations of the Emigration Office provided by its permanent head, A. C. Buchanan, before a legislative committee in 1860: "Report of the Select Committee to whom was Referred the Annual Report of the Chief Emigration Agent," *Journals*, Legislative Assembly, Canada, (J.L.A.C.), 1860, Appendix 4.

from 1838 until his death shortly after Confederation, revealed that at the outset "the office being a new one, the course to be followed by the Emigrant Agent was left in a great degree discretionary with himself." In special instances the Agent reported to the Civil Secretary who, it will be recalled, at the time of Union was virtually permanent head of the colonial civil service, reporting to the Governor of the colony.

In the decade before Union, the Quebec Office was supplemented by the appointment of inland agents first at Toronto and Montreal and later at Kingston, Hamilton, Ottawa, and Port Hope. The agent at Toronto, Mr. Hawke, whose connection with the service was as lengthy as Buchanan's, took orders from his superior in Quebec. Since the expansion of these inland agencies could not be financed from the capitation tax, the Imperial government provided a grant which averaged about £1,500 per year to meet their expenses. The other important addition to the local administrative arrangements for receiving the immigrant was the creation in 1832 by the colonial government of a quarantine station at Grosse Isle, down-river from Quebec. The salaries of the quarantine officials were paid from Imperial funds, but the expenses of the establishment were a charge against the colony.

After Union, this local administrative apparatus remained virtually unchanged until Confederation. Lord Sydenham—like Lord Durham before him—had been horrified by the lack of adequate facilities for dealing with the immigrants on their arrival in Canada and his bill of 1841 was designed to prevent them from being dumped under the Rock at Quebec and left to drift. The first immigration Act passed by the Union was sponsored by him.[2] It imposed a head tax of five shillings on each immigrant and directed that this tax fund should be used for three purposes: medical examination at the quarantine station on Grosse Isle; direct relief of the destitute; and transportation of such immigrants to their final destination in the colony. In 1842, at the suggestion of Buchanan, the Quebec Office was formally made the headquarters for all the inland agents and the disbursement of the fund arising from the capitation tax was removed from the private societies and placed in the hands of the Chief Emigrant Agent. Until 1853, however, the quarantine station was supplied by the Commissariat—an outpost of the Imperial government. By 1854, the British financial connection with the administration of immigration had been discontinued: the Imperial grant was dropped and

[2] 4 & 5 Vic., c. 13 (1841).

all expenses, including the rather heavy costs of the quarantine station, were met from the immigrant tax. Since the number of immigrants varied greatly, the tax in later years fell far short of the total expenses incurred and a substantial annual appropriation in aid of the immigration service was required.

It would appear that these local arrangements for coping with the flow of immigrants, once landed at Quebec, were reasonably adequate. The quarantine establishment was equipped to handle any normal epidemic, while hospitals at Quebec and Montreal were available for immigrants suffering from mild disabilities. The Quebec Office had money in hand for looking after immigrants who arrived destitute, arranging for their upkeep and transportation to their final destination. Spread out at strategic centres along the St. Lawrence route were half a dozen inland immigration offices whose agents were expected to keep in touch with local labour conditions, advise the newcomers, and direct them to areas where their services could be put to the best use. The minutely detailed reports submitted annually by these agents to Buchanan indicate that conscientious civil servants were on the job doing their best to keep statistics and provide real services for the newcomers.

Adequate as these arrangements on the Canadian side appeared to be, certain important elements remained beyond the control of Canadian officials. Most of the real problems encountered by the local agents arose at the point of embarkation, and the Imperial government, at least until 1848, argued that the colony could not interfere with the British emigrant. And yet it was vital for effective administration in Canada to have detailed and preferably advance information on three matters. First, how many intended emigrants could the Canadian office be expected to deal with each year? Second, as they were potential settlers, it was important to know something about the composition of the emigrant flow: age, sex, character, and practical skills were of real interest to Canadian authorities, so that they could make advance arrangements for absorbing them into the colonial economy. Finally, the Canadians were naturally concerned about the condition in which the passengers arrived at Quebec. Would there, for example, be a sudden pressure on the quarantine facilities or hospitals? How rigorously had the British authorities applied the regulations imposed by their own Imperial Shipping Act on the masters of the emigrant ships? To all these questions Canadian officials received inadequate answers, or were given to understand that it was considered none of their business.

It was the dramatically sudden and disastrous exodus of the Irish from their famine-ridden country in 1846-7 that brought the immigration issue to a head.³ Incidentally, it verified every suspicion that colonial officials had entertained about British control of the flow of emigrants from its shores. Dealing with this sudden migration would have been a stupendous task in itself; unfortunately, the deadly Asiatic cholera attached itself to this sorry mass of hungry humanity. The plague left its scars in Liverpool where most of the Irish had congregated awaiting ships for overseas; it left its mark as well on every Canadian community from Quebec to Niagara Falls. The quarantine station at Grosse Isle became a shambles of dead and dying, the Commissariat quickly ferried supplies and tents to the Island, emergency calls went out for more doctors and attendants. Lord Elgin, looking back on the episode, likened the province to a beleaguered garrison. Nor were there heroes lacking in the action: priests and nuns gave their lives succouring the diseased in the streets of Montreal, local voluntary societies mushroomed in every community and lent what aid they could to the stricken horde of immigrants as it gradually streamed inland. Months after the disastrous summer of 1847, the relatives of the victims of the plague crowded the larger centres and were dependent on the charity of the Canadian government. Those fortunate enough to have recovered from the dreadful disease could be recognized by their shaven heads as they roved the streets of Montreal. And, as the crisis abated, Canadian leaders began to believe that the whole colony would soon wear the same identifying marks—the symbol of victimization in this case being the colonial head, shorn financially by the Imperial authorities. For not the least unsightly of the sores opened up in the wake of the black summer of 1847 was the vituperation that now began to surge back and forth between Canada and the mother country.

The Canadian authorities, automatically assuming that the Imperial government would foot the bill for the enormous immigration, had spared no expense in attempting to cope with the dead, diseased, and destitute. The *ad hoc* local societies had been equally liberal— as the returns kept coming in, Elgin was forced to admit that they had been far too liberal. The colony emerging from its state of siege

---

³The details of this episode and its administrative implications are located in *Elgin-Grey Papers, 1846–52*, ed. by Sir Arthur Doughty (4 vols., Ottawa, 1937), vols. I, III, and IV; *J.L.A.C.*, 1847, pp. 113–15 and Appendix L; *J.L.A.C.*, 1848, Appendix W; *J.L.A.C.*, 1849, Appendix E.E.E.

expected kudos from the Imperial authorities; instead it received from Earl Grey a sharp lecture on the theme of the prodigal son, accompanied by a blunt refusal to pay the large immigration bill still outstanding. On receiving the minute of Executive Council in which this request for reimbursement was made, Grey angrily exclaimed that this was "about as unreasonable as anything I ever read. . . . "[4] In a series of despatches extending throughout 1847 and 1848, Grey built up an elaborate defence of the Imperial government's approach toward emigration to the Canadas. By March 1848 a more conciliatory, even resigned note emerged from the despatches and it was out of this new attitude that the colonists, under Elgin's able guidance, were able to acquire, first, more satisfactory regulatory powers over immigration, and then to assume the initiative in directing immigration to Canada from all possible sources on the Continent.[5]

In a lengthy post-mortem on the disastrous immigration of 1847, T. F. Elliot, Colonial Land and Emigration Commissioner in London, provided Earl Grey with a defence of the Imperial Government's actions and policies. Grey, in turn, submitted these arguments through Lord Elgin to the colonial legislature. From this memorandum and other despatches sent from the Colonial office the British position can be summarized. The British naturally expressed their horror and concern over the disastrous year. They were quick to point out that this "visitation of God" had (with Olympian dispassion) struck down not only colonists but citizens of the mother country as well. Every precaution that could reasonably be expected of the British authorities had been taken and, in view of the completely unforeseen plague it was unlikely that even the most rigorous regulations could have helped the situation. It was far better to have the great congested port of Liverpool disgorge its diseased human cargo on the spacious unsettled colonies than to confine the fearful famine-ridden Irish to an already overpopulated mother country.[6]

Canadian reaction to this argument was clear and violent. It was all very well for the mother country to throw up her hands in despair, open the ports, and release the great human tide. But Canada in her colonial dependency had no power to divert the flood as (they were prompt to emphasize) the state of New York was able to do most effectively. Indeed, so bitter was the reaction that many Cana-

[4] *Elgin-Grey Papers*, vol. I, Grey to Elgin, Nov. 3, 1847, p. 76-7.
[5] Again the *Elgin-Grey Papers* follow this gradual change in the Colonial Secretary's attitude, obviously influenced by Elgin's quiet urgings.
[6] Paraphrase of Elliot's memorandum, *ibid.*, vol. IV, pp. 1324 f.

dians were quite prepared to believe the most perverted explanations of the mass migration. The most pervasive of these was that Lord Palmerston and other Irish landlords had precipitated the disaster by trying to pawn off on the colony their unhealthy starved tenants.[7] To the Canadians, the ravages of the cholera proved the callousness and the want of discrimination exercised by the British government in the choice of emigrants.

The British had an answer to this last criticism. The completely *laissez-faire* approach to the problem of emigration had, after all, paid dividends. Suppose the Imperial authorities had embarked, as many colonists had suggested, on a scheme of government-aided emigration. How much larger, then, would the already oppressively swollen tide of emigration have become! As it was, all emigrants had come under their own financial steam, and the cost of the journey provided an automatic limitation on the numbers. Moreover, as Elliot ingeniously reported to Grey (although this report preceded the great exodus of summer 1847), the restricted number of ships available for the emigrants constituted a further rigorous limitation on the flow. Elliot never attempted to explain the discrepancy between his original estimate of a maximum of 20,000 additional emigrants and the actual excess emigration of well over double that figure in 1847. The well-placed Mr. De Vere, asked to report on immigration conditions in Canada, was able to provide that explanation. A thorough man, with a scientific curiosity that overweighed his native caution, he braved the rigours of a steerage passage on an immigration vessel in 1847 in order to obtain a first-hand impression of prevailing conditions. His description of the pestilential, floating Black Holes of Calcutta is a classic horror story.[8] The crowded conditions below deck explain how so many immigrants came across, despite Elliot's "natural" limiting factor—the restricted number of ships.

These were the ships, moreover, of which Elliot could speak quite complacently. The Imperial Passenger Act provided, as Elliot saw it "the best service which the Government can afford . . . to repress frauds on the poor emigrants before they sail, to prevent abuses in the ships by which they are conveyed, and in short to keep clear the channels in which emigration flows, without undertaking itself to

---

[7]*Ibid.*, vol. I, Elgin to Grey, March 2, 1848, p. 128; *J.L.A.C.*, 1848, Appendix W, where an interesting series of letters appears defending Palmerston and other Irish landlords.

[8]Stephen De Vere's interesting letter is in *Elgin-Grey Papers*, vol. IV, pp. 1339–47. For another description by a less influential person see Louise Wyatt, ed., "The Johnston Letters," *Ontario History*, vol. XL (1948), pp. 34–6.

conduct the stream."[9] And yet, according to De Vere's testimony and the experience of Canadian reception centres, the shipmasters ran their ships like modern "shake-down" racketeers and only by dint of several days' arduous scrubbing up just before reaching Quebec could the ships pass even the casual sanitary inspection of the authorities.

When it was suggested to the British authorities that they ought to tighten up the enforcement of the regulations, the official reply was: the colonists must remember that the pay load for British shipmasters is the Canadian lumber being exported to England. The only significant return cargo consists of human beings. If there are no emigrants the vessels will have to return empty to Canada. As a consequence the rates on transporting Canadian lumber to British markets will have to go up. In short, it would be unwise to compel the authorities to enforce the Passenger Act too rigorously.

Crowning this basic lesson in economics, Lord Grey added his own tart comment. It was really too bad of the colony to be complaining about this enormous emigration. Surely this was exactly what a struggling colony required. Far from finding fault with the British for opening the flood-gates, the colonists ought to be thanking them for this tremendous acquisition. Certainly, it was unthinkable that Britain should be asked to shoulder Canada's costs in absorbing these newcomers. As a matter of fact, Grey contended, the colonists were shockingly unsystematic in their whole approach to colonization. If they had shown some initiative in planning for mass colonization—as he himself had previously recommended—they would have encountered little difficulty in handling the emigration of 1847.[10]

Fortunately, the Canadians had in Lord Elgin an informed and sympathetic supporter. His replies to Lord Grey's arguments are typified by the following extracts from a letter written in August 1847:

I should at once assent to the justice of your remark "that it is far better to do too little than too much, and to allow a good deal of suffering to take place than to take away the motive to exertion by attempting to relieve everybody"—but these principles cannot be applied without large reduction and qualification to the present case. The great expenditure of this season has been incurred not with the view of transferring destitution to points where it may prove a help instead of a burden, but to stay the ravages of pestilence, and avert from the Province the direst of calamities.[11]

[9]*Ibid.*, vol. III, p. 1097.
[10]*Ibid.*, vol. I, pp. 63 f. and p. 77.
[11]*Ibid.*, vol. I, pp. 63 f., Elgin to Grey, Aug. 13, 1847.

Continuing his dispassionate survey of the situation, Elgin pointed out that every locality was crowded with destitute and plague-stricken exiles, that they could not be left to perish, that private charity was exhausted, and that there were no local rates to meet the expenses. There was no alternative but the expenditure of public funds.

But by whom is this charge to be borne? You say that when the first pressure is past the Province will derive in various ways advantages from this Immigration. . . . The benefit which the Province will derive from this year's Immigration is at best problematical . . . of the gross number of Immigrants who have reached the Province many are already mouldering in their graves. Among the survivors there are widows and orphans and aged and diseased persons who will probably be for an indefinite time a burden on Government or private charity. A large proportion of the healthy and prosperous . . . will, I fear find their way to the Western States where land is procurable on more advantageous terms than in Canada. . . . On the whole, I fear that a comparison between the condition of this Province and the States of the neighbouring Republic as affected by this year's Immigration would be by no means satisfactory or provocative of dutiful and affectionate feelings towards the Mother Country on the part of the Colonists. It is a case in which on every account I think the Imperial Government is bound to act liberally.

Throughout 1848, the local *ad hoc* relief agencies set up across the province to deal with the diseased tide of humanity sent in their expense accounts. As Elgin had foreseen, there had been some who profited from the enforced liberality of the government, but that did not detract from the over-all impression of a desperate situation bravely met by self-sacrificing individuals—many of whom had laid down their lives. It was not until 1849 that the Canadian government rendered its final account of the grossly swollen expenditures on the 1847 immigration. By this time the capable Sir Francis Hincks was in charge of financial affairs and his ingenious plan for settling this controversial issue was accepted by both sides. The Canadian government had long owed money to the British Commissariat in Canada for expenditures made as long ago as the Rebellion. Hincks proposed to offset this debt by dropping the Canadian claims against the British government for the balance still required to meet the final bill for the immigration of 1847. Grey and the British Treasury argued that this was not permissible under their system of parliamentary appropriation, but reluctantly agreed to let the matter stand.[12]

[12]*Ibid.*, vol. I, pp. 297–8, Grey to Elgin, Feb. 23, 1849.

The settlement of the irritating financial problem was less significant than the administrative victory which the colonists wrested from this whole unhappy episode. The Canadians could, first of all, find a rather sour satisfaction in the immediate tightening up of the Imperial Passenger Act. Obviously, the proud claims of the home authorities concerning the excellence of this Act had been substantially modified as detailed evidence of conditions on shipboard came to light. Even more important, however, was the Imperial government's sudden—almost precipitate—acknowledgment that the colony ought to be granted full control over its own immigration.

As we have seen, the capitation tax provided by Sydenham's Act of 1841, supplemented by the annual Imperial grant of £1,000 to £1,500, was able to take care of the normal flow of immigrants. But the pressure of the black year of 1847 not only exhausted this small sum but threatened to devour that small cash accumulation in the provincial treasury which was supposed to be used for paying the interest on the British Loan of 1841. The tremendous number of diseased and destitute immigrants made the colony conscious that the Act of 1841 could neither regulate the flow nor sift out the most desirable type of immigrant. What protection would they have in future against similar indiscriminate mass migrations which would leave the colony gasping for financial breath in a sea of nondescript cast-offs?

Governor Elgin was as quick to sense this problem as the Canadians and on Christmas Eve, at the end of the dreadful year 1847, he proposed the solution: ". . . for the future if Canada be permitted to enact such laws to guard herself against the evils of a pauper and diseased Immigration as she may see fit, I think the Mother Country may very properly decline to advance anything on this [the Immigration] account."[13] In February 1848 he renewed his plea to the British government to "wash their hands of all connexion with Immigration expenditure—and let the system support itself."[14]

But before the home government could make a clean break it had to assure itself that the colonial legislature had passed the legislation which would provide for a satisfactory continuation of the service. Elgin, operating under proposals set out by Lord Grey on December 1, 1847, steered such a measure through the Canadian legislature in 1848.[15]

[13]*Elgin-Grey Papers*, vol. I, p. 103.
[14]*Ibid.*, p. 124.
[15]*Ibid.*, p. 129; 11 Vic., c. 1 (1848); amended 12 Vic. c. 6 (1849).

It attempted to ensure sufficient funds for administering the Act by doubling the head tax. Its ingenious feature was the use of penalties to regulate emigration—not merely when the passengers reached Canadian shores but before they boarded the vessel in England. Protection against disease was provided by raising the rates in proportion to the number of days the ship had to stay in quarantine. As a check against the importation of paupers who would then burden the relatively slender resources of the Immigrant Tax Fund, the shipmasters were required to give sureties for every emigrant whom the authorities thought might become a public charge. The shipmaster could, and regularly did, elect another option—the payment of a 20-shilling "commutation" fee which immediately relieved him of any further responsibility. The agents stationed at the inland immigration offices were authorized to report within one year any case where the immigrant had become a public charge. This was about as far as one could go with legislation passed in Canada and without administrative agents for enforcement stationed in the mother country. On the Canadian side, the new measure empowered the provincial medical superintendent to board all emigrant ships, inspect their lists, and generally check on the shipmasters' adherence to the requirements of the Imperial Passenger Act.

This legislation, with certain amendments, remained on the statute books until Confederation. As the fear of mass inundations gradually disappeared, the head tax was progressively reduced and the penalties attached to the regulatory sections of the Act were substantially cut down. At the same time legislation conferred large discretion on the Governor in Council to provide quarantine regulations and extensive discretion was further delegated to the officials on Grosse Isle.[16] In matters such as quarantine where hasty improvisation may be required, the legislature, has always been prepared to give the executive a free hand.[17]

It is clear that the exodus of diseased Irish in 1847 convinced the British authorities that the Province of Canada should take over the regulation of its own immigration. Indeed, it was the dire emergency created by this migration which, in mid-1847, forced the Governor's Civil Secretary to drop out of the picture as the

---

[16] 16 Vic., c. 86 (1852).

[17] In the years after 1869, for example, the federal Department of Agriculture was accorded similar crisis powers in the matter of destroying diseased herds. See the "Report of the Minister of Agriculture for 1878," *Sessional Papers*, Canada, 1879, no. 9, pp. viii–ix.

formal head of the Emigration Service in Canada.[18] In the next year, 1848, the basic immigration Act just described was approved; but it was not until 1854 that the Imperial government finally cut itself adrift by dropping its annual grant. Meanwhile, in 1853, a newly constructed Bureau of Agriculture was made the titular head of the Emigration Service of Canada.[19] However, until about 1860, the various agents connected with immigration affairs appear to have been doubtful about the proper channels of authority. In 1859, for example, Mr. Hawke, the chief agent located in Toronto, thought that the Minister of Agriculture was his political head, but he contended that the Department issued no instructions and that all his reports went to the Chief Agent, Mr. Buchanan, in Quebec.[20] That official, in turn, retained until 1862 the title of Chief Emigrant Agent and reported to the Governor General. Not until the Bureau of Agriculture was reorganized in 1862 and converted into a full-fledged Department was the administration of immigration affairs assimilated into the Canadian departmental structure as an important branch of the Department of Agriculture and Statistics.[21]

By this time the major problem confronting Canadian authorities was the steady decline in immigration from the United Kingdom, apparently as a result of an improved domestic labour market. Canadian immigration was especially hard hit by this development. In the five years 1850–4 a total of 170,107 immigrants had come to Canada, but during the next five years the total was reduced to 71,343. In the evidence submitted to a legislative committee in 1860[22] the following reasons for the decline were adduced: (1) The re-

[18]See *Elgin-Grey Papers*, vol. I, p. 59, Elgin to Grey, July 13, 1847: "From the overwhelming nature of the calamity, and the large share which it has naturally occupied of the attention of Parliament and of the Public, the task of making arrangements to meet the necessities of the case has practically been withdrawn from the Department of Civil Secretary and fallen into the hands of the Provincial administration."

[19]At least Mr. Evelyn Campbell, Secretary of the Bureau, contended he had been placed in charge of emigration. See his evidence before Select Committee on Emigration, report and evidence appended to the "Annual Report from the Chief Emigration Officer," *J.L.A.C.*, 1859, Appendix 19. Also Act 16 Vic., c. 11, s. 6, had authorized the Bureau "to encourage Immigration from other countries."

[20]*Ibid.*, evidence of A. B. Hawke.

[21]See "Annual Report of the Minister of Agriculture and Statistics for the Year 1862," *Sessional Papers*, Canada, 1863, no. 4. 25 Vic., c. 7 (1862) made the Minister of Agriculture head of immigration affairs unless an Order in Council otherwise provided.

[22]See "Report of the Select Committee," *J.L.A.C.*, 1860, Appendix 4, pp. 7–9.

quirements of the new Imperial Passenger Act, 1855, were more stringent than the comparable American law and more rigorously enforced. (2) Lower passenger rates were charged on American ships which were plying on more regular and more frequent sailings to New York. (3) The prospect of picking up other return pay cargoes at New York encouraged "transient" ships to unload immigrants there rather than at Quebec. (4) Assisted passages for those emigrating to New Zealand and Australia diverted traffic to these colonies. (5) There was a lack of accurate information in the United Kingdom about the prospects and advantages of settlement in Canada. To most intending immigrants one route was as good as another, as long as it took them across the Atlantic. Unable to comprehend the vastness of the continent, it was not until they arrived at New York and began to consider the problem of proceeding to their inland destination that the relative merits of alternative sea routes could be properly appreciated.

It seemed clear to the legislative committee in 1860 that the Canadian government would have to embark on a positive immigration campaign. The first step, taken in 1860, was to send A. C. Buchanan, Chief Emigrant Agent, to Liverpool where, during the next two winters, he maintained a temporary agency. During the next few years, three more agents were appointed to serve in Ireland, Scotland, and Germany, while another agent covered France, Belgium, and Switzerland.[23] The bulk of Canadian immigrants still came from the United Kingdom but Canadians hoped to draw off some of the heavy emigration proceeding from the Continent to the United States. By 1863 nearly as much of the Department's budget was spent on these foreign agencies as on the salaries of immigration agencies within Canada.

Following on this sudden flurry of activity and obviously inspired by the optimism of Thomas D'Arcy McGee who had been the guiding spirit behind three or four special committees on immigration, there was a sudden retreat. The agents abroad were discharged: their expense accounts were considered abnormal; few positive results could be shown for their efforts; and the Canadian authorities appreciated for the first time some of the problems which the Colonial Office had once experienced in trying to supervise local agents when

[23]See "Second Report of the Committee on Emigration and Colonization," *J.L.A.C.*, 1863, Appendix 3, where a full review of the agency system appears. Interesting reports from these agents are printed in "Return re Copies of Instructions Given to Emigrant Agents Abroad, etc.," *Sessional Papers*, Canada, 1862, no. 21.

an ocean stood between them and headquarters' officials.[24] But apart from the disappointment with the overseas agents, there was another reason for the sudden cautious attitude toward positive efforts to entice immigrants to Canada. It appeared to many that, in the competition for immigrants, the agents abroad would merely foster a practice which Canadian authorities had always tried to check. Local authorities and individuals, as well as benevolently minded societies, were constantly pressing the human flotsam and jetsam of their own lands on Canadian shores. Canadians were not prepared to share the sentiments carved on the base of the Statue of Liberty in New York harbour: "Give me your tired, your poor, your huddled masses . . . the wretched refuse of your teeming shore."

The saga of the unfortunate "Limerick Union Female Immigrants" which gave rise to a long official correspondence in 1865 was a rather startling example of the kind of problem to which ambitious indiscriminate recruiting programmes might lead.[25] On May 12, 1865, some seventy girls sent by the Board of Guardians of the Limerick Union arrived on the *St. David* at Point Levis. The Chief Agent, having received neither money nor instructions for handling the girls, decided to ship them on to Montreal where they could be admitted for a few days to the St. Patrick's Home. In the interval between disembarkation and train time the girls "sold their boxes, bonnets, combs and any articles of clothing they could dispense with, to procure drink, and became not only shamefully intoxicated but were guilty of the most depraved acts of immorality." The party left its mark on the province as it was quickly passed from agent to agent, replete with 71 adults and 9 illegitimate children. At Montreal the agent, breathing heavily, reported back: "I am extremely thankful the girls have got away, that is those that were distributed—such a set I never wish to see again." The Reverend M. O'Brien, manager of the St. Patrick's Home in Montreal, averred that the shocked nuns would never again undertake a similar assignment. Arriving intoxicated at Ottawa, thirteen of the party were distributed around to protesting municipalities. Only one of the group possessed even a

[24]"Report of Minister of Agriculture and Statistics," *Sessional Papers*, Canada, 1863, no. 4; *ibid.*, 1864, no. 32; "Report of Minister of Agriculture," *ibid.*, 1865, no. 6; *ibid.*, 1866, no. 5.

[25]The history of this ill-fated group of immigrants is fully told in the "Annual Report of the Minister of Agriculture for 1865," pp. 11–13, 66a–66b, and in the Appendix to the Report, pp. 4, 23–36. It was ironical that McGee, who had long championed the cause of Irish immigrants, happened to be in charge of the Department when these unfortunate dregs of the Limerick Poor House arrived in Canada.

rudimentary training in household or farm work such as washing, ironing, and milking. The Kingston agent had his troubles with a flock of nine Limerick girls for they all refused to work and came back on his hands after he thought he had placed them satisfactorily. Some of the party went beyond Kingston but perhaps it is enough to have the picture which the Kingston agent has left us of the remnant of the party steaming for Toronto, "a number of them lying on the deck dead drunk, and several of them sitting on the laps and in the arms of some artillery soldiers that happened to be on board the boat, and this in broad daylight too."

Even for less susceptible Scottish consciences than that of Mr. Macpherson (the Kingston agent) this showed a shocking carelessness in the selection process which was supposed to be carefully followed by the authorities overseas. "If these be specimens of well-conducted girls," the Chief Agent sourly wrote to the Dublin Poor Law Commissioner, "I should be curious to see a few of the evil disposed."

With a few notorious cases of this sort, perhaps it is not surprising to find a parliamentary committee reporting shortly after Confederation: "Your Committee suggest that great caution and circumspection should guide any public effort to induce persons to immigrate. While Canada offers health, prosperity, and freedom to the industrious labourer and mechanic, she cannot, safely, assume any responsibilities on behalf of persons whose occupations or habits have been unfavorable to self-reliance or to the practical exercise of intelligent effort."[26]

Possibly there was another explanation for the rather timid approach toward any positive plan for immigration. Canadian authorities were really unable to determine how many of the immigrants docking at Quebec or entering overland via the Suspension Bridge at Niagara actually remained in the country. McGee was so dubious about the statistics hitherto presented by the Immigration Branch that he refused to publish them. However, we can assume that the number listed as remaining was in excess of those who actually did remain. Immigrants themselves, feeling that this answer was expected of them, often professed an intention to settle but soon went west. The local agents had no accurate means of checking on the veracity of the alleged settlers. But even if the figures are taken at face value they reveal an alarming state of affairs so far as the future of Canadian

[26]See "First Report of the Standing Committee on Immigration and Colonization," *Journals*, House of Commons, Canada, 1868, Appendix 8, p. 9.

settlement was concerned. In 1865, for example, just over 50,000 immigrants arrived in Canada and of these even the optimistic figures of the Department revealed that less than 19,000 remained in Canada. The highest proportion of itinerants was found amongst the immigrants from the German and Scandinavian ports, nearly all of whom moved directly into the American West.

This traffic touched off an interesting controversy. If the Quebec or St. Lawrence route was going to prove more attractive for immigrants moving into the interior, should efforts be made to admit only those who genuinely intended to settle in Canada? The other possibility was to make the best of the situation and think of the immigrants not as potential settlers in Canada but as so much remunerative up-bound traffic for the publicly owned canal system, the privately operated railways, and the local merchants who profited from the supplies sold to the newcomers.[27]

Even the chief immigration agent argued in favour of the second alternative. He admitted that many immigrants—particularly those coming from German, Norwegian and Swedish ports—were attracted mainly by the knowledge that Canada, unlike the United States, was prepared to pay the costs of transporting really impoverished immigrants to their destination. Logically, it seemed unwise to continue a scheme which in practice provided for the transit costs of immigrants from Quebec to some point on the American border. The Canadian railways further encouraged this traffic by selling "through tickets" from Quebec to Toronto, Detroit, Chicago, or beyond. These tickets could also be procured in Europe. On the other hand, if one were prepared to accept these newcomers as itinerants rather than immigrants, the best arrangement was to attract as many as possible and reap the financial benefits of the traffic. After all, the head tax levied at Quebec more than offset the amount spent in direct relief of indigent immigrants; the amount paid by foreign immigrants to railway and forwarding companies was estimated in 1866 at $100,000; while much more must have been spent on provisions and supplies purchased en route. More recent history reveals that this was not the last time the interests of transportation people directed the course of Canadian immigration.

By Confederation, then, Canadian immigration authorities had apparently fallen back on a conservative policy of receiving and for-

[27]See evidence of Grand Trunk officials before Select Committee on Emigration, *J.L.A.C.*, 1860, pp. 48 f. and the views of the Chief Emigrant Agent in 1866, quoted before the Standing Committee on Immigration and Colonization, *Journals*, House of Commons, 1868, Appendix 8, pp. 11-12.

warding immigrants, quite resigned to watching the greater number disappear into the American West, as one agent pettishly remarked, "to taste the joys of greenbacks, taxes and the other delights of the yet un-united Union." This lack of self-confidence contrasts oddly with the boundless energy and boisterous competitive push of the United States. It was well expressed in 1868 by the assistant immigration agent at Quebec: "Prudence would suggest," he wrote to a special committee, "that for the present matters should remain as they are, with the hope that we may shortly be in a position to offer such facilities and inducements as will secure a portion of this valuable immigration to settle in our country."[28]

What was the cause of this timorous attitude? Why was Canada unable to convert itinerants into immigrants who would settle happily in the country? The answer to these questions cannot be found in maladministration of the Immigration Service. Indeed, by contemporary standards, that service was quite efficient and manned by conscientious local agents. Many factors combined to make the Canadas less attractive to the immigrant than the United States. For example, the province, generally speaking, could offer neither superior climate and soil nor cheaper land to the farmer and certainly the internal market would not begin to compete with the expanding economy to the south. There may have been added attractions, also, in the allegedly classless society of the Republic which successfully captured the imagination of the underprivileged groups emigrating from Europe. Equally important was the long history of attempts to develop a satisfactory colonization programme. Such a programme was perpetually plagued by the ineffectual lands policies administered for the most part by Crown Lands. In turn, Crown Lands had inherited a sordid land-granting system which first developed under Imperial control and then became a convenient source of patronage for local politicians. Indeed, as we consider the colonial situation, it is clear that successful colonization depended not only upon the efforts of the Crown Lands Department and its surveys, lands and forests branches, but also on the building of roads and canals by the Department of Public Works, and the encouragement of agriculture and the distribution of maps, statistics, and other vital information by the Department of Agriculture. A consideration of the problems associated with the efforts to bring the flow of immigration to a happy and prosperous ending in Canada is now in order.

[28]*Ibid.*, p. 12.

Colonization

In the view of Imperial authorities colonization required skilled management and careful planning. While the United Kingdom was content to adopt a relatively passive attitude toward the emigrant (as revealed especially in the year 1847) it apparently found no inconsistency in pressing upon the colonies grandiose colonization ventures. Lord Grey, obviously badly bitten by the colonization bug, constantly urged Elgin to induce the colonists to support "measures for rendering the settlement of the territory more regular."[29] His views were coloured by the popular and well-publicized Wakefield-Buller-Torrens school of "systematic colonization."[30]

One of his first proposals would have done credit to the modern Ministry of Town and Country Planning.[31] He visualized several of the chartered land companies in the colony assuming responsibility for building what today have been known as "company towns." Each town was to consist of "100 to 200 cottages or log houses . . . a church and a house for the Clergyman." The costs of construction were to be borne by the Imperial government although Grey cannily suggested: "it w^d be highly desirable to have it given out that the money so advanced was not contributed by the public, but by landowners anxious to provide in America for persons sent from their estates, much better terms w^d probably be thus obtained."

Each village was to be "judiciously placed"—preferably "in the vicinity of some of the great public works that are going on, or some of the projected railroads upon which the emigrants might find work." The emigrants were to be moved in a compact group, their passages assisted by Scottish or Irish proprietors, their welfare in the hands of "a leader"—preferably a clergyman. The village was to have a business manager—a "director"— who was to supervise local road building by the new settlers, keep a regular account of the value of the work done by each man, divide the crops produced by the settlement amongst the villagers, and generally as a "superior intelligence" prepare the labourers for their "elevation" to the ranks of landowners. Once in the new town the immigrant was to earn a

[29] See *Elgin-Grey Papers*, vol. I, pp. 77, 117.
[30] For a classic summation and critical analysis of these views see Herman Merivale, *Lectures on Colonization and Colonies* (2 vols., London, 1841, 1842), especially Lectures IX, XIII, XIV, XV.
[31] This plan is outlined in the *Elgin-Grey Papers*, vol. III, pp. 1086-9, 1099-1100; the scheme was very much in Grey's mind throughout the latter part of 1846 and early 1847.

labourer's wage and from his savings purchase land as well as "pay weekly in advance the rent of his cottage."

This emphasis on importing labourers and making them pay for the land was the key to the so-called "Wakefield system." It operated on two assumptions: first, that only by securing a large labour force would British capitalists be induced to venture money in colonial projects; and second, that no Crown land should be given away but rather that the price be kept high so that the revenues obtained from sales could be spent on encouraging more emigrant labourers. An additional advantage claimed for the scheme was that the preliminary apprenticeship would test the mettle of the would-be settler and prepare him for taking up land as a responsible citizen.

Grey's planned settlements received no support in Canada. None of the major chartered land companies, such as the Canada Company, appeared anxious to act as agent for the government.[32] Some of their own experiments with rather limited group colonization projects proved unsuccessful—the settlers abandoned the sites and the settlements rapidly disappeared into the bush from which they had been chopped. Lord Gery's attention was called to the existence of a long Canadian winter which would leave the labourer without employment in his isolated settlement for six months. Company towns set up near a project like a railway, which changed its place as construction continued, would soon have been left isolated in the back woods.[33]

The principles underlying the Wakefield system also received general criticism. The view that labourers attracted capital was strongly denied. Such poor settlers might at any time become chargeable on their richer neighbours—this fear was all the more likely to be realized if work was intermittent and uncertain. Rich purchasers, for that reason, tended to shy away from villages made up of poor settlers.[34] The accompanying idea that labourers should not be put directly on free land, but should be made to earn money to pay for it at a fairly high price, was claimed to run against strong colonial prejudices. "It may perhaps be concluded," wrote T. F. Elliot, from the Colonial Land and Emigration Office in June 1847, "that there is little prospect of Establishing Village Settlements with any success in British North America."[35]

[32]See memorandum prepared by T. F. Elliot, in *ibid.*, pp. 1110-13, also at pp. 1055-6.
[33]See Lord Elgin's devastating criticism in *ibid.*, pp. 1133-5, May 7, 1847, and Elliot's Memorandum on Villages, *ibid.*, p. 1111.
[34]*Ibid.*, p. 1111.
[35]*Ibid.*

Grey accepted the voice of experience and dropped his planned settlements; but for the next few years he clung tenaciously to his Wakefield principles. During 1848 he was taken with a plan which ingeniously combined provision of a cheap defence for the colony with the cheap labour force which his Wakefield principles demanded.[36] A large reserve force was to be recruited in Ireland and sent to suitable locations in the colony where, working under military discipline for three years, the recruits would construct such necessary public projects as railways, later using their military pay to purchase land and settle down as farmers. The military discipline, Grey felt, might tame the "semi-barbarians of Mayo and Donegal" thus fitting them as useful settlers.

The official Canadian reaction to these various schemes and to the Buller-Wakefield principles of colonization was ably set out in two lengthy, closely argued memoranda prepared in 1848 by R. B. Sullivan, provincial secretary, and Francis Hincks, inspector general.[37] Sullivan's position, more conservative than that adopted by Hincks, constituted, until Confederation, Canada's answer to the problem of settlement.

There are certain long-range implications of the opposing views on colonization worth considering as a preliminary to a review of Sullivan's position. The Wakefield schemes required a bold policy in which an almost simultaneous application of new capital and labour to large-scale public projects, like modern pump-priming, would open up the colony, enhance the value of the remoter lands, and thereby encourage yet more capital and labour to flow in. The theory maintained that an initial investment of capital and labour, applied to suitable developmental projects, would set up a chain reaction which would populate and enrich the colony. To be effective the policy required a bold forward thrust into the unknown, in the hope that settlers and capital would line up in the rear and pour in along the route pioneered for them by the government. When Sir John A. Macdonald confronted the problem of opening the West to settlement after Confederation he operated on this principle. With a boundless faith in the future and a desire to see a Dominion united from sea to sea, he did not hesitate to send his surveyors out

[36]This plan was developed by Colonel Tulloch. Grey's endorsement of the plan is found in *Elgin-Grey Papers*, vol. I, p. 126, Grey to Elgin, March 22, 1848; again on May 18, 1848, at pp. 146 f.; on July 27, 1848, at pp. 206 f.

[37]For their far-ranging comments on settlement and its relationship to the whole colonial economy see *Elgin-Grey Papers*, vol. IV, pp. 1436-57 (R. B. Sullivan's memorandum on Colonel Tulloch's plans), and pp. 1427-36 (Hincks's "Memorandum on Immigration and on Public Works as Connected Therewith").

to map thousands of acres in no man's land and to bridge with thin steel rails an enormous empty land mass in order to connect British Columbia with the East. Pioneer the route, prepare the way, and let settlement take care of itself: this would appear to have been the guilding principle.[38] Not so with Alexander Mackenzie who replaced Macdonald. One of his first economy measures was to pull back the surveys and slow down construction on the railways to a snail's pace. Here was the cautious pessimist, fearful of over-extending the slim resources of the new Dominion, pursuing a careful policy of expansion only when a real demand became apparent.[39] Renewed vigour and optimism came back with Macdonald's restoration in 1879 and, on the whole, during the developmental period which followed, his bolder spirit prevailed.

Thus Lord Grey, with his Buller-Wakefield principles, was in effect expressing the views which took hold only after Confederation. At this time the solid weight of opinion in the colony was behind Sullivan and the policy of caution which later typified Mackenzie's reaction to the whole problem of national expansion. Even Lord Elgin was inclined to feel the higher merits of the Canadian case and disparagingly referred to the Wakefield schemes propounded by Grey, as "artificial systems of Immigration . . . more pompously styled, Colonization."[40]

Sullivan's position was pretty well the antithesis of the Wakefield principles. Public works, he contended, should not be undertaken by the colony merely as part of a plan to foster immigration and settlement. If they could not be prosecuted on their own merits in accordance with the present needs of the colony and its ability to pay for such works, then they should not be undertaken. Here no champion of the bold, debt-building entrepreneur is speaking but rather the honest conservative anxious to pay off old debts before incurring new ones and desirous of assimilating small gains before making further advances.[41]

Everyone could agree with Sullivan when he argued that the colony had already over-reached itself in constructing the canal systems.

---

[38]See Sir John's comments in Parliament on extending surveys in the new West, in *Debates*, House of Commons, Canada, 1880–1, pp. 1266–7.

[39]See David Mills's criticism of Macdonald's position in *ibid*. (I am indebted to William Bauer, former graduate student at Queen's, for calling my attention to this debate which is an interesting parallel to the pre-Confederation discussions on settlement.)

[40]*Elgin-Grey Papers*, vol. I, p. 129, March 2, 1848.

[41]*Ibid*., vol. IV, pp. 1440 f.

The revenues to be derived from the vast public works were not going to be immediately forthcoming and hence the provincial finances would be burdened by this debt for some time to come. There was no local source of capital for investment in large-scale public works, and consequently, if such a plan were envisaged as a necessary part of a settlement programme, money would have to be borrowed from Britain. Sullivan suffered from no illusions about the state of public morality when large Imperial expenditures were involved:

... large sums of money placed at the disposal of the Provincial Parliament, would be expended either in the construction of some gigantic undertaking, upon remote speculation of general benefit, or it [sic] would be compromised into a division of the spoils amongst the several localities having influence in the legislature. In any of these cases, quick and profitable returns would be in reality lost sight of, and the expenditure would depend upon strength of votes in Parliament, and the prevalence of local interests, and not upon the prudence or wisdom of the proposed measures.[42]

Sullivan's second line of criticism was directed against the policy of deliberate importation of labourers to be employed on such works. Under a system whereby the government furnished workmen for public projects "the conflict of authority, and the complication of mutual complaints, would make the whole scheme impracticable. Private contractors would never be satisfied with the daily labour of the workmen." On the other hand, if the workmen were to be under military authority, the contractors certainly would never be given the right to discipline the workers. A further question arose over the competitive position of such special imported labourers in the domestic market. They would either be in a more favoured position as to remuneration and permanence of employment or else held down by military discipline to accept poorer conditions, in which case they would probably desert.[43]

Having disposed of "systematic colonization" Sullivan went on to elaborate his own view of a scheme best suited to the Canadian situation. It was rooted in the widely shared local belief that the colony could not digest immigrants *en masse* but that during each immigration year (May to September) the colony would always be capable of absorbing the regular but rather thin stream of newcomers. Hence what was required of the colony was a policy that would keep that stream flowing steadily and prevent it from being diverted to the United States. The answer, according to Sullivan and his

[42]*Ibid.*, p. 1443.
[43]*Ibid.*, p. 1446.

colleague Francis Hincks, was to be found in adopting the right approach toward the public lands.[44] This approach was not to be found in the Wakefield principle of selling lands at a high price and devoting the proceeds to the encouragement of new immigration, thereby maintaining the mystical balance between land, labour, and capital. As Hincks clearly explained, so long as the United States was selling lands at moderate prices and so long as competitive private land companies existed, the government could not charge very high prices for land. Moreover, only the wealthiest settlers could be expected to be in a position to settle fully equipped alongside a newly opened road—these were not the typical settlers coming to Canada. In practice, as Sullivan graphically described the process, settlers first moving into waste land would construct "a rude and inexpensive way . . . through the forest, barely passable for foot passengers and ox carts."[45] Only when larger clearings had been made, old stumps decayed, and the swampy soil dried up could the settlers themselves make real progress on a good road. The next stage was the levying of a local tax for upkeep and the final step, to be taken "when the country becomes thickly settled with prosperous farmers," was the "turnpike" road.

Because of these local factors, Sullivan and Hincks believed that a modest homestead plan was one of the best inducements to immigration and settlement of the unoccupied lands. In 1840, such a plan had first been tried in a small way but with considerable success in the wild country surrounding Owen Sound.[46] The plan then adopted and subsequently broadened by legislation in 1845 was to grant fifty-acre lots to actual settlers free of charge along one side of a road—a road which the new settlers themselves were to build as part of the conditions surrounding the grant. Erection of a house, residence on the property, and cultivation of three acres annually were the main conditions required.

After 1847, this "Colonization Roads Plan," as it was officially called, became the province's chief answer to the problem of settling the less accessible portions of the Crown domain.[47] It violated the Wakefield principles in three ways. First, the land was given away rather than sold at a high price; second, the immigrants were able to get on the land immediately rather than labour on some public

[44]*Ibid.*, pp. 1449 f., and, for Hincks's views, pp. 1434 f.
[45]*Ibid.*, p. 1447.
[46]*Ibid.*, vol. I, p. 36, n. 1.
[47]A colonization roads branch was set up for both sections of the province and a local agent was appointed to superintend settlement and road building for each new road opened up.

work for wages with which they then would buy the land; third, the plan did not provide sufficient revenues for creating an immigration fund which could be used to assist the transportation of new settlers. Canadians argued, on the other hand, that giving away land was about the only kind of investment the province was financially capable of making and that in so far as the free grants developed settlements and roads, the value of the adjacent lands would be enhanced. As the colonization roads progressed, the government hoped to be able to sell either to the settlers already on the road or to newcomers now attracted to the settlement. "When there is abundance of land," Sullivan argued, "procuring the occupation of one lot by any means is a certain mode of making others saleable."[48] Hincks, too, contended that the colonization roads system actually provided "a Market for Immigrant labour." The free grants were most likely to be taken up by agricultural labourers already in the province or, as the settlements progressed, the adjacent lands along the roads would attract agriculturalists to invest their savings in the new land. So, as Hincks contended, "by the removal to the new settlements of a portion of the population, room is made for the Immigrants who are themselves unable from want of means to avail themselves of the privilege offered to them by the free grant system."[49]

Despite Grey's doctrinaire objections to this modified homestead plan, provincial authorities until Confederation experimented moderately with the plan in both the Upper and Lower Provinces. Indeed, as the period closed the Minister of Agriculture who was then in charge of the plan was prepared—had Confederation not upset his plans—to embark on a much more extensive homestead scheme.[50] After Confederation both Quebec and Ontario vigorously pursued the colonization roads projects which had been started some twenty years before.

The colonization roads plan was not an outstanding success. It probably worked better than any of the elaborate "systematic" schemes which Lord Grey had wanted the colony to try. However, Grey proved himself a good prophet in recording one major criticism of the scheme. Enforcement of the settlement conditions, especially with respect to occupying the land and performing road building duties, proved most difficult. In a short time the provincial government found that it could not get roads or increase the value of land merely by giving away 50-acre (or even 100-acre) lots. Soon extremely large sums were being spent on the roads and the manner of their spend-

[48]*Elgin-Grey Papers*, vol. IV, p. 1450.   [49]*Ibid.*, p. 1431.
[50]See "Report of the Minister of Agriculture for 1865," *Sessional Papers*, Canada, 1866, no. 5.

ing was very much as R. B. Sullivan had foretold in his memorandum of 1848.

The execution of the programme took on characteristically different forms in the two parts of the province. For Upper Canada the province passed an Act in 1853 giving approval to a road building programme for settlement purposes.[51] This legislation provided for an Upper Canada Improvement Fund which was to be made up of the proceeds from one-quarter of the sales of common-school land (less 6 per cent to cover costs of management) and one-fifth of the sales of Crown lands. For four years the Fund accumulated, until in July 1856 an Order in Council provided that the accumulation should be distributed among the townships in accordance with the actual sales of land within each municipality. This money was to be used by the local authorities to construct roads.[52]

Apparently the Fund was never distributed but was left in the sole charge of a Mr. David Gibson, Superintendent and Inspector of Colonization Roads in Upper Canada. In a most inexplicable manner this official appears to have acquired the right to dispose not only of the Improvement Fund but of the substantial legislative appropriations for colonization roads. Between 1856 and 1862 the legislature authorized nearly $600,000 for such purposes. His enormous financial independence was matched by the discretion which he arrogated unto himself. He determined the routes of most of the colonization roads, appointed the contractors (for the roads were no longer built by the settlers but only maintained by them), superintended them, and gave his final approval to the construction job. The ineffectual Bureau of Agriculture to whom, until 1862, Mr. Gibson was technically responsible, never called for vouchers and, indeed, never bothered to keep records of any description relating to this set of projects. When the Department of Crown Lands assumed administrative oversight in 1862, a more orderly system was introduced.[53] The evidence available does not explain how it was that Mr. Gibson was allowed to dispose of a large source of patronage which has traditionally been regarded as a standard method of repairing county political fences even as it improved the country roads. Presumably he enjoyed favour at court for when a special investigating body uncovered these facts about his irresponsible powers, he himself

[51]This development is outlined before the Financial and Departmental Commission in 1863 by James Bridgland (Clerk in the Crown Lands Department), *First Report* (Quebec, 1863), Evidence, Qs. 613–44.
[52]*Ibid.*, Qs. 642–3.
[53]*Ibid.*, Q. 641.

was never called in to testify, nor did the committee suggest he be discharged!

On the whole, Mr. Gibson's one-man rule produced fairly satisfactory results. True, contractors were often permitted to alter the route of a proposed road to take advantage of an easier terrain and casual inspection left some parts of the roads well below specifications.[54] Nevertheless, by Confederation the forbidding interior of the Upper Province had been criss-crossed with a network of colonization roads which opened up new lands and established connections with the older settlements. It is difficult to determine with any accuracy how many new settlers were encouraged to take advantage of the free grants system but it is clear that they were not jostling each other for the privilege held out to them. The scheme in Upper Canada was an extremely modest response to a small and not very noisy demand.

In Lower Canada the development followed a markedly different and, on the whole, much less successful path, though the need for vigorous aid to settlement was much greater.[55] Both sections of the province suffered from the problem of absentee landowners. The early prodigal alienation of Crown lands to various privileged individuals and companies was a sin of the fathers visited on the children. As late as 1860 in the Upper Province county officials estimated that there were nearly three and one-half million acres of "absentee lands" and that their presence was a real incubus, holding back settlement and the building of roads and schools.[56] The problem had been partly met by imposing local taxes on all unoccupied lands in order to discourage speculators and absentee landowners. But in the Lower Province the situation was more serious. The imperfect state of local government eliminated the possibility

[54]See the summary of Gibson's powers in *First Report of the Financial and Departmental Commission*, p. 29.

[55]The Commissioner of Public Works, J. C. Chapais, who was in charge of colonization roads in Lower Canada contended in his report for 1865 that the project had shown real progress during the first year or two there. See his "Report on Colonization Roads of Lower Canada," appended to Report of Minister of Agriculture, *Sessional Papers*, Canada, 1866, no. 5, pp. 21–3. But a more pessimistic picture is given by the Commissioner of Crown Lands, Alex. Campbell: "I regret to say that but little progress has been made in the settlement on the Colonization Roads either in Upper or Lower Canada. One hundred and sixty-three new and re-locations in Upper, and 94 in Lower Canada, indicate anything but a satisfactory advance." (p. xvii.)

[56]See "Report of the Select Committee to whom was Referred the Annual Report of the Chief Emigration Agent," *J.L.A.C.*, 1860, Appendix 4, p. 59, for table showing acres of "absentee lands" in 34 counties.

of using local taxation as a method of discouraging the large landowners. In the 1860's, in the Eastern Townships, settlers interested in purchasing some of these lands often could not locate the owners.[57] A paradoxical situation had thus early developed—especially in the Eastern Townships: as families enlarged they confronted a land shortage in the midst of great stretches of fertile unoccupied land. From the late 1840's on to Confederation parish priests constantly bemoaned the exodus of the younger sons to the United States in search of available land. It is not surprising to find the clergy in the forefront of any organization created for the purpose of sponsoring settlement—not, be it noted, of newcomers but of the children of old settlers.

Of course, when the demand is so strong and the land lies wild and close to hand, the temptation is very great to assert the old rule that possession is nine-tenths of the law.[58] Reliable witnesses testified in the 1860's that of the settlers in the waste lands south of the St. Lawrence, three-quarters were squatters. Some indication of the bottled-up frustration of the French Canadian at the existing obstacles to settlement may be found in the report of the Honourable J. C. Chapais, Minister of Public Works, for the year 1865.

What has so greatly retarded the opening of the great Saguenay territory? The exclusive right granted to the Hudson's Bay Company alone to tread that portion of Canadian soil!

What is it that has retained at the doors of the City of Three Rivers, for two centuries, the primitive forest which was frequented by the Indian Tribes contemporary with Jacques Cartier? The monopoly of the mining lands granted to proprietors of the St. Maurice Forges.

What is it, in our own day, that holds back from a great part of our wild land the poor and irresolute settler?—The egotism of the lumber masters, who, dreading to see their precious forests of pine disappear, do not hesitate to cry down even the soil that does not produce them.

Let but patriotism—that which is not a word but a deed—come to the assistance of colonization, and its future prospects are secure.[59]

While the serious barriers to settlement mentioned by Chapais were certainly present, it is nevertheless true that in the Lower Province the colonization roads programme was administered so in-

[57]*Ibid.*, p. 10. Also "Report of the Committee on Colonization," *J.L.A.C.*, 1860, Appendix 5, p. 9, where it is claimed that immigrants had access to better information about available lands than the inhabitants of the country. See also evidence of Rev. Messire Marquis before same committee, p. 20, Q. 9.

[58]Much sympathy for the squatter was expressed by various witnesses appearing before the Committee on Colonization and on Immigration in 1860.

[59]See "Report of the Commissioner of Public Works on the Colonization Roads of Lower Canada," appended to "Annual Report of the Minister of Agriculture of the Province of Canada for the Year 1865," *Sessional Papers*, 1866, no. 5, p. 23.

effectually that it did little to relieve the situation. The parliamentary grant was distributed to each county and then parcelled out as petty pabulum for the local authorities; the annual grants to each road ranged between $200 and $1,000, and in each case one or two local agents received a daily stipend of $2.50 to superintend these infinitesimal expenditures.[60]

To take a typical instance, in 1860 a parliamentary appropriation of $46,000 was split up among forty counties and these in turn allocated the funds to over 120 different local roads. Thomas Boutillier, Inspector of Colonization Road Agencies, found no fault in this system. Members of the legislature knew their own counties' needs and who was he to gainsay their superior local knowledge, or indeed why should he question the overseer recommended by the Member for that county![61] It was a cheap and gratifying method for all local interests. Boutillier's immediate assistant, Boucher de la Bruère, who had grown up with the colonization roads project in Lower Canada, frankly stated before a Committee in 1864 that he did "not know what better measures could be adopted for the distribution of the colonization fund."[62] Other expert witnesses begged to differ. A glance at the map was sufficient to reveal the ineptitude of this approach. Instead of a series of trunk lines with local roads branching off them, the colonization roads in Quebec appeared like short scratches of a hen's toes, grubbing in the dirt of the farm yard. Even these short, scattered strokes were deceptive, according to Mr. J. P. O'Hanly, testifying before the Committee on Colonization in 1860. "The money," he contended, "was spent in aiding old settlements, or roads long ago opened." Instead of main-line roads expertly surveyed so as to open up new tracts of country, the roads were built on a basis of county scrambles for miserable amounts that were then wasted on bits and pieces of useless local roads, badly constructed by local labour under the supervision of ignorant party hacks.[63] As the curé of a parish near Three Rivers remarked to the same committee, the government ought to appoint supervisors who were capable of doing something more than "keep off the flies."[64]

[60]For a scornful commentary by one irate Irish land surveyor, J. P. O'Hanly, see evidence before Committee on Colonization, *J.L.A.C.*, 1860, Appendix 5, pp. 15–16.
[61]*Ibid.*, p. 34.
[62]"Report on Immigration and Colonization," *J.L.A.C.*, 1864, Appendix 7, letter from de la Bruère, dated May 21, 1864.
[63]See "Report of Committee on Colonization," *J.L.A.C.*, 1860, p. 16, Q. 2.
[64]*Ibid.*, p. 30.

Apart from the local patronage aspects of this venture, the real problem rested in the sluggishness of municipal authorities; for even where roads were built for them they would not undertake repairs or upkeep. Consequently, while in Upper Canada the Crown Lands Department continued to handle the colonization roads project with reasonable success, in Lower Canada these roads were transferred to the Department of Public Works shortly before Confederation. This Department had for several years been engaged on governmental road building programmes largely confined to the Lower Province. It was natural that, with the failure of local government to undertake road building and with the failure of the colonization roads to build up a network of main-line communications, the task should devolve upon Public Works.

After Confederation the trunk roads built by Public Works were taken over by the Province of Quebec and were then treated like colonization roads, free grants of 100-acre lots being made available along their routes. In this fashion new land was opened up and the plan began to pay dividends in new settlements which under better management might have been obtained long before Confederation. In the interval not only had the immigrants landing at Quebec by-passed the province but younger sons had listened to the siren call of the United States and departed.

Confederation rang down the curtain on an immigration and colonization programme marked by cautious assimilation of newcomers a suspicious attitude toward grandiose schemes of planned settlement; the lack of co-operation of separate departments responsible for parts of the scheme; and, at the end, a fatalistic approach which admitted that the present and immediate future lay with the great pulsating nation to the south. But the rosy future was already at the doorstep of the new Dominion. Soon Canada was to have her own bright spasm of expansion and this time the conditions were more favourable to the optimistic adventurous outlook. The nation was prepared to commit its fortunes to glittering ribbons of steel, firm in the conviction that those vast unpopulated plains would soon produce a harvest home for the whole country. In many respects it was a return to the magnificent obsession of the Buller-Wakefield school: capital and labour established the beach head; the steel rails, with the surveyed land beyond, lay ready in the sun beckoning the immigrant to his fortune; and the government remained optimistic (though in debt) because it was certain this time that the immigrant could be brought to earth in Canada.

CHAPTER XVI

PIONEER PUBLIC SERVICE: RETROSPECT

Bureaucracy and the Pioneer Community

Pioneer communities, such as the two Canadas a century or more ago, presumably live under frontier conditions. It is part of the myth of the frontier that a sturdy self-reliant citizen flourishes there who will make few calls on the state and its servants. The frontier community, according to this view, provides the perfect environment for the philosophy of *laissez-faire*: self-help rather than state help is the motto. This was clearly the position of the Minister of Agriculture when he wrote in his annual report for the year 1863:

... must we not regret and condemn the fatal prejudice, too long prevalent, which is founded on the error that Canadians cannot live out of the shadow of the paternal roof [of the state], whereas, on the contrary, we find them, as hardy pioneers, plunging twenty, thirty, and fifty leagues into the forest . . . ?[1]

For this supporter of the *laissez-faire* tradition the services which the state could perform for a pioneer community were regarded as quite marginal and incidental.

Opposing this traditional view of the role of the state in a pioneer community is the far different conception which we find ably expressed by Alexander Galt in 1857, at the time when, as Minister of Finance, he was compelled to explain the heavy expenditures of the province.

Our Population [so ran his budget message], annually increased by Immigration, compels more extended arrangements for the Administration of Justice, and the wants of Civil Government. Our Infant Enterprises need to be fostered by the aid of Public Funds, and our great productive resources nurtured and expanded by the Erection of Public Buildings, the Construction of Light Houses on our Coasts, and the Improvement of Harbours and Navigable Waters.

And independently of these inevitable Expenditures which burthen the Public Treasury of every young Country, we have from the same Fund to draw means for the construction of Roads, the promotion of Agriculture, the support of Hospitals and other Charities, and the encouragement of

---

[1]"Annual Report of the Minister of Agriculture" (Mr. Letellier), *Sessional Papers*, Canada, no. 32, 1864.

Literary and Scientific Institutions, all of which in more populous and wealthy countries, are efficiently provided by individual enterprise and private benevolence.[2]

The thesis implicit in the foregoing chapters is that Galt's estimate of the role of the state is much more in accord with the facts of pioneer life than is the traditional *laissez-faire* view. The state and its servants did not operate simply on the fringe of the colonists' lives but in the very centre of their day-to-day concerns. What has recently been termed the process of accumulating "social capital" depended upon collective action and it was the state and its bureaucracy that served as the main focal point for such collective activities.

The Department of Public Works, the Post Office, and such agencies as the Colonization Roads Branch of the Crown Lands Department provided the colonists with the more expensive public works and the indispensable means of communication and transportation. In addition, the agencies which sheltered under the broad wing of the Crown Lands Department were intimately associated with those resources from which most colonists derived a living. On land and water the far-flung agents of this Department were in constant touch with the frontiers of settlement: the members of the Geological Survey, the land surveyors, the timber, mining, and land agents, the fisheries overseers. Selected groups in the community —typically the immigrants and the Indians—were also receiving special attention and services from the civil service. The record reveals that dishonest men, intent on personal plunder rather than public service, sometimes occupied these positions of trust, to the detriment of the colonists' vital interests; but, on the other hand, the government was also capable of commanding the services of devoted officials, some of them with outstanding administrative ability and an optimistic vision of Canada's potential greatness.

Not only did the pre-Confederation public service occupy an important place in the life of a pioneer community but also some of its more capable members contributed much to establishing lines of policy which persisted into the post-Confederation era. A brief case study of such a contribution was appended to chapter x where the policy-making role of the permanent officers of the Fisheries Branch was assessed. Such instances in other areas could also be found: John Langton in the Audit Office or Sir William Logan in the Geological Survey where he reigned in unmolested splendour throughout the whole period, an illustrious and world-renowned

[2]"Report of the Inspector General for the Year 1857" in "Report of the Select Standing Committee on Public Accounts," *J.L.A.C.*, 1858, Appendix 4.

figure. Dr. Pierre Fortin in the Gulf, William Gibbard and Richard Nettle in the Great Lakes, A. J. Russell in the Ottawa Valley: each of these officials in the Crown Lands Department through their formulation of regulatory policies and their administration of them contributed much to the protection of our wasting natural resources. Hamilton Killaly, presiding in somewhat unorthodox fashion over the engineer's empire—the St. Lawrence River route—was instrumental in committing the Canadas to a transportation system which, through no fault of his, was destined to be outbid by competitors and outmoded by the steam engine. In this work he was aided by the Keefer brothers, Thomas Begley, and John Page—all of the engineering fraternity. At headquarters, men like William Hutton and Dr. Taché built the foundations of that most vital of all services—the statistical branch. William Henry Lee and William Himsworth in the Privy Council Office, E. A. Meredith in the Provincial Secretary's Office, A. C. Buchanan with a life-time service in the Immigration Office at Quebec, William Spragge, Deputy Superintendent General of Indian Affairs, were also variously occupied—some in the colourless but necessary task of perfecting departmental routines, others dealing with the countless demands of people in trouble or in need. The enforced anonymity of these various officials should not lead us to overlook what emerges as an underlying theme of this study—their great contribution to the expanding needs of a pioneer community.

Bureaucracy and Responsible Government

The story of the winning of responsible government in the two Canadas has been fully recorded only at the political level. Briefly, it involved the efforts of one political group to implement its conviction that the Canadian people, at least in domestic matters, should be allowed to govern themselves. This theory of home rule, forcefully documented in Lord Durham's Report, was conceded in stages by successive Governors, culminating with Lord Elgin's acceptance of the principle of cabinet responsibility. After 1849, it became the recognized practice that a cabinet which had lost the confidence of the House must resign. Admittedly, this political achievement was important and embraced the main dramatic episodes in Canada's constitutional development. However, at the administrative level, less dramatic but equally essential reforms were being worked out that had an important bearing on the subsequent practical realization of the principle of responsible government.

In the first place, responsible government remained imperfectly realized as long as the province lacked complete control over its administrative services. While little has here been said about this particular development, the chapters on Indian affairs and immigration have indicated some of the complications arising from the transfer from Imperial to local authorities of certain services. In some instances, as with the Indians, the transfer was made gladly by the Imperial government and the new responsibility undertaken most reluctantly by local officials. In other instances, such as the Post Office and the immigration and customs services, protracted and often acrimonious negotiations ensued before the local authorities were able to assume full jurisdiction. This transfer of jurisdiction extended well over the decade following upon Lord Elgin's formal recognition of the principle of responsible government.

Secondly, responsible government could become a working reality only as a result of certain administrative reforms. It was observed in chapters II and III, for instance, that Durham's diagnosis of the weaknesses of colonial government was much concerned with administrative ineptitude and that Sydenham's major contribution to the evolution of a self-governing colony was the founding of a coherently organized bureaucracy. It was also suggested that without such preliminary rationalization of the administrative structure it would have been impossible to work the British cabinet system, relying as it does on ministerial heads of departments who are in a position to command the services of permanent public officers and to assume both individually and collectively responsibility to the legislature for all decisions.

If the Canadian cabinet, as was implied in the concession of responsible government, was to take over from the colonial Governor and his Civil Secretary the full direction of the public services, then the cabinet had to evolve the working methods and centres of power essential to that end. In chapter VI, the outlines of this development were sketched. It will be recalled that Sydenham had counted on an official with high legal attainments whom he entitled President of the Committees of Council to become the focal point within the cabinet. However, it is clear that his concern to keep inviolate his own central position prevented him from encouraging the accumulation of powers in this officer's hands. In fact, by the time responsible government had been granted, the offices of Attorney General for Canada East and Canada West had become the centres where parliamentary strategy was planned and major administrative decisions were reached. It was no accident, then, that found the two premiers most frequently operating from these two offices. But it could scarcely be said that the premiers had the power and influence in cabinet which their modern counterparts seem to have achieved. The factional quality of parties, the lack of party discipline, and the uncertainty of political tenure accounted in large measure for this situation. Certainly, individual members of cabinet were frequently found taking independent stands, thereby adding confusion at the Council table. Moreover, no single office could lay claims to pre-eminence—the Provincial Secretary and the President of Council, through the special duties conferred on them, often being as much in a position to direct the affairs of Council as were the two premiers. Joint responsibility—an essential feature of responsible cabinet government—was a principle easily enunciated but the party discipline and the overruling influence of a prime minister necessary to its ultimate imposition were not developed overnight.

Finally, the theme of evolving responsible government receives perhaps its most important addendum in chapter vii, "Tightening the Purse Strings." The ability of the legislature to hold the executive responsible has depended, traditionally, on its control of the purse. This aspect of the evolution of responsible government, apart from the early struggles over the Civil List, has hitherto been completely overlooked. It was suggested in chapter vii that there were really two stages in the development of Parliament's control of the purse. There was, first, the internal problem of devising adequate techniques of bookkeeping and of financial reporting together with the task of improving the methods of inspecting and auditing the public accounts. These reforms were largely a matter for public servants themselves to work out—hence the reference to this development as an "internal" process. Under the able tutelage of John Langton at the Audit Office the accounts were so improved and clarified that by the early sixties members of Parliament for the first time began to receive audited statements of the financial transactions of the government which they could understand. But not until 1864 was the executive compelled to estimate in advance its fiscal needs for the coming year. And only when this provision was added could Parliament expect to assert its full authority as guardian of the purse and ultimate controller of the executive's actions. Until this late date, Parliament had been forced to contemplate requests for money which the executive for the most part had already spent. Without this opportunity to approve appropriations before they had been spent, responsible government remained a somewhat unrealistic concession.

In summary, it may be claimed for the administrative approach that it emphasizes at least three neglected phases in the history of the winning of responsible government. First, the grant of autonomy in the administration of local services was a basic prerequisite, for without complete authority to guide their own public services provincial officials could not be expected to assume full responsibility to the legislature. Second, the development of the "top command" and the rationalization of the departmental system permitted the gradual growth of individual and collective responsibility of cabinet ministers which is so essential to the whole scheme of responsible cabinet government. The tendency to view joint responsibility as an automatic outcome of the recognition of the principles of responsible government has resulted in the neglect of a most important aspect of our constitutional development. Finally, the interdependence of responsible government and financial control warrants closer attention than it has yet received. By a complicated process, some of whose stages have been traced in this study, Parliament was able, just at the close of the period, to undertake its main duty as protector of the purse. Through this power it was then able to hold the executive responsible for the financial transactions which the law authorized it to initiate.

The Bequests of the Pioneer Public Service

What did the public service of the United Canadas bequeath to the public service of the new federal union in 1867? In the most immediate and practical sense the first legacy was that of the departmental framework designed by Lord Sydenham in 1841. The grouping of functions within the departments of the new Dominion was almost an exact replica of the arrangements in the United Canadas.[3] Moreover, the permanent officials, from deputy minister to the lowest clerical workers, were almost all ex-employees of the Province of Canada.[4] The fact that two Maritime Provinces had been added to the larger union was scarcely registered in the new bureaucracy.

Fortunately, the civil service of the United Canadas was well adapted to the needs of a federal union. It will be recalled that,

[3]The outstanding exception was the creation of a new Department of Marine and Fisheries; but, even here, the old personnel of the Department of Public Works and the Crown Lands Department of the United Canadas tended to predominate. See chart, "Chronological Perspective of Government Departments, 1841–1867," following p. 280.

[4]An analysis of the "Blue Book" just before and just after Confederation reveals that at least 220 out of 263 employees listed—mainly at headquarters—had previously been employees of the Province of Canada.

although the union of 1841 was termed a "legislative union," it continued to reflect the dualism of the two communities it was supposed to unite. This dualism found prominent expression in the adminstrative system which operated, for the most part, in two parallel but somewhat separate compartments, split from the Prime Minister down to office boy into sections for Canada East and Canada West. When the Canadas merged their interests in the broader federal union of 1867 their dualistic administrative apparatus possessed two advantages. In the first place, the task of providing the administrative agencies for strictly provincial functions of the new provinces of Quebec and Ontario was more easily handled, since the services were in many cases already divided to correspond with this division. Secondly, where the functions were transferred to the new Dominion some of the sting of centralization was removed because the branches were already organized to correspond with the two separate regions of the Upper and Lower Provinces: the "federalized" nature of such departments as Public Works, Indian Affairs, Immigration, Customs and Excise and the Fisheries Branch—all handling matters of Dominion concern—lessened the blow of the transition from provincial to federal jurisdiction.

However, by the same token, the heavy reliance of the new Dominion on the administrative staff and structure of the United Provinces tended to leave the Maritimes unrepresented in the new federal bureaucracy.[5] That there was surprisingly little outcry from the Maritimes for a share of the positions (read "patronage") in the new federal public service is probably due to the very slow development of centralized services.[6] As far as can be ascertained from a superficial examination of the record, during the first few years after Confederation the new Dominion's services to the more remote regions of its enlarged domain were directed by a handful of key

[5]The debates in the Canadian Senate on the bills setting up the new government departments contain some evidences of the Maritimers' dissatisfaction at this lack of representation. See *Newspaper Hansard* (microfilm in Library of Parliament), *Senate Debates,* p. 50 (Sen. Murphy on the bill organizing the Department of Marine and Fisheries); p. 58 (Sen. Bourinot on the Post Office Regulation Bill); p. 42 (a debate on the legal question of whether the new Dominion was bound by contracts made by the former provinces—e.g. with their employees); and again pp. 86 f. (debate on the question of continuing the officers of the Senate in their old positions).

[6]It was not until 1880, for example, that a Maritime member of the Canadian House of Commons asked for a breakdown of the federal civil service according to provincial origin. (This reply, unprinted, unfortunately perished in the Great Fire of 1916.)

officials aided by a nucleus of staff drawn from the old provincial services. Indeed, when British Columbia was drawn into the federation, the Lieutenant-Governor, Joseph Trutch, occupied a commanding administrative position comparable to that of the colonial Governors in the early 1840's. The case of British Columbia was somewhat exceptional, in any event, for it was grappling not only with the problems of membership in the federal union but also of its emergence as a self-governing unit.[7]

The history of the process by which the federal bureaucracy gradually lost its provincial coloration—particularly its heavy reliance on the two central provinces—and recruited its own more centralized civil service with wider loyalties still remains to be written. It will form an interesting commentary on Canada's progress in nation-building.

The second bequest of the pre-Confederation public service to the new Dominion was an outcome of the challenge posed by space. While improved means of communication tended to make the challenge less significant in the post-Confederation period, the decentralization of administrative activities which it had originally stimulated remained a constant feature of the bureaucracy. In chapter x, decentralization was singled out as one of the important features of the Crown Lands Department. While this department was most affected by the need for decentralization it was by no means unique in having to employ far-flung agents in the field. Given the problems created by time and space, administrators had little alternative but to accept decentralization, even though this decision brought many serious defects in its wake. Indeed, the inability of the adolescent bueaucracy to overcome these defects suggests that the evils of administration at arms' length by Imperial authorities located in Whitehall were only slightly reduced by the transfer of responsibility to local authorities. Headquarters' officials were often as remote from the actual application of policies as were their former Imperial masters.[8]

With the benefits of hindsight and more experience, it is possible for us now to see why decentralization—although unavoidable—had rather disastrous results in the adolescent bureaucracy. Decentraliza-

[7]The files of the Department of the Interior and the Macdonald Papers contain much revealing information on this neglected episode in the expansion of the federal union.

[8]It is worth noting that for a few years after Confederation there was a Department entitled The Secretary of State for the Provinces whose function was to handle all correspondence between the federal and provincial governments. The analogy with the British Colonial Office seems very close.

tion requires delegation of authority to local agents. Normally, such a delegation can be achieved only in a mature bureaucracy where policies have settled down to routine and standardized practices, and where the abilities and experience of local officials can be relied on by headquarters' staff. Even a mature bureaucracy possessing these features insists on other precautionary checks such as periodic inspection and careful central audit. The pre-Confederation public service was forced to decentralize at a time when scarcely any of these prerequisites was present. Often, there was no clearly defined, settled policy to be administered; the staff in the regions was often of inferior calibre and more amenable to patronage; the central safeguards, which were all the more necessary under such circumstances, were of the most rudimentary or cumbersome type. The situation called for first-class book-keeping practices, intelligent, independent departmental auditors, and full-time inspectors. Instead, departmental books were consistently in arrears and often not very enlightening, departmental financial controls were very slack, and inspection was normally regarded as a subordinate, part-time activity of over-worked headquarters' officials. Yet the amount of paper work was prodigious, apparently on the assumption that the extent of headquarters' control was proportionate to the number of reports and accounts submitted by the local agents. Nor was the situation improved by the steady partisan pressure on the integrity of local officials. Controlling large stakes in the public domain at a time when a rather loose code of public morality prevailed, these agents were often tempted to take advantage of the semi-autonomous position which all these factors combined to confer on them. Lack of consistency in the administration of policies conceived by headquarters was the inevitable outcome of the personal discretionary powers with which local agents tended to invest themselves.

The post-Confederation public service, for some years, confronted the same imperatives of time and space for, although transportation and communication were improved, the tasks of administering a Dominion that stretched from sea to sea could only be undertaken by the same extensive and somewhat autonomous field service. The experiences of the adolescent bureaucracy of the pre-Confederation period at least provided valuable guides for the new Dominion in the ultimate disposition of its regional services. In the earlier post-Confederation period, it is difficult to assert that the Dominion learned much from the mistakes of its predecessors, for many of the same difficulties reappeared. However, as the Dominion civil service matured, the techniques of central control were improved: better book-keeping, auditing, accounting, and inspection methods began to show results. In fact, it would be a tenable thesis that the history of the developing federal civil service reveals a gradual curtailment of powers delegated to local agents and the substitution of a centralization at headquarters which, under modern conditions, has tended to place a few key officials under an unbearably heavy burden. It is probable that the search for the appropriate balance between the authority of headquarters' officials and the powers delegated to regional officers is still not ended, even though some of the major defects accompanying decentralization at the adolescent stage have been eliminated.

The third important legacy of the pre-Confederation bureaucracy consisted of the introduction of a number of instruments whose object was to improve the co-ordination and supervision of the entire public service. In part, these instruments were designed to counteract some of the disabilities created by the decentralization just noted. But other factors also encouraged the search for a means of developing greater unity of command at the top. The rapid turnover of political heads of departments, the Imperial legacy of semi-autonomous agencies whose heads were most reluctant to submit to the suzerainship of new departmental overlords in Canada, the impact of the dual claims of the French- and English-speaking portions of the community on the administrative structure: all of these conspired against co-ordination and control. At least four expedients were adopted in the effort to improve the situation and each of these, in more elaborate form, became important features of the new Dominion bureaucracy.

First, the cabinet began to use subcommittees to handle its central duties as budget maker and budget controller. The two outstanding examples of such committees were the one to consider expenditures on public works and the tentative experiment with control over appropriations which directly after Confederation was formalized in the creation of Treasury Board.[9] Closely related to the whole problem of asserting a central control in financial matters was the evolution of the second supervisory device—the Audit Office. This agency at the outset, and for some time after 1867, remained too closely identified with the Department of Finance, but provided,

[9]On July 2, 1867, P.C. 3 provided for the establishment of "a Board of Treasury with such powers and duties as may from time to time be assigned to it," by the Governor in Council. The original membership consisted of the Ministers of Finance, Customs, and Inland Revenue, and the Receiver General. In 1870, the Board was established by statute and the debate on the Finance Bill indicates widespread ignorance, even on the government benches, as to its real duties.

nevertheless, a continuing central source of critical information and advice on all matters of departmental finance. In the immediate post-Confederation period the Auditor was much more the informed expert advising Treasury Board on all budgetary matters rather than, as he is today, the independent agent who enables Parliament to exercise its vital role of guardian of the public purse.

The third central agency created by the pre-Confederation bureaucracy was important not so much for its achievements at the time but because of its potential value to the enlarging public service of the future in which greater demands were to be made on the competency of civil servants. In the Civil Service Act of 1857 provision was made for an Examining Board, consisting of the permanent heads of every department and provided with a secretary. After Confederation this agency was continued intact, with the same terms of reference—providing simple pass examinations for new candidates to the civil service. This forerunner of the modern Civil Service Commission, like its counterparts of the same period in Great Britain and the United States, had a humble beginning but an influential future in the difficult task of elevating proficiency above patronage.

Finally, within each department after 1857 there emerged the important figure of the deputy minister. Like the Civil Service Examining Board created in the same year, the value of this new office was not immediately revealed. Amongst the deputies in the pre-Confederation bureaucracy there were several outstanding men who would probably have become centres of power even without being dignified as "deputies." There were others, however, who scarcely rose above the level of office manager at headquarters and were quite prepared to permit the branch heads to exercise their powers almost autonomously. This was clearly the situation in the largest department, Crown Lands, where, as was suggested in chapter x, the problem of internal co-ordination was attributable to the independent attitude of the branch heads who were incorporated under the Department. Departments similarly placed, like Interior and Marine and Fisheries after Confederation, showed signs of the same disparate forces produced by autonomous branches, and the co-ordinating powers of the deputies were similarly weakened.

In the Department of Public Works, however, the problem of central control was related, as chapter xii has tried to make clear, to the inability of the technician and the political layman to communicate properly with one another. The incompatibility of the irresponsible technician and the responsible layman produced several major scandals in the Department each of which pointed to the same moral—that the claims of ministerial responsibility could be met only if the technically trained experts would conscientiously try to keep their political chief fully informed of every major decision. Could this situation best be guaranteed by placing in the Deputy Minister's office an engineer who was qualified to pass judgment on the technical matters raised by his subordinates and advise his amateur political chief accordingly? Both the pre-Confederation bureaucracy and its Dominion successor argued that the Minister was best served by a technically competent Deputy, despite the evidence, particularly that provided by the Parliament Buildings Scandal, that the engineer-deputy often failed to perform those liaison functions which were necessary to the preservation of ministerial responsibility. While a final judgment on this problem is difficult to make, it would appear that the experience of the pre-Confederation bureaucracy fortifies the view long popular in Britain that the scientific and technical personnel should be subordinated to a permanent head whose competence is that of the "generalist." The permanent head with a non-specialized training is much more likely than the specialist to be conscious of those outside considerations which must be weighed by the politically responsible Minister, and these are considerations which the expert is most likely to regard as extraneous.

In summary, it would appear that the pre-Confederation bureaucracy of the United Canadas not only gave the original impetus to the public service of the new Dominion but also contributed much to shaping its administrative agencies and working practices. That the adolescent civil service had many failings cannot be denied. But they appear, in retrospect, to be no greater than those of its contemporaries in other democratic countries. Moreover, many of its administrative defects sprang from the forces of dualism which, since Confederation, have never been so concentrated or quite so divisive. Finally, some of the major administrative blunders were attributable to failures to solve problems of decentralization, co-ordination, and expert-to-layman relationships which still plague our modern administrators and still await more adequate solutions. Within the limitations imposed by time and space, by rudimentary methods of accounting and book-keeping, and by prevailing standards of public morality, the response of the public service of the United Canadas was, on the whole, commendable. The early public servants deserve more of us than the mantle of silence in which their labours have hitherto been wrapped.

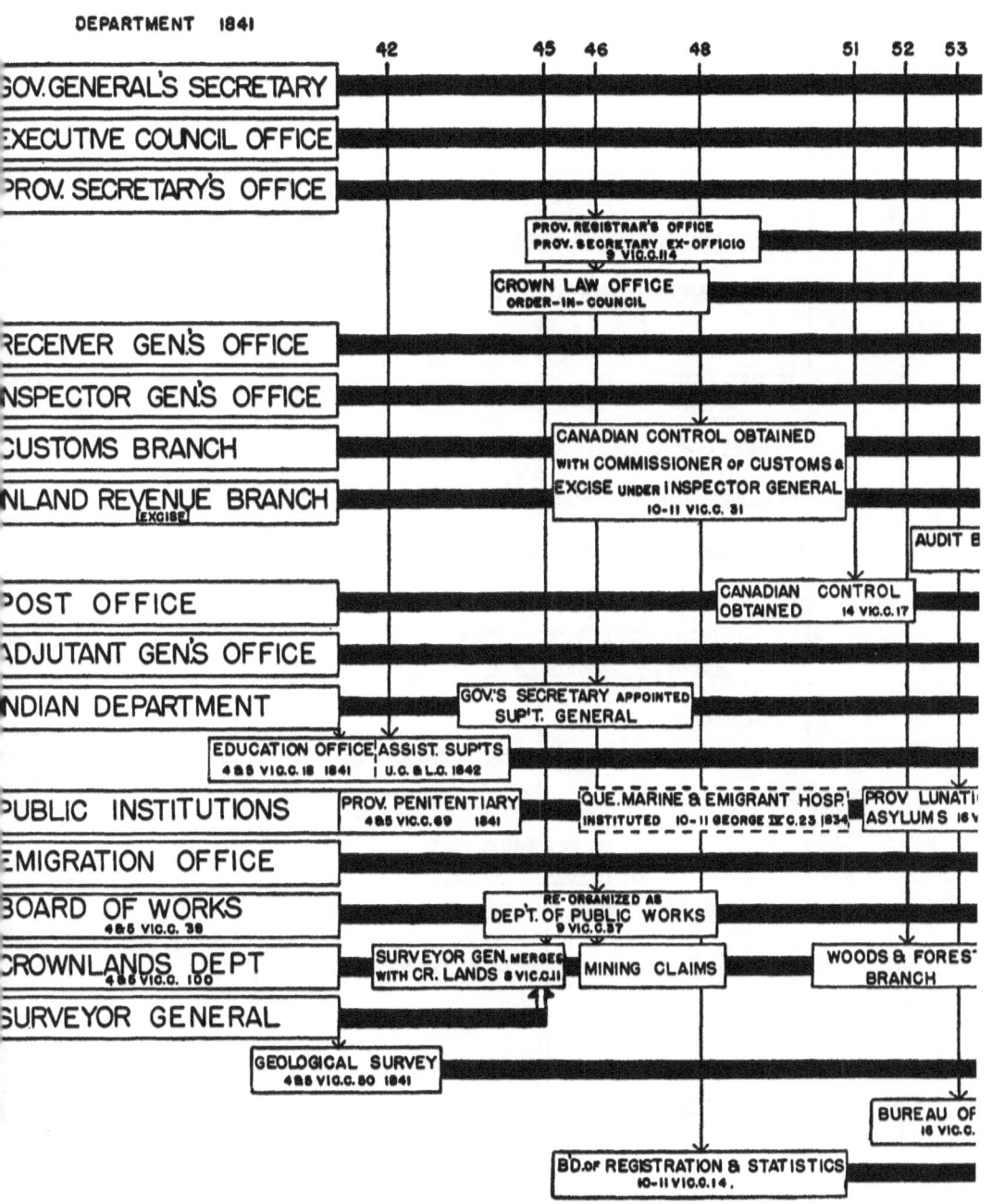

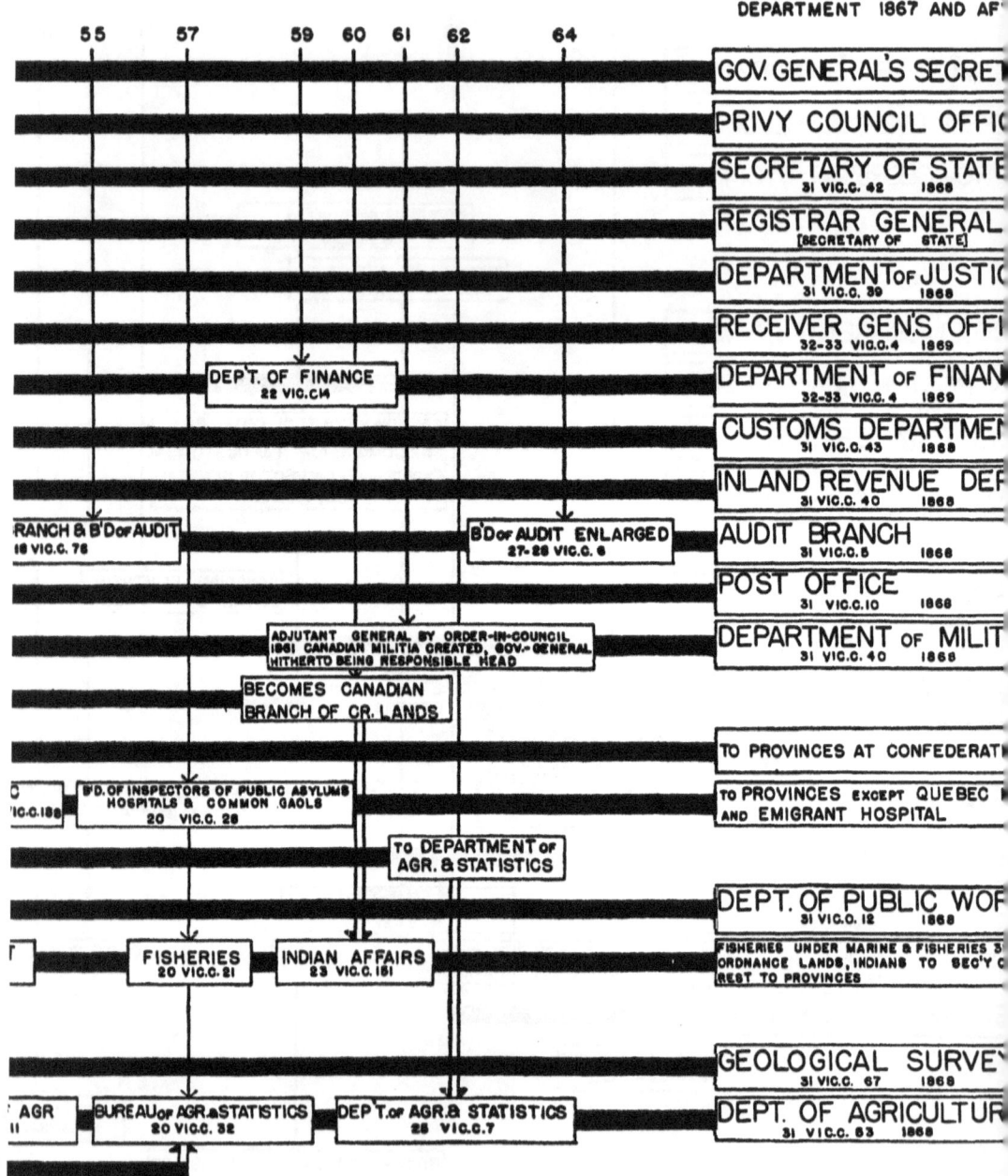

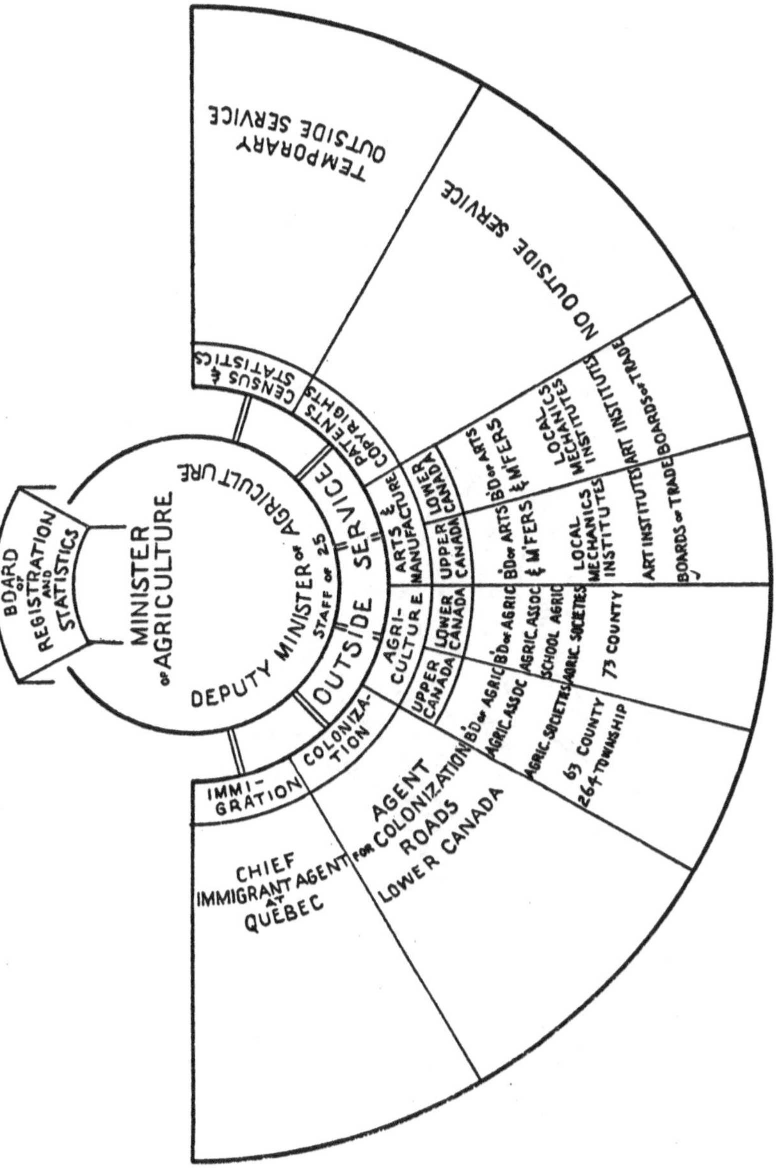

APPENDIX 281

DEPARTMENT OF AGRICULTURE – ORGANIZATION IN 1867

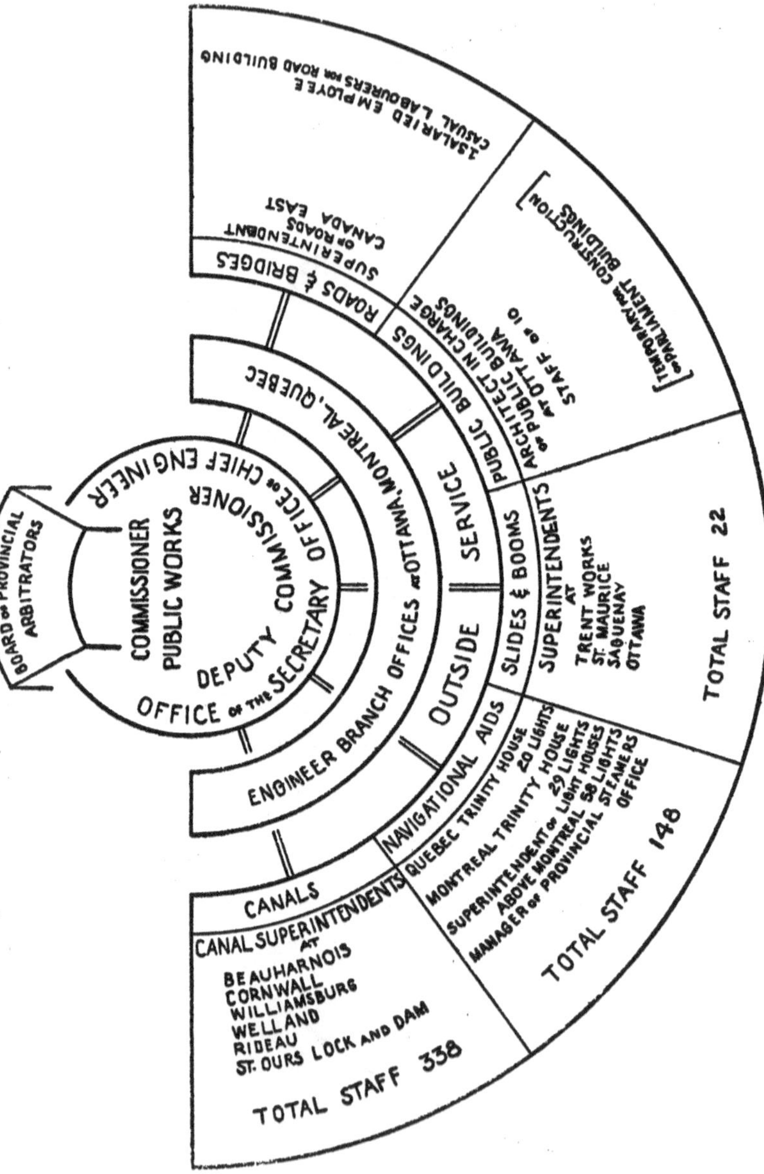

282 APPENDIX

DEPARTMENT OF PUBLIC WORKS — ORGANIZATION IN 1867

BOARD OF PROVINCIAL ARBITRATORS

COMMISSIONER PUBLIC WORKS
DEPUTY COMMISSIONER
OFFICE OF THE SECRETARY
OFFICE OF CHIEF ENGINEER

ENGINEER BRANCH OFFICES AT OTTAWA, MONTREAL, QUEBEC

OUTSIDE SERVICE

ROADS & BRIDGES
SUPERINTENDENT OF ROADS CANADA EAST
3 SALARIED EMPLOYEE
CASUAL LABOURERS FOR ROAD BUILDING

PUBLIC BUILDINGS
ARCHITECTS & PUBLIC BUILDINGS AT OTTAWA
STAFF OF 10
(TEMPORARY CONSTRUCTION OF PARLIAMENT BUILDINGS)

SLIDES & BOOMS
SUPERINTENDENTS AT
TRENT WORKS
ST. MAURICE
SAGUENAY
OTTAWA

TOTAL STAFF 22

NAVIGATIONAL AIDS
QUEBEC TRINITY HOUSE 20 LIGHTS
MONTREAL TRINITY HOUSE 29 LIGHTS
SUPERINTENDENT OF LIGHT HOUSES ABOVE MONTREAL 58 LIGHTS
MANAGER OF PROVINCIAL STEAMERS OFFICE

TOTAL STAFF 148

CANALS
CANAL SUPERINTENDENTS AT
BEAUHARNOIS
CORNWALL
WILLIAMSBURG
WELLAND
RIDEAU
ST. OURS LOCK AND DAM

TOTAL STAFF 338

APPENDIX

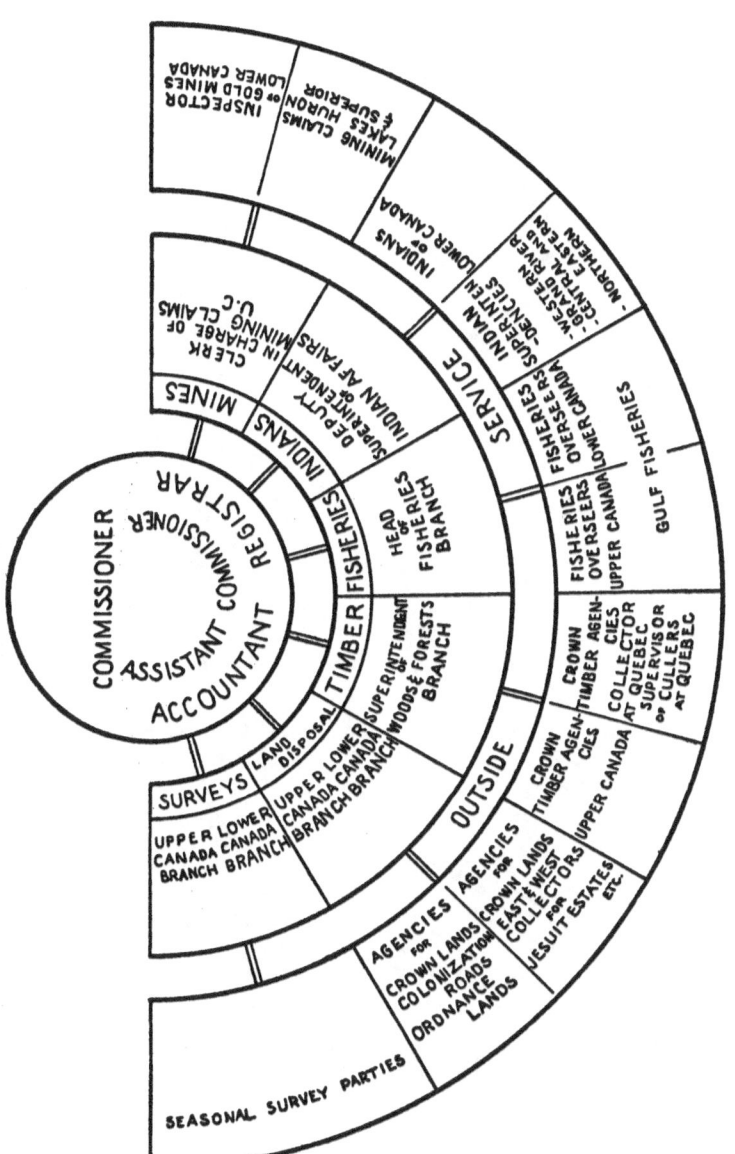

DEPARTMENT of CROWN LANDS — ORGANIZATION in 1867

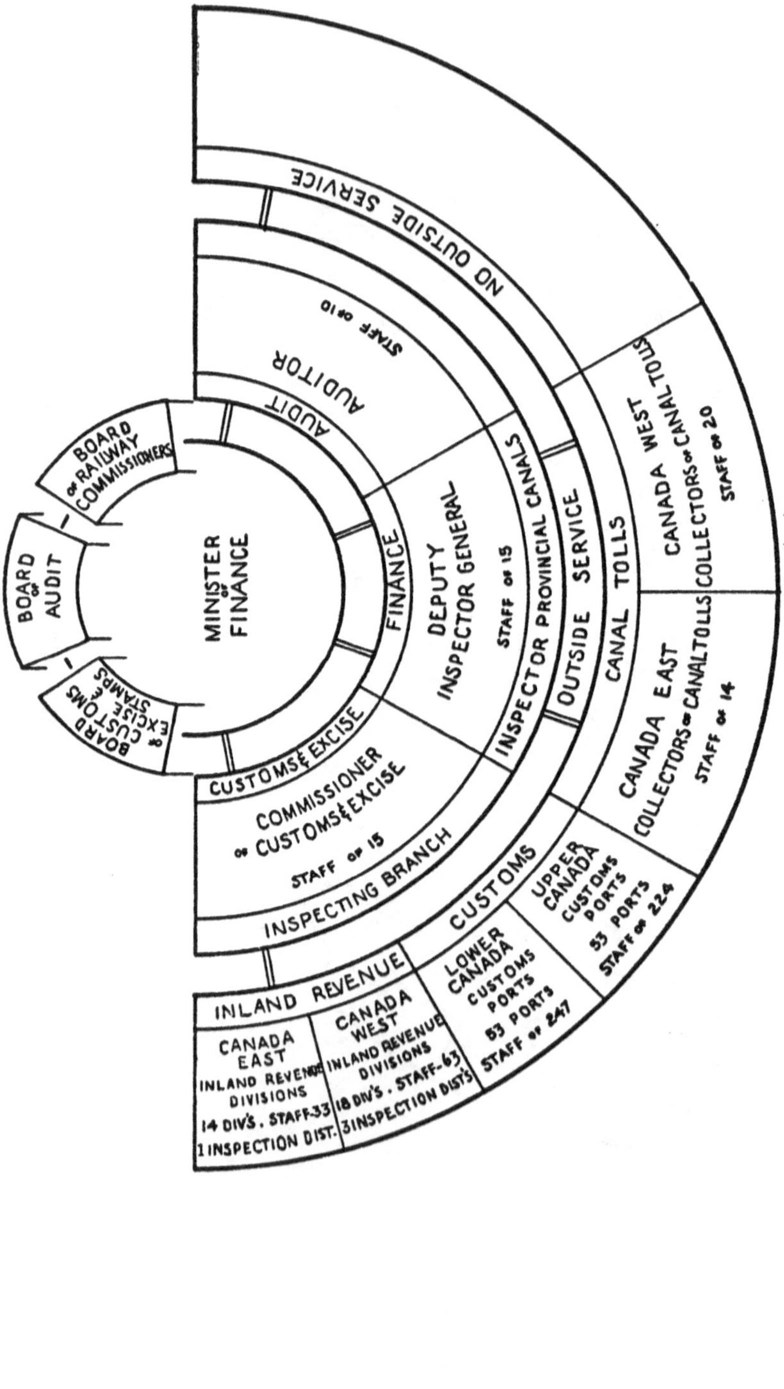

284 APPENDIX

DEPARTMENT OF FINANCE — ORGANIZATION IN 1867

INDEX

ACCOUNTANTS, departmental, 99–100, 103, 106
accounts, 39; of Inspector General and Receiver General, 98–9; of Public Works, 106, 193–4, 196–7; of Crown Lands, 159–60; of Indian Dept., 220, 223, 273; *see also* Public Accounts
Act of Union, 1841, 11, 27, 80, 108, 110, 176, 205
Adjutant General, 13, 24, 39, 61
advances, accountable, 100, 113
agriculture, in Canadas, 6–7; and lumbering interests, 121; administration of, 226–39; legislation on, 230–3
Agriculture:
 Boards of, 232, 235
 Bureau of, 40, 94, 131, 226, 232, 235–6, 251, 264
 Department of, 35, 42, 61, 226–39, 251, 263
 Local associations of, 226, 229–32, 234
 Societies, U.C. and L.C., 42, 227–8, 230–2, 234–6
annuities, *see* Indians
appropriations, parliamentary, 113–14; *see also* legislature; financial control
architects, 52, 201–2
Arthur, Sir George, 24, 34, 216
Attorney General, 15, 37, 55, 64, 82–4, 272–3
auction: of beaches, 125–6; of Crown lands, 133, 161; of timber berths, 140; of fishing rights, 146, 149
audit: committee of cabinet on, 90–1; Act of 1855, 101, 104; Act of 1864, 101, 103–4, 106–8, 115, 273; procedure, 101–4; and fiscal year, 114–16
Audit, Board of, 104, 107–8
Audit Office, 102, 104, 214, 273, 278–9
Auditor General, 96, 114
Auditor of Canada, 32, 39, 99–103, 106–8, 115, 117, 159

BAGEHOT, WALTER, 78
Bagot, Sir Charles: and resp. govt., 28n; and civil secretary, 74–5, 78; and Geological Survey, 126; and Bd. of Works, 176n, 191; and Indian affairs, 216
Baines, Thomas, 125, 165
Baldwin, R., 55, 64, 68, 88, 92–3
banks, 99
Begley, T. A., 103, 192–5, 271
Bentham, Jeremy, 25, 50
Blue Book, 94, 239
Board:
 of Agriculture, *see* Agriculture, Board of
 of Arts and Manufacturers, 228–9, 233, 236–7
 of Prison Inspectors, 238
 of Railway Examiners, 41, 181–2
 of Registration and Statistics, 228, 232, 234, 238–9
 of Works, 15, 31, 176–81, 190, 192; *see also* Public Works, Dept. of
book-keeping, 52, 99, 103, 160, 273, 277–8
Boutillier, T., 158n, 267
British civil service, 22, 44, 50, 86, 92, 94, 172
British North American Land Company, 133
Brown, George, 66
Bruce, Colonel, 212
Bruère, Boucher de la, 267
Buchanan, A. C., 241–2, 251–2, 271; *see also* Emigration, Chief Agent of
Buchanan, Isaac, 69–70
Buller, Charles, 16–17, 24, 33, 257–9, 269
bureaucracy: internal features of, 35–54; external factors affecting, 55–72; and policy formation, 63, 170–5; signs of maturing, 166; relations with layman, 195–204; *see also* civil service; civil servants
Burke, E., 110
businessmen: in cabinet office, 67–70;

285

INDEX

support self-sustaining service, 70–1, 159; favour "working" heads, 93–4; views on Public Works, 194n

CABINET: and Exec. Council, 22; lack of solidarity, 22–3; Russell and Sydenham on, 28; dualism in, 55; instability of, 62–3; lawyers in, 64–5; and formation of, 64, 69, 170n; journalists in, 65–7; businessmen in, 67–70; as co-ordinating agency, 73, 81; joint responsibility of, 68, 73, 81–2, 274; procedure of, 82–6; dominance of law officers in, 83–4; secretarial assistance for, 86–9; committees of, 89–91, 108, 278; Merritt and, 186; and administrative reform, 272–3
Cameron, Malcolm, 19n, 194, 235–6
Campbell, Alex., 265n
Campbell, Evelyn, 251n
Canada Year Book, 239
Canals, 177–9, 184–8
Cartwright, Sir Richard, 55, 59, 65
Cathcart, Lord, 76, 79
Cauchon, Joseph: criticized by Keefer, 57–8; as journalist, 65; as administrator, 67; character and career, 118–19; and Crown Lands, 118–23; on timber regulations, 138, 140n; on fisheries administration, 145, 174; and reform of local agencies, 158n; on maps, 161; on office practices, 163–4; on direction of Crown Lands, 167; criticized by Spragge, 170
Cayley, William, 90, 97, 101, 103, 108
Census, 3, 4n, 42, 227n, 228, 234, 236, 238–9
Chapais, J. C., 265n, 266
Christie, Robert, 69
Civil List, 8–9, 79, 108–10, 112, 188–9, 273
Civil Secretary: Sydenham on, 29–30; Colonial Office on, 30–1; functions of, 35–7; changing role of, 77–80, 91; and Indian affairs, 216, 221–2; and emigration, 212, 242, 250–1
civil servants: contributions to pioneer community by, 14, 269–71; statistics of, 36, 42, 157n; paper work by, 38, 52–3; recruitment of, 42–7; regulation of, 47–9; salaries of, 49–50; pension for, 50–1; promotion system for, 51–2; quadrennial removal of, 60–1; influence of, 63, 270–1; relations with ministers, 170–5
civil service: conditions in, 47–54; disproportion of English in, 57; effect of small size, 63; personalities in, 64–70; self-sustaining idea, 70–2; contributions to responsible government, 271–4; legacy to new Dominion, 274–80
Civil Service Act, 1857, 20n, 42, 166, 279; McGee's indictment of, 43–4, 49; provides for deputy ministers, 91–2, 94, 168
Civil Service Commission, 43, 73, 185, 279
Civil Service Examining Board, 43n, 279
clergy reserves, 9–10, 128–9, 131, 218
Coffin, Colonel William F., 169
Colborne, Sir John, 207
Colonial Office: criticism of other departments, 23n; on rules of administration, 25; on Civil Secretary, 30–1, 77, 79, 91; and resp. govt., 81; and Indian affairs, 213–14, 222; and statistics, 239; and emigration, 240, 252–3
Colonial Secretary, 23, 74, 78, 213–14
colonization, 227, 257–68
colonization roads, 42, 120–1, 124, 127, 133, 157, 181, 262–8, 270
Commissariat, 13, 214, 222, 242, 244, 248
Commissioner of Crown Lands: commission appointing, 20n; discretion of, 48, 125–6; Cauchon as, 66–7, 118–19; on cabinet committee, 90; relations to Assistant Commissioner, 93–4; and disputed claims to land, 161; heads Indian affairs, 211, 213; *see also* Crown lands
Commissioner of Public Works, 57; Cauchon as, 67; on Bd. of Railway Examiners, 182; and canals, 185–8; office created, 192; struggle with engineers, 192–204; *see also* Public Works
Comptroller General, 73, 98, 101
conservation: of timber, 138, 141–3; of fisheries, 144–6, 149
Consolidated Revenue Fund, 109–10
contingencies, 79, 114, 217
co-ordination, 60, 84, 168–71, 278–80
copyrights, *see* patents and copyrights

INDEX

Crown lands: as source of revenue, 17, 71, 109, 128–9; policies re, 128–36, 258, 265–6
Crown Lands Dept.: Durham criticizes, 15, inheritance of, 16; reorganized by Sydenham, 31–2, 41–2; regulations in, 48; dualism in, 56; moving of, 61; deputy minister of, 93–4; retention of gross revenues by, 99–100; domain of, 118–27; patronage in, 125–6, 162–6; land policy of, 128–36; timber policy of, 136–43; fisheries policy of, 143–50; mining policy of, 150–5; administrative problems in, 156–75; centralization in, 161–2; and office procedures, 163–4; control over Indians by, 211, 217, 223; responsibility for colonization roads, 264, 268; and pioneer community, 270; and decentralization, 276
Crown Law Office, 36–7, 55, 82–4, 86
Cullers, 45–6; Superintendent of, 45–6, 70, 124, 142, 166
customs: administration of, 16n, 18–19, 71n; committee on, 16n, 28–9; as source of revenue, 17–18
Customs Dept.: operations of, 38–9; patronage in, 47; retention of gross revenues by, 99–100

DECENTRALIZATION: in Crown Lands Dept., 156–62; as legacy to Dominion, 276–8
delegation of judicial powers: to fisheries overseers, 143, 146, 149; to mining inspectors, 158; to Indian agents, 208–9
departmental system: Durham on, 12, 19–21; Sydenham on, 13, 25–34; McGee's report on, 37n, 85n; as bequest to Dominion, 274–6
departments: functional analysis of, 35–42; clientele, 41, 206, 210, 219–25; housing for, 58–60; holding company, 118, 166–71; housekeeping, 177, 183–4; see also under individual departments
deputy minister: salaries of, 50; promotions for, 52; development of office, 91–4, 279; in Crown lands, 168–9; reticence of, 171; in Public Works, 195–204; in Indian affairs, 216–17, 223; need for in Dept. of Agriculture, 236–8

DeVere, Stephen, 246–7
Devine, T., 118
dualism, administrative, 30, 55, 58–62, 93, 231, 275
Durham, Lord: general conclusions of Report, 10; criticizes civil service of Canada, 12–20; proposes departmental system, 20–1

ECONOMY, of Canadas, 5–7
education, 16–17, 24, 129, 131, 207, 209, 228–9, 234
Education Office, 39–40, 57
Elgin, Lord: resp. govt. acknowledged, 23; views on French representation in civil service, 57n; on Governor's role, 75–7; on resp. govt., 82; on Indian presents, 206, 211; on Irish immigrants, 244–5, 247–9; on colonization, 257–60
Elliot, T. F., 245–6, 258
Emigrant Office, 39, 70, 240; and Chief Agent of, 40, 241–2, 251–2; and agents, 242, 251–3; and financing of, 242
emigration, see immigration
engineers: growing professionalism for, 44–5, 52; in Public Works, 182, 189–90; as administrators, 192–204
Erie Canal, 186–8
estimates: reform in procedure of, 106–8, 111, 273; supplementary, 107, 114; and fiscal year, 115–16
Evanturel, F., 237–9
examinations, 42–7, 279
Executive Council: procedure of, 15–16, 82–6; relations with Governor, 21; contrasted with cabinet, 22; investigation of, 24; relations with legislature, 26–8; duties of, 31, 80–2; supplements to, 86–91; control over finance, 98–9; relations with Bd. of Works, 191–2; see also cabinet
Executive Council Office, 37, 86–7

FIELD SERVICE, see decentralization; local agents
Finance, Dept. of., 73, 91, 98, 104, 107, 278–9; Minister of, 73, 111, 113, 116, 269; see also Inspector General
Financial and Departmental Commission, views of: on audit, 103, 105; on Commissioner of Crown Lands,

125-7, 164; on application for land grants, 135; on Woods and Forests Branch, 139, 165; on local agencies, 160; on surveys, 164; on deputy minister of Crown Lands, 168-9; on Public Works, 196-7
financial control, 96-117; and resp. govt., 273
financial departments, 38-9
fiscal year, 114-16
fisheries: overseers, 122-3, 127, 145-6, 161; bounties, 126, 148, 150; policies, 142-50, 172; legislation, 143n, 144-6, 173-5; artificial propagation in, 145-6, 149, 173; proposed addition to Agriculture, 227
Fisheries Branch, 70, 126, 145-6, 149, 151, 169, 172-4
Fortin, Pierre, in charge of Gulf fisheries, 124, 147-9, 169-70, 173-4, 271

GALT, ALEXANDER: and salary committee, 49; as reformer, 91, 97, 105-6, 117; on land disposal, 132-4, 164; on seat of govt. removals, 158
Gaspe, 124
Geological Survey, 126, 169, 270
Gibbard, William, 151-4, 271
Gibson, David, 265-6
Glenelg, Lord, 207, 209
Gourlay, Robert, 3, 9
governor: relations with legislature, 20, 27n; with Executive Council, 21; with departmental heads, 21-2; as Commander in Chief, 39; changing role of, 74-80; re public works, 191; re Indians, 212-16, 222; re immigration, 251
Governor's Secretary, see Civil Secretary
Grand Tour, 3
grant in aid, for agriculture, 230-3
Grey, Lord: on functions of Council, 74; on Indian affairs, 205, 208, 212; on immigration, 245-7; on colonization, 257-60, 263
Grievances, Committee on, 33, 96, 112
Griffin, W. H., 94
Grosse Isle, see quarantine station
Gulf fisheries, 124, 143, 146-8, 173-4; see also Fortin, Pierre
Gzowski, B., 177

HARBOURS, 180-1
Hawke, A. B., 242, 251

Head, Sir Edmund, 173, 176n
Himsworth, William, 271
Hincks, Francis, 97; and salaries, 50; and cabinet making, 64, 69, 171n
Home Office, 30n
homestead plan, 120-1, 130-3, 262-8; see also colonization roads
horticulture societies, 228, 233
Howland, J. P., 97, 117
Hudson's Bay Company: and fisheries, 123, 144, 146, 173; and mines, 152; and timber, 266
Hutton, William, 233n, 236-7, 271

IMMIGRANTS, 16, 240-1, 244-7, 249, 251-5
immigration: administration of, 39-40, 131, 228n, 240-56; agents, 40, 241-3, 249, 252-3; Act of 1841, 242, 249; Act of 1848, 249-51
Imperial loan, 31, 176, 191n
Imperial officials: criticisms of, 18, 20, 29; changes in control by, 35, 39, 272; changes in appointment of, 77; and forerunners of deputy ministers, 92; and Crown lands, 109n, 128-9, 169; and Indian affairs, 205-6, 208-19; and immigration, 240-51
Imperial Passenger Act, 241, 243, 246, 249, 250-2
Indian Acts, 210, 213; agents, 213-14, 217, 220-1
Indian Affairs, Dept. of: investigation of, 24, 29; functions of, 39-41; Imperial authority transferred to, 77, 80, 211-19; financing of, 217-19, 225; later history of, 223-4
Indians: reserves, 119, 208-9; and land revenues, 131; and Proclamation of 1763, 205-6; administration of, 205-25; civilization of, 205-6; policy towards, 205-11; and presents, 206-8; Six Nations, 218
Inland revenue, 17, 19
Inspector General: in charge of customs and inland revenue, 19; investigation of, 24; Sydenham's reform of, 32; as financial agency, 39, 90-1, 98-9, 101; on cabinet committee, 90; on Bd. of Agriculture, 232; on Bd. of Registration and Statistics, 238; see also, Finance, Minister of
Irish, 244, 253-4
issue, of public money, 98-101

INDEX 289

Jarvis, S. P., 214n, 220
Jesuit estates, 123
journalists, 65–7
justice, administration of, 13–14, 70, 80

Keefer, S., 177, 193, 195, 200, 203–4, 271
Keefer, T. C., 177, 271
Kempt, Sir John, 206–7
Killaly, H. H.: Langton's views on, 103, 176n; heads Public Works, 176–7, 191–2, 193n, 194–5, 204; as arbitrator, 202
King's Domain (Posts), 123, 144, 146, 173
Kingston, 4, 40, 58, 179, 254
Knaplund, Paul, 29n

laissez-faire: and immigration, 16, 246; and regulation of timber trade, 142; and fisheries, 149; and evolution of civil service neutrality, 172; and administration of agriculture, 226–35; and collection of statistics, 234; in pioneer community, 269–70
land: sales, 121–3, 125, 131–6, 164, 217–8, 220; agents, 122, 126–7, 134–6; policies, 128–37, 172; and colonization, 258, 262–3; *see also* Crown lands
Langton, H. H., 102n
Langton, John: first auditor, 90–1; financial reformer, 96–7; as auditor, 101–6, 108; view of Killaly, 103, 176n; improves accounts, 113–16, 159–60; contributions of, 270–3
Law Department, *see* Crown Law Office
lawyers, 19n, 44, 64–5
Lee, W. H., 52, 94, 271
legislature: interference with executive, 19–20; control over civil service, 20n; relations with executive, 28; control over finance, 72, 96–7, 100–1, 106–17, 273; and Civil List, 188–9; and road building, 267
Latellier de St. Just, Luc, 237–8, 269
Lieutenant-Governor, 13, 20, 30, 34, 213–15
lighthouses, 179–80, 184
Limerick Union girls, *see* Irish
local agencies, 33, 42, 119–20; Cauchon's reform of, 122–5; maladministration by, 125–6, 158; in Crown lands, 125–7, 156–62; benefits of, 126–7, 136, 270; for immigration, 242–3
local government: lack of, 14–15; Sydenham's proposals, 33; Provincial Secretary's relations with, 37; and land revenues, 129; and harbours, roads, canals, 179–81; and taxation, 265–6
Logan, Sir William, 152, 270
Lower Canada: conditions in, 3–11; administration in, 13–14, 29; and feudal tenure, 30; and legal profession, 44; and Education Office, 57; animosity towards, 57–8; and land sales, 134; and fisheries legislation, 144–8; and local agents, 160; and roads, 181; agriculture societies in, 230–1; and immigration, 241; and colonization roads, 265–8
lumbering, 5, 120–1, 247; *see also* timber; Woods and Forests Branch
lump sum votes, 115–16

Manitoulin Island, 209
maps, 118–20, 161
Maritimes, and administrative representation, 274–5
mechanics' institutes, 228–9, 233, 237
Meilleur, Dr. J. B., 57
Meredith, E. A., 271
Merritt, W. H., 97, 177; on public works, 15; on red tape, 53; on cabinet making, 67–8; as cabinet minister, 68–9; on gross revenues, 72; on cabinet procedure, 82–4; on revenues, 129; on canals, 186–7
Metapedia, 124
Metcalfe, Lord: and resp. govt., 28n; on overtime pay, 47–8; shifts caiptal, 58; relations with Council, 75–6, 81; and Civil Secretary, 78–9, 101; and audit, 101; and Bd. of Works inquiry, 192
military: control over Indians, 213–15; and colonization plans, 259; *see also* Commissariat
militia, 13, 39, 77
mines: claims on Lakes Superior and Huron, 119, 152, 154; gold, 124, 153–4; and speculation, 126, 151, 154; policy re, 150–5; practices in, 154n, 155; proposed addition to Dept. of Agriculture, 227
ministerial control: and turnover, 62–3;

over finance, 111–12; over Crown lands, 166–75; in public works, 189–204, 279–80
money bills, executive initiative on, 27, 34, 89–91, 110
Montreal: population of, 3–4; govt. in, 12, 14; and immigration agent, 40; as seat of govt., 58–9; and canal system, 178–9; Trinity Board, 180; and metropolitan rivalry, 186–8; and Irish immigrants, 244–53
Montreal Mining Company, 151–2
Morin, A. N., 131–2

NATURAL RESOURCES, administration of, 41–2, 118–203, 226–39
navigational aids, 41, 179–80, 184; see also Trinity Boards
Nettle, Richard, 150n, 170, 173, 271
New York, 186–8

ORDERS IN COUNCIL: procedure with, 37, 76, 84–6; for money grants, 101–2, 107; for regulating mining, 152–3, 155
Ordnance: lands, 169; canals, 179
Ottawa: canal routes, 4, 178–9; timber regions of, 5, 122, 137–8, 140; immigrant agency, 40; as capital, 62; see also parliament buildings

PAGE, JOHN, 202–3
parliament buildings: in Toronto, 60, 62; in Ottawa, 62, 183, 193, 198–204, 280
parliamentary assistant, 92–3
party, political, 22, 82, 88
patents and copyrights, 227–8
patronage, 20n, 46–7, 53–4, 162–6, 261, 264–5, 267–8
pensions, 50–1
population, of Canadas, 3–4, 8
Post Office: as source of revenue, 17–18; Imperial administration of, 20; commission on, 28–9, 33; expansion of, 38; patronage in, 47; moving of, 61; retention of gross revenues by, 99–100
presents, see Indians
President of Committees of Executive Council, 31, 37, 87–9, 232, 273; see also Executive Council
prime minister, 27, 34, 64, 73, 83–4, 87–8, 273
Prince, Dr. A. E., 174

Privy Council Office, 73
professions, 44–5
promotions, 51–2
Provincial Secretary: office created by Sydenham, 30; functions of, 37; dualism in office of, 55–6; moving of, 61; and Civil Secretary, 77; and cabinet, 87; and control over money, 99–100; on Bd. of Registration and Statistics, 238, 273
Public Accounts: select committee on, 96, 105, 111–12, 116–17, reports from, 116n; improvement in, 100, 104–6, 111, 112–16; see also accounts
public corporation, 190–1
public institutions, 37
public works: importance of, 14–15; supervision of, 15; viewed as self-sustaining, 71; committee of cabinet on, 89–90; and colonization, 260–1
Public Works, Dept. of: functions of, 41, 177–84; dualism in, 56; paper work in, 58; and seat of govt. removals, 58–62, 183; deputy minister in, 93; and audit, 103; Cauchon and, 119; patronage in, 162–3; servicing functions of, 182–3; and policy re canals, 185–8; administrative problems in, 189–204; and overexpenditure, 189, 196–204; procedures in, 198–204; and colonization roads, 268; see also Bd. of Works

QUARANTINE, station at Grosse Isle, 16, 183, 242, 244, 250
Quebec, city: population of, 3, 12; govt. in, 12; seat of govt., 59–60, 198; headquarters for Emigration Office, 40, 240–3; Marine and Emigrant Hospital, 70–1, 183, 241; timber merchants of, 137–8, 140–1; Trinity Board, 180; and metropolitan rivalry, 186–8

RAILWAYS, in Canadas, 4, 8; Bd. of Examiners for, 41, 181–2; lands used to finance, 130; guarantees for, 181–2; and immigration, 255–6; and settlement, 257
Rawson, R. W., 78
rebellion, in Canadas, 8–9
Receiver General: investigation of, 24; office reorganized, 32; as financial

agency, 39; on cabinet committee, 90; and control of money, 98–9; on Bd. of Registration and Statistics, 238
religion, in Canadas, 8–9; and Indians, 206–7
representation in civil service: for the French-speaking, 56; for the Maritimes, 274–5
reserves, 206–10, 225; *see also* Indians
responsible government: Russell on, 25–6; Governors' views on, 28, 74–7; and Exec. Council, 81–6; and Indian affairs, 211–13; and administration, 271–4
revenues of Canadas: sources, 17–18; administration of, 32; gross, 32, 100, 112–13, 160; under Civil List, 109; land as source of, 128–36; from timber dues, 137, 139–41; from canal tolls, 186–8
roads, 4, 119, 123–4, 180–1, 264; *see also* colonization roads
Rose, Sir John, 200–2
royal commission:
 on Bd. of Works, 1845, 190–2
 on Civil Service, 1881, 171
 on Civil Service, 1892, 92
 on Crown Lands Dept., 1845–6, 157n, 158, 160–1, 163
 on Indian Affairs, 1842–4, 206n, 210n, 214–16, 220–1, 224
 on Indian Affairs, 1857–8, 205n, 208–9, 216–18, 222
 on Mineral Resources of Ontario, 1889, 151, 153
 on Ottawa Buildings, 1862–3, 198–204
 on Post Office, 1842, 28, 29n
 on Prevailing Mode of Keeping Public Accounts, 1862–4, *see* Financial and Departmental Commission
 on Public Depts., U.C., 1839–40, 12n, 24–5, 87–8, 219–20
Rubridge, F. P., 196–7
Russell, A. J., 140n, 271
Russell, Andrew, 161
Russell, Lord John, 12–13, 23, 26–8, 75
Ryerson, Egerton, 17, 57

St. Lawrence canal system, 177–8; policy issues re, 185–8; as immigration route, 240, 255
salaries: under Civil List, 109–10; and commissions, 159

Scott, D. C., 210–11
seat of government: removals, 47, 157–8, 177, 183; perambulating, 58–62
Secretary of State for the Provinces, 276n
self-sustaining civil service, 70–2, 159
settlement, in Canadas, 5, 7; frontiers of, 120–1, 123–4; and timber interests, 121, 138–40; and lands, 130–6; and immigration, 240–1, 255–6; and Imperial policy, 257; *see also* colonization; colonization roads
Sicotte, L. V., 174–5, 194–5
Solicitor General, 13–14, 37–8, 55
statistics: responsibility for collecting, 42; and Dept. of Agriculture, 227–8, 234, 238–9; provided by local associations, 231–2
Stayner, Thomas, 18, 29n
Stephen, Sir James, 23n, 29n
Sullivan, R. B., 64, 88, 259–63
Superintendent General of Indian Affairs, 212–16, 220–2, 224; *see also* Indian Affairs, Dept. of
supply, vote of, 101, 111–12
Surveyor General, 15, 32, 56
surveyors, 44–5, 119, 126
Surveys Branch, 52, 56, 125, 164, 166, 169–70
Sydenham, Lord (Charles Poulett Thomson); and Niagara Falls, 3; and stage coach trip, 4; and Union, 10–11; and civil service reform, 12–13; and public works, 15; and Imperial emigration policy, 16, 242; and departmental system, 23, 25–34; character of, 25; on Governor's role, 27n, 74; views on Secretary's office, 74; on Council, 81, 88; selects Killaly, 176; on Bd. of Works, 191; on Indian Dept., 216–17
systematic colonization, 257–61

Taché, Sir Etienne, 192–3, 194n
Taché, Dr. J. C., 66, 91n, 94, 238, 271
Taché Road, 123, 181
tariff, 5n, 6, 18, 140n, 142, 185–6
timber: industry, 5–6, 45–6; agents, 120, 122, 124, 126, 139–40, 165; berths, 120–1, 126, 138–40; policy, 137–43; slides, 182–4; *see also* cullers; lumbering; Woods and Forests Branch
tolls: canal, 186–8; and roads, 181

Toronto, 4, 5, 40, 47, 59–60, 181
trade, of Canadas, 6–7; *see also* tariff
travel, in Canadas, 3–4
Treasury Board, 31n, 73, 90–1, 101–2, 106, 108, 278–9
Treasury, British, 18, 23n, 32, 207, 214, 222, 230n, 248
Trinity Boards (Houses), of Quebec and Montreal, 41, 180
Trudeau, Toussaint, 196
Trutch, Joseph, 276
Tupper, Sir Charles, 174

UNITY OF COMMAND, 19, 28, 34, 73–95, 156, 166–71
Upper Canada: conditions in, 3–11; and Education Office, 57; animosity re Lower Canada, 58, 170; and fisheries, 144; and mining locations, 151; and roads, 181; and agriculture societies, 230; and colonization roads, 264–5

VANKOUGHNET, P. M., 46, 51n, 122

WAKEFIELD, G., 16, 257–60, 268
War Office, 13
warrants, 100, 104
welfare agencies, 39–41, 205–25
Whitcher, W. F., 145n, 169–70
Woods and Forests Branch, 120–1, 137–9, 142, 164–6, 182; *see also* timber
Wright, Ruggles, 182n

YOUNG, JOHN, 69, 97

www.ingramcontent.com/pod-product-compliance
Lightning Source LLC
Chambersburg PA
CBHW030306080526
44584CB00012B/455